GEOPOLITICS

GEOPOLITICS

Impact on Energy Transition and Energy Security

Edited by

R.N. Prasher

ink | OCCAM

ISBN: 978-93-6547-294-3

First published in India 2025
This edition published 2025

BluOne Ink Pvt. Ltd
A-76, 2nd Floor, Sector 136, Noida
Uttar Pradesh 201301
www.bluone.ink
publisher@bluone.ink

Printed and bound in India by Gopsons Papers Pvt. Ltd., Noida

Kali and Occam are imprints of BluOne Ink

ink | OCCAM

Contents

Preface

Geopolitics has been described as a complex global game where nations are like chess pieces and continents are like squares. The game is characterised by strategy, continuous power dynamics, and extremely high stakes. Every successful grand strategy and colossal blunder changes the international order, making some nations gain global influence and dominance while others lose it.[1] If that is true, then who are the players at the two ends of this giant chessboard? As with a conventional game of chess, the moves are ultimately decided by a human on each side, and the rest of humanity is obliged to take sides and watch as the spoils or the losses fall to their fate. In dictatorships, the player on one side may be a single megalomaniac who makes all the decisions while the nation pays the price, whereas in a democracy, the leader may take the advice of a small group of advisors, but he alone makes the final decision.

Chess is a game that can be played by only two players and no more. This situation once existed in the world which remained bipolar for a long time, although the nations represented by the players at the two ends kept changing. Size, natural resources, economy, technology, and an unquantifiable factor called 'national character' can boost or diminish the players' chances of winning, and yet, these are not the sole determinants. The individuals sitting at either end of the board play a larger-than-life role in diplomacy and in war, a role that has been euphemistically called 'diplomacy by other means', notwithstanding the scenes of death and destruction on the battlefields and even in the cities. What further distinguishes this game from the benign moves on a chessboard is that not playing is not an option. An abdication on one side results in the seat being taken by someone else. One can play chess with a computer, though that is an unequal game, generally resulting in the defeat of the human. 'Experts' have designed predictive models for geopolitics and wars too, but human nature and the outcome of diplomatic manoeuvres remain largely unpredictable.

The period comprising the Cold War stretched from the final months of World War II to the collapse of the Soviet Union, at which point the world started believing that it had become unipolar, although that is a theoretical impossibility. Soon after, we saw Russia attempting to claw its way back to the high table, while China more or less declared that the second place belongs to it now. With a weakened Russia making the suicidal move of taking on the North Atlantic Treaty Organization (NATO) and asserting the right to decide who can join that alliance and who cannot, Putin has placed himself in a position clearly subservient to China, thereby strengthening China's claim of being the other superpower. The new Cold War has the US and China as the main adversaries, with more and more countries facing the decision to join one side or the other.

One development distinguishes the new Cold War from the old one: The world is a lot more interconnected, and countries, even those at or near the top, are more dependent on each other than at any other time in history. Communications and international trade have made the term 'global village' a reality. Yet, in this 'village', there are hegemons who think and act as if they are the village heads. The panchayat or the council of elders that the United Nations was supposed to be has turned out to be as toothless against the hegemony as village councils are against the powerful. To add to the conundrum, there are multinational corporations which, by their very definition, have no nationality and recognise no other morality except market dominance and profits.

Since the harnessing of steam power, energy has played a big role in geopolitics among nations. Nations grew strong through coal extraction and use, then through oil extraction and its processing, and later merely through their control over the trade in energy. Nuclear power was no exception, with nations that had fuel enrichment facilities trying to manipulate and profit from other nations' dependence on them. This state of affairs would have continued until the fuel sources were depleted, but the degradation of the environment caused by the use of coal and oil, along with three major nuclear reactor accidents—Three Mile Island in the US, Chernobyl in the then USSR, and Fukushima in Japan—gradually put off even the nuclear club countries. Those dependent on these countries were already frustrated by their tantrums in supplying fuel. In the era of oil and gas, we also had the rentier states that rode on the bounties of nature to become obscenely rich without producing anything.

It is in this scenario that a cry was heard about the future of the planet being in danger. The cry itself is subject of partisan interpretations, ranging from an existential threat to being called the great climate hoax. Yet, it has been taken seriously enough, and coal, oil, and gas have been held guilty of creating this threat to human existence. The transition to non-fossil sources of energy, such as nuclear, wind, solar, hydrogen, waves, tide, and geothermal, is unquestionably the accepted goal of all nations, and the race for hegemony in these areas is already on. Such hegemony in control over oil and gas sources had disrupted the energy security of nations in the past. The new energy sources are more evenly distributed across continents and nations, but the resources, including technology differentials to harness these sources, bring back the spectre of hegemony. The manufacture of solar panels at competitive prices, wind turbines, batteries for storage, and electrolysers for making hydrogen to permit continuous use of intermittent wind and solar power is again giving a few nations control over the rest.

Ensuring energy security while the transition to green energy takes place is not a matter of economics alone. In this book we argue that national security is heavily dependent on energy security, and therefore it should play a part in determining what is a 'cheaper' source. Europe's dependence on Russia for gas showed that ignoring the strategic costs while choosing/deciding the 'cheaper' source can be very costly for a nation. When we factor in the costs being borne by Europe for assisting Ukraine, the Russian oil bought in the past may not appear to be so cheap. Thus, energy transition has the potential to bring about major shifts in geopolitics.

Countries, including the rentier states, that controlled traditional fuels, as well as those countries dependent on others for such fuels, have to make many adjustments in their geopolitical paradigm to ensure that their energy security is not jeopardised by the changes. Energy security has become synonymous with national security, as consumption levels are so high that storage provides only temporary security to importing nations. Simultaneously, the rentier states that lived solely on the proceeds from the sale of energy also have to change their economic paradigm to remain in the game. Green energy is more evenly distributed across continents than conventional energy sources. Deserts, which had little economic value unless there was oil beneath them, have vast potential for producing wind and solar power. The next two decades shall see the world undergo a quantum shift in comparative national powers because of energy transition.

The strategic costs of buying from countries run by ideologies diametrically opposite to democracies go beyond energy costs, as these encompass food security, disinformation, cyber disruption, terrorism, and actual wars. There has been a lot of talk of decoupling, de-risking, offshoring and friendshoring, yet trade between democracies and dictatorships continues to grow. As the doors remain open, technologies developed with huge investments of time, capital, and human resources flow, mostly in a clandestine manner, to dictatorships, adding to the strategic cost of engagement with totalitarian regimes. Globalists may disagree, but there appears to be no benign way of doing business with totalitarian regimes. Democracies have been hesitant to take this issue head-on, but the era of energy transition may no longer permit this luxury.

This book brings together policymakers, concept analysts, and industry leaders who are in the business of energy generation and management. All the contributors have vast experience in their respective fields. In Part I, policymakers share their vision, and in Part III, those who implement these policies through national organisations present the scenario in specific sectors with an emphasis on action. In Part II, the concepts are laid down to delineate the directions in which the policies and action are moving or ought to be moving.

In Part I of the book, Shri Nitin Gadkari has written in great detail about his vision to reduce the carbon footprint of road transport—a large part of which has already been implemented. Shri Suresh Prabhakar Prabhu has written on the geopolitical implications of the fact that nature's resources are very unevenly distributed across nations. Shri Raj Kumar Singh chronicles how he successfully worked to decarbonise the power sector in spite of coal being the traditional mainstay of our power generation. Shri Ghanshyam Prasad lays down the vision for the generation and distribution of power in India in the era of energy transition.

In Part II, the contours of the three interrelated themes in this book—geopolitics, energy transition, and energy security—have been delineated. Three countries have been selected for a detailed description of their historical geopolitics: China, Russia, and Iran, the first being the largest consumer and the other two, major producers. There are many other important energy producing and consuming countries, but one common characteristic distinguishes these three in that subset. While the energy policies of the others are more or less transparent, making their future course predictable to a large degree, these three have been black holes as far as information sharing goes. They publish information officially, but because their statecraft is shrouded in layers of secrecy, the veracity of this information requires corroboration from other sources. Iran and Russia have been under Western sanctions on energy exports, and both have been using stealth to sell oil and gas. This is supplemented by the secrecy surrounding the import of energy by China from these two dictatorships. While some secrecy has also surrounded India's purchases from Russia and Iran, democracy ensures that India's economic indicators, including production, export, and import, are ultimately reflected in the records. Any policymaker dealing with energy transition struggles with the data from China, Russia, and Iran, hence we have given extra space to these three countries.

A chapter on hydrogen has been added to Part II of the book. More of hydrogen's potential to play a decisive role in energy transition and security still lies in the future rather than on the ground. Yet, every country in the world is focussing on that potential. For policymakers, the future of energy transition must necessarily negotiate the unknowns of cheap and green hydrogen manufacture and use. However, it is now clear that batteries alone may ultimately prove to be less than adequate in terms of capacity, cost, and environmental repercussions/cost, to transform the entire green generation, which is mostly infirm power, into firm power available around the clock.

In Part III, Mrs Manjula Prasher has written about the disruptive role that disinformation can play both for energy transition as well as for energy security. Shri Sanjeev Chopra shares the remarkable role he played while working with the Ministry of Agriculture in moving the country towards a food-surplus status and enabling export-oriented growth in this sector. Shri Rabindra Nath Sen, through his numerous writings, has reminded us of the perils of the poor being left behind in the march towards prosperity. Here, he has dwelt on the need to maintain an inclusive perspective in energy transition. Dr Brij Behari Dave draws on his experience of writing about geopolitics to elaborate on the huge impact that energy transition shall have on international relations. Shri Ajit Balaji Joshi, who is also working in the agriculture sector, gives us a peep into the potential of this sector in aiding and promoting energy transition, exposing the myth that agricultural land has to be necessarily reduced to provide space for green energy production. Shri Vivek Kumar Dewangan tells us how India, including the Rural Electrification Corporation, has a few lessons for the world in making the energy transition sustainable. Shri Gurdeep Singh has written about the National Thermal Power Corporation that ensures firm coal and gas power for India and is now also moving into nuclear power. He describes the crucial role this organisation plays in making India energy self-sufficient and energy secure. Shri Manoj Tripathi and Shri Charanpreet Singh delve into the Bhakra Beas Management Board (BBMB) project that led India's transition from a food-deficit country to a food-surplus country. He also elaborates on the role of this project in

India's energy security. Shri Dip Kishore Sen offers the perspective of the private sector as India moves on the path of energy transition.

In Part IV, Shri Harry Dhaul shares a dream of a global utopia where energy does not pollute the environment, and instead of dividing the world and causing wars and strife, it contributes to peace and tranquillity.

We thank all these personalities who have contributed to this book. As is common with a group of such distinguished personalities, there may be some divergence of opinion across chapters. We have made no attempt to harmonise their viewpoints, as we believe that diversity is more conducive to transparency as well as to fertilising new ideas.

We hope this book proves useful to all those involved with the energy transition and energy security issues at this defining moment in human history.

Part I
The Policymakers

1

Road Transport and Highways Steer India towards Energy Security

Nitin Gadkari

In the context of nation-building, we talk of three Es as the most important pillars: ethics, economy, ecology/environment. The last is particularly important and has three critical aspects of pollution: air, water, and sound. As far as air pollution is concerned, I feel that the responsibility lies all the more with me, as I am the minister in charge of transport, including automobiles. During the last ten years, we have tried to make improvements, and some success has been achieved. Fossil fuels are problematic not only in the context of pollution but also for our economy. We are importing fossil fuels to the tune of Rs 16,00,000 crore every year, and in the coming years this will increase to Rs 25,00,000 crore. Our country has been adding to the number of automobiles at a rapid pace. In December 2013, we had less than 2.5 crore vehicles; ten years later, we had more than 35 crore, of which 27 lakh were electric vehicles. All the major global automobile brands have entered India, and I frequently receive invitations to launch new models.

Atmanirbhar Bharat, a $5-trillion economy, and becoming the third-largest economy in the world—these three goals have been set by the Honourable Prime Minister Shri Narendra Modi for the nation by 2025. The automobile industry will play a major role in achieving these goals, as it contributes to employment, exports, and tax revenue, but it could simultaneously lead to a substantial increase in the already high levels of pollution, with adverse consequences on the health of our people. It could also result in an avoidable increase in accidents, leading to the loss of life and limb. Therefore, we have accepted the challenge that, along with the growth in this sector, we will not only prevent an increase in pollution but also make a substantial reduction in the existing levels of pollution, despite the growth in the number of vehicles. To achieve this difficult goal, we are focussing not only on electric vehicles but also on vehicles running on alternative fuels. I have been working in this field since 2000 when Shri Atal Bihari Vajpayee was prime minister. He had sent a delegation under the leadership of Shri Ram Naik, then petroleum minister, to Brazil. I was part of that delegation and had the opportunity to observe Brazil's efforts in blending ethanol into automobile fuel. I realised that it had the potential to reduce our imports, lower fuel prices for consumers, and also reduce pollution. Shri K.S. Sudarshan, the then sarsanghchalak of the Rashtriya Swayamsevak Sangh (RSS), had frequently talked about using this admixture of biofuels and petroleum products, but it took somewhat longer to convince the people concerned of the benefits of out-of-the-box ideas. Subsequently, I became the president of the Bharatiya Janata Party and repeatedly emphasised the need for diversification in agriculture towards the energy and power sectors, but people were still sceptical. It is now, after almost two decades, that the importance of this transition is being fully appreciated.

The present and the future of rural India are linked to four Js: jal, jungle, jameen, and janwar (water, forests, land, and animals). Unfortunately, in the past, these aspects, which have a great bearing not only on our food security but also on our energy security, have not received due attention. As a result, rural areas have become more impoverished in comparison to the prosperity of cities. Agriculture contributes only 15 per cent to the GDP, while manufacturing adds more than 28 per cent, and the service sector accounts for over 54 per cent. The last two have been increasing, while the contribution of agriculture has been falling, creating a huge gap in the per capita income and spending power between rural and urban areas. While the latest survey shows that the percentage gap in consumption between the two has fallen, the average urban monthly per capita consumption expenditure is still roughly 70 per cent higher than in rural areas.

Bio and alternative fuels have great potential to transform the economics of agriculture, thereby bringing prosperity to rural areas. This will have two immediate benefits: It will enable rural areas to contribute to our GDP at par with urban areas, and it will slow down the migration to urban areas. At one time, 85 per cent of Indians lived in villages; that figure has now dropped to 65 per cent, despite the huge population growth. This shows the extent to which villagers have been migrating to cities in search of livelihood. This migration has led to the proliferation of slums in cities and has strained the resources of municipal administrations in providing basic amenities like housing, water, electricity, sewerage, education, and health to these internal migrants. These people left the villages because of a lack of roads, safe drinking water, sanitation, and other amenities, coupled with low income, primarily because of small land holdings, a lack of focus on highly remunerative commercial crops and alternative commercial uses of their existing crops, residues, and wastes. Unfortunately, they are confronted with the same problems after migration. While improvement in amenities in slums would better the lot of existing migrants, preventing future migration will continue to depend on whether agriculture becomes a source of sustainable rural prosperity through a rapid increase in farmers' income, particularly by diversifying into the energy sector.

If the agriculture sector's contribution to GDP growth increases to 24 per cent, migration will be reduced, and even reverse migration may take place. After all, the environment in rural areas is cleaner and more attractive than in cities and urban people have been going to rural homestays for relaxation. To achieve the mission of Atmanirbhar Bharat, migration to cities must become less attractive, and for that to happen, water, electricity, roads, education, and health facilities need to be provided in rural areas at the same standards as those available in cities. Like smart cities, we need smart villages too. The most important contribution to this transformation can be made through biofuels, for which we have already made a start. Eighty-five factories for biofuel are under construction, of which thirty-five have been completed. Rice straw can give us bio-CNG and bio-LPG. At Panipat, we have been making one lakh litres of ethanol and 150 tonnes of bitumen every year. So far we had been making ethanol from molasses. Now, technology is emerging where sugarcane juice can be converted directly into ethanol. We can also make ethanol from corn, broken rice, and even from food grains that may have somewhat deteriorated and become unfit for human and cattle consumption, making it a case of 'waste to wealth'. Ethanol can now be made from segregated municipal solid waste too, thus converting a source of urban air and water pollution into a valuable asset. The refinery in Numaligarh in Assam has started making ethanol from bamboo. Seeing these emerging sources of ethanol, we have decided that petrol shall be blended with 20 per cent ethanol. By producing cheaper pollution-free import substitutes indigenously, our oil import bill can be reduced by Rs 1,00,000 crore. We are exporting petrol to Bangladesh through a pipeline. If we blend it with 20 per cent ethanol, it will not only make petrol cheaper for our neighbour, but it will also reduce pollution in that country while providing extra income to our farmers. This will reduce our crude oil import bill and enhance our energy security.

We are not stopping at making only ethanol from biomass. Of the total requirement of 80 lakh tonnes of bitumen, we produce 50 lakh tonnes indigenously and the remaining 30 lakh tonnes have to be imported. Now, we are producing bitumen from rice straw, the burning of which has been a contentious issue. We are also producing aviation fuel from biomass, and in August 2018, an Indian budget carrier flew its turboprop Q400 aircraft from Dehradun to Delhi on fuel made from biomass. Then in December 2018, the Indian Air Force flew its An-32 transport aircraft using blended bio-jet fuel, and they are working on flying fighter jets on blended fuel. The International Air Transport Association (IATA) believes that biofuels have the potential to reduce greenhouse gases emissions by 80 per cent compared to the present aviation fuel over their entire lifecycle. Thus, soon, the aviation sector will increase farmers' incomes, reduce flying costs, lower our import bill, and decrease environmental pollution caused by airplanes.

Logistics costs are crucial for Bharat to gain a competitive edge in exports. Our logistics cost is 14–16 per cent, primarily due to road conditions, which lead to slower traffic and more consumption of high-priced imported fuel. If we could reduce the logistics cost to 9 per cent, we would be able to produce the cheapest trucks, buses, cars, and scooters without compromising on our high-quality standards. This will make our exports competitive. If there is any doubt about our potential to dominate the vehicle export market, let it be known that even today Bajaj Auto and TVS Motor Company are exporting 50 per cent of their production. The boost to GDP from the automobile sector will help us reach the goal set by NITI Aayog of a $30-trillion economy by 2047 and a per capita income of $17,590.

The transport sector plays a vital role in any economy. The movement of people and goods is a critical component of any production process as well as for import and export. The primary dependence for this movement within the country and to neighbouring countries, such as Nepal, is on road transport. Even when goods are transported by rail, air, or sea, the road network provides the last-mile connectivity. The quality of roads determines the efficiency of road transport. Poor quality of roads results in suboptimal speeds, traffic jams, and higher accident rates. All these contribute to pollution, longer travel time, and increased transport costs. Furthermore, they increase the turnaround time of rolling stock, which reduces its efficient utilisation. In the past, our country lagged behind in providing a nationwide high-speed road network. The absence of good roads connecting towns to villages diminishes the ability of our farmers to efficiently market their produce. The absence of fast transport discourages them from diversifying into high-value but perishable commodities like flowers, fruits, and vegetables. Fuel efficiency increases considerably on smooth roads that are free of bottlenecks. That reduces our oil imports and adds to energy security.

When our former prime minister, Shri Atal Bihari Vajpayee, took office in 1999, he recognised this bottleneck in our economic development as well as in the prosperity of our rural areas. He conceptualised the Golden Quadrilateral to connect the four corners of the country by expressways. He also accelerated work on the East–West and North–South corridors that are now effectively bringing most of the country within reach of expressways. The projects slowed down after Shri Vajpayee demitted office in 2004. During the next ten years, not many of the national highways were converted from two-lane to four-lane. The total length of the national highways, including two-lane ones, at that time was 91,287 kilometres. This shows how inadequate our road transport network was more than sixty-five years after Independence.

With the painful realisation of this major transport bottleneck that was holding back the development of our country, in 2014, the new government took a pledge to more than double the national highways to 2,00,000 kilometres. Since then, we have already achieved 1,61,350 kilometres. We increased the average construction per day from 11.6 km to 37 km. In 2013, the four-lane national highways constituted about 18,000 km of the total of 91,287 km. Now this figure has gone up four times to more than 72,000 km out of 1,61,350 km. This has been possible through various models involving tolls, the yearly collection of which has increased from Rs 4,770 crore in 2013–14 to Rs 41,342 crore in 2022–23. We expect that this figure shall reach Rs 1,30,000 crore by 2030. This was facilitated by the 'One Nation, One FASTag' initiative, which was introduced as a pilot project in 2014 on the portion of the Golden Quadrilateral between Ahmedabad and Mumbai. We quickly extended the network throughout the country over the next seven years and made it mandatory for all four- or more-wheeled vehicles in February 2021. This has made the passage through toll points smoother, and the average waiting time at these points has come down from 734 seconds in 2014 to forty-seven seconds in 2023. The waiting period is highly detrimental to the environment, as vehicles move at a crawling speed, resulting in avoidable fuel consumption. A study by the Indian Institute of Management Calcutta (IIMC) revealed that the waiting and crawling at the tolls resulted in fuel wastage of Rs 70,000 crore. We are trying to further reduce the waiting time to thirty seconds.

The frenetic pace of highway construction has earned us seven world records. In May 2021, the National Highways Authority of India (NHAI) established world records recognised by the *Guinness Book of World Records* by building a 2.5-km four-lane concrete road within 24 hours. Another feat of completing 25 km of a one-lane road within 24 hours was also recognised as a world record. Completing both works simultaneously was also a world record. In June 2022, NHAI was again recognised by the *Guinness Book of World Records* for laying 75 km of bituminous concrete in a single lane of NH53 in 105 hours and 33 minutes between Amravati and Akola districts. The work began on 3 June 2022 at 7.27 a.m. and was completed on 7 June 2022 at 5 p.m. In this project, 36,634 metric tonnes of bituminous mix were used by a workforce of 720. The previous record was held by Qatar for building 25.75 km of road in Doha. Another record was set in May 2023 when the Ghaziabad Aligarh Expressway Private Limited, a Special Purpose Vehicle (SPV) of Cube Highways Trust, in collaboration with EPC contractor Larsen & Toubro Limited, completed the laying of 112.5 lane kilometres of bituminous concrete within 100 hours, from 15 May 2023 at 10 a.m. to 2 p.m. on 19 May 2023. A total of 51,396 tonnes of asphalt was used in a single operation, and both achievements were recognised as world records.

Our contracting models have evolved from build-operate-transfer (BOT), build-own-operate-transfer (BOOT), toll, operate and transfer (TOT), etc., to the Hybrid Annuity Model (HAM). To monetise completed highways, we have now sponsored the InvITs (Infrastructure Investment Trust). The Canada Pension Plan Investment Board and the

Ontario Teachers' Pension Plan have each subscribed 25 per cent, with the remaining 50 per cent allocated to domestic investors. The confidence of investors in us can be gauged from the fact that we had kept ten days for subscription, but it was subscribed within seven hours, and by the end of the subscription period, it was oversubscribed seven times. We pay an annual interest at 8.05 per cent, which is credited to the investors' accounts every month. Many retired people have invested their retirement benefits with us, and their pensions are being supplemented by this regular income. Thus, our senior citizens are contributing to India's efforts in creating a world-class road network and ensuring our energy security, while also securing their own financial future.

Many areas in Uttarakhand, Himachal Pradesh, Ladakh, Jammu and Kashmir, and the northeastern states are mountainous. Road construction in such areas can leave a massive ecological footprint, as these mountains are part of the Himalayan ranges that are relatively very young and mostly soft. Such mountains also have water pockets, and road construction can lead to landslides. As we are committed to taking India forward on the path to prosperity while safeguarding the environment, we are constructing tunnels wherever feasible. In addition to saving the mountains, these tunnels reduce travel time, pollution, and wear and tear of vehicles. It used to take more than three hours to cross the Rohtang Pass between Manali and Keylong, and the pass used to remain closed for more than half the year. During winter, when the pass was snowbound, patients in Lahaul-Spiti had to be airlifted to hospitals. Now, the Atal Tunnel has reduced travel time to just a few minutes, making these valleys accessible around the year. Adventure enthusiasts who visit Rohtang Pass now find it to be pollution-free.

Tunnels are expensive to construct, but we are tweaking the process to reduce construction cost. The original cost estimate for the Zojila tunnel was Rs 12,000 crore, but we were able to finally get bids that were Rs 5,000 crore lower. Similarly, the cost of the Majuli–Jorhat Bridge has been reduced from Rs 4,000 crore to below Rs 1,000 crore. Where tunnels cannot be constructed due to feasibility or cost factors, we are stabilising the mountains by learning from technologies developed in Switzerland and Norway. Landslides damage mountains by carrying away the topsoil, which can take up to a hundred years to form. This topsoil is the foundation for the vegetation that stabilises the mountains. Landslides uproot trees, and trees like deodar take hundreds of years to mature. All of this ends up in rivers, causing reservoirs to become silted up quickly. I have suggested to the Himachal Pradesh government that we can desilt the riverbeds by a few feet and use the excavated material for road construction. The siltation of riverbeds affects not only the availability of irrigation water and flood protection capability of these reservoirs, but it also impacts power generation. Hydropower is renewable, green, and low cost. Once the capital cost of the project is recovered, the only cost of power is the variable cost, which is very low. This low-cost power will aid our transition to methanol, electric vehicles, and hydrogen vehicles, and will contribute to our energy security. Therefore, the cost of tunnels, though seemingly high, should be considered in light of high fuel consumption on mountain roads, damage by landslides, and other costs associated with increased travel time and closures of passes in winter.

The Delhi–Mumbai Expressway, which is nearing completion, will significantly contribute to the economy of the nation by facilitating fast road connectivity between the national capital and the financial capital of the country. This 1,386-kilometre expressway, with a maximum permissible speed of 120 km/h, will reduce the travel time between the two metros to twelve hours. Costing Rs 1,11,420 crore, it is already operational between Delhi and Jaipur, and the entire project will be completed by the end of 2025. Travel time between other important cities is also being reduced by faster highways. Delhi to Amritsar will come down from ten hours to four hours; Kanpur to Lucknow will be reduced to thirty-five minutes from the present two hours; Delhi to Katra from fourteen hours to six hours; and Delhi to Srinagar, currently a day-long haul, will only take eight hours thanks to the fourteen tunnels between Srinagar and Jammu, with four more tunnels to be added. Once the projects are completed, inter-metro distance will also be reduced. For example, the distance from Delhi to Chennai will be 300 kilometres shorter. We are also connecting ports with expressways to facilitate export and import, and to reduce logistics costs to make Bharat competitive in the world. For example, the six-lane Raipur–Vishakhapatnam access-controlled road of 464 kilometres, costing Rs 17,000 crore, is under construction. This will boost exports from central India, particularly from Madhya Pradesh, Chhattisgarh, and Odisha. This will also boost tourism to India's eastern seaboard, the potential of which has remained underutilised compared to the western seaboard. For the development and maintenance of strategic roads in border areas, we have created the National Highways and Infrastructure Development Corporation Ltd. (NHIDCL), which is helping improve the highway network in the northeast of the country. This will accelerate the development of Chhattisgarh as well. To ensure the use of the latest technology, the quality of construction, and maintenance of the large number of bridges built under the national highway projects, the Ministry of Road Transport and Highways (MORTH) has set up the Indian Bridge Management System (IBMS) at the Indian Academy for Highway Engineers in Noida.

Construction of good highways leads to improvement in the quality of life and acceleration of economic activities. We have planned 670 amenity centres along the national highways, and work has already started on about 200 of them. These centres feature pleasant architectural designs and offer facilities such as food, rest, and recreation, along with petrol, CNG, and electric charging stations. There is also provision for adding hydrogen stations in the future. Logistics parks are being developed along these highways, and these are expected to attract an investment of Rs 2,00,000 crore. We are also planning electric highways where articulated buses (two or three buses connected together) can run by drawing power from overhead cables. This will lower ticket costs by 25 per cent, make public transport noiseless, and eliminate air pollution. Additionally, we plan to provide passenger amenities similar to air travel at much lower costs, which will reduce the environmental burden of personal cars and air travel. All these efforts will decrease our dependence on imported fuels and make us more secure in the energy sector.

A major cause of delay in road transport and accidents were the level crossings in the country. In coordination with the railways, road over bridges (ROBs) have been constructed under the Setu Bharatam project that was launched by the Honourable Prime Minister Shri Narendra Modi on 4 March 2016 with a budget of more than Rs 10,000 crore to make the national highways free of level crossings. On 11 November 2014, the Ministry of Road Transport and Highways signed an MOU with the Ministry of Railways for safe and seamless travel on national highways. This provides for the construction of subways under the railway tracks to facilitate pedestrian and vehicular traffic, so that all level crossings can be permanently closed. Where subways are not possible, foot over-bridges (FOBs) shall be provided. Wherever national highways are diverted to bypass urban areas, the level crossings in the city shall be closed by providing an ROB or FOB.

Another area linked to improvement in the efficiency and cost of road transport is the automobile industry, which is also under my charge. We are currently in third place, having pushed Japan to fourth place. This industry provides jobs to 4.5 crore people and is the highest contributor to the Goods and Services Tax (GST). Globally, we are the largest manufacturer of tractors, the second largest of buses and two-wheelers, the third largest of heavy trucks, the sixth largest of passenger vehicles, and the seventh largest of commercial vehicles. Our goal is to elevate our automobile sector to the first place in the world, ahead of China, which is currently at number two, and even ahead of the US, the leader in the sector. We have introduced a new scrapping policy for very old vehicles that burden the environment with air pollution due to outdated technology and consume more of precious imported fuel. These old vehicles are also more prone to breakdowns and accidents, both of which can lead to traffic jams. The scrapping policy is coupled with the recovery of rubber, plastic, steel, aluminium, and copper, which will reduce component costs by 30 per cent. This mantra of waste to wealth and knowledge to wealth will drive the progress of our country in the coming future.

Increased awareness about the environment and global warming, as well as more vehicles, more roads, and increasing economic activity, higher standards of living and greater prosperity must be accompanied by mitigating actions to ensure that this positive trend is sustainable. Some of our road projects get delayed due to issues related to environmental clearances. It is unavoidable that in order to increase the road network and widen existing roads, some trees have to be removed. While compensatory afforestation is always adopted wherever forest lands are affected by road construction, trees take a long time to mature to the same level as those that were removed. We are taking two steps to ensure that we get mature trees faster: We are transplanting old trees instead of cutting them, and we are planting new trees that are already three metres tall. For example, in 2022, there were more than a thousand banyan trees on the right of way (ROW) along Sant Tukaram Maharaj Palkhi Marg in Maharashtra. We transplanted 1,025 trees, of which 870 survived. Similarly, while widening the road from Chhatrapati Shivaji Nagar to Paithan National Highway, fifty-one banyan trees that were up to 100 years old were transplanted. On Dwarka Expressway, 12,000 trees have been transplanted. So far, we have transplanted more than 70,000 trees. Some people are not comfortable with the cost of transplanting large trees. But can we really put a price on a 100-year-old tree when the choice is between cutting it down and relocating it? During the execution of highway projects, we have planted more than 3.8 crore trees, ensuring that these are at least three metres tall. We are not leaving this important aspect to contractors.

We have field-tested crash barriers made from bamboo and have also had them tested at an institute in Indore. Their strength compares well with metal crash barriers. We are using municipal solid waste, after segregation, for road construction. Three million tonnes of such waste have been removed from the Ghazipur landfill in Delhi for this purpose. In this way, a public nuisance is being used to build roads, for which the earth would have otherwise been dug up. The process of segregation yields plastic, glass, and metals, and these are recycled to create additional value. Prime Minister Modi's Swachh Bharat Mission is thus being realised through road construction projects. Where the earth has to be dug up, we are creating ponds and lakes that are contributing to groundwater recharge. Delhi suffered due to the burning of paddy straw in surrounding areas. We are now making bio-bitumen from paddy stalks, which were previously a nuisance, and it is now being sold at Rs 2,000 per tonne. This will help reduce our dependence on imports for bitumen, which amounts to 30 lakh tonnes every year. Paddy stalks are now contributing to import substitution, and our farmers, who are called 'anna daatas' or providers of food, are now also becoming 'bitumen daatas', and foreign exchange savers.

The bulk of pollution caused by road transport can be substantially reduced by the use of methanol. Methanol costs only Rs 25 per litre, while petrol and diesel cost four times more. We have started testing a 20:80 blend of methanol and diesel in Karnataka State Transport buses and have received a test certificate confirming its success. Ashok Leyland has made a truck that runs fully on methanol. I had asked the chief minister of Assam to try an admixture of methanol and diesel for trucks and buses. The experiment has succeeded and 15 per cent methanol is being added to diesel. This is reducing running costs as well as pollution. We are shifting to electric buses on a large scale and hope to convert the entire intra-city bus fleet to electric in five years' time. We are also working on hydrogen. In order to increase people's confidence in this fuel, I am using Toyota's hydrogen car, the Mirai. At present, we are producing some blue hydrogen and are working towards green hydrogen in a big way so that vehicular pollution can become a thing of the past. If we succeed in our efforts, a major portion of the foreign exchange, to the tune of Rs 16,00,000 crore, which we currently use for importing oil, will be saved. Moreover, this import is subject to price fluctuations and shipping disruptions due to geopolitical events like wars and other international incidents which compromise our energy security. Thus, switching to alternative fuels not only adds to farmers' incomes and reduces pollution but also saves foreign exchange and enhances our energy security.

Road safety is a major area of concern in our country. It causes immense pain and suffering to the victims and their families. Half a million accidents kill more than 1,60,000 people every year, rendering families destitute, as 60 per cent of these deaths are in the age group of 18 to 35 years. Nearly 4,00,000 people are seriously injured every year, placing a large burden on healthcare. All these tragedies slice off more than 3.1 per cent of our GDP and substantially lower our country's happiness index. We have set ourselves the goal of reducing these accidents by 50 per cent by 2030. We are placing emphasis on all the four Es of road safety: engineering (of roads and vehicles), enforcement, education, and emergency response. Simple steps such as regular eye check-ups for commercial vehicle drivers can make a significant dent in the grim accident statistics. In addition, we are tapping into the corporate social responsibility (CSR) funds of the corporate sector for this purpose. The negative strokes of law alone will not produce the required results, and the positive social recognition of good behaviour will go a long way in bringing about the necessary attitudinal changes for road safety. We are also encouraging the use of resources of NGOs, self-help groups, and student bodies in this direction.

Despite comprising 18 per cent of the world's population, India has access to only 4 per cent of the world's water resources. The country has 4,000 billion cubic metres of rainfall, but it is concentrated over a few months of the year. As a result, rivers are in flood during the rainy season and carry very little water during the rest of the year, making water transport impractical. Shri Vajpayee's vision extended even to water transport. In 2002, he envisaged the Interlinking of Rivers (ILR) project, which included the 9,300-km-long Garland Canal. This canal would make the water bodies and rivers across the length and breadth of the country complementary to each other. It would make water transport a feasible alternative, prevent situations where there is drought in one part of the country and floods in another, and facilitate optimal utilisation of river water, a large part of which still flows into the sea. Unfortunately, this idea was not followed up as enthusiastically by the new government after Shri Vajpayee left office in 2004. After 2014, many components of the river interlinking project were revived.

When one thinks as a politician, it is mainly about the next election; socio-economic thinking, however, has to focus on the next century. Such thinking propels us to make use of yet uncharted opportunities. Prime Minister Modi's vision of Amrit Kaal, for which we have twenty-two years until 2047, is a mission goal for MORTH, and our team is working to achieve it. The aim is to make Indians more productive, prosperous, happier, and healthier by ensuring comfortable, pollution-free, fast, and safe road travel for people and goods. In the process, we are making our rural areas as comfortable and economically attractive as urban areas to stem rural-urban migration. Simultaneously, we are contributing to India's national security and economic strength by enhancing our energy security.

2

Geopolitical Implications of Lopsided Natural Resource Endowment

Suresh Prabhakar Prabhu

Countries not endowed with sufficient natural resources lament the inequity of nature. On the other hand, economists talk of the 'resource curse', also known as the paradox of plenty or the poverty paradox. It is based on some empirical evidence that countries with abundant natural resources have worse development outcomes than countries with fewer resources. In modern times, this idea was crystallised by Richard Auty in his book *Sustaining Development in Mineral Economies: The Resource Curse Thesis.*[1] The concept is debatable, but it does appear that when a less-developed economy becomes mineral rich, it becomes what has been called a rentier state. It is defined as a state that generates a majority of its revenues from the sale of valuable resources to foreign clients, and such revenues are called external rents. It has been observed that such states pay scant attention to domestic agriculture and industrial development, since they have the foreign exchange to import what they need.

Lenin considered rentier states as usurers and the practice of living on external rents as a form of imperialism, saying that the rentier states were a 'state of parasitic, decaying capitalism, and this circumstance cannot fail to influence all the socio-political conditions of the countries concerned'.[2] Lenin, of course, had the Marxist obsession that nothing good can come out of capitalism, though experience has shown that capitalism and democracy have thrived together, while Marxism leads to extinction of democracy. Whether the resource curse theory has general application, or it operates only when certain other conditions are present simultaneously, the fact remains that most countries dependent on the export of natural resources are undemocratic. It does appear that their natural resources often strengthen a dictator, a king, or any other form of totalitarian regime. If we take the example of oil, as of today, all the states that have thrived mainly on oil revenues have been undemocratic. The US may seem like an exception, but the fact remains that at no time in its history has the export of oil been the basis of its prosperity.

That brings us to a few questions: What are the geopolitical implications of rentier states for themselves and for others? Does the resource curse arise solely from internal factors, or does it also have transnational causes and effects? How does the resource curse lead to erosion of democracy? Can the external rents obtained from the export of natural resources be ploughed back into the domestic economy to stimulate domestic agricultural and industrial growth?

One obvious conclusion emerges when we look at the nation that allows other nations to dig its resources and ship them away: it has income without effort. However, this income accrues to the state, while most of the digging may be done by people who are paid a much smaller wage by the foreigner than the wage in his own country. Thus, the foreign entity, state, or corporate gets a licence to exploit the local labour. Since the rentier state is so dependent on what is paid to it by foreigners, it develops a collusive relationship with the foreign entity and ultimately becomes complicit in the exploitation of its own citizens. Thus, are sown the seeds of a totalitarian state, which eulogises the exploitation of its masses by a foreign state, packaging it as the sacrifice being made by the people. The state may then lean on religious or sectarian divisions in the society and side with the more powerful faction to project goals other than prosperity. Alternatively, it may demonise another nation that is in some way on the other side of the fence, whether the difference is ideological, religious, or sectarian. All this makes the probability of a rentier state being at peace with other nations rather low.

Other countries look at the resource-rich state with a totalitarian government as one that can be easily exploited. They can offer personal inducements to the dictator, provide weapons to fight the nations the dictator has demonised, or assist in suppressing voices of democracy. They can finance tinsel projects to awe the population and raise the stature of the ruler. As the competition among buyers increases, so do these efforts to curry favour with the undemocratic ruler, along with rising geopolitical tensions among the rich buyers. Many of the conflict zones in the world have their foundation in the concentration of natural resources in a country, which allows it to become a pawn on the geopolitical chessboard.

That is where the idea of 'democratic peace' strengthens this hypothesis. Britannica defines it as 'the proposition that democratic states never (or almost never) wage war on one another'. However, democracies, in general, are certainly not more peaceful than non-democratic countries, but between themselves, democracies have institutional mechanisms that provide alternatives to hostilities, with the legislature, judiciary, civil society, and a free press operating as modulators. The absence of these modulators, when one or both of the parties are undemocratic, creates a higher probability of violent conflict. As far back as 1776, Thomas Paine had said, 'The republics of Europe are all (and we may say always) in peace.' Immanuel Kant believed that a majority of people will never vote to go to war, unless in self-defence. He said that a world that had only constitutional republics was a necessary condition for peace. Alexis de Tocqueville, too, subscribed to the peace dividend of a democratic society: 'When the principle of equality spreads, as in Europe now, not only within one nation, but at the same time among several neighboring peoples, the inhabitants of these various countries, despite different languages, customs, and laws, always resemble each other in an equal fear of war and love of peace.'[3]

Thus, we can reasonably conclude that in a less developed state, a surfeit of a natural resource that is not so abundant in the rest of the world leads to erosion of democracy and geopolitical machinations that impinge negatively on world peace.

Domestic Causes of the Resource Curse

One obvious factor is the state of development of a nation that finds itself endowed with an exceptionally large share of a natural resource in demand by rich countries. If it is already developed, with institutional mechanisms in place for processing the resource and adding value for its own people, it is unlikely that it will export it in raw form. The institutional mechanisms will prevent exploitation in terms of low prices or low wages. If the country is democratic, many voices and ideas will ultimately produce an optimal solution that gives maximum advantage to the local economy.

Botswana is often cited as an undeveloped country that rode on democracy to fully capitalise on its natural resources for the benefit of its people. When it gained independence in 1966, few believed in its viability. As documented by the World Bank, '[Botswana] was one of the poorest countries in the world, with per capita annual income of just $70 a year ...

There were only 12 kilometres of paved roads, and agriculture (mostly cattle farming for beef production) accounted for 40 percent of gross domestic product (GDP). By 2007, Botswana had 7,000 kilometers of paved roads, and per capita income had risen to about $6,100 … making Botswana an upper-middle-income country.'[4] The World Bank report further states that life expectancy had increased from thirty-seven years to sixty years. The share of agriculture in GDP had fallen to 2.5 per cent. There were some negatives too: income inequality had increased, and there was rural to urban migration. Yet, all segments of society had gained, and the country had reduced its dependence on international aid from 60 per cent to 3 per cent. The report adds, '[M]any countries in Africa, including Zambia, Nigeria, the Democratic Republic of Congo, Sierra Leone, and others, have squandered vast amounts of their natural wealth … Mineral-based countries seem to be prone to bad government.'[5]

The prosperity of Botswana was fuelled by the discovery of diamonds and other minerals. The country was lucky that it is relatively homogeneous ethnically. Yet, the World Bank asserts, '… most of the credit must be given to the leadership, which, since independence, has designed and fostered the conditions of governance that have ensured stability and social and economic progress.'[6] The World Bank has enumerated the steps taken by the leadership: respect for property rights, rule of law, high degree of transparency and consultation, all of which created a trust in the government. It concludes, 'To a large extent, Botswana overcame the threat of the resource curse.'[7]

The United Nations Economic Commission for Africa has praised this bright example on what was once called the dark continent with these words: 'Botswana is a shining light and beacon of hope in the fight against corruption in Africa and has one of the best anti-corruption profiles on the continent.'[8]

Thus, while the resource curse has destroyed the socio-economic fabric of many countries that became rentier states, democracy not only saved Botswana from that fate but also made it a model that other African states could aspire to follow if they moved on the path of democracy. The curse of unequal endowment of natural resources in a less developed economy and its deleterious impact on the geopolitics of the world thus requires only one mantra for exorcism: democracy.

3

Ensuring India's Energy Security and Transition to Green Energy in the Face of Geopolitical Upheavals

Raj Kumar Singh

Electricity is the most important infrastructure and a sine qua non for development. We have traditionally generated electricity from coal, with nominal contributions from nuclear and gas. Our coal has relatively lower calorific value, and domestic coal production has not kept pace with rapidly increasing consumption. As a result, we have to import a part of our coal demand. We also have huge domestic consumption of oil and gas, with very little domestic production, making us import-dependent for these hydrocarbons. Of course, some of our imports are re-exported after processing and value addition. However, our hydrocarbon requirement is highly dependent on the security of shipping lanes, and that security has been under question in recent times. There are geopolitical disruptions on the Red Sea–Suez Canal route and in the South China Sea. Not only has fuel been import-dependent, but we have also faced legacy issues of low manufacturing capacity for generation equipment, as well as the fact that domestic manufacturing costs more than imports. This trend continued as we began shifting to solar and wind energy, with substantial import of solar panels and wind turbines. This import dependence remained a threat at the core of our energy security.

As we face the challenge of ensuring a smooth transition to green energy, we must ensure that the transition does not jeopardise our economic growth and energy security. On this energy journey, we encounter the apparently conflicting requirements of long-term investment as well as rapidly evolving and often disruptive technologies. We have to strike a balance between environmental concerns and the need to provide firm and reliable power for our growing economy. There are geopolitical upheavals that threaten to upend our energy security. There are also the expectations of the poorer sections of society, and the small and marginal farmers. In the face of all these apparently contradictory demands, we are adopting innovative solutions to achieve all these goals simultaneously.

Our Strategy

- Create sufficient generating capacity that corresponds to the growth targets of our economy and meets the comfort-level expectations of our 1.4 billion people. Simultaneously, we aim to create and sustain a national grid that eliminates continuous regional imbalances in generation and consumption.
- Transition towards our goal of peaking emissions by 2050 or before and moving towards net-zero emissions by 2070 while ensuring quality power 24x7. While undertaking this balancing act, we should not look upon fossil fuels as an evil to be banished but as supplements to be used until needed.
- Enabling small consumers' and farmers' involvement in this transition to green energy, so that they get cheaper or

even free power without anyone else paying for it, thus, removing the burden on distribution companies and state governments.

- Improve energy efficiency in all consumption sectors by encouraging and enabling device transitions and process transitions, while improving the energy intensity of production processes to achieve the highest standards and achievable norms prevalent in developed economies.
- Facilitate indigenous production of thermal, solar, and wind generation equipment and infrastructure, and support R&D for promising storage technologies, including batteries and hydrogen, to reduce costs and make them viable at grid scale.
- Enable our transport, steel, cement, and other legacy consumers of fossil fuels to make a smooth transition to hydrogen without adding to operational costs.

I shall elaborate on each of these steps to show how, during the last decade, we have made steady progress and have even overachieved/overshot our ambitious targets.

The Goal of Sufficient Generation and Transmission Capacity

At the beginning of 2014, there were wide demand-supply gaps when it came to the time of day and seasons. The gap was 4.2 per cent in terms of energy, going up to 4.7 per cent at peak. Within two years, by 2016–17, we had reduced these to 0.7 per cent and 1.6 per cent respectively,[1] and further reduced them to 0.3 per cent and 1.4 per cent in 2023, despite peak demand increasing from 136 GW to more than 243 GW during this period.[2] Earlier, we used to struggle with peak management while there was simultaneous backdown of generation. We frequently encountered very low grid frequencies, equipment damage, and even grid failures. Theoretically, the nation had 'one grid, one frequency', but Interregional transmission capacity constraints had created this inefficient scenario. We targeted this issue, and interregional transmission capacity was increased from 38,000 MW in 2013 to 1,16,540 MW in March 2024, an increase of 224 per cent. Now, the country is truly on a national grid, handling surpluses and shortages in real time. In the process, we have created the world's largest integrated transmission system that has 4.81 million circuit kilometres of transmission lines and 12,25,260 MVA of transformation capacity, with the ability to transfer 116.5 GW from one corner of the country to another.[3] During this period, we have spent Rs 2 lakh crore to construct 3,000 new substations, upgrade 4,000 substations, and add 8.5 lakh circuit kilometres of high tension (HT) and low tension (LT) lines, and 7.5 lakh transformers.[4]

For access, we have made the rules and regulations business-friendly through measures like General Network Access. Connectivity will be allotted immediately, and once you are connected at one point, you will be connected to the entire country. You can generate power anywhere and buy and sell anywhere. Furthermore, you do not need a transmission licence to get connected. We have also introduced the Green Energy Open Access Rules, which guarantee that you can buy energy from anyone you want.

India has invested Rs 20 lakh crore in the power sector over the past nine years, and in the next five to seven years, an additional Rs 17 lakh crore is expected. We have added 190 GW to the generation capacity, bringing the total to 436 GW. Eighty-five gigawatts of thermal capacity and 14 GW of hydro capacity are under construction, while another 15 GW of hydro energy is under clearance. As a result of all this, we have been able to increase rural power availability from 12.5 hours in 2015 to around 21 hours today, and in urban areas to 23.8 hours. I have publicly said that the days of generators are over. We have rules that state that 24x7 power is now a right. Unwarranted load shedding is an insult to the people. No distribution company will be allowed to indulge in gratuitous load shedding; if they do, they will have to pay penalties and consumers will be compensated. During the last ten years, peak demand has grown from 130 GW to 243 GW. It has been growing at the rate of 9 to 10 per cent every year and is likely to exceed 400 GW by 2030.[5] We have to be prepared for this in all sectors, be it generation, transmission, distribution, and the manufacture of equipment for these activities.

We used to be dependent on foreign equipment suppliers for the bulk of our capacity additions, both for thermal and renewable power. A significant amount of our generation and transmission equipment, including control systems, has been bought from China. There are attendant national security and energy security risks due to this dependence. The world is looking at China plus one, and we want to be that one. The year 2024 represents a decade of 'Make in India'. We want to manufacture the equipment for our needs and benefit from economies of scale, and we want our equipment to be competitive in the export market as well. We have already put in place policy instruments, such as a tariff barrier of 40 per cent on modules and a barrier of 25 per cent on cells, so that industry is protected. We have put quality barriers, so that externally manufactured equipment takes as much time to qualify as domestic equipment. To provide a level playing field to protect our industry from artificially low prices coupled with low quality from countries like China, in 2018, we came out with a circular stating that all imported equipment needs to undergo strenuous tests. For thermal equipment, we started the phased manufacturing programme, encouraging domestic manufacturing.[6] New production capacity for thermal, wind, and solar generation equipment has been established within the country. We have modified our bidding system to encourage indigenous production. The earlier system of giving the entire engineering-procurement-construction (EPC) contract to a single bidder was not producing an encouraging response from Indian manufacturers, as their specialisation was fragmented. To overcome this, we have encouraged splitting of tenders and bidding by consortia of companies.

We have taken steps which have further brightened the business environment in the power sector. A payment security mechanism, which has no parallel anywhere in the world, has been introduced. Payments are guaranteed within seventy-five days, and current dues are 100 per cent up to date. Even legacy dues are being paid. The demand and supply balance for the next 20–25 years will create a suppliers' market. My advice to the industry is to ramp up manufacturing capacities to meet demand, so that they are ready for the huge capacity that is coming.

While we are a leader in manufacturing of wind power equipment, there is a need to domestically manufacture wind turbines with larger capacities. We have informed manufacturers that there will come a time when we will not accept any turbine of less than 5 MW. We want entrepreneurs to enter the field of high-voltage direct current (HVDC) transmission lines. We have taken steps to improve investor confidence in power projects. Earlier, there were problems of stranded capacity, and the generation sector was in dire financial straits. We had about 60 GW under the National Company Law Tribunal (NCLT), but today, all power companies have doubled or tripled their share prices, and the market caps have increased three to four times, indicating how viable they have become. I have told investors very clearly that those in the power business will miss out if they are not adding capacity. Demand will continue to grow at a rapid pace, and prices in exchange will remain high. Those who add capacity will gain, and those who don't will miss out on a golden opportunity.

Achieving Emission Goals while Ensuring Energy Security

At our stage of economic development, to ensure our energy security, we cannot wish away thermal power, and we offer no apology for saying this. Simultaneously, we are committed to adopt a climate friendly and cleaner path. We shall, however, chart our own course which may be different from the one followed hitherto by others. We are a leader in our own right in energy transition and the narrative to the contrary being spread by some NGOs in the developed world is false and misleading. We are a huge country of 1,400 million people and comparing our emissions with countries of less than 100 million is ridiculous. A small island country may be consuming huge quantities of energy per capita, yet its total emissions will be less than ours. Just as we talk about GDP on a per capita basis, we must also discuss emissions in the same way. India's per capita emissions in 2023 were around 2 tonnes, while the global average was 4.6 tonnes. Advanced economies have per capita emissions that are substantially higher than the global average. For example, the figure for the US is 14.7 tonnes, and for China, it is 8.9 tonnes. Ten per cent of the global population with the highest income accounts for 48 per cent of global emissions. What is more worrying is that the per capita emissions in these high-emission countries are still increasing, even as India is given sermons on further lowering its already very low per capita emissions. The US had a 1.9 per cent increase in 2023 compared to 2022, while China's increased by 4.7 per cent over the same period. China's total emissions accounted for 35 per cent of the world's total, while India's were about 8 per cent. In 2023, the total CO_2 emissions of India were comparable to those of the European Union, even though India's population is more than three times that of the EU. Thus, it seems rather unfair to expect India to cut down on its economic growth while affluent countries continue to have increasingly higher emissions.

In spite of India being among the lowest per capita emitters, we are achieving exceptional results in creating renewable generation capacity. Our rate of new capacity creation is the fastest after China. In March 2013, we had renewable generation capacity of only 28.1 GW. In March 2024, it was 190 GW, including 47 GW from large hydro projects. We had pledged that by 2030, 40 per cent of our energy capacity would come from non-fossils. In January 2024, it already stood at 44 per cent—180.7 GW out of a total of 427 GW. Almost all of this is from renewables, as our nuclear capacity is just 7.80 GW. Thus, we are six years ahead of our target. Not resting on our laurels, we have shifted the goal post forward: We have now pledged that 50 per cent of our capacity will come from non-fossil sources by 2030. We shall surpass the target of adding 500 GW renewable capacity by 2030, and within that year, we expect 65 per cent of our energy capacity to come from non-fossil generation. As president of the International Solar Alliance, I am acutely aware of the fact that 80 per cent of the global population resides in countries that depend on fossil fuel imports—that is a staggering 6 billion people. Renewable energy sources have the potential to supply 65 per cent of the world's total electricity needs by 2030 and to decarbonise 90 per cent of the power sector by 2050.[7]

Most of the renewable energy will come from solar and wind generation, which can supply round-the-clock power only through storage, which is expensive at present. We are dedicating resources for R&D to bring down storage prices, both for batteries and hydrogen. This is going to take time. Meanwhile, our demand growth cannot be kept waiting; it will have to be met through either thermal or nuclear power. We are working hard on nuclear power too, but that has a long gestation period, and there are issues with fuel availability. Hence, we look upon thermal and renewable energy not as alternatives but as complementary. We will have to keep adding to our thermal capacity until cheaper storage becomes available. We have 27 GW of coal capacity under construction and will start work on another 55 to 60 GW. We hope to have coal and lignite capacity of 283 GW running by March 2032, against the present 214 GW. We have asked that all states with thermal capacity must maintain and run them. Those states that wish to add additional thermal capacity shall be supported in doing so. We have assured thermal equipment manufacturers that they shall get a steady line of orders for the next five to seven years.

In addition, we have issued several policy documents to guide the transition to renewable energy. The National Action Plan for Climate Change (NAPCC) serves as the top-level guidance. We have issued the National Electricity Plan 2023 (NEP 2023) and also announced the National Green Hydrogen Mission in the same year. In December 2022, we amended the Energy Conservation Act. It lays the groundwork for a potential domestic carbon market and includes provisions for the establishment of a carbon market through the introduction of a Carbon Credit Trading Scheme (CCTS). The Bureau of Energy Efficiency (BEE), which has been given the responsibility to create the Indian carbon market, will work in collaboration with the Ministry of Power and the Ministry of Environment, Forest and Climate Change. The pilot carbon market, which is expected to cover petrochemicals, iron, steel, cement, pulp and paper, is expected to be operational by April 2025.

At COP 26 in 2021, Prime Minister Shri Narendra Modi announced a 2070 net-zero target for India, and during COP 27 on 18 December 2023, India submitted its long-term low carbon development strategy. As a party to the United Nations Framework Convention on Climate Change (UNFCCC) and its Paris Agreement, India submitted its first Nationally Determined Contribution (NDC) in the year 2015, comprising these quantifiable targets:

- To reduce the emissions intensity of its GDP by 33 to 35 per cent by 2030 from the 2005 level; and
- To achieve about 40 per cent cumulative installed electric power capacity from non-fossil fuel-based energy resources by 2030.

We achieved these two targets of the Nationally Determined Contribution well ahead of time. In fact, the target of a 33 per cent reduction in the emissions intensity was achieved as early as 2019, that is, eleven years in advance. During the period of 2005–2019, India's GDP grew at a cumulative annual growth rate of 7 per cent, while emissions rose by only 4 per cent. As of 31 October 2023, the cumulative installed generation capacity from non-fossil fuel-based energy resources was 186.46 MW, which is 43.81 per cent of the total cumulative installed electric power capacity. As per the third national communication submitted by India to the UNFCCC in December 2023, the emission intensity of its GDP was reduced by 33 per cent between 2005 and 2019. Then, we adopted updated NDCs:

- An emissions intensity target of 45 per cent below 2005 levels by 2030;
- A target of achieving 50 per cent cumulative installed electric power capacity from non-fossil fuel-based energy resources by 2030; and

- Creation of a carbon sink of 2.5 to 3 $GtCO_2e$ through additional forest and tree cover by 2030.

While India indicated in its updated NDC that achieving the 50 per cent non-fossil capacity target would require international support, even without that support, we are already on track to achieve 60 per cent or more non-fossil capacity by 2030 under current policies.

We have introduced several policy initiatives in recent years that demonstrate our commitment to climate change mitigation. The minimum Renewable Purchase Obligation (RPO), which was 24.6 per cent in 2023, will be gradually raised to 43.33 per cent by 2030. To demonstrate our focus on facilitating storage projects, NEP 2023 includes measures for the adoption of battery storage systems, and guidelines have also been issued for pumped storage. We are proactive in boosting the domestic manufacture of solar modules. Incentives have been formulated for the manufacture of electrolysers for producing green hydrogen, with a production target of 5 million tonnes per year by 2030. Similar to the RPO, a green hydrogen purchase mandate has also been formulated.

The United Nations Development Programme (UNDP) has noted our efforts in transitioning to green energy.[8] Taking note of our updated NDC to reduce the emission intensity of our GDP by 45 per cent, the UNDP has said that it is an important step towards achieving net-zero emissions by 2070. It has mentioned the steps we have envisaged for the decade 2021–2030, which will increase green jobs, boost manufacturing of low-emission products, such as electric vehicles and super-efficient appliances, and promote innovative technologies such as green hydrogen. It has also acknowledged our focus on sectors and areas vulnerable to climate change, disaster management, the Himalayas, and coastal regions. Additionally, it has expressed confidence that India will build capacities for the rapid diffusion of cutting-edge climate technology. The International Renewable Energy Agency (IRENA) has termed India as a 'renewable energy powerhouse and a country whose energy transition actions speak lounder than their words'.[9]

The UNDP has highlighted that worldwide employment in renewable energy stood at 11.5 million in 2019, with women holding one-third of these jobs. This number is expected to increase to more than 40 million by 2050. India is playing, and will continue to play, more than its fair share in this effort to generate employment through climate change.

Transition from Small Consumers and Farmers to Energy Generators

Due to differences in the paying capacities of consumers belonging to different economic strata, differential tariffs and cross subsidies are allowed by the State Electricity Regulatory Commissions. Although our long-term goal of abolishing these cross subsidies remains on the horizon, significant economic growth will be required before the paying capacity of the poorest households enables them to pay the same tariff as richer households. These differential tariffs, however, neither burden the distribution companies nor do they require any subvention from the state government, as the cross subsidy covers the difference.

The position with agricultural supply is, however, different. For the size of our country and the need to grow food for 1,400 million people, our surface water is very limited, and farmers have to rely on groundwater extracted through electric pump sets for irrigation. In certain areas, the groundwater is very deep, requiring powerful motors to pump it out, resulting in heavy consumption. Unfortunately, farmers find growing water-intensive crops like rice to be highly remunerative.

Many states provide free power for agriculture or charge a very nominal tariff, taking responsibility for paying the difference to the distribution company. Some states end up spending far more than their available resources and make up the difference through heavy borrowing. The liability of debt servicing further deteriorates their financial health, and they become remiss in paying the distribution companies for the cheap power supplied to the fields. This has severely hurt the financial health of the distribution companies, which then fail to pay the generators for the power purchased. As a result, the generators cannot buy coal or gas for power generation, and the supply in the system is reduced.

We have taken a tough stand on this issue. If any state wants to provide free or subsidised power to any category, it may do so, but it must pay the distribution company in advance. I have also warned the states against heavy borrowing to pay for power, as they could end up in a debt trap. For example, the state of Punjab has borrowed Rs 47,000 crore for giving freebies during 2022–2024, and debt servicing is eating into the development of infrastructure, as well as health and education expenditures. By addressing the issue of states' payments to distribution companies, we have brought the arrears down from Rs 1.45 lakh crore to Rs 40,000 crore, while the payment of current dues is now up to date. The outstanding dues of the generating companies will now be cleared within the next ten to twelve months. To introduce an element of competition in the distribution sector, we are trying to get an amendment passed for the separation of carriage and content. Different suppliers can sell to consumers on the same distribution lines. The regulator will fix a ceiling tariff, and the suppliers can compete below that.

We have taken steps to reduce the aggregate technical and commercial (AT&C) losses and have brought them down from 27 per cent to 15 per cent. A substantial part of these losses is due to inefficient distribution systems. That is where solar power generation by small consumers and farmers comes into play. The Pradhan Mantri Kisan Urja Suraksha evam Utthan Mahabhiyan (PM-KUSUM) is a nationwide initiative that aims to provide clean energy to farmers through solar pumps and grid-connected solar power plants. It has three components, and the targets are to be achieved by 31 March 2026:

- Component A: Setting up of 10,000 MW of decentralised ground/stilt-mounted, grid-connected solar or other renewable energy-based power plants by farmers on their land. Solar energy-based power plants (SEPPs) of 500 kW to 2 MW capacity will be set up by individual farmers/group of farmers/cooperatives/panchayats/Farmer Producer Organisations (FPOs)/Water User Associations (WUAs). The distribution companies (discoms) will notify surplus capacity at the sub-station level, which can be fed from the SEPP to the grid. The solar power generated will be purchased by discoms at a feed-in-tariff (FiT) determined by the respective State Electricity Regulatory Commission (SERC).
- Component B: Installation of 14 lakh standalone solar agriculture pumps. Individual farmers will be supported in installing standalone solar agriculture pumps with a capacity of up to 7.5 HP in off-grid areas where grid supply is not available. A Central Financial Assistance (CFA) of 30 per cent ((50 per cent for the northeastern states, Sikkim, Jammu and Kashmir, Himachal Pradesh, Uttarakhand, Lakshadweep, and Andaman and Nicobar Islands) of the benchmark cost or the tender cost, whichever is lower, for the standalone solar agriculture pump will be provided. The state government will give at least a 30 per cent subsidy, and the remaining up to 40

per cent will be borne by the farmer. Farmers can avail of bank finance so that they initially pay only 10 per cent of the cost, with the remaining 30 per cent of the cost provided as a loan.

- Component C: Solarisation of 35 lakh grid-connected agriculture pumps, including feeder-level solarisation. Individual farmers with grid-connected agriculture pumps will be supported in solarising their pumps. A solar PV capacity of up to twice the pump capacity in kW is allowed under the scheme. The farmer will be able to use the generated solar power to meet irrigation needs, and the excess solar power will be sold to discoms. The financing pattern shall be the same as in component B.

There is also a component for feeder-level solarisation. Instead of individual solar pumps, states can solarise agriculture feeders. Solar plants with a capacity to meet the agriculture load requirements of the selected feeder can be installed through the capital expenditure (CAPEX) or open expenditure (RESCO) model for a project period of twenty-five years.

To enable small consumers to become solar power generators, Finance Minister Nirmala Sitharaman included the Rooftop Solar Scheme or the PM Surya Ghar Muft Bijli Yojana in the 2024–25 budget. Consumers from low- and middle-income categories will receive subsidies ranging from Rs 30,000 to Rs 78,000 to install rooftop solar generation systems and will be given 300 kWh of free electricity every month. Nationwide, this group will save up to Rs 18,000 crore every year from free electricity and will be able to sell surplus power, through a net meter, to the distribution company.

Symbolic steps towards shifting to green energy play a big role in conveying the message to the people. Following the vision of our prime minister, the famous Sun Temple at Konark has been fully solarised and the town of Konark is being developed as Surya Nagri or Sun City.

These schemes, while providing reliable power to farmers and low-income consumers, will supplement the green generation capacity of the nation.

Improving Energy Efficiency

Energy efficiency has to be tackled at the consumption, device, building, and process levels. A simple example of increasing energy efficiency at consumption level is rationally setting the thermostat of air conditioners. Every degree raised in this setting saves 6 per cent of the energy consumed. If people set the thermostat at no lower than 24 degrees Celsius instead of 21 degrees Celsius, 18 per cent energy is saved. Currently, this consumption accounts for about one-tenth of the total energy consumption of the country, which means that keeping the thermostat at 24 degrees Celsius instead of 21 degrees Celsius saves approximately 2 per cent of the total power consumed in the country. The total air conditioner capacity in India reached 80 million tonnes of refrigeration in 2022, having increased by 21 per cent in just three years, from 2019 to 2022, according to estimates from the International Energy Agency (IEA), published in October 2023.[10] By 2050, air conditioning consumption is expected to exceed the total power consumption of entire Africa today. These estimates may turn out to be on the lower side, as the incidence of heat waves are becoming more frequent. Therefore, consumer behaviour will be critical in ensuring avoidable consumption. All homes, commercial establishments, offices, public spaces, and workplaces have to cooperate in this endeavour. The IEA had recently observed that 'India's Lifestyle for Environment (LiFE) initiative aims to conserve energy by shifting the behaviours of at least a billion people in the coming years'.[11] The LiFE movement seeks to transform each individual into a 'pro-planet person' who would adopt sustainable lifestyles.

India is working towards energy efficiency under the National Mission on Enhanced Energy Efficiency (NMEEE), which has four components:

- Perform, Achieve and Trade (PAT): This is a regulatory instrument to reduce specific energy consumption in energy-intensive industries, with an associated market-based mechanism to enhance cost-effectiveness through the certification of excess energy savings, which can be traded.
- Market Transformation for Energy Efficiency (MTEE): This scheme proposes accelerating the shift to energy-efficient appliances in designated sectors through innovative measures to make the products more affordable.
- Energy Efficiency Financing Platform (EEFP): This is for creation of mechanisms that would help finance demand side management programmes in all sectors by capturing future energy savings, as well as for capacity building of financial institutions and Energy Saving Companies (ESCOs)/industries. Excess energy saving can be traded.
- Framework for Energy Efficient Economic Development (FEEED): It is for the development of fiscal instruments to promote energy efficiency.

India's Bureau of Energy Efficiency (BEE) is spearheading the goal of improving energy efficiency. It has prescribed star ratings and norms for devices that have yielded remarkable results in containing increases in energy demand. Through energy efficiency schemes, India saved more than 50 million tonnes of oil equivalent in 2022–23 and saved electricity to the tune of more than 307 billion units in the same year, which represents 3.5 per cent of our total energy consumption. In the process, we reduced carbon emissions by more than 306 million tonnes.[12]

Our climate goals and transition to green energy have a circular relationship with energy efficiency. As we reduce inefficiency, each unit of energy goes farther; as we go green, energy generation moves closer to consumption points, making the system more efficient.

Supporting R&D and Indigenous Production

We are fully committed to enabling energy generation and the manufacture of storage equipment under the 'Make in India' initiative of the government. No country can be fully self-sufficient; every country needs to import something, for which it needs to be able to sell to another country. In order to export, we have to be competitive. This competition can be achieved by reducing costs through research and development (R&D) and increasing volumes to enjoy economies of scale. We are committed to supporting R&D to enhance quality at lower costs, enabling us to not only meet domestic demand but also to capture a slice of the export market and leverage economies of scale.

We support R&D in the power sector through the National Perspective Plan (NPP). The NPP is a joint project between the Central Electricity Authority (CEA) and the Central Power Research Institute (CPRI) that focuses on new products, process development, and technology development. We reconstituted the standing committee on R&D (SCRD) in the power sector in 2015 to identify and prioritise important strategic areas of research and development, including inter-sector research projects to be considered for implementation. These projects are formulated under three categories: in-house R&D, research scheme on power, and R&D under NPP. The committee also aims to identify leading researchers and domain experts in diverse areas of the power sector and engage them in the research schemes.

The CEA has created a chair at IIT Delhi, and CPRI has established a chair professorship at the Indian Institute of Science (IISc), Bangalore, to invite highly qualified professionals in power engineering from foreign universities and research institutes to share their expertise with our professionals. For applied research specific to the power sector, an autonomous body under the administrative control of the ministry, namely, CPRI has been created to carry out and encourage essential research. Some of the areas being supported for R&D include green hydrogen production and storage, developing alternatives to lithium-ion storage batteries, nano technology for EV batteries, modifying electric cookers, green hydrogen for mobility, carbon capture, sequestration and use, geothermal energy, and solid-state refrigeration.

Our special focus is on R&D for enabling us to manufacture equipment for the production and storage of green hydrogen. In January 2023, the Union Cabinet approved the National Green Hydrogen Mission (NGHM) with an outlay of Rs 19,744 crore, aiming to make India a global hub for manufacturing this clean source of energy. The mission is expected to lead to the development of 5 million metric tonnes per annum of green hydrogen production capacity by 2030. We are open to international cooperation and collaboration in this field, as it holds great promise for the energy transition, both as a storage option and directly as fuel for the mobility and manufacturing sectors. India and Saudi Arabia signed an MoU in the fields of electrical interconnection, green/clean hydrogen, and supply chains on 8 October 2023. This strategic collaboration is expected to be advantageous for both countries, as they can leverage each other's capabilities to foster the growth of the green hydrogen ecosystem within their respective nations. The G20 New Delhi Leaders' Declaration affirmed the G20 High-Level Voluntary Principles on Hydrogen to build a sustainable and equitable global hydrogen ecosystem that benefits all nations. The declaration also emphasised a free and fair trade of hydrogen in line with World Trade Organization (WTO) rules, supported by resilient and diversified supply chains.

India's electrolyser market potential is projected to grow from $4 billion in 2030 to $78 billion in 2030,[13] and that does not include our export potential. The Ministry of Ports, Shipping and Waterways has identified three major ports—Deendayal, Paradip, and V.O. Chidambaranar (Tuticorin)—to be developed as hydrogen hubs. A working group has been constituted under the chairmanship of the secretary of the Ministry of New and Renewable Energy (MNRE) for the establishment of a robust framework of regulations, codes, and standards for green hydrogen. The government is introducing a production-linked incentive scheme for grid-scale storage, which will further bring down the price of storage. We have also been working to reduce our dependence on imports for solar equipment. Due to interventions such as custom duties on solar modules and cells, as well as the Approved List of Models and Manufacturers (ALMM), the capacity for module manufacturing has increased from about 20 GW to about 50 GW. By 2030, we will have about 24 GW of polysilicon-to-module manufacturing capacity.

Our dependence on imports for battery energy storage systems is also diminishing due to our R&D support. In September 2023, the Union Cabinet approved the scheme for viability gap funding (VGF) to develop battery energy storage systems (BESS). Under this scheme, projects will be approved over a three-year period, from 2023–24 to

2025–26, with the disbursement of funds extending until 2030–31 across five tranches. The anticipated cost for the BESS system ranges between Rs 2.40 crore to Rs 2.20 crore per MWh for the development of 4,000 MWh capacity, totalling a capital cost of Rs 9,400 crore, supported by a budget of Rs 3,760 crore. The central government will provide up to 40 per cent of the capital cost for BESS as viability gap funding. These storage systems, when charged with renewable energy, will contribute to a substantial annual reduction in carbon emissions. Additionally, this storage system will provide up to 4,000 MWh of energy during peak hours.

Transition in the Mobility, Steel, and Cement Sectors

We had signed the Glasgow Declaration on Zero-Emission Cars and Vans—a pledge made by more than 100 countries, cities, financial institutions, and multinationals at COP 26 to end the sale of internal combustion engines by 2040. For this transition, we are targeting two- and three-wheeled vehicles also, which are the fastest-growing mode of transport in India in terms of sales. In June 2022, NITI Aayog had released a report titled 'Forecasting Penetration of Electric Two-wheelers in India' that stated there could be a 100 per cent penetration of electric two-wheelers in the Indian market by March 2027. We have introduced the Faster Adoption and Manufacturing of (Hybrid &) Electric Vehicles (FAME) scheme, which incentivises consumers and manufacturers to promote electric vehicle (EV) adoption. This has increased demand for electric two-wheelers and encouraged manufacturers to invest in new technologies and supply chains to produce EVs. Infrastructure for fast charging of electric vehicles is also being put in place nationwide.

Under the National Green Hydrogen Mission, Rs 455 crore have been already allocated for the steel sector. I had assured the stakeholders in January 2024 that, if required, additional funds will be allocated for decarbonisation of the steel sector under this mission. This will include funds to develop technology for the integration of hydrogen in steel making. This shall be done through a transparent selection process. Encouraged by our promise of support, some manufacturers have already started experimenting with green hydrogen in the steel sector. All efforts should be made to zero in on the right technologies and pathways for decarbonising this sector. In light of trade barriers imposed by some developed countries and the dumping of cheap steel by others, we must rapidly adopt technology to decarbonise this sector while maintaining cost competitiveness.

With determination and prudent realism, we shall be able to meet the multiple geopolitical challenges and maintain the pace of our transition to green energy without compromising our energy security. We are undertaking the transition along with the goal of moving from import dependence to becoming an exporting country by adopting cutting-edge technologies that make our prices competitive in the global market. Our export capability will enable economies of scale, which will further make us competitive, and this virtuous circle will lead us towards becoming a developed economy and the realisation of Amrit Kaal in our Bharat.

4

Challenges of Renewable Energy Integration and Energy Transition

Ghanshyam Prasad

India has emerged as a major force in the global energy economy. As the world grapples with the challenge of climate change, India is committed to reducing its carbon footprint in line with the global response to tackle this challenge. India's approach to growth in the power sector aligns with the global demand for a shift towards green generation and a transition to cleaner energy sources.

India has already fulfilled its Nationally Determined Contributions (NDCs) submitted at COP 21[1], achieving 40 per cent of its installed capacity from non-fossil fuel generation sources nine years before the target year of 2030. The country has set an ambitious goal of achieving 50 per cent of its generation capacity from non-fossil fuel sources by 2030. Additionally, India has committed to achieving net-zero goals by 2070 and has taken several policy measures to achieve the goal. There is a strong realisation that achieving the goal of net zero will require transfer of technology from the developed world and removal of market barriers imposed by different countries.

India's renewable energy (RE) programme is one of the most ambitious and extensive programmes in the world. The country has recognised the importance of transitioning to clean and sustainable energy sources to address energy security, climate change, and economic development. The programme has set a target of installing 500 GW of non-fossil energy capacity by 2030. To decarbonise the energy sector, the share of electricity in total energy consumption is anticipated to rise to 38 per cent in 2047, up from 17 per cent in 2019, with increasing electrification of different sectors of the economy. To achieve this target, we aim to reach 2,528 GW of installed electricity capacity by 2047, up from the present 442.8 GW (as of 31 May 2024), with the percentage of non-fossil capacity increasing to 88 per cent, from the present 43 per cent. This is likely to ensure energy security, and the future capacity added is expected to be largely indigenous. Consequently, emissions will decrease to around 560 million tonnes by 2047. This is approximately a 40 per cent reduction compared to 2022, when emissions were 905 million tonnes. The emissions intensity per unit of electricity generation, which is likely to be about 0.400 kg CO_2/kWh in 2032, may decrease to 0.079 kg CO_2/kWh by 2050.

India has been emphasising the need to focus on reducing the reliance on fossil fuels, which includes coal, gas, oil, in order to achieve the energy transition towards green sources. This includes electrifying various sectors of the economy as much as possible, such as electric mobility, electrification of railways, replacement of diesel generating sets, diesel pumps, shift towards a green hydrogen economy, co-firing of hydrogen/ammonia and bio-pellets in thermal power plants, biomass generation, blending hydrogen with gas in gas power plants, and enhanced production of fuel resources in the country. However, there are challenges associated with the import of technology, equipment, and materials, as well as supply chain issues in this new paradigm of energy security.

The downward trend in the cost of solar panels and newer technology options, like battery energy storage systems (BESS), have led to energy transition in the power sector in a cost-effective manner. The capital cost of renewable energy technologies (solar photovoltaic [PV] and wind) for power generation has become competitive day by day via-à-vis coal-based generation. However, the intermittency associated with renewable energy technologies is a limitation that needs to be addressed in the power system. Large-scale integration of renewable energy generation sources can be achieved through the adoption of grid-scale energy storage solutions. Storage hydropower plants and pumped storage plants (PSPs) can be highly useful for facilitating the integration of high-variable renewable energy power into the power system. Besides storage solutions, massive investments may be required to strengthen the transmission system to ensure grid stability and reliability. The cost of renewable energy integration is expected to rise substantially in the future as the percentage of variable renewable energy (wind, solar PV) in the generation mix increases.

The central and state governments are implementing various policies and regulatory measures to promote renewable energy in India. This includes the renewable purchase obligation (RPO) procured from renewable energy sources by obligated entities, along with conducive measures such as competitive bidding processes, foreign direct investment (FDI) through the automatic route, and various fiscal and financial incentives to attract investment in renewable energy projects. To address the intermittency of renewable energy sources, India is also focusing on energy storage technologies, in addition to promoting renewable energy hybrid projects, forecasting and scheduling, demand-side management, and integrating renewable energy projects at different locations through the national grid. Decentralised renewable energy is being promoted to provide reliable power near load centres, along with mandating flexible operation of coal-based generation for absorption of maximum renewable energy. Further, regulations on ancillary services have been notified to, inter-alia, take care of variable renewable energy resources. Through these sustained efforts, the country plans to achieve the ambitious goal of reaching net zero by 2070.

The transmission utilisation factor is low for the transmission lines evacuating the renewable energy generation, as their capacity utilisation factor (CUF) is low. A corrective policy needs to be in place to signal the right price for the renewable energy capacity addition in the country. This will optimise the overall cost of power supply to consumers.

Cost economics is very dynamic. Initially it was thought that it would lead to a cheaper solution as well. However, if we look at the overall costs, such as transmission and balancing costs, the economics is different. Perhaps, once the cost of storage is considerably reduced, it could be the cheaper solution.

Plan of RE Integration in India

The electrical energy demand has grown at a compound annual growth rate (CAGR) of 4.5 per cent, while peak demand has grown at a CAGR of 5.6 per cent during 2018–23. Technological innovations are driving sectors such as transport and industry towards increased reliance on the electricity system. This may lead to further unforeseen growth in electricity demand, leading to a shift in energy usage patterns towards electricity. Therefore, future demand growth rates are likely to be higher due to the electrification of the economy, electric vehicles, green hydrogen, etc. According to the 20th Electric Power Survey of India projections[2], peak electricity demand and energy requirement are expected to grow at a CAGR of 6.42 per cent and 6.67 per cent, respectively, during 2022–2027, and at a CAGR of 5.74 per cent and 5.33 per cent, respectively, during 2027–32. Additionally, peak electricity demand and energy requirement are projected to grow at a CAGR of 4.34 per cent and 4.23 per cent, respectively, during 2032–2047.

The current installed capacity of India, as of 31 May 2024, is 444.8 GW, comprising 201.76 GW from non-fossil fuel-based resources and 243 GW of fossil fuel-based resources. As per the National Electricity Plan (2022–32), the likely installed capacity for the year 2031–32 will be 9,00,422 MW, consisting of 3,04,147 MW of conventional capacity (coal 2,59,643 MW, gas 24,824 MW, nuclear 19,680 MW) and 5,96,275 MW of renewable-based capacity (large hydro 62,178 MW, solar 3,64,566 MW, wind 1,21,895 MW, small hydro 5,450 MW, biomass 15,500 MW, pumped storage plants [PSPs] 26,686 MW, excluding 5,856 MW of likely hydro-based imports). Additionally, there will be a battery energy storage system (BESS) capacity of 47,244 MW/2,36,220 MWh. The share of non-fossil fuel-based capacity is likely to increase to about 69 per cent, up from the current 43 per cent, with a significant addition of renewable energy generation sources in the coming years.

The installed solar and wind-based capacity of the country was 82 GW and 46 GW, as of March 2024, contributing to 19 per cent and 10 per cent of the total capacity, respectively. Solar and wind capacity accounted for about 6 per cent and 4 per cent of the total generation mix during 2022–23. Additionally, large hydro-based capacity currently stands at 47 GW (with additional 5 GW of small hydropower and 5 GW of PSP), which is around 10 per cent of the total capacity mix. According to the National Electricity Plan[3], renewable energy capacity is likely to grow to 553.7 GW by 2032, with solar capacity of 364.6 GW and wind capacity of 121.8 GW, and the remainder coming from large and small hydropower).

The shift towards green sources, leading to energy transition, is likely to continue beyond 2032 in order to achieve India's net-zero vision by 2070. The generation planning studies for the horizon until 2047 outline one of the likely trajectories for capacity addition beyond 2032 to meet the country's increasing energy requirements, while fulfilling India's ambition of an energy transition within the ambit of energy security.

The projected installed power generating capacity of India under least-cost development is anticipated to increase from 442.8 GW, as of 31 May 2024, to 2,528 GW by 2047, with the percentage of non-fossil capacity increasing to 88 per cent from the present 43 per cent.

Solar power is expected to dominate the buildout of capacity and reach unprecedented rates of installation after 2032 due to the expected long-term cost development, reaching a capacity of 1,191 GW by 2047. This represents a 15-fold increase from current capacities by 2047. The second-largest increase in capacity can be observed in onshore wind power, which will reach 422 GW in 2047, corresponding to a 9-fold increase. Large hydro capacities are expected to double, reaching 92 GW in 2047.

The share of renewable energy in the generation mix is likely to increase to 78 per cent in 2047. The major development is coming from an unprecedented buildout of power-generating capacity from solar PV. Consequently, solar PV may provide 50 per cent of electricity generation by 2047, and combined with onshore wind, these variable renewable sources will account for around 70 per cent of electricity generation by 2047. Large and small hydro projects are expected to contribute to about 7 per cent of electricity generation by then.

By 2047, the substantial deployment of renewable energy capacity will necessitate a significant need for storage in the power sector to ensure proper grid and supply balancing. The likely storage requirement of 480 GW/2,709 GWh is expected in 2047, which comprises 116 GW/703 GWh of pumped hydro capacity and 364 GW/2,006 GWh of battery energy storage systems (BESS). Given the dominating share of variable renewable energy (VRE) generation (primarily solar and wind) in 2047—most of which is inherently intermittent and variable on a diurnal and seasonal basis—grid stability and reliability will be a key challenge. This may require significant investments in grid-stabilising elements and transmission systems to enable seamless integration of RE into the national grid.

The Challenges: Intermittency, Variability, and Grid Stability

- Between January 2022 and March 2024, there have been approximately fifty-five incidents of generation loss of more than 1,000 MW in renewable energy complexes.[4] Analysis of the events reveals that the actual behaviour of the plants, particularly under transient conditions, are often inconsistent with the response exhibited in the simulation-based studies submitted in the pre-commissioning stage. In several cases, limitations in the equipment's capability under prevailing ambient conditions and gaps in the adopted settings for controllers at the field level have been observed. In addition to the above, there is also non-compliance of the RE plants with specified CEA standards, low system strength in remote RE pockets, and a lack of coordination between RE developers and inverter/WTG/PPC manufacturers.
- In addition to the generation loss events, there was a generation reduction of about 8,000 MW within one hour due to cloud cover in Rajasthan on 28 May 2023. In the

case of large-scale renewable capacity in the close vicinity, the possibility of losing a large chunk of solar generation due to disturbances or large cloud cover also increases significantly.

- Development of field/onsite testing facilities must be prioritised for conducting periodic compliance verification of RE plants, including low voltage ride through (LVRT) and high voltage ride through (HVRT) testing.
- Primary, secondary, and tertiary reserves shall be maintained for handling contingencies. These reserves need to be maintained at both interstate and intrastate generating stations. The aggregate requirement at a pan-India level is in the range of 19,000 MW. However, the availability of reserves in the conventional generating stations is often constrained during non-solar hours. It has been observed that most of the commissioned solar and wind plants do not operate with margins or additional earmarked storage to provide generation-up reserves. At a later date, the RE plants may be required to provide frequency response.
- The increasing addition of non-synchronous renewable energy plants to the grid is expected to reduce the system inertia that is inherently provided by synchronous generators. Synthetic inertia through fast frequency response will be required to address the higher rate of change of frequency during any load-generation imbalance.
- Going forward, it is important that renewable energy plants and battery energy storage systems (BESS) also participate in the primary and secondary frequency control. BESS has the capability to operate with very low droop (1–2 per cent) and provide fast response, which can be effectively harnessed. Furthermore, the intermittency and visibility of RE generation can be addressed by the development of pumped storage plants (PSPs) and by adding flexibility to thermal generation.

- Synchronous condensers that can provide multi-fold benefits in terms of inertial support, dynamic reactive power support, and short-circuit current contribution, or any other suitable technical solution, may also be timely planned and implemented in view of the envisaged decline in inertia in the near future.
- Low frequency oscillations are already being observed at the Rajasthan renewable energy complex, possibly due to the interaction between different controllers of the RE plants. The problem may exacerbate if further converter-based devices are added in the vicinity without corrective measures. It is important that these controller interaction issues are identified at the planning stage itself. However, this would require extensive power system simulation studies on accurate models. The original equipment manufacturer (OEM) must ensure that their device is capable of operating reliably under different operating conditions at the interconnection point and has the ability to damping the dominant oscillation frequency in the system. It is suggested that these controller interaction studies be carried out at the planning/design stage, before the interconnection of the plant, and during the operational phase, as per requirement.

RE Proximity, Generation Loss, and Non-Compliance

With a large quantum of renewable energy generation connected in close vicinity, a voltage drop due to any nearby fault would be reflected in most of the plants. In case of a fault-ride through failure, there is a possibility of losing a significant amount of generation during a fault.

A large number of generation loss events—fifty-five events of over 1,000 MW generation loss between January 2022 and March 2024 at the interstate transmission system level—have already taken place in large RE complexes, especially in Rajasthan. One of the major reasons for these events was non-compliance with the specified standards by the RE plants. With around 20 GW of installed capacity in Rajasthan, the largest contingency in the RE complex was approximately 7,000 MW. As significant RE capacity is added to the complex, the size of credible contingencies and generation losses may also increase considerably.

In order to overcome the above challenges, the following measures are suggested:

- Strict compliance with specified standards and regulations by the RE plants.
- Robust compliance verification before interconnection of any new plant to the grid.
- Periodic compliance testing and provisions for disconnection in case of persistent non-compliance.

Controller Interaction Issues

Solar, wind, BESS, HVDCs, and FACTS devices (STATCOMs) are all power electronic converter-based devices. With a large number of converter-based devices getting connected in close vicinity, there can be various issues of interaction among the controllers of these sources. Low-frequency oscillations are already being observed in the Rajasthan RE complex, possibly due to the interaction between different controllers of the plants. This problem may exacerbate with the further addition of converter-based devices in the vicinity without corrective measures.

Suggested Mitigation Measures

The identification of controller interaction issues would require extensive power system simulation studies from the planning stage itself. The availability of accurate models (both RMS and EMT) of the network elements is also important for successfully conducting these studies. Periodic tuning of controllers would also be required based on the simulation studies. In summary, detailed controller interaction studies and tuning of controllers are of utmost importance for reliable interconnection of a large quantum of RE in close vicinity.

International Commitments

COP 26 Pathway: India upgraded its Nationally Determined Commitments (NDCs) at the COP 26 in Glasgow in November 2021 and formally communicated its updated NDCs to the United Nations Framework Convention on Climate Change (UNFCCC) in August 2022. The updated NDCs include:

- Reduction in emissions intensity of its GDP by 45 per cent by 2030, from 2005 levels;
- Achieve about 50 per cent cumulative installed electric power capacity from non-fossil fuel-based energy resources by 2030, with the help of transfer of technology and low-cost international finance, including from the Green Climate Fund (GCF);
- And promote 'Mission LiFE' (Lifestyle for Environment).

India's RE Capacity Addition and Targets to Achieve the COP 28 Pathway

Events where the decision was taken	Agreement/ Commitment	Present Status	Target by 2030	Remarks
Conclusion of the 1st Global Stocktake (GST) during COP 28 (November 2023)	Tripling RE capacity by 2030 (from the base year of 2023)	180.8 GW (as of 2023) (RE installation rate was 13.5 GW in 2021–22)	540 GW	Require an installation rate of RE capacity of 51.5 GW/ year

The Road Ahead

- India added around 13.5 GW renewable energy capacity during the calendar year 2023, corresponding to an investment of about Rs 74,000 crore.[5] It needs to add around 50 GW each year until 2030 to achieve the 500 GW target by 2030.
- The annualised growth rate of wind power installations remains close to 5 per cent while the growth of solar installations is around 10 per cent.
- The plans ahead are promising, and we are on track to achieve our targets. Significant capacities are already under construction, with plans in place to complete all bids by 2028.
- From the buyers' side as well, the resource adequacy plans have mandated them to makes the purchases. Once both buyers and sellers have a clear roadmap, the country will achieve its targets.

Further Steps to Forge Ahead

India's solar module manufacturing capacity was 67 GW by 25 September 2024,[6] and India's annual production capacity of domestic wind turbines was about 15 GW.[7]

According to the Confederation of Indian Industry's CII-EY report on 'Atmanirbhar Bharat in RE Manufacturing',[8] India's solar PV cell and module capacity is likely to exceed 59 GW and 110 GW, respectively, by 2026. Therefore, India is on the right trajectory to considerably expand its RE manufacturing capacity.

The Government of India consistently brings out policies to enhance domestic manufacturing capacity in the renewable energy sector. Some of these are listed below:

The Production-Linked Incentive (PLI) Scheme[9] under the National Programme on High-Efficiency Solar PV Modules aims to achieve domestic manufacturing capacity at gigawatt (GW) scale in high-efficiency solar PV modules, with an outlay of Rs 24,000 crore. The scheme is being implemented in two tranches. Tranche I has an outlay of Rs 4,500 crore, under which letters of award have been issued for setting up of 8,737 MW of fully integrated solar PV module manufacturing units. For Tranche II, with an outlay of Rs 19,500 crore, letters of award have been issued for setting up of 39,600 MW of fully/partially integrated solar PV module manufacturing units.

Under some of the current schemes of the Ministry of New and Renewable Energy, namely the CPSU Scheme Phase II, PM-KUSUM Component B, and Grid-connected Rooftop Solar Programme Phase II, where government subsidies are provided, it has been mandated to source solar PV cells and modules from domestic sources.

Through the implementation of the Public Procurement (Preference to Make in India) Order, procurement and use of domestically manufactured solar PV modules and solar inverters have been mandated for the government and government entities.

Waiver of Interstate Transmission System (ISTS) charges for the interstate sale of solar and wind power for projects to be commissioned by 30 June 2025.

Reduction of CO_2 Emissions

- Presently, coal-based generation accounts for around 73 per cent of the total electricity generation in India. Coal-fired thermal power plants (TPPs) emit CO_2 gas during their combustion process, which is a major greenhouse gas (GHG). CO_2 from the power sector alone accounts for around 40 per cent of the total greenhouse emissions in the country.
- Coal, as an indigenous mineral, plays a crucial role in ensuring energy security and affordability. Therefore, coal-based power plants are expected to remain an integral

part of the energy mix in the near future to meet baseload generation demand. However, decarbonising these plants would be essential to achieve the environmental commitments of the country.

- In this direction, some technological interventions have already been introduced, such as the use of supercritical/ultra-supercritical (USC) technology, and biomass co-firing, which are contributing to CO_2 emission reduction from coal-based power plants.
- According to the National Electricity Plan of May 2023, the total CO_2 emissions are projected to increase from 1,002 million tonnes in 2021–22 to 1,057 million tonnes in the year 2026–27, and 1,100 million tonnes in 2031–32 due to rising energy demand. The average emission factor is expected to reduce to 0.548 kg CO_2/kWh by 2026–27 and drop further to 0.430 kg CO_2/kWh by the end of 2031–32.
- The peaking of CO_2 emission can be expected by the year of 2034–35.
- The actual CO_2 emissions would depend on the rate of achievement in renewable energy capacity addition and the corresponding rate of increased demand for electricity generation.
- India needs to accelerate the growth of renewable energy installations to fulfil its targets. As of January 2025, renewable energy sources, including large hydropower, have a combined installed capacity of around 217.62 GW[10], with about 127 GW at various stages of implementation and around 89 GW in the bidding process.[11]

Need for Balancing Power

The large-scale addition of renewables into the grid will require balancing from other energy sources with the ability to ramp up and ramp down quickly, depending on grid requirements, such as conventional hydro and pumped storage power stations, battery energy storage systems (BESS), etc. The source could not be located.

The role of thermal power stations will change from providing baseload supply to supporting the power system by providing balancing and flexibility services, especially during the days and seasons with low variable renewable generation. They may need to frequently ramp up/down generation depending on the renewable energy generation and system demand. This may require retrofitting thermal power plants for operation at partial load.

Hybrid renewable energy power plants also provide a simple balancing approach in which the production of intermittent renewables, such as wind and solar, is monitored and intermixed to utilise the available energy from both sources at any given time. This approach allows the maximum possible power to be delivered by combining dominant and non-dominant resources at all times, mitigating the intermittency of individual resources.

Storage has various advantages, such as balancing the grid against load fluctuations and addressing intermittency in generation. Energy storage can provide energy time-shifting, which can be useful with the large-scale deployment of variable renewable energy sources. However, the storage requirement depends on the shape of the demand curve and the extent of renewable energy penetration. Energy storage technologies can also provide operating reserve requirements, balancing, ramping, and renewable energy integration services.

Gas power plants operate on established conventional technology and are more flexible than coal, lignite, or nuclear power plants. Gas-based plants, with their quick ramping up/down capabilities, can support the balancing power requirements of the grid. Gas-based capacity will minimise the need for other alternative modes of power generation during peak hours of power shortage, such as using diesel generators, which are not only costlier but also result in more environmental pollution. Additionally, gas-based power generation would reduce carbon emissions, as emissions from gas-based power generation are lower compared to those from diesel or coal-based generation. However, due to acute shortage of domestic gas and higher price of imported natural gas, gas-based power plants are unable to run efficiently nor help in reduction of environmental pollution. To address this, commercial and regulatory bottlenecks in enhancing the consumption of natural gas in the power sector need to be resolved. This would enable gas-based power to act as balancing power, together with renewable-based power. The use of a combination of domestic gas, imported LNG, and APM/non-APM gas may be considered for the optimum pricing of power production.

Recently, gas-based plants have been utilised to meet peak demand during high-demand days (around 20 to 30 days). We have used them through the bidding route, ancillary services, and have even invoked section 11. We are also working on using them in the future as well.

Down the line, as the Indian power system becomes increasingly dominated by renewable energy generation to meet the projected demand, the high seasonality of wind and hydropower will create variation in the regional power generation throughout the year. Transmission will play a pivotal role in mitigating these seasonal variations and balancing power distribution.

Addressing the Challenges: Flexibility in Thermal and Nuclear Generation

The Central Electricity Authority (CEA) has already issued a gazette notification on 30 January 2023 regarding flexible operation of coal-fired generating units. As per the CEA gazette notification extraordinary, part III, section 4, no. 61 (CG-DL-E-31012023-243299), the coal-based thermal power generating units will have flexible operation capability with a minimum power level of 40 per cent, along with a ramp rate of 1 per cent between 40–55 per cent, 2 per cent between 55–70 per cent, and a ramp rate of 3 per cent above 70 per cent. The implementation of the flexible operation (40 per cent minimum thermal load [MTL]) will be according to the phasing plan specified by the authority from time to time.

In view of the aforementioned, for the smooth integration of renewable energy, the CEA has prepared a phasing plan (pilot phase and four phases) and notified the same in the Gazette of India on 15 December 2023 to achieve the minimum load operation (40 per cent MTL).

Summary of the Phasing Plan is given in the following table:

Phase	Timeline	Total Units	Total Capacity (GW)
Pilot Phase	May 2023–March 2024	10	5.85
Phase 1	July 2024–June 2026	91	51.08
Phase 2	July 2026–June 2028	100	46.825
Phase 3	July 2028–December 2029	101	37.215
Phase 4	January 2030–December 2030	191	55.767
Total		493	196.737

Solutions to Address the Challenges: Flexibility in Thermal Generation

Challenges	Solutions
Inability of the units to achieve 55% minimum thermal load (MTL) along with prescribed ramp rates	To achieve 55% MTL, the CEA has already published and circulated the standard operating procedure (SOP) to all concerned parties. As suggested in the SOP, the response of all critical loops should be studied at 55% of the load, and further necessary corrections should be carried out prior to 55% load operation. Additionally, the ramp-up and ramp-down rates should also be considered for tuning the critical loops.
Lack of confidence among the operators to run the units at 55% MTL	Training programmes for power plant operators have been finalised in consultation with the National Power Training Institute (NPTI), which is also included in the SOP. Plant operators and trainers must train on the simulator for 55% load operation, with a 3% ramp rate above 70% load and a 2% ramp rate below 70% load, all without oil support. Simulator training for power plant operators will enhance their skills and prepare them for low-load operation without oil support, helping to stabilise the plant during ramp up and ramp down at lower loads. Operators of central, state, and private utilities can also be trained at NPTI training centres or the training centres of major utilities to gain confidence. Further, utilities that have achieved 55% load operation without oil support in their units can extend support to other utilities that are facing difficulties in achieving the same.
Lack of/ inadequate compensation to utilities for running at low load by respective regulatory commissions	The issue of compensation has been taken up with CERC, SERC, and the Joint Electricity Regulatory Commission (JERC) for units operating at 40% MTL.

Challenges	Solutions
Non-availability of designed coal quality	The supply of coal with a stable gross calorific value (GCV) will enable the generators to efficiently comply with the 55%/40% MTL.

Focus on Expeditious Commissioning to Increase Generation Capacities

Plans are in place for the expeditious commissioning of the generation capacities under nuclear, hydro, and hydro PSP categories. We have taken several measures to facilitate this process. Nuclear capacity will be doubled by 2030 to around 15 GW. Under hydro PSP, the main focus is on the closed-loop hydro PSP, which can be commissioned in approximately four years, with a reasonable cost of around 4 to 5 rupees per unit of storage.

Benefits of Hydro Pumped Storage Power Plants

- PSPs are key enablers of the clean energy transition, as they provide environmentally friendly large storage capacity compared to other storage options.
- They also provide ancillary benefits, such as peak shaving, load levelling, frequency regulation, voltage control, black start facility and spinning reserve to supplement grid stability.
- This reduces the need for operating reserves from thermal power plants (typically high-carbon coal and gas).
- It increases the capture of renewable over-generation by compensating for their variability.
- This reduces renewable energy curtailment during oversupply of variable renewables like wind and solar.
- In addition, off-river, closed-loop PSPs supply power for the future needs of our country without affecting the existing water/irrigation systems or river basins. They can

be set up faster and at a much lower cost compared to conventional PSPs, as they do not involve construction of huge dams, spillways, structures, or desilting chambers and are located away from the main rivers.

- India has a potential of 1,33,690 MW of PSPs. Currently, 4,746 MW of capacity has been installed, and 4,050 MW is under construction. Around 67,996 MW of the capacity has been allotted by states for development. It is anticipated that about 50 GW of PSP capacity is likely to be installed by 2031–32.

Battery Energy Storage System Plan

Status of BESS in India (≥ 1 MWHr)				
Serial Number	Category of Project	Number of Projects	Capacity (MW & MWHr)	
			MW	MWHr
1	In Operation	7	88.5	182.8
2	Under Construction	6	665.00	1,939.00
3	In Tender Stage	23	2,731.60	13,070.50
4	In the Pipeline (2+3)	29	3,396.60	15,009.50

Issuance of Guidelines for Hydro PSP & BESS

The Ministry of Power, via a resolution dated 10 March 2022, issued detailed guidelines for the procurement and utilisation of BESS as part of generation, transmission, or distribution assets, or along with ancillary services.

The guidelines

- Provide standardisation and uniformity in the procurement of BESS.
- Offer a risk-sharing framework between various stakeholders.
- Ensure transparency and fairness in procurement processes.

- Based on these guidelines, the Solar Energy Corporation of India (SECI) has carried out bidding of a 500 MW/1,000 MWh BESS pilot project.
- Gujarat has also successfully conducted a bid for a 500 MW/1,000 MWh BESS.

The revised standard bidding document (SBD) for BESS and PSP is also under finalisation.

Suggested Future Strategies

- Promote distributed renewable energy (already mandated through renewable purchase obligation [RPO])
- Installation of dynamic compensation (STATCOMs), filters
- Grid-forming inverters
- Accurate forecasting and scheduling
- Wind turbines, as per Indian weather conditions
- Market-based renewable energy capacity addition
- Mandating minimum storage with the installation of RE (solar and wind)
- Optimal use of the transmission system to keep the transmission cost reasonable
- Capacity addition aligned to the electricity demand growth in the country
- Strategy for long-term use of existing gas-based power stations
- A clear, dynamic strategy for achieving net zero by 2070 or earlier. The plan will be dynamically revised at least once every year to ensure corrective action in time. This will align with the dynamic Resource Adequacy Plan being prepared by the distribution licensees, the Central Electricity Authority (CEA), and load despatch centres.

Part II
The Concepts

5

Facets of Geopolitical Disruption

R.N. Prasher

Until the implosion of the USSR, geopolitics used to be generally stable, predictable, and prone to occasional surprises, much like the weather. The surprises were exceptions to the rule of stability and predictability, and hence, strengthened the rule. Nations, speaking through their leaders, as a rule eschewed contradicting their past pronouncements. Even when a contradiction became unavoidable, considerable diplomatic effort was involved in preparing a fertile field for sowing the exception. Threats were held out in private, but in public, enemies shook hands, and even completely disastrous summits were described as 'free and frank' discussions, with the palliative that more discussions would be held in the future.

Take the history of the conflict between Taiwan (Republic of China [ROC]) and Communist China (People's Republic of China [PRC]) over the Kinmen Islands—also called Jinmen or Quemoy—which are next to PRC's eastern shore and more than 150 kilometres to the west of Taiwan. In 1949, as the communists advanced, the forces of Chiang Kai-shek retreated to Formosa—as Taiwan was known then—but left a garrison on Kinmen, from where individual Chinese could be seen strolling on the PRC beaches, while the main island of Taiwan was not even visible. It was a thorn in the side of Mao Zedong, and his forces shelled Kinmen repeatedly in 1954. At that time, Taiwan still occupied the permanent seat in the Security Council, representing the whole of China, and was an ally of the US, then as now.

The US sent substantial military aid to Kinmen and sailed the Seventh Fleet through the Taiwan Strait, where Kinmen is located. In September 1954, the US formed the Southeast Asia Treaty Organization (SEATO), which, despite its name, included only two Southeast Asian countries, the Philippines and Thailand. Other members were Pakistan from South Asia, Australia and New Zealand from the Pacific Rim, and France and Great Britain from Europe, but neither Formosa nor Hong Kong was included. The stated aim of SEATO was to prevent the expansion of communism—the quintessential Cold War goal. The US even signed the Mutual Defense Treaty with the Republic of China (Taiwan). Yet, all this would not have prevented Mao from occupying Kinmen. What stopped the communist leader from that adventure was a threat discretely conveyed through diplomatic channels: the US would nuke mainland China if attacks on Kinmen were not stopped. The USSR, not keen on that scenario, which would have put it on the horns of the dilemma of either joining the nuclear war or abandoning its communist ally, quietly advised Mao to back off.

In April 1955, Zhou Enlai, the then foreign minister of the People's Republic of China, who later became the prime minister, sought negotiations with the US. The two sides met in Geneva in September of that year and the conflict was reduced to simmering levels. Compare this with the public pronouncements of Biden, Putin, and Xi Jinping in recent times. The US has, in the past, engineered regime changes in many places but without making an announcement about it.

Yet, on 26 March 2022, Biden said this about Putin: 'For God's sake, this man cannot remain in power.' It was all the more dramatic that this declaration was made in Warsaw where, in 1955, the Warsaw Pact was signed by the Soviet Union with seven Eastern European countries, which remained the counterweight to the North Atlantic Treaty Organization (NATO) until the Soviet Union's dissolution. The Russian response, too, was made publicly through its spokesperson: 'This is not to be decided by Mr. Biden. It should only be a choice of the people of the Russian Federation.' Earlier, on the 100th anniversary of the founding of the Communist Party of China, Xi Jinping had said, 'At the same time, the Chinese people will never allow any foreign forces to bully, oppress or enslave us. Anyone who dares try to do that will have their heads bashed bloody against a Great Wall of steel forged by over 1.4 billion Chinese people.' On 15 November 2023, Biden had a four-hour summit with Xi Jinping. While the latter was still on US soil, Biden was asked if he still considered the Chinese leader a dictator. Without blinking an eye, Biden said, 'Look, he is. He's a dictator in the sense that he's a guy who runs a country that is a communist country.'

Russia, for its part, has been obliquely threatening the use of nuclear weapons if the West does not back off from arming Ukraine. All pretence was, however, shed by Putin on 29 February 2024, when he reacted to Macron's suggestion of putting the West's military boots in Ukraine. Putin said that there would be 'tragic consequences' of any such move, adding, 'All this really threatens a conflict with the use of nuclear weapons and the destruction of civilization. Don't they get that?'[1] Donald Trump, never one to be left behind, is on record saying that he will encourage Russia to attack NATO members that do not spend enough on defence, thus undermining Article 5 of the NATO Charter, which states that an attack on one is an attack on all.

These undiplomatic outbursts are just one facet of the rapid and disruptive changes that have taken place in the geopolitical universe over a relatively short time. All of them have resulted in frequent disruptions in geopolitics and have forced policymakers to resort to continuously course-correct, subtracting from the erstwhile relative stability of foreign policies. All such disruptive factors have a bearing on the energy security of every nation; therefore, an understanding of these disruptors of geopolitics helps us place the issue of energy security in proper perspective. We list here a host of them:

- The decline of diplomacy
- Geopolitics in the era of political pendulums
- Speed of change
- With technology, small may be formidable, powerful may be diffident
- Spooks, cyber threats, and AI: Winning the war without fighting
- Geopolitics and supply chain disruption
- Nuclear proliferation, proxies, multipolar world, and the ideological divide
- Illegal migration
- Connected world, unforeseen consequences
- A silver lining: reduced probability of biological war

Let us now consider each of these disruptive factors.

The Decline of Diplomacy

'Diplomacy is the art of telling people to go to hell in such a way that they ask for directions.' Winston Churchill is often 'credited' with these words, though falsely. However, the words, by themselves, have a loud ring of truism. Diplomatic speak comprises dropping of barely concealed hints, while leaving enough room to manoeuvre out of any situation those words may create. Diplomatic chatter at parties has been described as the art of being able to say nothing, especially when speaking. P.G. Wodehouse described the lowest rungs of any hierarchy as 'nodders' and 'yes-men', with the former not being allowed to open their mouths even to express agreement; they may just nod their heads. Career diplomats spent years as 'nodders' and 'yes-men' before they were allowed to open their mouths to 'say nothing'. At international summits, national leaders spoke only after diplomats had prepared a smooth ground for interaction; they never ventured into territory not yet charted by diplomats, hence, there were no surprises. Even the leaders reached the summit level after having been 'nodders' and 'yes-men' for decades. All that has changed very quickly. In large parts of the world, we have princelings who become leaders by entitlement, without going through the mill.

Take the case of Canadian Prime Minister Justin Trudeau, who inherited the mantle from his father. The junior was born and brought up in the prime minister's residence and cares nothing for tradition or diplomatic etiquette. In the old days, leaders never took a vacation unless the visit was dictated by the needs of diplomacy, so summits were often held in salubrious locations famous for vacations. Justin is extremely fond of going on vacations, and one such vacation in December 2016–January 2017 blew up in his face when, ignoring the tradition of the prime minister spending the Christmas holidays with his countrymen, he decided to forego the white Christmas in frozen Canada for the blue seas around the balmy Bahamas and enjoy the hospitality at the palace of the Aga Khan IV. To compound the faux pas, after returning to Canada, he made a gift of $50 million to the Aga Khan Foundation. Found guilty by an ethics commission, he escaped with an apology. He has endangered relations with India by making accusations on the floor of the Canadian Parliament that the Indian state was complicit in the murder of a Sikh separatist in Canada. His government has not been able to provide any evidence so far, despite repeated demands from an angry Indian government.

Justin was forty-three when he became prime minister, making him the second youngest in Canada's history. Similarly, Giorgia Meloni was forty-five when she assumed office as Italy's prime minister, Emmanuel Macron was thirty-nine when he became president of France, and Jacinda Ardern was thirty-seven when she became prime minister of New Zealand. Ardern resigned, saying she 'no longer had enough in the tank' for the job. Macron was the first leader to meet Meloni after she became prime minister, but she threw away the friendship by directing a migrant ship to France. Macron returned the 'compliment' by excluding Meloni from a meeting between him, Ukrainian President Zelensky, and German Chancellor Scholz. Meloni responded by calling Macron's invitation to Zelensky 'inappropriate'. Macron has stood out for more than his share of upheavals, including one in which he advocated for Western troops in Ukraine, bringing focus to 'his reputation as a diplomatic disruptor who likes to break taboos and challenge conventional thinking'.[2] When the allies reacted strongly to Macron's suggestion, he urged the allies not to be 'cowards', prompting Germany's defence minister, Boris Pistorius, to say, 'We don't need really, from my perspective at least, talk about boots on the ground or having more courage or less courage.'[3]

At the other end of the spectrum are leaders who are too old to remain lucid, keep committing diplomatic faux pas, but refuse to step down. We are not talking about a dictator like Zimbabwe's Mugabe, who ruled for thirty-seven years and finally quit only when the country's army placed him under house arrest at the age of ninety-three. Joe Biden, who was eight-two years old when the US presidential elections were held in 2024, doggedly sought another term, hoping to hold the US's nuclear button until he turned eighty-six.

Xi Jinping, who has been in power for twelve years, has entrenched himself in the leadership role for life through a constitutional amendment that overcame a provision restricting the tenure to a decade. Putin has continuously held supreme power as prime minister or president since 1999 and shows no indication that he will ever abdicate. Cameroon's Paul Biya, ninety-one, has been prime minister or president continuously for forty-nine years since 1975.

These very young and very old leaders sit over the fortunes of mankind, take decisions of war and peace, and put their foot in their mouth frequently, endangering diplomacy. Simultaneously, the cardinal principle in democracies, which restrained opposition leaders from criticising their nation's foreign policy when visiting other countries or meeting leaders of other nations, is being ignored more often. In India, Rahul Gandhi, leader of the oldest political party, has been speaking at universities and other forums abroad, castigating the government for its foreign policies and even putting a seal of approval on the policies of countries like China. Such utterances create uncertainty and even encourage foreign powers not only to actively cultivate such leaders but also to use their heft for regime change.

In times of war, nations used to present a united front to the enemy; not anymore. Since the Vietnam War, opposition to war has been considered patriotic, perhaps even more patriotic than supporting war effort. Draft dodging and escaping to another country to avoid enlistment is no more an act of treason in the eyes of many. Each individual is free to decide the justification for a particular war, while leaders keep looking at the way the wind is blowing at the moment. It is organised advocacy that often tilts the scales for leaders. Crowds are fickle and have been swayed by clever rhetoric since at least the day Mark Antony delivered his speech, immortalised by Shakespeare, eulogising Julius Caesar, who harboured ambitions of becoming emperor by subverting democracy. His words gave a positive spin to the dictatorial aspirations of Caesar and turned the masses against patriotic Brutus within minutes. In India, we witnessed such dissenting rhetoric when India responded with lethal force against Pakistan in retaliation for a terror attack. Such organised dissent weakens the voice of diplomats before the world.

All these developments have increased the content of passion in international relations—a serious drift away from the staid, dispassionate, cold, and calculating world of diplomats. The world was violent even in the heydays of diplomacy, but the decision for hostilities was taken with many experienced heads coming together, and the beginning of war was more often predictable. That soothing breeze of diplomatic finesse has given way to fire-breathing by leaders, who are often either inexperienced or senile, disrupting geopolitics with increasing frequency.

Geopolitics in the Era of Political Pendulums

Leaders are being seen more often at one of the two extremes. With a change of leadership, national policies swing from one extreme to the other extreme like a pendulum. This used to be a regular feature of dictatorships, where a change in the helmsman could result in wide-ranging reversals of policy. The designation of Prince Salman as the heir to the Saudi throne resulted in major swings in the oil giant's policies almost overnight. Continuity in foreign policy used to distinguish democracies from dictatorships. That dichotomy now seems to be giving way to a far-left versus far-right divide, and an election may swing the nation from one of these extremes to the other. Labour and Conservatives in the UK have opposite views on foreign policy, including about the European Union. The Labour Party leaders had declared before elections that if they came to power in 2024, they would rework the Brexit deal.[4] When Lula loses power or comes back in an election in Brazil, it results in drastic changes in foreign policy. The same is true of Maduro in Venezuela or of Javier Milei in Argentina. Taiwan, Indonesia, and many democracies in Asia and Africa display the same swing when the party in power changes after an election. The trend is not confined to Asia, Africa, or Latin America. The last elections in Italy have thrown up a far-right government, and the consequent changes in policies are visible. In Europe, the policies of the EU did create a degree of stability, but the recent surge of far-right parties may result in that ideology becoming mainstream in the EU. Parties on the opposite side of the pendulum are waiting in the wings in France and Germany, and if and when they win, there could be major upheavals, particularly in their approach towards Putin. We have seen such swings in Slovakia and Hungary. Similar developments are unfolding now that Trump has returned to the White House.

Twenty twenty-four was an election year for half of the world's population in fifty countries, including the US, India, Mexico, Indonesia, Bangladesh, and South Africa. It gave jitters to those in charge of keeping a nation's foreign policy on a stable course. In all these countries, the elections produced a leadership from one or the other extreme. It appears that only dictatorships' policies could be predicted in 2024, but that is a false hope. China and Russia have shown that powerful dictators can perform policy somersaults that are more difficult to predict than those happening when far-left and far-right leaders replace each other.

Far-right politics are more inward looking, while the far-left relies on rigid theories that may have originated in far-off lands and for a different set of socio-economic parameters. In groups like the European Union, which had been left-leaning for a long time, great disruption is caused when the democratic process produces a far-right ruler in a member state. Brexit was one such upheaval caused by the Conservatives, and the Labour Party had vowed to rework it when they came to power. The far-right Viktor Orbán of Hungary has held up Ukraine's membership of the EU and has made no secret of his admiration for Putin. Orbán is known as a far-right leader, and Putin has projected himself in a similar light. Trump's 'America First' pronouncements have earned him the label of far-right, but there are also accusations of collaborating with Putin. The far-left pays lip service to groups like the LGBTQ, and such policies have caused fissures in the EU.

There are notable exceptions to this divide. China, a communist dictatorship, is today closer to the far-right Putin than to left-leaning democracies. The godless communists of China are comfortable with the clerics in theocratic Iran and in the Islamic states of Pakistan and Afghanistan. It does appear that the far-left and far-right divide hurts only democracies. Be it as it may, it is a nightmare for a foreign policymaker to wait with bated breath for the outcome of election results in a democracy, large or miniscule, far off or next door. This was demonstrated in April 2024 when the 1,400 million people of India were anxiously waiting for the election results in Maldives, which has a total population of about half a million. Urban settlements with that many people in India are not even called cities; they are called towns. One of the two contending groups in the fray was pro-India, while the other was pro-China. Victory of the latter led to a declaration of victory for China and a setback for India. The same is true for the elections in the Solomon Islands, a country with a population of three-quarters of a million and a geopolitical footprint that is disproportionately large, where the pro-China incumbent was in an electoral fight with the anti-China opposition.

At least ninety countries of the world hold free and fair multi-party elections, and in most of them, the main contending groups hold opposite views of world events. The periodic swings between the two extremes in these countries have a strong disruptive effect on geopolitics.

Speed of Change

Lenin had famously said, 'There are decades where nothing happens, and there are weeks where decades happen.' Less than two hundred years ago, monarchs travelled by horse-drawn carriage to Rome to confabulate with the Pope. The journey to and fro could take more than a month. Messages were sent with riders who travelled a little faster, changing mounts along the way, but it could still take a few weeks. Before the advent of the telegraph in 1851, British officers in India received their instructions from Westminster and copies of London newspapers by sea. Diplomats were cut off from their governments and had to proceed according to their best judgement, free from pressures of any quick changes in the sentiments of the home population. In the present era of instant communications, diplomats have to synchronise with the changes in the domestic situation in real time, making geopolitics infinitely more fluid. One utterance by Putin or Xi Jinping may stop diplomats around the world in their tracks the very next moment, requiring a course correction or even a reversal.

Technology has not only made communications real time, it has also enabled trade deals to be sealed more quickly and goods to move faster, both of which suffer from increased uncertainty. Ships laden with Australian coal were anchored off China for months due to a change in mood of Xi Jinping, because after the ships had left Australia, the prime minister of that country had demanded an inquiry into the origins of the COVID pandemic. Veteran diplomats must be missing the pleasure of leisurely parleys at seaside resorts even as guns boomed on the battlefields. Today, Blinken has been shuttling between Washington, Amman, Tel Aviv, and Cairo on a weekly basis. Biden announced that aid would be airdropped in Gaza, and it happened less than twenty-four hours later.

Yet, all this technology is vulnerable. Critical internet cables connecting Europe to Asia pass through the Red Sea. Ships drop anchor, and sometimes these anchors get dragged, damaging the cable. The damage may be worse if a sunken ship falls on a cable, as happened during one of the attacks by the Houthis. The damage may be deliberate; the sea here is not very deep and advanced technology is not needed by a terrorist to access the cables. Somebody did blow up Russia's underwater gas pipelines, Nord Stream I and II, and until today, the jury is out on who did it. Damaging fibre optic cables is much easier than blowing up gas pipelines. The world has become too dependent on internet connectivity, and the possibility of major disruptions shaking up security pillars that were once taken for granted is a growing concern.

There is another dark side to the speed of change: obsolescence, not only of products but also of whole factories. We are not talking about fly-by-night investors—and there are plenty of them in China—who pretend to set up manufacturing units to take advantage of huge state subsidies and then declare bankruptcy. In China, this has happened in chip manufacturing in the past, with 10,000 chip companies closed in 2021 and 2022[5] and 22,000 chip-related firms having disappeared since 2019, and it is now happening to the electric car and battery sectors. But let us move past such criminal activities and focus on mainstream manufacturing, where companies conduct large due diligence exercises before investing their billions. Hyundai, a technological and manufacturing giant of South Korea, set up an engine manufacturing and car assembly unit at Chongqing in China in 2017. The facility, spread over a square mile of land, cost more than a billion dollars. The plant was fully automated and employed thousands of employees. It was shut down five years later and sold in 2023 for a fraction of the investment. It is lying desolate, and weeds have taken over the premises.[6] This will be the near future of a hundred other factories in China that were designed to manufacture 40 million internal combustion engine (ICE) vehicles every year. China is not alone in witnessing the demise of its ICE vehicle industry; many plants in Europe, North America, and other parts of the world will soon face the same fate. It will not only be the carmakers who find themselves in this sinking boat; it will be the fate of lubricants and coolants too, which will no longer be required as the world transitions to electric and hydrogen vehicles. This shift will require major adjustments in the relationships between producing and consuming countries, as well as the oil supply chain.

Technology has always progressed; horse carriage makers would have faded into the sunset when ICE cars came, but the transition took a very long time, spanning a few generations, which helped individuals transition occupationally and allowed the industries concerned to make a non-disruptive shift. A much faster world has clearly increased the probability and intensity of geopolitical disruptions.

With Technology, Small May Be Formidable, Powerful May Be Diffident

Bigger guns were never a sure recipe for victory. but they did make the odds better. Europeans colonised Asia, Africa, and the Americas with superior technology. Bigger guns prevailed on land, and bigger ships with bigger guns prevailed on the seas. That history is not repeating itself in the 21st century. Digital technology has changed the equations between large and small, and between offensive and defensive capabilities.

Traditionally, the ratio between offensive and defensive capabilities was 3:1. Today, missiles that cost a million dollars are being used to destroy a kamikaze drone costing less than 25 per cent of that figure. These drones, mostly from Iran, are packed with half a tonne of explosives and go on a one-way mission, flying at an altitude of more than 7 kilometres to a target more than 3,000 kilometres away, guided with pin-point accuracy. A toy drone, refitted by an amateur in a garage, carrying a grenade designed by another amateur, both costing a total of $500, can destroy the most advanced tank costing $4 million. Artillery pieces and armoured personnel carriers costing a fortune, in addition to the priceless lives sheltering behind these steel hulks, are sitting ducks for these cheap drones. When they come in swarms, no defence system exists that can take down all of them, and some will always reach their target. Within a short time, the intercontinental ballistic missile (ICBM) silos with their nuclear warheads will be within the destructive reach/capability of these drone swarms, with smaller drones distracting countermeasures as the larger ones reach the target. In the Ukraine War, these small drones have chased soldiers into their bunkers and then destroyed everyone inside. Slipper-wearing Houthis, numbering barely 2,00,000, are holding half of the international trade to ransom by attacking ships in the Red Sea, even as human rights' proponents hold back the hand of the largest powers from carpet-bombing their desert territory into submission.

During the Cold War, there was immense confidence in the effectiveness of defensive countermeasures. US's HIMARS, Russia's S-400, and Israel's Iron Dome were legendary. The Ukraine and Gaza wars have shattered that confidence. No defence system is foolproof. Israel's Iron Dome radars have been hit by Hezbollah with low-cost rockets; US bases have been hit by Iraqi militants; and Russia's S-400s have been hit by cheap Ukrainian drones. In 2023, Putin boasted of a new deadly weapon that turned out to be a hypersonic missile. He said that these could travel up to a speed of Mach 10 or 12,250 kilometres per hour. The technology was quickly picked up by every nation that matters: the US, China, and even India appears to be working on it. Technological superiority lasts only months. India is exporting supersonic BrahMos missiles and is working on a Mach 5 model that is technically hypersonic. Also, technical superiority is no longer guaranteed. On 16 May 2023, Ukraine claimed that it had managed to destroy six of these new Russian war toys in a single night.

All these developments have shaken the concept of superpower. The erstwhile superpower Russia is relying on North Korean ammunition and Iranian drones. As the drones develop intercontinental distance capability, attack will be cheap and precise; defence will be unreliable and expensive.

Spooks, Cyber Threats, and AI: Winning the War without Fighting

A large chunk of global power production relies on Chinese equipment, including thermal, solar, and wind energy systems. With their low prices, Chinese electric vehicles are beating the likes of Tesla. Fears have been expressed that all these devices feed information to China and can be controlled from China whenever needed. On 7 May 2021, one of America's largest pipelines that carried fuel from Texas along the coast to New York had to be shut down due to a ransomware attack.[7] Colonial Pipelines, the operator company, said that the closure affected 8,800 kilometres of this pipeline, which carries 45 per cent of the East Coast's fuel supplies. The hackers demanded $4.4 million in bitcoins as ransom, which was apparently paid, yet it took several days to bring the system back online. A day before the attack, the hackers had stolen 100 GB of data from the company servers. A month later, about 84 per cent of the bitcoins were recovered by investigative agencies, and the hacker group DarkSide stated, 'Our goal is to make money and not creating problems for society.'[8] If private groups could cause such disruptions just for money, what disruptions could be caused by a rival nation?

The banking system is highly vulnerable to hacking. Power grids, water supplies, city traffic lights, and airports have all become susceptible. It was bad with rogue groups engaged in these activities. It will be disastrous if the might of China and Russia is used for this purpose, and the criminals, even if identified, will enjoy the protection of these states. A cyberattack is cheaper than an attack with weapons, and it is becoming increasingly certain, since, as with conventional weapons, cyber defence is expensive and never guaranteed. In every form of terrorism, the attacker has to succeed only once; the defence has to be successful all the time.

In recent times, large-scale cyberattacks by rogue states have moved from the realm of rare possibilities to real events. Reports emerged in December 2023 that 'hackers affiliated with China's People's Liberation Army have burrowed into the computer systems of about two dozen critical entities ... to sow panic and chaos and snarl logistics in the event of a U.S.-China conflict in the Pacific'.[9] Among the targets breached were a water utility in Hawaii, an important West Coast port, oil and gas pipelines, and an attempted penetration of the Texas power grid. Speaking at the Vanderbilt Summit on Modern Conflict and Emerging Threats on 18 April 2024, FBI Director Christopher Wray said that China's 'targeting of our critical infrastructure is both broad and unrelenting' and the goal of the Chinese Communist Party's hacking programme isn't just aimed at stealing American intellectual property; it is to 'physically wreak havoc on our critical infrastructure at a time of its choosing'. The facilities on China's targets are 'vital sectors—everything from water treatment facilities and energy grids to transportation and information technology—[that] form the backbone of our society'.[10]

Cyberattacks from states like Russia and China have always been a threat to secret research and strategic documents. Now, these are emerging as a threat to day-to-day life. Communications, power, water, oil and gas, port operations, train management, and city traffic lights can all be hit by hackers. Testing equipment made in China has been found sending patients' data, including genetic information, to unauthorised recipients. When COVID cases began rising exponentially, a Chinese company, Beijing Genomics Institute (BGI), reached out to some states of the US with an offer of setting up testing labs with the intention of harvesting US citizens' DNA data.[11] The US National Counterintelligence and Security Centre, a wing of the Office of the Director of National Intelligence, reached out to the authorities concerned and warned them of the dangers ahead. Yet, BGI managed to set up labs in eighteen other countries and collected DNA data. Fire-fighting measures like black-listing the Chinese communication giant Huawei or the entertainment application TikTok may seem symbolic, as opposed to doing nothing. These have limited utility in terms of preventing a determined rogue state's penetration into the innards of a democracy's life. If important international trading partners that play a critical role in supply chains and energy supplies are hit by cyberattacks, it will affect the economies of many other countries too. Of course, in times of war, such cyberattacks will have disastrous consequences, making them perhaps the most potent disruptors of geopolitics and energy security.

China might not have to fight a war to disrupt the national security and economy of the West. 'To subdue the enemy without fighting is the acme of skill,' said Sun

Tzu, the 5th-century BC. Chinese general. China has become powerful without fighting a war with the West; the wars that it fought with Vietnam and Russia made it weaker. It has avoided fighting the US despite fuming at American warships sailing in the South China Sea and even in the Taiwan Strait, both of which it claims as its exclusive preserves. China routinely issues warnings to US warplanes and warships in this area, and the Americans routinely reply that they are exercising freedom of navigation in international waters. There may be a valid reason for China's continuous restraint, and the reason is certainly not that China does not want to overwhelm the West. The reason may be that China has found a way of achieving its goal of grabbing victory without fighting a military or economic war.

Another pearl of wisdom attributed to Sun Tzu is, 'If you know the enemy and know yourself, you need not fear the result of a hundred battles.' With the goal of knowing everything about its own citizens, China has become the perfect surveillance state with 700 million surveillance cameras in place, every citizen's mobile phone under constant watch, and a 20-million-strong monitoring crowd keeping real-time tabs on everything that the citizens read or post on their smart devices. Sun Tzu will approve that Xi Jinping knows the minutest details of his country and is able to instantly block what should not be there. Now that Xi's goal is to take the lead in AI, his capabilities to 'know' his people will further take a quantum leap.

Xi Jinping also excels in the other part of Sun Tzu's advice: know the enemy. Firstly, the world is his enemy because there are other hegemons and aspiring hegemons around. They labour in the laboratories to take the lead in various aspects of science and technology, spending a considerable part of their GDP on this endeavour. If China were to do that, it would seriously reduce the wealth available to spend on its armed forces, their equipment, and toys of war. So, China and its 'friend without limits', Russia, have resorted to shortcuts with two objectives: to steal technology from the West and replicate it, and to sabotage social stability in the West to prove that democracy is not as fruitful as it is made out to be. They have achieved considerable success on both fronts.

Since 9/11, the spy-busting agencies of the West have been focussed on terrorism, particularly that emanating from Islamist groups. However, in the last few months, realisation has dawned on these countries that espionage by Russia, China, and Iran poses an immediate and more serious danger, not only to their economic progress but also to their national security and their capability to be prepared to meet the challenge posed by these countries. A report's headline in the *Sunday Telegraph* on 2 June 2024 said it all: 'Focus on Russia and China spies rather than terrorists, MI5 told.' The British government has two agencies, MI5 and MI6. While the former is responsible for catching foreign spies, the latter is used to spy on other countries. It appears that thanks to liberal immigration policies, Britain is swarming with foreign spies, particularly from Russia and China, while Iran has been using organised criminals to gather information and conduct sabotage. Language is a significant factor in identifying spies, and Chinese-speaking spy busters are expensive; MI5 has been hiring them with starting salaries of around £44,000.

Britain is not alone in ringing the alarm bells. The Chinese PM landed in Wellington, New Zealand, on 13 June 2024. His 'welcome' included the release of a documentary, *The Long Game*, which focuses on China's spy networks in New Zealand. In the film, the then minister-in-charge of the Security Intelligence Service (SIS) states that half of the intelligence effort goes into foreign interference, and 'the country that gets most attention from our authorities is China'. Jiang

Yang, a Chinese-born member of Parliament, is accused of spying for China and having links with Chinese military academies.[12] A real-life espionage story that seems straight out of the movies took place in the Philippines. Alice Leal Guo, the mayor of Bamban town, claimed to have been born in the country. Upon interrogation by the country's senate, she could not provide proper answers about her birth, childhood, and schooling, leading even President Marcos to say, 'We are wondering where she came from.'

In the US, open borders have permitted entry of almost 50,000 illegal Chinese immigrants since last year. Since leaving China with an entire family is not possible without state connivance, there is legitimate suspicion that many of them arrive with the connivance of the communist state. Many of them never return for their immigration hearings and manage to find jobs in sensitive industries. Reuters quoted a US counterintelligence officer as saying, 'China and Russia are among the leading foreign intelligence threats to the US space industry.'[13]

But placing assets in a foreign land for intelligence gathering is a primitive method, and China seems to have moved ahead. In the world of espionage, one method of gaining entry to a well-guarded establishment has been as a member of the maintenance crew. No establishment can have all the specialised maintenance staff on its rolls, so they must rely on outsiders. Today's world relies heavily on commerce and communications through fibre optic cables crisscrossing the seabed, with researchers interacting with each other via the internet, even when they are in the same building. These cables are vulnerable to damage from marine life, such as sharks and whales, accidents like ships sinking on the cables, and even acts of sabotage. While the world was developing the internet, China was developing ships to repair these undersea cables.

A report dated 17 June 2024 in the *National Enquirer* bears the headline, 'China spying at bottom of the sea!' It mentions that 'the Chinese are using cable repair ships to install remote devices that allow them to eavesdrop on data flow'. This enables China to not only steal commercial and technological secrets but also military secrets. Owners of the cables, which include giants like Google and Meta, unwittingly use companies partly or indirectly owned by the Chinese. Alarm bells rang when some of these repair ships began disappearing from radio and satellite tracking, with one such ship, *Fu Hai*, vanishing a dozen times during the last five years.

The US's FBI director Christopher Wray went on record on 7 July 2020, saying that the Chinese spy campaign is so broad and diverse that his bureau opens a new Chinese counterintelligence probe every ten hours.[14]

Geopolitics and Supply Chain Disruption

A new threat to the stability and predictability of international trade emerged during the disruption caused by the COVID pandemic between 2021 and 2023. The events sensitised policymakers to the deleterious effects of supply chain disruption on national economies. These disruptions can occur not only during a pandemic but also due to natural disasters and international conflicts. Some of the disruptions during COVID were deliberately caused by China, which sought to profiteer from its virtual monopoly of some personal protection equipment (PPE) by hoarding and manipulating prices through restricted supplies. Prolonged lockdowns in various cities of China, which supplied critical components to production facilities around the world, further contributed to supply disruptions at a later stage of the pandemic.[15] One example was the non-availability of semiconductor chips used in cars, for which

China was the main source. The chip shortage hit more than 160 different types of industries, ranging from automobiles to computers, washing machines, phones and TVs. This led to production cuts, unemployment, price increases, and disruptions in areas like car rentals.

The situation finally eased in the third quarter of 2023. This crisis has created a positive change too: before 2021, supply chains were taken for granted. It was presumed that when there was a demand, supply would be generated. The criticality of supply chains was understood during the pandemic not only in the context of economic disruption but also with regard to national security. Countries realised belatedly that the little price advantage offered by China could result in a much higher cost in terms of national security. There have been calls for decoupling from China, with the EU coining the term de-risking. Homeshoring, reshoring, and friendshoring are new terms in the lexicon referring to the movement of Western industries from China to their home country, a third country, or an allied country. On 21 March 2024, US Senator Mitt Romney, along with three other Republicans and two Democrats, introduced a bipartisan legislation titled the 'American Economic Independence Act'. If passed, it would require the president to submit to Congress a 'comprehensive threat analysis of the national security risks posed by economic integration with China in key economic sectors'. Romney warned, 'We must consider the national security threats posed by U.S. economic integration with China—from critical minerals to manufacturing and everything in between—to effectively craft a strategy that mitigates these threats.'[16] Senator Young, a co-signatory of the bill added, 'In recent years, we have experienced the economic and national security risks associated with relying on a strategic rival's supply chains for a wide variety of industries.' The bill lists the following sectors, covering almost the entire gamut of economic activity, where economic engagement with China creates national security risks for the US:

- Financial services
- Critical minerals, including rare-earth elements
- Semiconductors and microelectronics
- Artificial intelligence
- Communications, including telecommunications, social media applications, satellites and other space-based systems, and undersea cables
- Quantum computing
- Cloud-based systems, including computing services and data storage
- Biotechnology
- Pharmaceuticals and medical technology, including medical devices
- Manufacturing, including casting, machining, joining, and forming.

In March 2023, the president of the European Commission, Ursula von der Leyen, had called for de-risking the EU's economies from the effects of economic engagement with China. She said that the de-risking would include 'stress-testing our relationship to see where the greatest threats to our resilience, long-term prosperity and security lie'.[17] She pledged that Europe will produce at least 40 per cent of its clean technology and will take into account Europe's economic security interests when exporting to China. Earlier, the European Council had recommended to the EU to 'continue to reduce critical dependencies and vulnerabilities, including in its supply chains, and … de-risk and diversify where necessary and appropriate'.

In just a few years, India's story of economic engagement with China has undergone a qualitative change, although enough quantitative change is not yet visible. The Indian government has restricted or placed extra scrutiny on China's role in India's economy, technology, telecommunications, civil society, and media. It has been recognised that cheap Chinese products are double-edged; on the one hand, they have increased household consumption, but on the other hand they have created an increasing trade imbalance as well as a security risk. China was not inclined to buy from India in areas where we have strength, such as pharmaceuticals and IT services, blocking these with various non-tariff barriers. Simultaneously, India shares the suspicion of the rest of the democracies that China uses its exports to snoop and create possibilities of sabotage when desired. While cracking down on the likes of Huawei and TikTok, India imposed a very high level of scrutiny on Chinese investments in India. In addition, some of the investments leaving China came to India, such as from Apple. India had not joined the Belt and Road Initiative (BRI) and had withdrawn from the Regional Comprehensive Economic Partnership (RCEP) in 2019. At that time, India's Home Minister Amit Shah had written an article explaining India's decision. He said that 'the agreement didn't seem to accommodate India's concerns on issues like trade losses and dumping'. He added that the agreement, as negotiated by the previous government of the Congress Party, would have led to unhindered imports. He concluded that by rejecting RCEP, 'India has firmly protected its industries from any adverse effects that Chinese interests would have caused.'[18]

Thus, the recent experience of supply chain constraints and various coercive steps taken by China have compelled the world to take a step back from the earlier mantra of universal globalisation. Countries have realised that the adverse costs imposed on economic and national security by China's trade practices are unacceptable, and they have been looking for alternative models. A churning has been going on about what the new model shall be, as seen in this title of a 2021 analysis by the World Economic Forum: 'Regionalization vs globalization: what is the future direction of trade?'[19] Whatever be the future direction, the issue of overdependence on China seems to have altered geopolitics permanently.

Nuclear Proliferation, Proxies, Multipolar World, and the Ideological Divide

The number of countries with proven or known capability of making and delivering nuclear weapons has increased steadily. North Korea remained in denial mode on the issue of developing nuclear weapons, but it withdrew from the Non-Proliferation Treaty (NPT) in 2003 and came out in the open with its underground nuclear test on 9 October 2006. Israel's not-so-secret nuclear hoard has at least ninety warheads, but it may be as high as 400, and the country has missile capabilities for their delivery. South Africa, too, had produced six warheads, but it ended the programme in 1989 and signed the NPT in 1991. Libya's Gaddafi had an active nuclear weapons programme until he announced the destruction of all weapons of mass destruction (WMDs) in 2003. The dictator signed the Chemical Weapons Convention in 2004 when it was revealed that the backward country had stockpiles of mustard gas and chemical precursors to make the poisonous nerve gas sarin. The latest to join the fray is Iran, after Trump nullified the nuclear deal, accusing Iran of violating its provisions.

In the new geopolitical environment, undeclared wars are being fought by proxies of countries like Iran, Syria, Iraq, Saudi Arabia, and Pakistan. These proxies do not represent any state, are not parties to conventions and treaties that regulate the conduct of parties in times of war and are laws unto themselves. Yet, they attack nations, hiding among civilian populations, and retaliations by the regular armed forces draw criticism for causing excessive collateral damage. The rapid rise of groups like Al-Qaeda and the Islamic State caught policy planners by surprise, even when the terrorist organisations were, to some extent, their own creations. Iran has been propping up Hamas to hurt Israel, much like the US had propped up Osama bin Laden to hurt the Soviet Union. Ultimately, the Frankenstein monster often turns against the hand that fed it. Hamas is a Sunni organisation, and given the millennia and a half of bloodletting between the Shia and the Sunnis, its long-term proximity to Iran is virtually impossible.[20] Sooner than later, Hamas may shift its allegiance to Saudi Arabia, the leader of the Sunnis in the Muslim world, and then fight the Shia Houthis in Yemen, who are making common cause with Hamas since 2024. Proxies are tools; a tool does not have a mind of its own and can change hands. Yet, it makes the task of long-term geopolitical reckoning a nightmare.

When the Soviet Union imploded, there were loud proclamations that the world had become effectively unipolar. However, these 'expert' voices had spoken too soon; there had to be two superpowers contending against each other, although this may have seemed otherwise during the interregnum. Simultaneously, sooner or later, a third power would emerge, trying to replace the relatively weaker of the two at the high table. The continuation of Russia in the superpower role was enabled by the West when it handed over the permanent seat of the USSR in the Security Council to Russia, even though the latter was much pruned in size, influence, and economic clout to be eligible for such automatic succession.

Initially, Putin showed an inclination to join the West, in conformity with the fact that historically Russia has been a European country and Tolstoy's characters from the nobility frequently speak in French. The Cold War threat of communism had already been diluted with the dissolution of the Soviet Union, and for a time, it was seriously believed that the successor state, the Russian Federation, would truly become ideologically European. Yet, it was the US that rebuffed all such attempts. It may sound unbelievable, but even the Soviet Union had expressed a desire to join NATO. On 1 April 1954 (and it was not an April Fool's Day prank), the Associated Press (AP) had published the text of a Moscow broadcast of the same day on the question of European collective security, with a focus on German militarism. It said, 'The Soviet Government, guided by the unchanged principles of its foreign policy of peace and desirous of relaxing the tension in international relations, states its readiness to join with the interested governments in examining the matter of having the Soviet Union participate in the North Atlantic Treaty.'[21] By this time, however, the US's loathing of the Nazis had been replaced by a fiercer loathing of the communists, and the US refused to even examine the idea.

Russia's eastern parts in Asia were seized much later by the imperial rulers. Parts of Qing dynasty's territories were ceded to Russia under the 1858 Treaty of Aigun and the 1860 Treaty of Peking, and this has continued to rankle Xi Jinping as part of the 'Century of Humiliation'. Russia formally applied for membership in the Council of Europe on 7 May 1992. Although the request ran into rough weather due to the atrocities committed in Chechnya, Russia provided lengthy assurances of better behaviour in the future and was finally invited to join on 25 January 1996.[22] The issue cooled off after Russia invaded Georgia in 2008 and went into cold storage after it annexed Crimea in 2014. Now, with the invasion of Ukraine, Russia is back to claiming its superpower status. Simultaneously, as China increased its economic and military heft, it has been contending for Russia's place on the superpower table. As luck would have it, Putin has become dictator for life, and history tells us that such self-centred megalomaniacs, from Nero to Hitler, end up hurting their countries. While Putin annoys the West with his frequent threats of using nuclear weapons, Xi seems to be waiting for Russia's economic and military depletion. Gradually, China's prospects of being the second superpower, displacing Russia, are brightening. While the West tries hard not to have either of these dictatorships as a superpower rival, other democracies are forced to negotiate the tortuous geopolitical bylanes that run between the US, Russia, and China.

The end of the Cold War signalled the slipping of the ideological divide, giving way to the compulsions of economy and trade. It was during this time that Samuel P. Huntington presented his thesis on the 'Clash of Civilizations' and published the book by the same name in 1996, postulating that the religious divide would take precedence over the ideological divide. Huntington's thesis was initially criticised as being too simplistic and reductionist. After the terrorist-commandeered planes hit the Twin Towers of the World Trade Center on 11 September 2001, some called the idea a self-fulfilling prophecy.[23]

For a while, during the conflicts in West Asia and Afghanistan, it did appear as if the West was fighting a war with Islam. Gradually, however, as Russia, China, North Korea, and Iran increasingly confronted the West, it became clear that the religious divide alone could not explain much. If it were the driving force, then Russia's pounding of Chechnya's Muslims and China's atrocities on Muslims in Xinjiang would have kept Iran away from Putin and Xi Jinping. The fact that the relations have become even closer after these atrocities shows that the real divide in the world is between ideologies of total control and democracy.

There is no meeting ground between the totalitarian and democratic regimes. It is true that undemocratic regimes like Saudi Arabia are allied with the West, but that is an offshoot of the religious divide within Islam between the Shias and the Sunnis. Even emerging economies like India, which have been close to Russia, are gradually thickening their bonds with the democratic block, and dysfunctional electoral democracies like Pakistan, which were firmly with the West, have drifted closer to China, Russia, North Korea, and Iran. The multinational corporations of the West, which by definition, have no nationality, are still creating a smokescreen to show that economic entanglement across this ideological divide can still work. The sooner the policymakers and analysts of geopolitics in the democratic world realise the futility of looking for trust where none can exist, the better it will be for the future of democracy.

Illegal Migration

During the Cold War, communism raised physical barriers, such as the Berlin Wall, and administrative barriers, such as restrictions on travel and the flow of information, to keep the two worlds apart. Gradually, technology made many of these walls porous. It is a connected world now, and nothing can insulate any part of the world from the rest. Yet, the goal of the undemocratic block is the demolition of democracy. Therefore, there will have to be limits on the permitted porosity if disaster is not to be courted by democracies. Let us consider an example of porosity that is going to hurt the US severely in the near future. On the one hand, US intelligence agencies are fighting hard to minimise the impact of China's clandestine activities on influencing elections and elected representatives in the country. Yet, on the other hand, bowing to international conventions relating to refugees, US law enforcement authorities felt compelled to 'receive' illegal Chinese entrants into the US and provide them with food, shelter, and even telephones. More than 37,000 Chinese citizens entered the US illegally in 2023 through the border with Mexico. After a legal formality, they were given a date for court appearance and released into the country. Most of the illegal migrants simply melt into the country and never bother to appear before the courts for their asylum hearing. Twenty twenty-three was not an exception; the rate of illegal border crossings by Chinese nationals and others will continue to increase, particularly when the Democratic Party is in power.

It is true that most of these Chinese have become disillusioned by the impossibility of a decent life in China and are escaping that oppressive system. However, the probability is very high that the communist state is actively complicit in sending some of its agents in the garb of refuge seekers. Even if only 1 per cent of the illegal entrants are saboteurs, that means 500 saboteurs from a rival country have entered in less than eighteen months. It is time that the sanctity of the borders and the passport-visa regime is restored if democracies do not want to face unmanageable levels of internal sabotage.

Illegal migration has caused tensions within Europe, with the point-of-entry countries like Italy not getting enough cooperation from other countries for sharing the burden of illegal migrants. Many European countries are facing the prospect of their social fabric being torn apart due to the refusal of the large number of migrants to assimilate. The illegal migrants can even be weaponised, as was attempted by Belarus in 2021 when it tried to push migrants into Poland,[24] and by Russia when it facilitated the entry of migrants into Finland, with the latter calling it a hybrid attack.[25]

Connected World, Unforeseen Consequences

In the connected world, an event that appears to be a trade deal between two nations may have far-reaching consequences for other nations or even the whole planet. Consider how China's large demand for pork is warming the earth. China has the largest pig population in the world, with almost half a billion pigs—about two-thirds of the world's total. It used to buy soybeans for these animals from the US, but due to trade tensions, it began importing from Brazil. Large areas of the Amazon basin were deforested to grow this food for Chinese pigs, significantly contributing to global warming. This tightening of the bond between China and Brazil led to China implementing its Belt and Road Initiative (BRI), which accelerated deforestation to create infrastructure such as ports, roads, power plants, and railways to transport soybeans to China.[26] The country's hunger for pork has resulted in massive forest fires in the Amazon, adding emissions and heat, while creating a Chinese outpost that is altering geopolitics on the South American continent.

Let us consider another example of the unforeseen consequences of an interconnected world divided by ideology. Indonesia has huge reserves of nickel—21 million tonnes or about 22 per cent of the world's total. Most of it was converted into nickel matte, which was then sent to Japan's Sumitomo Metal Mining Company for refining into pure nickel, while some ore was also exported. In January 2020, Indonesia completely banned the export of nickel ore and matte to encourage the setting up of domestic processing facilities. This led to a flood of Chinese investment, and by July 2023, forty-three nickel smelters were operating in Indonesia, with twenty-eight more under construction and twenty-four additional smelters on the drawing board.[27] It was a great success story in terms of investment and production. There were, however, many issues caused by the Chinese lack of concern for safety standards and environmental impact. The Chinese mainly used coal in their smelters, and there was a major explosion in one of the units. The flooding of the market with Indonesia's nickel led to a price crash of up to 40 per cent, resulting in the closure of some facilities in Australia. Protests against mining in Indonesia increased in intensity. Some restrictions were imposed on mining, forcing the Chinese to import nickel ore from the Philippines. There is no ban on the export of ore from the Philippines, and earlier China had been importing directly from that country as well. This created a new opening for China in its relations with the Philippines, which had been tense due to the country permitting more US bases in addition to the existing ones. US policy think tanks have called for setting up nickel processing units by US companies in Indonesia.[28] Indonesia has been trying to formulate a Critical Minerals Agreement with the US and take advantage of the avenues available under the Inflation Reduction Act, but Chinese investment stalled the negotiations.[29] In April 2024, the US and the UK imposed sanctions on Russian metal supplies, which gave a boost to Chinese nickel. If the sanctions are extended to nickel produced by Chinese companies in Indonesia, it will severely hurt the Indonesian economy. All these changes have taken place in less than three years. Maybe someday, the Indonesian government will be forced to do what the US is doing to TikTok: ask China to sell its Indonesian smelters.

Imagine the plight of a geopolitical policymaker formulating even a medium-term policy for electric vehicles, given that nickel is a critical component of batteries in the currently dominant technology!

Another example of the unforeseen effects of geopolitical disruptions is liquefied natural gas (LNG). With the Ukraine War and the damage to the Russian gas pipelines supplying gas to Europe, the democracies on the continent rushed to shift to LNG, which is easy to transport by ships due to the smaller volume in liquid form, as compared to the compressed gas form (CNG), which was carried in pipelines. The rapid increase in liquefaction and LNG shipping capacities saved Europe during the winters but disadvantaged India, which had already been importing its gas as LNG. The large European demand raised the import costs for India; while LNG import volumes in 2022–23 decreased by 15 per cent, the value of its import increased by 27 per cent![30]

Another spin-off of the Ukraine War was India's and China's ability to buy discounted Russian oil, rendered surplus due to sanctions imposed by the West. This further added to India's foreign exchange earnings, as the country used its large crude processing facilities and exported more refined products to European countries, helping them mitigate the effects of Russian sanctions. India and China were thus insulated from the spurt in energy prices due to Russian sanctions, but Bangladesh could not avoid it. Bangladesh is highly dependent on imported fuel for power generation, and higher fuel prices cut generation, leading to blackouts. This hurt its textile and garment industries, which are the major earners of foreign exchange. Many Bangladeshis worked in Russia and sent money back home. They have all returned, causing unemployment and drastic fall in remittances. The cause-and-effect chain resulting from a single geopolitically disruptive event passes through points that had earlier remained below the radar.

A Silver Lining: Reduced Probability of a Biological War

Among all these dark effects of geopolitical disruption, there is a silver lining. Ironically, it is the effect of an event that has caused more economic disruption and human suffering than any other event since World War II. The COVID-19 epidemic, despite China's efforts to block an inquiry into its origins, was caused by China's actions, whether by an act of commission or omission. Yet, within a month, it began impacting the rest of the world. Viruses and bacteria cannot be confined by borders; they travel on trains, planes, ships, and cars without the operators' consent. They are carried by goods moving along the lines of foreign trade and by vectors like wind, birds, animals, and insects. This should have always been known to mankind, but arrogance in the capability of science and technology convinced militaries that they could confine these organisms to 'enemy' territory and insulate their own. In that misplaced belief, they developed and stockpiled biological weapons. COVID-19 has exposed the hollowness of these assumptions; an epidemic in any country, if the virus is resilient and potent enough, shall soon become a worldwide pandemic. With this realisation, even rogue states like North Korea, Iran, China, or Russia would be deterred from using or further stockpiling biological weapons. They will remember that even heads of states became infected. Thus, a geopolitical crisis had a positive effect on the world's future, although if China had an active hand in it, Xi Jinping would not have foreseen it.

6

China: The Great Disruptor of the Global Geopolitical Order

Radha Krishna Mathur and R.N. Prasher

Xi Jinping runs a dictatorship, and dictators do not like to be advised. Under his totalitarian rule, economic experts have been marginalised. The feedback that earlier leaders used to receive has been replaced by flattery.[1] China's cabinet, the State Council, is headed by the prime minister, technically the number two man in the country. Yet, China's rubber-stamp Parliament amended the Organic Law of the State Council, making it explicitly subservient to the Chinese Communist Party (CCP) and its supreme leader Xi Jinping. The amendment states that 'the council shall uphold the leadership of the ruling party and be guided by Marxism-Leninism, as well as the political doctrines of previous and current party leaders'. It further stipulates that the State Council shall resolutely safeguard the authority and centralised, unified leadership of the party's decision-making Central Committee, which is led by Xi Jinping, and fully implement its decisions and instructions.

Dictators are always insecure, worried about the power enjoyed by those around them. The former prime minister, Li Keqiang, who was also a member of the party's Central

Committee, did give Xi cause to worry. Li was an economist and is remembered for a fateful statement made on 28 May 2020 while addressing his annual press conference: 'The average per-capita annual income in China is 30,000 yuan ($4,193), but there are over 600 million people whose monthly income is barely 1,000 yuan ($140), not enough to rent a room in the Chinese cities.'[2] This appeared to run counter to the party propaganda that officially stated in 2020 that extreme poverty had been eradicated. Speaking in February 2021, Xi had called this achievement a 'miracle'. Obviously, he was not amused by the prime minister choosing to state the facts as they were.

The party 'elected' a new Central Committee on 22 October 2022 that did not include Li Keqiang. Then in March 2023, Li Keqiang was removed from the post of prime minister and replaced by Li Qiang. In October 2023 it was announced that Li Keqiang had died of a heart attack. The curtailment of the powers of the cabinet and the prime minister, and perhaps even the latter's life, was Xi's way of telling the new PM that his post is ceremonial, and he should not speak out of turn. The new cabinet will now ensure that the only advice given to Xi is that which is pleasing to his ears.

Thus, decision making by Chinese dictators continues with little input from experts. Since each individual, even a dictator, has limitations on what he can know and foresee, there is a long litany of crucial mistakes that have been made since the days of Mao.

The Great Leap Forward and Its Geopolitical Impact

Mao's socio-economic campaign, which lasted from 1958 to 1962, focused on the rural areas for the collectivisation of agriculture. By that time, collectivisation had already failed in the Soviet Union. Mao eulogised Stalin as the ideal Communist leader and ascribed the failure of collectivisation in the Soviet Union to Stalin's death in 1953 and to the liberal policies of his successor Khrushchev, with whom Mao could never develop a rapport. Managers of the collectives in China kept reporting high production figures, and the official news agencies released reports of a huge surplus of grain and concerns about what to do with it. The state increased the tax rate (in kind) to 28 per cent of the inflated figures and resorted to increased exports of the collected grain. In reality, collectivisation had led to a drastic 30 per cent decline in agricultural output between 1958 and 1960, and after the collection of the levy, which was based on the presumed high production, nothing was left with the farmers. As reports of mass starvation began coming in, a patriotic Peng Dehuai, a hero of the Korean War, had the courage to inform Mao in a deferential letter that mistakes had been made in the Great Leap Forward and correction was necessary. Mao felt threatened and Peng was arrested for being a counter-revolutionary. The Great Leap Forward resulted in the Great Famine that killed around 50 million Chinese, all because of the ideas of one man.

The Great Famine threatened Mao's control, and he needed a distraction around which the masses could be rallied. Early in 1962, he went into retreat and during that period there was talk of a change in leadership. Alarmed, Mao returned to centre stage and took full control by the end of September 1962. He denounced the 'bourgeoisie right in the party ranks', hinting at those who had tried to change leadership. He also decided to attack India; some of Nehru's utterances were deemed to be the immediate provocation. All other senior leaders had acquiesced in Mao's statement that 'since Nehru sticks his head out and insists on us fighting him, for us not to fight with him would not be friendly enough. Courtesy emphasizes reciprocity'.[3]

Then, a larger meeting was held in Beijing on 6 October, during which some pointed to the danger of China being isolated. Mao replied, 'China need not fear isolation as long as the front line troops fight well...'[4] The attack on India took place on 20 October 1962. The Chinese then decided to terminate the war 'with a unilateral Chinese halt, ceasefire, and withdrawal'.[5] The Chinese military believed that the domestic situation in China demanded that the PLA troops 'would quickly disengage and end the fighting as quickly as possible'.[6] That is exactly what happened; the war had started on Chinese terms, it ended, too, on their terms. The Chinese rallied around Mao once again, and opposition to him was decimated. The hunger and death were forgotten, and Mao remained the unquestioned leader until his death in 1976.

Opinion is divided about who was more responsible for the 1962 war, Nehru or Mao? Neville Maxwell is inclined to lay the blame on Nehru's door,[7] while Bertil Lintner feels that Nehru's actions on the border in 1961 were not so relevant to Mao's decision to attack India.[8] According to Lintner, Mao was cut to the quick by India giving refuge to the Dalai Lama in 1959. Be that as it may, it was a dictatorial Mao pitched against a dictatorial Nehru in taking decisions for war and peace between two nations that represented one third of the human population. While the dictatorship of Mao is evident, that of Nehru has been less talked about. Neville Maxwell is unsparing in this regard. He said that so much of Nehru's reputation was 'the projection of his charisma that when he was alive it was not easy for those in contact with him to separate policies from personality so as to weigh the former in isolation. The affection he aroused in those who knew him and the emotional response to his personality blurred judgment .... Nehru dominated the cabinet when he did not ignore it .... foreign policy, in its conceptualization, articulation and execution, was his private monopoly'.[9] The two dictators, Nehru and Mao, ended up adding another intractable issue, the India–China border conundrum, to the already muddled world of geopolitics.

The Sino-Soviet Split

Mao owed much to the Soviet Union for the roots of the Chinese Communist Party (CCP) as well as for gaining power in 1949. It is important to remember that in the matter of revolution, China was a few years ahead of the Russians. The Xinhai Revolution had deposed the last emperor in February 1912, while the Russian czar was deposed in 1917. The beginnings of the CCP can be traced to Tiananmen Square, where on 4 May 1919, just two years after the Bolsheviks came to power in the Soviet Union, around 3,000 students gathered to protest the terms of the Treaty of Versailles, which had allowed Japan to retain Chinese territories in Shandong. This May Fourth Movement sowed the seeds that would sprout as the CCP in 1921. A secret 1952 document of the CIA, declassified in 2004, throws considerable light on Sino-Soviet relations in the 1950s.[10] It concluded:

- The Peiping regime accepts Moscow leadership in the world Communist movement, and is becoming increasingly dependent on the USSR economically and militarily.
- The Peiping regime retains some capability for independent action, and is in a position to influence the formulation of Communist policy in the Far East.
- The Kremlin will be able by non-military means to achieve a degree of control over Communist China comparable to that which it exercises over the European Satellites.... The Kremlin will not attempt to achieve such control by military force.

- Over the long run, Sino-Soviet solidarity might be weakened as a result of efforts by the USSR to intensify and extend its control over Communist China … (and) divergent views concerning the border areas.

Meanwhile, immediately after coming to power in 1949, Mao's forces invaded Xinjiang, which was called East Turkestan Republic and was a de facto independent state aligned with the Soviet Union. It could not be accomplished without Soviet help, and Stalin was proactive in providing all help as soon as Mao requested for assistance, pleading 'the railroads in this region are poor, the conditions difficult, there are few people, and there is no food. We acutely need and hope that you will help us with 30–50 transport aircraft to ship food, clothing, key personnel, and some of the troops'.[11] When the planes arrived, Mao further requested fuel and food for the 90,000 soldiers invading Xinjiang, and Stalin obliged. Thus emboldened, Mao's forces marched into Tibet in 1950 where Thubten Gyatso, the 13th Dalai Lama, had made a declaration of independence in 1913. The Dalai Lama requested India for help, but Nehru did not oblige.

The Soviet Union actively helped China with nuclear technology, while China exported uranium ore to them. The Chinese propagated the idea that the Soviet bloc would survive a nuclear attack by the West and would live to fight. Mao said that even if our 'enemies conquer the European part of the Soviet Union, then in that case the USSR will still have the vast and rich regions of Siberia and the Far East'.[12]

With the death of Stalin and Khrushchev's attempts at de-Stalinization and peaceful coexistence with the West, all the Soviet help was forgotten, and tensions arose between the Communist parties in Moscow and Beijing. Khrushchev's closeness to India and his supplying of weapons to India also played a role in this breach. By 1961, the Chinese denounced the Soviets as 'revisionist traitors'. The continuation of the Cold War led Mao to take advantage of the West to isolate the USSR, which led to Kissinger and Nixon visiting China in 1971 and 1972, respectively. Simultaneously, the two Communist states were cooperating in supporting North Vietnam in the long Vietnam War. Yet again, once the two-decade US–Vietnam War was over in 1975, China and Vietnam clashed in 1979, and Vietnam prevailed with Soviet help.

Thus, Mao came to power with Soviet help and grabbed Xinjiang and Tibet with their support. He also developed nuclear weapons and missiles with Soviet assistance. Yet, he turned to the West to weaken the USSR. A few decades later, having enriched itself with Western technology and markets, China turned against the West and is now again claiming a 'friendship without limits' with Russia. Simultaneously, it is publishing maps with Chinese names of places in Russian Siberia and is encouraging illegal migration to those regions, ostensibly preparing future ground for reclaiming at least those areas that were originally part of China before the treaties of Aigun and Peking transferred them to Russia.

Over the last seventy-five years of Communist regime, China's roller-coaster relationship with Russia has had a profound impact on geopolitics. Both of these large nations have historical grievances about humiliation by the West and the thrusting of unequal treaties down their throats. Ivo Daalder, former US ambassador to NATO, claims Xi Jinping is obsessed with the century of humiliation,[13] starting with the Opium Wars, and Putin keeps lamenting the disruption of the Warsaw Pact and the implosion of the USSR in 1991. He calls it the demise of historical Russia, the greatest 'geopolitical catastrophe' of the 20th century and the loss of 'what had been built up over 1,000 years'.[14] Both blame the

West for these misfortunes and are making common cause by joining hands in the 21st century. In March 2023, Xi had told Putin, 'Right now there are changes the likes of which we have not seen for 100 years. And we are the ones driving these changes together.'[15] Xi and Putin have met sixty-three times, and high-level consultations are held between the two countries every two weeks or so.[16] Their countries have held joint military exercises and simulated nuclear runs. They have been mostly voting together in the Security Council. China has not only helped Russia with its purchase of oil, but it has also been helping its war effort through the sale of chips and parts through third countries. In April 2024, Julianne Smith, the US Ambassador to NATO, said that the US was increasingly seeing materiel support from China to Russia through dual-use technology and this was playing a critical role in Russian successes against Ukraine.[17] NATO put its seal of approval on these accusations on 10 July 2024.[18] But are these two giants really aligned or is the present bonhomie just a blip caused by the present circumstances? Are there disruptive factors in their relationship when we look beyond the compulsions of trade, multilateral diplomacy, shared geography, lack of faith in democracy, and their tendency to violate not only the social contract with their citizens but also the norms of international conduct?

Philipp Ivanov, a senior fellow at the Asia Society Policy Institute, believes that there is a lot that pulls Russia and China apart despite the many areas of convergence. He explains, '... Russia and China are also driven apart by historical animosities, power asymmetry, competition in overlapping spheres of interest, deep cultural differences, and shallow societal links.'[19] He says that the Ukraine War has increased Russia's economic dependence on China, altering the power asymmetry between the two nations. Simultaneously, it has damaged China's relations with Europe and the US. Both the dictators, Xi Jinping and Putin, resent dependence and the present proximity may be the high point of their partnership.

The history of these two behemoths does not instil confidence in their long-term partnership. The 1989 armed conflict between the two on a small island in the Ussuri River may not be the last collision in the clash of these two empires. China covets areas in eastern Russia, populated by Chinese immigrants. Manchuria has been another region of discord between China and Russia. Geographical proximity meant that Russia always had a large interest in Manchuria. The Manchu, who constituted the Qing dynasty that lasted two and a half centuries, came from Manchuria, an ancient geographical name that has now been obliterated from Chinese maps. The Manchu were as distinct from the Chinese Han as two cultures can be, religiously, culturally, and linguistically. They even had a script that was completely different from the Chinese script and much closer to the Mongolian script. The mutual hatred between the Chinese and the Manchu led to the construction of the Willow Palisade on the border between Manchuria and China to prevent the Han from 'polluting' the Manchu. This also extended to the enforcement of the Manchu hairstyle on court officials in Beijing, and the imperial court frowning upon the Han tradition of binding their women's feet.

In the second half of the 19th century, when China was in decline and Russia was in ascendance, the Qing Dynasty was forced to sign the unequal treaties of Aigun and Peking with Russia, ceding large areas that had previously been ceded to China under the Treaty of Nerchinsk, when the power equation favoured the Chinese. These treaties are part of the century of humiliation that Xi Jinping keeps lamenting. The 'humiliation' continued with more areas ceded to Russia for constructing the Trans-Siberian Railway. The rankling in Chinese minds is so strong that even in these heydays of 'friendship without limits' between the two powers, China published a map of the area, reiterating Chinese names for the cities and places under Russian sovereignty today.

What do we make of these contradictory gestures in Sino-Russian relations? Until the USSR imploded, it was unquestionably one of the two superpowers. With the USSR gone and replaced by a Russia that is not only smaller but also has a smaller sphere of influence in Europe, for some time it appeared to be a monopolar world. However, China was soon seen as a contender for one of the two seats at the high table. China's ambition can only be achieved by replacing Russia. If Xi Jinping wants to accelerate that process, he needs to take steps that will weaken Russia without strengthening the US. China's encouragement of Putin in the Ukraine War must be seen in this context. The longer Russia has to fight this war, the more dependent it becomes on China directly[20] and also through Iran and North Korea, over which China has considerable influence. In addition, the war is causing disagreement between Europe and the US, as well as within the US between the two major political parties, the Republicans and the Democrats. These developments weaken both NATO and the US. The stalemate in the US Congress over aid to Ukraine and the consequent reversals being suffered by Ukraine on the battlefield undermines the credibility of the US as a trustworthy fallback in any crisis.

Thus, by supporting Putin in this war without actually getting involved militarily, Xi Jinping is winning many other wars, which he hopes will pave the way for him to displace Russia as a superpower in the near future. Meanwhile, the democracies of the world have the unwelcome prospect of constantly being wary of the intentions of both Putin and Xi Jinping.

Geopolitical Disruption Caused by China's Demographic Blunder

Demography is an imperfect science, as the variables that determine human propensity to reproduce are too numerous and unpredictable. Yet, in no other case have demographic projections turned out to be farther from reality than in the case of China, and the fault does not lie with the demographers. The unpredictability of human propensity to reproduce was sought to be regulated by the Communist state by a draconian policy that made it a criminal act to reproduce at will.

The UN's World Population Prospects (WPP) annual report is prepared by the world's top demographers and is used by policymakers. The 1992 report estimated China's population to reach 1.52 billion by 2025. The 2022 report revised this figure to 1.42 billion; the actual numbers may be even lower. The projections for 2100 were even more off the mark: The 2019 report predicted a population of 1.06 billion, while the 2022 report suggests it could be as low as 767 million!

In 1970, the average fertility rate of Chinese women was six. The country had come out of the Great Famine that had lasted until 1962, and the surge in birth rates immediately after the famine was beginning to peter out. By 1980, the fertility rate had fallen to 2.74 births per woman. Demographers would have been aware of this trend, although the rocket scientists and the economists might not have been. Yet, it was rocket scientist Song Jian and economist Tian Xueyuan who predicted in 1980 that China's population would exceed 4.2 billion by 2080. Deng Xiaoping became chairman in 1978 after the dust of the Cultural Revolution had settled. He aimed at making China rich and did not want a large population to obstruct the path to that goal. Song and Tian had Deng's trust, so all the other demographers nodded in agreement, except for one, who had no audience, as he was not trained as a demographer. Dr Yi Fuxian, a gynaecologist and obstetrician by profession, had the courage to question Song and Tian's projections. He later wrote in *Big Country with an Empty Nest* in 2007 about the prospects of China's population decline; it was promptly banned in China. Song and Tian, who had succeeded in imposing the one-child policy with their dire predictions, went hammer and tongs after him. He was dubbed a 'national traitor' and had to flee China just before he would have been arrested. He became a professor at Wisconsin University and continued to write about the impending economic doom of China due to its one-child policy. His logic was simple: As the population ages, people will have an increased sense of insecurity about their old age, as a single child would not be able to bear the burden of supporting parents and grandparents. This would result in a lower propensity to consume, with increased savings and investment. However, lower domestic consumption would lead to greater dependence on exports. The experts had labelled China a rising star, and nobody believed the dark forebodings of Yi.

By 2012, the adverse effects of the one-child policy were becoming apparent. The demographers had begun ringing the alarm bell that China would get old before it got rich. Yi was invited to China and visited Henan, his home province, where officials had earlier threatened that he would be arrested upon his return. Bloomberg carried a story with this headline on 25 June 2012: 'Traitor treated to lunch as one-child China seen softening.' He gave an interview in Beijing and delivered twenty-three talks at universities and forums in China. Old enemies were still scheming against him, and he returned to the US, but his message had resonated. In 2015, the disastrous policy was abandoned, and Yi made another trip to China in 2016. On 23 March 2016, the *New York*

Times carried the story: 'Yi Fuxian, Critic of China's Birth Policy, Returns as an Invited Guest.' It noted Yi's transition from 'pariah to V.I.P.' in just six years. He spoke at the Boao Forum, a prestigious gathering of intellectuals, businesses, and writers.

The irrepressible Yi again got in trouble with the Communist Party. At the Boao Forum, he said that due to the one-child policy, there is no way the Chinese economy is going to overtake the US's. It was 2016; China was rising every day, and his words were like poison to the party. Yet, he emphatically declared, 'People say we can be two to three times the size of America's economy. I say it's totally impossible. It will never overtake America's because of the decrease in the labor force and the aging of the population.'[21] He further added that China's population had already begun declining in 2016. The 2015 census results had not yet come out, but he predicted that the fertility rate would be 1.25, as against the official expectation of 1.8. Although the official figure after the census was 1.6, many experts believe that the actual figure was close to Yi's estimate. There were calls again for his arrest.

In an article published on 4 April 2023, Yi wrote about the Communist Party inflating the birth figures. He showed that there were more 14-year-old children at school in 2014 than were born fourteen years ago. He gave several reasons for this falsehood: Local governments get more funds from Beijing if they report a larger population, and households receive more benefits from the local government if they report a bigger family. The local party gets recognition for reporting a population increase under the new policy of encouraging more children. In 2016, some provinces reported a 75 per cent increase in births compared to the previous year. The UN's WPP faithfully reproduced these figures. Yet the truth is like the sun; clouds may cover it for some time, but it will peep out soon. The bamboo curtain and the Great (Internet) Firewall of China have not succeeded so far in preventing the truth from being known to the world. The Chinese, of course, live in a different world where clouds perpetually veil the truth.

The effect of China's diktat of one child and the subsequent obfuscation has been profound on China, but it has misled the world too. Henry Kissinger and Richard Nixon had gravitated towards China, attracted by the potential consumption power of its large and ever-rising population. Investment flowed to China in the belief that its large population would provide cheap labour forever. Clinton believed that once China became rich, this large population would not remain subjugated, and China would gradually drift towards democracy. The Chinese military believed that it would have an inexhaustible pool of young men and women to sustain its goal of dominating the world. Even when it became clear that demographic implosion was on the way, the Chinese leadership was so smug in the belief that it controlled Chinese reproductive behaviour that it simply changed the policy to a two-child policy, and when even that did not work, to a three-child policy. Now it is clear that the social contract between the CCP and the Chinese people—that they can have a good material life as long as they stay away from politics—has finally been breached.

Once Russia's dependence on China crosses a threshold, the latter may move to actualise its claims over Taiwan and in the South China Sea with the full backing of the former. If that goal is achieved, then the door will be open for China to move northward to assert control over the Arctic Sea route, which will soon be open year-round thanks to the rapid melting of Arctic ice. By that time, Russia will be so subdued that China can easily take control of large parts of Russia that lie in Asia to the east of the Urals.

These are Xi Jinping's dreams, but geopolitical variables rarely move along predictable tracks. The Chinese economy has been unsteady and has not shown much resilience. Demography is expected to hurt China particularly due to its reluctance to allow much migration from high-population growth areas of the world like Africa. Consumer and investor confidence in the Chinese economy has taken a nosedive, and coupled with calls for decoupling or derisking, the long-term prospects for exports are not very bright. The surplus manufacturing capacity can be sustained for some time by state-subsidised low prices, but not for very long. Once the Chinese economy enters a long-term contraction, none of the geopolitical dreams will be within reach. Meanwhile, India, too, is working towards a position from which it can become a credible challenger to China. In the midst of all this uncertainty, only one thing remains certain: For a long time ahead, China shall remain a geopolitical disrupter.

Other Geopolitical Disruptions by China

China's insistence on enforcing its nine-dash or ten-dash line in the South China Sea has resulted in considerable realignment in the region. Chinese coast guards hit a Vietnamese vessel in 2014, and they were engaged in similar incidents against the Philippines in 2024. They are now using powerful water cannons against smaller boats, which are getting crippled. Chinese soldiers are also intimidating the Filipinos with long knives and hammers. Against the explicit Chinese commitment that the artificial islands created by them in the South China Sea would not be militarised,[22] they have added military infrastructure, including runways, on these islands. While China's border disputes with India are well known, it has conflicts with every country with which it shares a boundary, whether land or maritime:

Bhutan: China has a disputed border with Bhutan on the Doklam plateau and has been building settlements in contested areas in the Jakarlung and Menchuma valleys. In 2021, the two countries signed an MoU for expediting border talks, except on the tri-junction with India. In all likelihood, Bhutan will have to cede the areas, because the settlements have, de facto, made them Chinese territories.

Nepal: There have been reports of China gradually encroaching on Nepalese territory despite the 1,400-km-long Sino-Nepalese border being laid out after treaties were signed between the two countries. The area is close to Mount Kailash, which is considered sacred in Hinduism, Buddhism, and Jainism.[23]

Taiwan: China denies Taiwan's sovereignty and treats it as part of China, despite the fact that the current Communist regime has never ruled the island. It claims a right to use force if peaceful unification is not possible. Taiwan is a major geopolitical hotspot due to Chinese threats and aggressive displays by its navy, air force, and rocket force in the exclusion zone of the island. Five of the missiles fired by China in protest against US House Speaker Nancy Pelosi's visit to Taiwan landed, for the first time, in Japan's exclusive economic zone (EEZ) after flying over Taiwan.[24]

South Korea: China has a dispute with South Korea over the Socotra Rock, which is located 149 km from the nearest South Korean island and 287 km from the nearest Chinese island. Both claim the area to be a part of their exclusive economic zones.

Japan: The dispute with China over the Senkaku Islands, which China calls Diaoyu Islands, has been simmering for a long time. The island chain is 190 nautical miles southwest of Okinawa, well within the 200-mile limit of Japan's EEZ. Japan has accused China of 'relentless' intrusions around the islands and of placing buoys in its EEZ. A white paper released by Japan in July 2020 accused China of 'continuing to attempt to alter the status quo in the East China Sea and the South China Sea'.[25]

Philippines: The dispute between China and the Philippines over the ownership of the Spratly Islands has intensified in recent times, in spite of the ruling in the latter's favour by the Permanent Court of Arbitration in 2016. Parts of this island chain are claimed by Brunei and Malaysia also, while the Philippines, China, Taiwan, and Vietnam have overlapping claims over the entire chain. China, however, is the only country that has used violence in this area against the vessels of other countries. All the islands fall in the EEZ of the Philippines but also overlap with the EEZ of Vietnam, Taiwan, Brunei, and Malaysia. In 1999, the Philippine Navy ship *BRP Sierra Madre* was deliberately grounded at the Second Thomas Shoal in the Spratly Islands and is since then being used as an outpost of the Philippine Marine Corps to assert the nation's sovereignty.[26] Small boats deliver supplies to the troops on the ship, and these are regularly attacked by Chinese coast guard vessels, which ram them and use water jets, resulting in injuries and damage to the vessels.

The US already had five military bases in Philippines: Cesar Basa Air Base in Pampanga, Fort Magsaysay Military Reservation, Lumbia Air Base, Antonio Bautista Air Base, and Mactan Benito Ebuen Air Base. In 2023, an agreement was reached to add four more: Naval Base Camilo Osias in Santa Ana, Cagayan; Camp Melchor Dela Cruz in Gamu, Isabela; Balabac Island in Palawan; and Lal-lo Airport in Cagayan. The purpose of the bases, as made ominously clear in a handout by the Pentagon, is to 'strengthen the interoperability of the United States and Philippine armed forces and allow us to respond more seamlessly together to address a range of shared challenges in the Indo-Pacific region'.[27] The crumbling ship *BRP Sierra Madre* is becoming a hotspot in the South China

Sea, with China increasing its belligerence against Philippine vessels, and the latter, reassured by the new bases and the US-Philippines Mutual Defence Treaty (MDT) of 1951, refusing to give in. The MDT mandates both nations to support each other if either is attacked by another nation.

Indonesia: China's nine-dash line asserts its claim over the Natuna Sea around the Natuna Islands that lie within Indonesia's EEZ. Indonesia's significant economic entanglement with China through the BRI keeps both parties circumspect about the dispute. Yet, the two sides maintain rigid positions, a high degree of military deterrence, and continue making diplomatic representations on the issue. Chinese fishing vessels keep encroaching on the EEZ, while Indonesian fishermen demand that Jakarta keep them away.[28] Indonesia's efforts to keep tensions low may eventually be thwarted by an act of violence by fishermen from either side.

Malaysia: China's dispute with Malaysia overlaps with others over the Spratly Islands. Malaysia reacted angrily to China's 2023 edition of the national map, which reasserted its ownership of all areas within the nine-dash line in spite of a judicial verdict against it. Malaysia said that it 'does not recognise China's claims in the South China Sea as outlined in the "2023 edition of the standard map of China" which extends into Malaysian maritime area. The map has no binding effect on Malaysia'.[29] Malaysia has asserted that it will continue exploration of gas and oil in its EEZ in the South China Sea in spite of China's objections to its flagship company Petronas producing lots of oil in this area, while keeping a muted response to Chinese patrols[30] intruding into its claimed exclusive economic jurisdiction.

Brunei: This Islamic sultanate has been marked by its 'silent claims' against China for the Spratly Islands. It has become increasingly economically dependent on China, which is involved in its infrastructure development, setting up of petrochemical facilities, joint oil and gas explorations, and the establishment of the Brunei-Guangxi Economic Corridor.[31] Despite long-standing relations with the US, which permitted the use of Brunei territory during the Vietnam War, Brunei has bowed to the changed reality. It is now following 'a hedging strategy with the United States and China, maintaining strong relations and working to obtain the best possible economic, political and defence deals from both sides'.[32]

Vietnam: China had invaded Vietnam in February 1979 in order to force Vietnam out of Cambodia, where the Vietnamese had ousted the pro-Beijing murderous Pol Pot regime. A month later, Chinese forces had to withdraw without achieving their aim. The border remained tense and heavily militarised until in 1999, the China–Vietnam land border treaty was signed. Remaining issues were settled in December 2008. However, disputes over the Spratly Islands continue, and there have been hostilities between the vessels of the two communist countries. In April 2020, a Chinese coast guard vessel deliberately hit a Vietnamese fishing boat and sank it.

China's island building in the South China Sea has reclaimed 16 square kilometres of land in this area. Vietnam is the only nation to respond with its own island-building activities since 2022. It has created an island at Pearson Reef in the Spratly Islands and has increased the area of Tennent Reef, where it has also built a port. The atoll at the Barque Canada Reef, which previously had a negligible area, has now grown to 0.8 square kilometres with reclamation. A total of twenty reefs have been reclaimed by Vietnam, covering a total area of 3.5 square kilometres.[33] Due to Chinese aggression, Vietnam has come closer to the US, its erstwhile nemesis, and considerable American investment fleeing China has moved to Vietnam. If China invades Taiwan, Vietnam's role will be crucial for countries such as the US, Japan, Philippines, and South Korea, and even Australia, which may join the fray on Taiwan's side. When China invaded Vietnam, Taiwan had supported the latter. Today, the economies of high-tech Taiwan and Vietnam are increasingly intertwined, with a surging Vietnam becoming the fourth-largest exporter of high-tech goods after China, Taiwan, and Germany. If Vietnam opens the 1,297 km border front with China, when the latter invades Taiwan, the scales will be tilted against China. Whether it is manufacturing consumer goods, high-tech goods, or playing the balancer, Vietnam will play a significant role in managing the disruptions being created and likely to be created by China in global geopolitics and geoeconomics.

Russia: There have been serious border conflicts between Russia and China. They had a seven-month-long armed conflict on an island at the confluence of the Amur and Ussuri rivers. Both countries signed border agreements in 1991, 1994, 1997, and finally one in 2004, which divided the island between them. These agreements have, for the record, ended the border disputes between the two countries. In 2006, they signed another agreement for practical modalities of managing the border. China, however, continues to eye large areas in eastern Russia. It has been light-heartedly suggested that China's acquiescence to Russia's land grab in Ukraine is to prepare the ground for action on China's claims on Russian areas in Siberia.[34]

North Korea: The most significant border dispute between China and North Korea is over Mount Paektu, a 2,744-metre-high volcano at the source of the Yalu and Tumen rivers.[35] The mountain has been sacred to the Koreans throughout their history as well as to the Communists, who consider it 'the sacred mountain of the revolution', where Kim Il-Sung, the grandfather of the present dictator, operated as a guerrilla in the 1930s. China occupies a part of the mountain and demands more as compensation for providing military support during the Korean War. There are border disputes at the mouth of the Yalu and Tumen rivers, as well as along these rivers, which serve as borders between the two countries. On the Tumen River, China claims the right to cross the river over North Korean territory to access the Sea of Japan. At the mouth of the Yalu River, the two countries differ over economic and fishing exclusion zones. The Koreans signed agreements with the Russians to settle the border in this area, adding to China's discomfort.

On 28 August 2023, China published the latest edition of the 'National Map of China' showing many areas of its neighbours within its borders. It also showed many place names across these borders in Chinese language, different from the names used in the countries where these places are located, causing consternation in the neighbouring countries, including Russia.[36]

Why is China antagonising so many countries in order to assert its sovereignty over their EEZs, knowing that the rights of those countries are in conformity with the United Nations Convention on the Law of the Sea (UNCLOS)? In addition to the fact that it boosts China's strategic position towards the Pacific, there are compelling economic reasons. It is perhaps the most important trade route for the world, and certainly for China. In 2023, ships carrying 10 billion barrels of oil and 6.7 trillion cubic feet (Tcf) of gas passed over it. Yet, what lies beneath this body of water may dwarf what passes over it. So far, 3.6 billion barrels of oil and 40.3 Tcf of gas have been proved.[37] The explorations have been hindered by the disputes; ultimately, the hoard may exceed all expectations. If China is able to assert sovereignty according to its nine-dash line, its energy imports—which remain its Achilles Heel in any conflict scenario—may drop to zero. China is the world's largest importer of oil and the second-largest importer of gas. Its self-sufficiency in these hydrocarbons will crash the market. Cheap oil and gas will heavily hinder the transition to green energy and lead to a serious setback in environmental goals. Of course, it is unlikely that China will be able to enforce its nine-dash line unchallenged any time soon.

China has been a great disrupter of geoeconomics and geopolitics and has made subversive inroads in many democracies over the last few decades. Having taken full advantage of Western technologies and markets after Clinton enabled it to enter the World Trade Organization, the China of the Xi Jinping era bared its wolf warrior fangs at the West and indulged in large-scale subversion of the democratic process and influenced peddling among the elected and corporate leaders, press, academia, sports bodies, as well as in Hollywood. Bowing to immense corporate pressure, Western democracies had, until recent times, persevered and resisted taking protective measures against the Chinese maelstrom, but the COVID-19 pandemic broke the back of their tolerance. Movements to impose tariffs on state-subsidised cheap Chinese products as well as efforts to break Chinese monopoly on critical supply chains have resulted in a flow of capital out of China, the imposition of restrictions on technology cooperation, and an emergence of practices like decoupling, derisking, homeshoring, reshoring and friendshoring.

Thus, in less than seventy-five years of its existence, Communist China has redefined global geopolitical relations and, along with countries like Russia, North Korea, and Iran, is leading to an unbridgeable chasm between democracies and undemocratic regimes. While there is hope that someday democracy may return to countries like Russia and Iran, there is no such hope for China in the near future. The other dictatorships, by themselves and without help from

China, are not capable of altering or subverting the global order. China, on the other hand, is putting all its energies into subverting democracies with money, cyber, and military power. Its Belt and Road Initiative (BRI) loans have burdened some of the countries with non-performing assets and have caused domestic upheavals in those countries. Its efforts at encircling India with the so-called pearl of strings, and India's efforts at responding with a necklace of diamonds,[38] show the scale of conflict between the two ideologies.

Nazi Germany gave us the Führerprinzip, which can be translated as the 'leader principle'. This principle was declared the law of the Nazi Party as early as July 1921. It states that the word of the leader is above all written law and that the entire government works to realise that leader's will. Irrespective of the name of the ideology, Stalin's Russia and Mao's China were examples of the Führerprinzip. Today, under Xi Jinping, China is becoming a classic example of this concept. Xi Jinping Thought on Socialism with Chinese Characteristics for a New Era, abbreviated as Xi Jinping Thought, was launched in 2017 and incorporated into the Constitution of the Chinese Communist Party. Next year, it was made a part of the preamble of the Constitution of the People's Republic of China. In 2021, it was declared 'a new breakthrough in Sinicization of Marxism'. Top filmmakers, actors, and pop stars are being indoctrinated, so that all productions are in line with Xi Jinping Thought.[39] Reminiscent of the *Little Red Book* of Mao's thoughts, a condensed version of Xi's thoughts is being carried by many. Although it appears that Xi has stepped into the shoes of Mao, his thoughts do not enjoy the same veneration as those of the latter,[40] and therein lies the danger.

We could slightly modify William Congreve's line in the play *The Mourning Bride* to read 'Hell hath no fury like a dictator scorned'. Or closer home to Xi Jinping, Sun Tzu, the

6th-century BC Chinese general, strategist, and philosopher, who carried the honorific 'Master Sun', had said, 'An evil man will burn his own nation to the ground to rule over the ashes.' That is even more destructive than the Marxist idea that capitalism contains seeds of its own destruction, and the new order rises from its ashes like the phoenix. Having subverted the Chinese Constitution to remove the term limits, Xi Jinping is a ruler for life, obsessed with the ideas of taking over Taiwan, by force if necessary, and creating in his lifetime a world order in which China will be at the apex. He is an evil man in a hurry; no wonder, China is the principal disruptor of geopolitics today.

7

Geopolitics: Russia

R.N. Prasher

'Geopolitics was considered in the USSR until the last years of its existence as a reactionary bourgeois science aimed at justifying the expansion of international imperialism.'[1] This is the insider view of the field of geopolitics in Russia. It is only with the collapse of the Soviet Union that geopolitics became a subject of intense inquiry in Russia. In the Western mind, events in Imperial Russia, the Soviet Union, and present-day Russia are all related to Europe. Napoleon's invasion of Russia and his defeat by 'General Winter' is one of the most prominent events in Russia's interactions with Western Europe. The latter was acquiescing to the aggressive designs of Hitler after the failure of the collective security talks at the Munich Conference in September 1938. Facing the grim prospect of having to confront Hitler on his own, Stalin also took the path of appeasing Hitler. In May 1939, he dismissed his foreign minister, Maksim Litvinov, who was Jewish and would not have compromised with Hitler. The new foreign minister, Vyacheslav Molotov, then began negotiations with Hitler. This resulted in the German–Soviet Non-aggression Pact of 23 August 1939, signed in Moscow, which included a secret protocol to divide Eastern Europe between German and Soviet spheres of influence, the latter including large parts of Poland, Lithuania, Latvia, Estonia, and Finland. It was another disastrous foray by Russia into the treacherous quagmire of geopolitics. On 22 June 1941, Hitler launched Operation Barbarossa against the Soviet Union, using 80 per cent of Germany's armed forces. After adding the Axis troops, the invading army numbered over 3 million troops. It was the naivety of Stalin in geopolitics that such a huge operation—the largest single military adventure of World War II—caught him by surprise. The Moscow Pact had so antagonised Western Europe that Hitler shifted almost all his forces to the Russian front, confident that the European nations would not come to Stalin's aid. Interestingly, Russia's folly in dealing both with Napoleon and Hitler ultimately hurt the aggressors, and the invasion of Russia by Napolean and the Soviet Union by Hitler was the beginning of the downfall of both leaders.

The Ethnic Divide in a Synthesised Russia

Both China and Russia have expanded manifold, gobbling areas of neighbouring ethnicities. While 'China proper' was enlarged by the Qing dynasty by amalgamating Manchuria, Mao increased its size further by occupying Tibet, Xinjiang, and Inner Mongolia. Imperial Russia expanded its empire by occupying Asia to the east of the Urals, Outer Manchuria, and almost all of Central Asia. The Communists expanded it further by taking complete control of many Eastern European countries and indirect control of the rest under the Warsaw Pact. Russian language and culture have very little overlap with most of the countries of Eastern Europe, barring a few like Ukraine and Belarus. In the case of the areas east of the Urals, the overlap is almost zero and antipathy aplenty. Russian migration to these areas and imposition of the Russian language in education was parallel to the

Han migration to Tibet, Manchuria, Xinjiang, and Inner Mongolia, and imposition of the Chinese language and script on these regions. While the heavy-handed Chinese regime has had a fair degree of success in this 'sinicisation' of areas outside 'China proper', Russia has not been so successful with its campaign of 'Russification'.

Yakutia is a republic in the Russian Far East; its capital Yakutsk has the distinction of being the coldest large city in the world. Under Russian pressure, these hunting people superficially paid homage to the Russian Orthodox Church but kept practicing their shamanism. They have their own language, attire, dance, and music, making them an ethnic group that is very distinct from the Russians. According to their mythology, the east is the realm of *aĭyy*, the bright spirits, and the west of *abaasy*, the dark harmful spirits; Russians from the far west of Yakutia clearly being *abaasy*. Russia occupied Crimea in 2014 following the call of 'ethnic Russians' in that territory, which was originally part of the Ottoman Empire and from where the Soviet Union had forcibly deported 2,00,000 Tatars in 1944. As Russia continues its brutal invasion of Ukraine ostensibly to prevent the alleged genocide of 'ethnic Russians' in eastern Ukraine, questions arise: Are the Yakuts or the Sakhas, as they call themselves, Russian? Are Chechens, who are Sunni Muslims—a Turkic people like the Sakhas, with their own language, culture, dress, and social norms—Russian? Are the Muslim natives of the Republic of Bashkortostan ethnically Russian? Or are the Mongolians in the Republic of Buryatiya, many of whom are even now Buddhists and shamanic, ethnic Russians? The war in Ukraine is a milder version of the two wars that Russia waged on the Chechens. Russia lost the 1994–1996 war and concluded a peace treaty with the Chechens, granting them territorial autonomy. However,

Russia invaded again in 1999 and virtually flattened the 'Republic'. A Chechen quisling, Ramzan Kadyrov, now lords over it as Putin's henchman. As Russia flaunted ethnicity as the main ground for the invasion of Georgia in 2008, and now in Ukraine, and possibly in Moldova in the near future (where there is already a de facto Russian Republic called Transnistria, a thin sliver of land where the Moldovan government's writ does not run), it may be stoking another ethnic implosion similar to the one in 1991 that brought down the Soviet Union, a much bigger and mightier power than Putin's Russia. It is tempting to use ethnicity to stoke nationalism, but ethnicity has the last laugh, as it had in 1991, with numerous ethnic groups escaping the clutches of the Soviet bear.

Let us have a look at the crossed wires of Russia with Islamic countries. It was involved in the Syrian war on the side of the Shia, the faction of Assad (now deposed), and was supported in this venture by the Shiite regime of Iran. The involvement of Russia and Iran in Syria's bombing of its Sunni areas was a major cause of the rise of the Islamic State (IS), a Sunni enterprise. Turkey supports the remnants of the Ottoman Empire in Crimea and has a large population settled in Turkey who were victims of the Russian pogrom against Tatars in Crimea in 1944—all of them Sunnis. On that ground, Turkey has its empathies with the Chechens, while Putin is trying to draw Turkey into the golden ring, which includes Sunni-dominated Pakistan and Shia-dominated Iran. Chechen soldiers have been sent by Ramzan Kadyrov to fight alongside Russians in Ukraine. The leading Chechen, Mufti, Salakh Mezhiyev, has called Kadyrov the Lion of Allah and has declared that there will be no other branch of Islam in Chechnya except Sunni. Mezhiyev accuses Iran and Russia of distributing Shiite literature in Chechnya. There is a simmering independence movement in Chechnya, and some of these Sunni 'freedom fighters' have joined Ukrainians in the fight against their common enemy, Russia, making it a fratricidal battleground between Kadyrov's Chechen soldiers and pro-independence Chechens. To make things even more complicated, Russia is bringing Shia Syrian fighters also to Ukraine. The Crusades seemed so uncomplicated compared to this conundrum!

Russian language and culture were imposed by the czars upon the minorities, and that policy continued under the Soviet Union. Even today, the former Soviet republics in Central Asia use the Russian script, although their languages are related to Turkic, except for the Tajiks, whose language is Iranian. Russia never showed interest in these cultures; the Kazakh, Uzbek, Tajik, and Kyrgyz people were looked down upon as uncultured and uncouth, as people who needed to be civilized through Russification. Even after the collapse of the Soviet Union, Russia maintains its leadership over these states through the Commonwealth of Independent States (CIS) that was formed in 1991. China has tried to penetrate this Russian sphere of influence through its Belt and Road Initiative, but the Russian imprint still dominates. There is a substantial Russian population in Central Asian countries, estimated at 7 million, in addition to half a million Russians in Ukraine. The historical context of Hitler invading neighbouring countries to 'save Germans' and the pretext used by Russia to invade Ukraine is causing concern in these countries. If Russia can invade Ukraine to 'save' one branch of Christianity from another, it could certainly do so to save Eastern Orthodox Russian minorities in these countries from the majority Muslims. With Turkey trying to wrest the mantle of leadership of the Sunni world from the Saudis, these Turkic former Soviet republics may see a saviour in that country, as the Uyghurs of China already do. After all, during the early years of Russian influence, this entire region was called Turkestan by the Russians, and the Xinjiang independence movement is still referred to as the East Turkestan Independence Movement. The consequences of stoking an ethnic divide to strengthen Russian nationalism may be much larger than Ukraine, Georgia, or Moldova.

Russia and China

Soviet folly repeated itself when the Soviet Union sowed the seeds of Communism in China and propped up Mao. Without Stalin's support, the communist revolution would never have finally succeeded in China. Even after Mao came to power in 1949, Stalin helped him with weapons, missiles, and nuclear technology, enabling him to survive despite the West's full support to Taiwan. Mao's loyalty was to Stalin, and not to the Soviet Union. Soon after Stalin's death in 1953, relations between the two soured, with Mao branding Khrushchev's Russia as 'reactionary'.

During all these events, the West perceived the Soviet Union as the sole threat and went to the extent of joining hands with China and abandoning Taiwan to contain the Soviet Union. Moscow was contained, not as much by geopolitics, as by the failure of its Marxist economic policies that led to popular discontent. With the collapse of the Soviet Union, serious attention was paid by scholars in Russia to geopolitics, and after repeated attempts to integrate with the West and join the European Union, Russia evolved a policy of 'pivot to the east', much as Obama had announced his 'pivot to Asia' in 2011. Though at that time it was perceived that Obama's pivot would weaken transatlantic synergy. In the intervening years since 2011, US policy has evolved to create synergy between the Atlantic powers and the nations of the Asia Pacific, spurred by the policy of containment of

China. On the other hand, by the time Russia articulated its pivot to the east and the idea of a Greater Eurasia, China had become its real contender for supremacy in Asia, with India following behind at some distance. The economic growth of Russia has lagged behind that of the US, China, and India. Its population has been declining and its influence in Central Asia is being rapidly encroached upon by China. India's dependence on Russian arms is being replaced by a much larger group of arms sellers with better technology. Russia's oil hegemony over Europe, too, turned out to be illusory, as when confronted with difficulties in importing Russian CNG through pipelines (two of the major ones were blown up, possibly by Russia itself), Europe could quickly transition to LNG brought in by ships.

Yet, the most glaring failure of Russian geopolitics continues to be in its relations with China. Pressed against the wall by the combined might of the US and Europe after its invasion of Ukraine in 2022, Russia has almost become a client state of China, while also becoming dependent on China's closest 'friends', Iran and North Korea. The US is convinced that Putin cannot continue with the Ukraine War without Chinese support. On 2 May 2024, Avril Haines, the US director of national intelligence, said at a hearing of the United States Senate Committee on Armed Services that 'China's provision of dual use components and material to Russia's defense industry is one of several factors that tilted the momentum on the battlefield in Ukraine in Moscow's favor, while also accelerating a reconstitution of Russia's military strength after their extraordinarily costly invasion'.[2] Haines added that this war is unlikely to end anytime soon. Irrespective of the impact of this war on Ukraine's fortunes, every day of this war strengthens Russia's dependence on China and is one more nail in its coffin as a superpower.

There is an important reason why China is standing behind Putin in his aggression in Ukraine, even though this support has become the most important reason for increasing antagonism between Europe and China, with the former calling for de-risking from China. To know why Xi Jinping is so eagerly waiting for a weakened Russia we have to go deeper into the history of Sino-Russian relations and China's major territorial grievance against Russia. Before the Manchu foreigners began ruling China as the Qing Dynasty, China was less than one-fourth of its present size. The Qing expanded China's territory to include Manchuria, Tibet, Outer Mongolia, and Xinjiang, thereby creating the large and resource-rich country we know today. These regions remained restive and were frequently outside the effective control of Beijing until Mao asserted firm military control. Until the 20th century, writers used the term 'China Proper' to designate the smaller area populated by the Han people, which was under the control of various dynasties before the Qing, including the fabled Ming. The regions included by the Qing were all non-Han, even as the Qing themselves were Manchu. All these regions had their own distinct languages, scripts, culture, hairstyle, dress, and cuisine. The animosity of the Han majority towards these regions continues to this day, with the Han, now in control, doing everything in their power to extinguish the language and culture of the Tibetans, Uyghurs, and Mongols. As it is, they have already succeeded in obliterating the Manchu.

During the sunset days of the Qing Dynasty, China suffered what Xi frequently refers to as the 'century of humiliation', when unequal treaties were imposed on them by the Western powers and Russia. Atrocities were inflicted on the Han during the Japanese invasion and large parts of China were occupied, including Beijing. Events like the

Nanjing Massacre have become a part of the painful memory of the collective Chinese psyche and play a significant role in rallying the Han around the Communist Party.

Yet, one part of this century of humiliation has so far received less attention than the rest, because the West was not the culprit. The huge Russian territory to the east of the Urals became part of Russia only recently in the 19th century when the tsars moved in militarily. The area had previously been ruled by the Mongols, who inhabited it alongside the Turkic tribes. A large portion of this territory was part of Manchuria, which had its own Manchu emperor and was later ruled by the Manchu as the Qing dynasty from Beijing. This area, known as Outer Manchuria or Russian Manchuria, was part of the Chinese empire until 1860, when the weakened Qing were compelled to sign the unequal treaties with the tsars that allowed Russia to annex 3,50,000 square kilometres of this territory. This Amur annexation is as much a thorn in the Chinese memory as Hong Kong and Macau, but also much bigger. The People's Republic of China's Ministry of Natural Resources renamed eight areas and cities in Russia's Outer Manchuria region on 14 February 2023. China's apparently unexpected move to rename Russian towns, mountains, and rivers has to be seen in this context. Even the crucial port of Vladivostok is in China's sights; the Chinese name for it is Hǎishēnwǎi; Sakhalin Island has been renamed as Kuyedao; Khabarovsk is now Boli; and Stanovoy Mountain Range will be Outer Xing'an Range. In spite of the pious declaration of 'friendship without limits' between Xi and Putin, and the fact that China is Russia's largest trading partner, China has not recognised the annexation of Crimea by Russia and the latter does not recognise China's nine-dash line.[3] Simultaneously, China has not condemned the Russian invasion of Ukraine, while Russia has not commented on the legality of Chinese island-building in the South China Sea.

Siberia comprises 77 per cent of Russia's geographical area but has only one-fifth of its population. This thinly populated area to the east of the Ural Mountains contains the bulk of Russia's natural resources. It has huge deposits that comprise 80 per cent of Russia's coal, 80 per cent of oil, 85 per cent of natural gas, and 40 per cent of timber. It has an abundance of iron ore, diamonds and other precious stones, gold, mercury, copper, nickel, asbestos, etc. China is deficient in many of these resources, particularly coal, oil, gas, and iron ore. This huge land, equal in area to the US and India put together, is what makes Russia large and runs its industrial complex and economy. This area has a border of more than 4,400 kilometres with China, sparsely populated on the Russian side, with just 6 million people who have 90 million Chinese staring at them from the other side. There has been large-scale illegal Chinese migration and intermarriages, leading to a significant presence of Chinese genes on the Russian side, but hardly any Russian genes on the Chinese side. In the book *Frontier Encounters: Knowledge and Practice at the Russian, Chinese and Mongolian Border*[4] there's a chapter by Frank Billé, meaningfully titled, 'On Ideas of the Border in the Russian and Chinese Imaginaries'. He explains, 'While for Chinese, the north-eastern border with Russia appears to be seen, predominantly, as a frontier of opportunity where commercial ties can be created and valuable contracts concluded, in the Russian media the border is most often associated with illegal migration and criminality…' The book is more than a decade old, and the situation has tilted considerably further in favour of the Chinese. There are Chinese-owned factories on both sides of the border with hardly any Russian workers on the Chinese side, but a host of Chinese on the other side, making the region de facto a part of China's 'factory empire'. The French geographer M. Foucher had called borders a 'factory of identities'; it does appear that the identities on this border are 'manufacturing' a greater Chinese empire.

In 1891, an arch was erected in the border town of Blagoveshchensk to welcome the Russian Crown Prince Nicholas. It was renovated in 2015, and a declaration was etched onto it, stating 'The earth along the Amur was, is and always will be Russian.' That reiteration notwithstanding, the renaming of places in Outer Manchuria at a time when Russia is internationally in its most dire phase since Putin came to power, reminds one of Caesar's shock when he saw that Brutus was one of his assassins. On seeing the Chinese order, Putin, too, must have exclaimed, 'Et tu, Xi?' Yet, it was Putin's naivety in the first place—as it was Nehru's naivety much earlier with Mao—to presume that Chinese leaders can be taken at their word. When the time comes to pay the price for Xi's support for the annexation of Ukrainian territory, Putin will realise that the Chinese have traditionally been astute traders, and the joke is always on the party that trusts them. If he can read Xi Jinping's lips, the message is clear: 'You give me Siberia, I will give you Crimea.' There is another silent message in this map game: Geopolitical maps are perishable; a nation may be relying on them for long-term strategy without noticing that the expiry date is close at hand.

The Significance of Russia's Geopolitics to India

Under British rule, the Indian leadership's geopolitical approach was ambiguous and amorphous, and knee-jerk reactions were not exceptions but the rule. Before Mahatma Gandhi fully evolved his doctrine of non-violent struggle, he supported Indian soldiers' participation on the side of the British and against the Germans in the First World War. He said, 'Home rule without military power was useless, and this was the best opportunity to get it.' As a result, when the king sent his message asking the 'Princes and people of My Indian Empire' to support the war effort, not only did the princely states respond enthusiastically but even the political elite were in favour of it.[5] By 1918, India had sent over one million Indian soldiers for the war, not including Imperial Service Troops from the princely states, sailors, and Indian Labour Corps. Around 7,700 had died, 16,400 were wounded, and 840 went missing.[6] Gandhi's support was, however, fickle as was evidenced by his reaction to the Ottoman sultan joining the Germans. The British, after their victory over the sultan, were worried that Indian Muslims would support the Islamic caliphate of the sultan. Yet, while even the nizam of Hyderabad and the begum of Bhopal were wavering in their support for the caliphate, it came from an unexpected quarter: Gandhi declared his support for the Khilafat movement, which had been started in India by the brothers Muhammad Ali and Shaukat Ali. Gandhi's well-known Non-cooperation Movement against the British was in many ways an offshoot of the Khilafat movement.

Russia, too, was greatly affected by the First World War. It joined the war on Britain and France's side in July 1914, and by the end of that year it had lost over one million men, suffered numerous defeats, and its economy was ruined. All these factors led to the end of Imperial Russia and the success of the Bolshevik Revolution in 1917. Initially, the Bolsheviks considered Gandhi a revolutionary of their ilk and held high hopes that India would soon have a similar revolution. In 1918, Bolshevik ideologue K.M. Troianovsky wrote, 'If Russia is justly considered to be a citadel of the world revolution, then India can be definitely called a citadel of the revolution in the East, a revolution which is bound to resound most strongly in the East and in the world in general.'[7] Even Lenin had declared, 'In that same India, where 300 million of Britain's serfs are oppressed, awareness is awakening and the revolutionary movement is growing every day. They are all looking at one star, the star of the Soviet Republic because they know it has made tremendous sacrifices in the cause of the struggle against the imperialists and has withstood terrible trials.'[8]

Bolshevik supporters in India, however, were not enamoured with Gandhi. M.N. Roy labelled Gandhi as 'purely reactionary' and a 'religious and cultural revivalist'. Stalin supported Roy's view. When Gandhi suddenly called a halt to the mass movement after the burning of a police station at Chauri Chaura, Roy denounced it as a 'betrayal of the revolutionary rank and file by the non-revolutionary and reactionary leadership'. Even Nehru, an ardent follower of Gandhi, said, 'For the National Congress as a whole the non-violent method was not, and could not be, a religion or an unchallengeable creed or dogma.' Gradually, the antipathy between the Bolsheviks and Gandhi grew, and in 1921, Gandhi wrote in *Young India*, 'I have never believed in the Bolshevik menace.' Three years later, he wrote in the same publication, 'I am yet ignorant what exactly Bolshevism is ... in so far as it is based on violence and denial of God, it repels me.' He turned down an invitation to visit Soviet Russia, saying 'an attempt to use me for a violent purpose is bound to fail'. The schism was in the open when in 1928 the Comintern said, 'Gandhism is more and more becoming an ideology directed against mass revolution. It must be strongly combated by Communism.'[9]

Even during the interwar period, there was a geopolitical divide among the leaders of the freedom movements. Subhas Chandra Bose, who believed in military means to win independence for India, had thrown in his lot with the Axis powers. He was also inclined towards Russia and had condemned Hitler for invading it. On the other hand, the Congress leadership under Gandhi and Nehru relied on the goodwill of the Allied powers, who promised that in exchange for Indian support with soldiers in WWII, freedom would follow. Gandhi's geopolitical ambiguity was in play when he opposed Hitler's persecution of the Jews as well as the Jewish claim for a homeland in Palestine.[10]

The Soviets did not give up on India despite all these utterances by Gandhi. In fact, the Soviet Union established diplomatic relations with India on 13 April 1947, four months before India changed from a colony of the British to a British dominion and even used its veto in the Security Council in favour of India in 1951, even though Stalin had a negative view of the Indian National Congress and its leaders. After Stalin's death in 1953, his successor, Khrushchev, was extremely friendly towards India and supported the establishment of state enterprises in steel, heavy machinery, mining, and power generation. Soviet Union and India signed a Treaty of Peace, Friendship and Cooperation in 1971, which marked a major deviation from India's policy of non-alignment and may have established the pre-eminence of India in South Asia.[11] The treaty might seem like a knee-jerk reaction to the crisis in erstwhile East Pakistan and the impending war that created Bangladesh, even as the US Seventh Fleet was menacing India in the Bay of Bengal. Yet, it had been in the making since 1969, and a close look will show that it was aimed at China. In subsequent decades, the Soviet Union and its successor, the Russian Federation, repeatedly voted in favour of India and exercised its veto power when the West tried to push a resolution favouring Pakistan on the Kashmir issue. India, too, consistently refrained from voting against Russia in the Security Council until 25 August 2022, when it abstained from a minor procedural vote regarding the invitation for Ukraine's President Volodymyr Zelenskyy to address the UNSC via a video teleconference. India has consistently abstained on every vote in the UN on resolutions that sought to condemn Russia for the Ukraine invasion, though Prime Minister Narendra Modi had politely told Putin on the sidelines of the Shanghai Cooperation Organisation (SCO) summit at Samarkand, Uzbekistan, that 'I know that today's era is not an era of war, and I have spoken to you on the phone about this,' adding that democracy, diplomacy, and dialogue kept the world together. Putin also responded diplomatically: 'I know your position on the conflict in Ukraine, your concerns that you constantly express. We will do our best to stop this as soon as possible.' The exchange showed the level of understanding between the two nations and the confidence that they shall not be misunderstood. That confidence comes from more than seven decades of cooperation, since the beginning of the Khrushchev era and has sustained in spite of changes brought about in New Delhi by the electoral process, which have brought parties in power with diametrically opposite views on Communism and socialism.

In addition to diplomatic cooperation at the UN, the other highlight of India's relations with the Soviet Union and the Russian Federation has been their military cooperation as strategic partners. In 2000, the two countries established the India–Russia Inter-Governmental Commission on Military Technical Cooperation (IRIGC-MTC). Under it, the defence ministers meet annually, and there are two working groups and nine subgroups. The agreement has been periodically renewed, and the current one is for 2021–2031. The India–Russia 2+2 Dialogue, involving the defence and foreign ministers of both countries, was set up in 2021. Much of India's defence production, such as the T-90 tanks, Su-30-MKI aircraft, MiG-29 aircraft and its upgrade Kamov-31, and AK-203 rifles, fall under this cooperation.[12] A geopolitically significant outcome of Indo-Russian defence cooperation is the establishment of the BrahMos Aerospace, a joint venture between India's Defence Research and Development Organisation (DRDO), which holds 50.5 per cent share, and Russia's Joint Stock Company NPO Mashinostroyenia, which holds 49.5 per cent share. BrahMos Aerospace has designed, developed, and produced the BrahMos supersonic cruise missile with active participation of a consortium of Indian and Russian industries, and is now marketing it.[13]

Over these seven decades, Indo-Russian cooperation has continued despite the disruptions to regional geopolitics caused by China. In view of China's long-term goals in Russia, India and China have followed somewhat different trajectories in their response to the Ukraine War. India has kept the window open to both belligerents and kept bilateral trade flowing to its advantage, without doing anything about the war effort that may draw an action relating to the West's sanctions against Russia. China, on the other hand, seems to have crossed the Western red line on aiding the Russian war effort. Biden had warned China in 2022 against providing material support to Russia's war against Ukraine. On 27 April 2024, US Secretary of State Antony Blinken said that China has ignored that warning and has become 'overwhelmingly the No. 1 supplier' of Russia's military industrial base, which has fundamentally changed the course of the war.[14] Surely, Iran and North Korea will be watching the US's reaction to this conclusion, and a tepid response from the US will embolden the two rogue regimes, while encouraging China towards its unification with Taiwan 'by using force if necessary'.

The Ukraine War Woke Up the World to Russia

The Ukraine War is a point of unexpected inflexion in global geopolitics, and even a few months before the invasion, it was not considered feasible that Russia would launch a full-scale invasion. Since the collapse of the Soviet Union, the world had paid very little attention to Russia, even as it invaded Georgia in 2008, annexed Crimea in 2014, and assisted in the crackdown protests in Belarus in 2020–2021. In the preface to his 2020 book, *The Dynamics of Russia's Geopolitics: Remaking the Global Order*, published shortly before the invasion of Ukraine, David Oualaalou states, 'The lack of debate about Russia within the Washington establishment alarms me.' The Ukraine War, which Putin expected to be over in a few days, has upended all future projections of the global geopolitical order made before the invasion. The so-called golden ring of China, Iran, Russia, and North Korea has become a reality, and it does appear that if Erdogan is on the scene for much longer, Turkey may become its active supporter. Turkey has given enough indication of its closeness to Russia, a far cry from the twelve Russo-Turkish Wars during the three-and-a-half centuries from 1568 to 1918. USSR's mass deportation of 2,00,000 Crimean Tatars of Turkic origin in 1944 is generally classified as genocide. From the beginning of the unrest in Crimea to its culmination in the annexation by Russia, Tatars have been at the receiving end of Russian brutalities, which Human Rights Watch (HRW) has referred to as 'the revolving door of persecution in Crimea'.[15] Yet, Erdogan does not see much of a future for himself with the West and is willing to join the currently strong but, in all likelihood, temporary Russia–China alignment. In the process, Turkey has preferred to turn a blind eye to China's persecution of the Uyghurs in Xinjiang, which has sent thousands of Uyghurs as refugees to Turkey. It was established in 2024 that North Korea, another element in the golden ring, has been facilitating the Russian war effort not only with artillery shells but also with ballistic missiles and even soldiers, and may be using the Ukraine War as a testing ground for its weapons.

The golden ring, along with Turkey, Syria, Iraq, and Iran's proxies in Lebanon and Yemen, represents a hugely destabilising force for global geopolitics. All these actors are a law unto themselves, going to the extent of denying the sovereignty of other states, as Russia does with Ukraine and Iran does with Israel. Of late, they have been acting in unison at the UN and have a large number of small states that act as their camp followers. A silver lining is that theirs is a marriage of convenience and there are fundamental differences in their perceptions of the future global order. Moreover, their geopolitical perceptions are based on those of the individuals currently heading these states, Russia being one of the most personalised states. What will be the geopolitical approach of Putin's successor is a big black hole for diplomats and statesmen around the world.

8

Iran: Geopolitics in the Persian Gulf

R.N. Prasher

Most discussions of geopolitics are projections of the past and the present onto the future. As the wag said, the only certainty about the future is that it is uncertain—and so are geopolitical discussions. People lead nations, and people and their ideas are perishable. The future continues to sprout from the debris of the memory of those people and their ideas. The roots of the West Asian conflict are generally seen through the prism of Israel. The conflict, however, is much older than the modern state of Israel and is rooted in Shia-Sunni dichotomy that is as old as Islam itself. It was the Arabs' conquest of Iran in the 7th century that converted Zoroastrian Persia to Sunni Islam, and it continued that way for 850 years during which Iran remained part of the Sunni Ottoman Empire, the sworn enemy of the Shia. Some Shias in Persia considered this foreign Arab rule as subjugation and longed for the return of Persia's former glory, even though that was pre-Islamic. Their dream of 'self-rule' came true when Shah Ismail I of the Shia Safavids swiftly gained control of many parts of the Persian Empire, such as Armenia, Azerbaijan, and Dagestan, between 1500 and 1502, and within the next eight years, took control of all the territory that now constitutes Iran. This change was the beginning of the forcible conversion of Iranian Sunnis to Shia. Ismail had realised that unless all of Persia became Shia, it would not be able to assert itself against the powerful Sunni Ottomans to the west and the Uzbeks to the north-east. Colin Turner describes how under Ismail, cursing the caliphs became a religious duty and Sunnis were labelled impure, reducing them to 'dogs, swine, infidels and other such Islamically-defined objects of impurity'.[1] Sunnis were given only three choices: convert, leave, or be executed. Nearly 20,000 were killed in Tabriz alone for resisting conversion. Ismail created the office of the Sadr as the link between the state and religion and laid the foundations for the power of the clerics in Persia. The two Shahs of the 20th century, Reza Shah Pahlavi (1925–1941) and his son Mohammad Reza Shah Pahlavi (1941–1979), had the twin aim of claiming all the Arab lands where the Shia had a presence and simultaneously reducing the power of the clerics by modernising Iran. Chelsi Mueller narrates how the Shah refused to recognise the independence of the sheikhs of the Gulf.[2] Pahlavi Iran claimed Bahrain as Iranian and even hinted at similar claims over Kuwait, Qatar, Abu Dhabi, Dubai, Sharjah, Ras al-Khaimah, as well as Muscat and Oman.

The Shia mullahs of Iran could have no dispute over these hegemonic claims, but it was Shah's second goal of marginalising the mullahs that raised their hackles, leading to the last Shah's ouster and the return of Khomeini. Thus, the ambitions of Iran were, and continue to be, based on twin objectives: restoring Iran to its days of long-lost Persian glory and engaging in continuous confrontation with the Arabs and Turkic Sunnis to expand the area of Shiite influence. The nine-year Iraq–Iran War has to be seen in this context of Iran's intolerance of a Sunni Saddam lording over a Shia-majority Iraq. Iran's steadfast support for Bashar al-Assad of

Syria stems from the fact that he was a Shia leader ruling over the Sunni-majority population of Syria. That majority was encouraged by Sunnis all around Syria to turn rebellious, leading to the creation of the Islamic State of Iraq and Syria (ISIS). Those who see a change of heart in Iran's support of the Sunni Hamas in the Gaza conflict miss the wood for the trees; the goal of Iran in Gaza is the weakening of Israel and the US, and in the process, they are achieving attrition of Hamas. It may someday facilitate inroads of the Shia Hezbollah into Sunni Palestine. It is an arena of eternal war, with peace just a transient pause between the last and the next conflict.[3]

When Yemen's Houthis began attacking Red Sea shipping, there were many voices predicting disruption in the movement of Gulf oil, shortage of oil, and a spurt in its prices. The Houthis had started firing missiles towards Israel on 19 October 2023, and in late November 2023, drones and missiles were aimed at Red Sea shipping with increasing frequency. Yet, on 9 January 2024 reports appeared that the oil traffic in the Red Sea was stable in spite of the Houthi attacks.[4] Oil prices also remained steady, because the extra cost of shipping was only about $40,000 for a million-barrel ship or 4 cents per barrel per day. Oil has seen more volatility than that without ruffling feathers.

Let us rewind to the past. It is the year 1988. Iraq and Iran have just ended their eight-year-long war, and both are exhausted. A million people have died, and the economy is in shambles. So, what do the experts in geopolitics say? The leaders of Iraq and Iran will focus on reconstruction and economic development. Wasn't that the goal of Japan and Germany post their defeat and surrender in World War II? But history does not merely repeat itself; it simultaneously moves forward, much like a car that moves ahead with each rotation of its wheels. Yet, it moves ahead because there is firm ground under it that provides traction;

on a quagmire, the wheels rotate endlessly in the same spot, digging deeper with each rotation. The victors in World War II, minus Russia and China, laid the foundations of democratic structures in West Germany and Japan, and contributed to rapid reconstruction of not only these two countries but also of such parts of Europe, as had not been taken under the wings of the Soviet Union. In the Iraq–Iran War, there were no victors and there was no one to promote democracy and reconstruction. Both Iraq and Iran have been digging their feet deeper into the quagmire for a long time, and now Syria has also joined the ranks of the 'stuck nations'. Lebanon, with Iran holding its strings through the Hezbollah, has metamorphosed from a swinging entrepôt to a nation constantly at war with itself.

Why do we bother about Iran? Iran is located in the heart of the Middle East (It prefers West Asia to the Middle East, as it considers the latter to be too much of a part of the European worldview.). Its central position means that no nation, friend or foe, can ignore it; it has more foes than friends, particularly among those that share a border with it or are in close proximity. Iran has fifteen neighbours, and it has not been a silent bystander to conflicts in its neighbourhood, whether in Afghanistan, Pakistan, Iraq, Syria, Yemen, Armenia, or Azerbaijan. It controls the Strait of Hormuz and many islands in the Persian Gulf. The Strait of Hormuz is a narrow choke point between the Persian Gulf and the Gulf of Oman, and is the transit route for more than 30 per cent of international oil movement by ships and also for 25 per cent of the world's LNG. With 34 trillion cubic metres of established gas beneath its ground, Iran sits over 17 per cent of the world's total oil reserves and 50 per cent of OPEC's oil. It has more than 208 trillion barrels of established oil reserves, which is 9 per cent of the world's total, and is not sitting idle on those reserves.

It produces 26 billion cubic metres of gas every year and 24 million barrels of oil daily.

On 28 January 2024, a drone attack on a US base by militias based in Iraq and Syria, owing allegiance to Iran, killed three US soldiers. Once again, fears were raised about the escalation of the conflict and the US getting trapped in it.[5] Shia militias in this area, over which Iran has a strong influence, include Al-Ashtar Brigades of Bahrain, Kata'ib Hezbollah, Badr Organisation and Asa'ib Ahl al-Haq of Iraq, Fatemiyoun Brigade, Zainabiyoun Brigade, Quwat al-Ridha and Baqir Brigade of Syria, and the Houthi movement of Yemen. It was said that there was a risk of a direct US–Iran confrontation as these attacks and reprisals escalated. But a few days later, on 30 January 2024, Kata'ib Hezbollah, suspected of the attack on the US base, announced 'the suspension of military and security operations against the occupation forces in order to prevent embarrassment to the Iraqi government'.[6] These militias have, in the past, been at loggerheads with the Iraqi government, and it was clear that the restraining hand has been Iran. Given their precarious position at home, the Iranian regime was not in a position to launch a full-scale confrontation with the West.

Iran is wary of the intentions of Sunnis in every country in its neighbourhood and in every major nation in the world—with good reason. It carries the baggage of its history of fights with the Sunni Ottoman Empire since the days of Shah Ismail. But it has an even more bitter history of dealing with Europe, particularly Britain, France, and Russia. At various times, one of these three countries signed a pact with Iran against another one of these three. Soon, the two European nations patched up, and Iran was not only left high and dry, it was attacked, defeated, and humiliating treaties were imposed on it. Several such humiliating treaties imposed on Persia rankle the Iranian mind. Under the 1813 Treaty of Golestan, Persia had to cede to Russia most of its possessions in Caucasus, such as Dagestan, parts of Georgia, parts of Azerbaijan, and parts of Armenia—territories it had possessed for more than three centuries. Then fifteen years later, on 10 February 1828, it was compelled to sign the Treaty of Turkmenchay, which deprived Iran of many of its northern territories and separated the Iranian speakers in Azerbaijan from Iran. With the 1857 Peace of Paris, Iran had to give up all claims to Afghan areas, followed by the 1881 Treaty of Akhal, under which most of what is today called Turkmenistan was ceded to Russia from Iran. This steady dismemberment of the Persian Empire is in the mind of every Iranian diplomat when they talk to their European counterparts.

Bruno Reynaud de Sousa has referred to Iran as an 'antifragile state' in the 2021 book *The Geopolitics of Iran*.[7] The Joint Comprehensive Plan of Action (JCPOA) signed between China, Russia, France, Germany, the US, the UK, and the European Union on 14 July, 2015, commonly called the Iran nuclear deal, was to stop Iran from processing uranium to weapon-grade level in return for the lifting of crippling economic sanctions imposed on it. History, however, repeated itself when just three years later, Trump reimposed all the bilateral sanctions on Iran, which were operational from 1996 until 2015 and had crippled the Iranian economy. Trump acted in spite of almost a dozen reports from the International Atomic Energy Agency until 2018 that Iran was fully complying with the terms of the JCPOA. In 2019, the US declared Iran's Quds Force a foreign terrorist organisation and this was used to justify the killing of its commander, General Qasem Soleimani. Bruno Reynaud postulates that Iran has used ideology, ingenuity, and asymmetry to convert the threat of sanctions and the ignominy of being called a rogue state into an opportunity to create national unity and strengthen its theocratic hardline policy.[8] The regime has survived international pressures for a long time and is unlikely to succumb any time soon, although the same cannot be said of internal pressures. Rogue nations have fallen more often due to internal dynamics; the Soviet Union being a prime example.

What is the significance of Iran's geopolitics for India in general and for India's energy security in particular? India has had a long history of engagement with Persia, even before the advent of Islam. There is a significant overlap between the Zoroastrian faith and ancient India's belief systems, with enough evidence of a common origin. Fire is central to all the Vedic rituals and is also central to the Zoroastrian faith, with its representation of purity being identical in both. While expanding their empire in all directions of the compass, Persians did not invade India in the pre-Islamic period, and there were enough indications that the Indus was the boundary between the two, which was respected by both sides. Even Cyrus had kept his invasion limited to west of the Indus. It was only Darius who, in 518 BC, attacked some areas east of the Indus but then withdrew, just as Alexander had done earlier. With Persia's conversion to Islam, the attacks became more frequent, leading to some Zoroastrians seeking refuge in India, creating the enterprising Parsi (a variation of Farsi, the name by which Persians called themselves) community, who are even now called 'Irani' by the local people in Maharashtra. Post Islam, the invasions increased, and the depredations of Nadir Shah and Mahmud of Ghazni were extremely destructive.

Indo-Persian trade was extensive, with the balance of trade generally in India's favour. Indian exports were up to three times greater than Persian exports to India, and the difference was made up by Persian gold and silver flowing into India, as had been the case with the Roman Empire for millennia. The trade declined with the advent of the East India Company and the Industrial Revolution, as Britain became India's major trading partner and also the controller of that trade. The trend has continued, with trade between India and Iran remaining restricted to the export of rice, tea, and sugar from India and the import of some petroleum products like bitumen and ethanol from Iran. In spite of US sanctions, some Iranian oil continues to flow into India through traders.

The Middle East conflict and Iran's involvement in it, spanning Gaza, Lebanon, Syria, Iraq, and Yemen, makes the geopolitics of Iran highly significant to India. It directly affects India's policies in Afghanistan and Baluchistan, as well as India's energy security. Iran's geopolitical significance for India lies in its location, from where it controls the flow of oil, and the possibility of a land route to Europe through it. In spite of the 2012 attack on an Israeli diplomat in India's capital by Iranian operatives, relations between the two countries have not deteriorated. India has invested half a billion dollars in Iran's all-weather Chabahar Port. In addition to providing connectivity to land routes in Afghanistan and Europe, this port is India's answer to China's investment in Gwadar Port in Pakistan, which is the terminal point for the China–Pakistan Economic Corridor (CPEC). In January 2024, India and Iran announced a new agreement for this port that is valid for ten years and will be renewed automatically. Someday, when the international environment permits, India may like to import CNG from this port; its proximity to India makes it a viable alternative to LNG, the latter requiring much higher investment to set up a liquefaction plant.

The world should remember that superpower rivalries are not the genesis of eternal conflicts in West Asia. These conflicts are internal, mainly driven by the schism and hatred between the Sunni and the Shia. Outside powers are externalities that try to take advantage of that conflict. Yet, conflicts shall arise even when such externalities are absent. Syria is one such example: The mutual hatred between Assad and the Sunni majority was not created by outside powers. The rebellion was the result of Assad's atrocities on the cities held by the rebels. These atrocities included indiscriminate bombing of towns held by the rebels, resulting in nearly 2,00,000 civilian casualties and the displacement of 14 million people. The weapons included barrel bombs filled with shrapnel dropped from helicopters, and chemical weapons—both illegal under international conventions. If the rise of ISIS can be attributed to one most important factor, it is the conduct of the Assad regime.

On 30 September 2015, Russia launched its military intervention in Syria, while Syria began bombing rebel towns in early 2011 and continued to do so even in 2024. Syria had been using barrel bombs on rebel towns since July 2012. The Syrian government started using chemical weapons against the rebels on 21 August 2013, when Eastern Ghouta, the rebel-held suburb of Damascus, was attacked with the nerve agent sarin. The gas killed more than 1,400 people, including many children, and thousands of others suffered from serious respiratory complications. Thus, blaming the superpowers' actions as the primary cause of the conflict and suffering in this region misses some vital facts. The establishment of a Sunni regime in Damascus in January 2025 after the overthrow of Assad's Shia regime is a new twist in the Shia-Sunni dichotomy in this region. It has weakened Russian and Iranian influence and has added to Turkish footprint. Since the new regime controls only a slice of Syria, the saga of sectarian conflict may go on.

The only silver lining on this foreboding dark horizon is that the people of Iran do not seem to have completely succumbed to Iran's theocratic rulers and their henchmen in uniform. The people's pride in the glory of the pre-Islamic Persian Empire is still alive; they still take pride in their music, dance, and poetry, much of which is frowned upon by the Islamists on both sides of the divide, Shias and Sunnis. The deaths of two women in police custody, who were detained for the offence of not wearing their hijab properly, had erupted into violent confrontations with the clergy and law enforcement. Despite the severe oppression, arrests, torture, and execution of the protestors, the issue did not die out completely and continues to simmer. It does appear that Iran is not completely lost to democracy forever, and at some point not far off in the future, another mass movement may bring democracy to this country. Iran's proximity to the rogue states of Russia, China, and North Korea may make the transition difficult and bloody. Yet, the arrival of democracy in most of the Warsaw Pact Europe/countries as the Soviet Union lost steam shows that the flame of democracy waits and erupts into a full-blown conflagration when the opportunity arises. With this hope, India's engagement with Iran should continue as, when that time comes, India will perhaps be the one and only true democracy in the region that could be the inspiration as well as provider of succour to the seekers of democracy to the west of India, as had happened in 1971 in the east in Bangladesh.

9

The Promise, Perils, and Pitfalls of Energy Transition

R.N. Prasher

Energy transition is a rage, even as fossil fuels continue to dominate the energy sector. In 2023, fossil fuels still accounted for 80 per cent of the world's energy generation. It is true that nations have added a significant amount of renewable generation capacity, mainly in solar and wind. It is also true that the cost of energy generated from renewable sources is now competitive with that from fossil fuels. However, because of renewable energy's inherent dependence on the sun and wind, the hours during which consumers can enjoy the benefits of nature's bounty remain limited. During those hours, not all of the renewable generation may be needed; beyond those hours, renewable energy is not available. The first part of the problem can be handled by increasing the capacity of national and transnational grids so that surpluses can be shared with areas of high demand. The second problem is addressed to some extent by the complementary nature of solar and wind; wind tends to blow when the sun goes down. But the bulk of this imbalance will require storage at the grid level, which is too expensive at present. The issues confronting energy transition are political, social, geoeconomic, and technological.

Political and Geopolitical Dimensions of Energy Transition

It may not seem intuitive, yet fundamental technological changes are not ideologically neutral. At COP 26, Al Gore had said, 'In order to solve the climate crisis, we have to address the democracy crisis.'[1] He was speaking in the context of American democracy and juxtaposed the difficulties in passing climate-friendly legislation with the problems in another favourite subject of the Democrats: gun control. He followed it up with a hard-hitting speech at a TED event in June 2023, decrying the powerful actors on the climate-change stage who have been, since COP 26, putting 'short-term profit over activities that destroy the planet'. In December 2023, in an interview with the Associated Press, Gore accused the person handling the UN climate talks of running one of the dirtiest oil companies. He was alluding to Sultan al-Jaber, the president of the National Oil Company of UAE and the president of UN climate talks.

These three statements by a former vice president of the US show how intimately and intricately climate issues remain connected to both domestic politics and geopolitics, and how energy transition could either remain a camp follower of these two political arenas or become their vanguard. Adnan Z. Amin, director-general of the International Renewable Energy Agency (IRENA), has said that the production, distribution, and utilisation of energy 'are deeply embedded in the fabric of our economies and central to relations between states.... The rapid development of renewable technologies and their widespread deployment is certain to have significant long-term effects on geopolitical dynamics'.[2] In 2019, he had lamented that 'to date no systematic efforts have been made to examine (renewables') geopolitical implications comprehensively'.[3] Ólafur Ragnar Grimsson, chairperson of IRENA's Global Commission on the Geopolitics of Energy Transformation, echoes the same sentiment about domestic and international politics being affected by energy transition, and in turn, affecting this transition. He says that 'energy transformation is also driven by the policies and action of governments, businesses, cities and civil society … (and) is already becoming a major geopolitical force: changing the power structures of regions and states …'[4]

One fundamental factor that seems to determine whether a nation shall enthusiastically and genuinely pursue energy transition or will only pay lip service followed by cosmetic action seems to be democracy. This apparently counterintuitive link has been attracting the attention of scholars and analysts in the recent past. Research has indicated that 'democracy continues to be an important driver of low-carbon energy use' but 'economic development plays a role in shaping the effect of democracy within individual countries'.[5] High-income democracies are more likely to transition towards nuclear energy, as increased influence of democratic institutions in these countries tends to inhibit solar, wind, and hydro energy. It can be presumed that a participatory political process will lead to decisions that are equitable, sustainable, and by and large, socially acceptable. The higher value placed on the individual in a democracy, compared to a country like China, allows the possibility of environmental voices being heard in public spaces, which works in favour of a transition to low carbon alternatives. But it can be argued that China has surged far ahead of democracies in installing solar and wind capacity. A closer look will show that these decisions in China were driven by economic and hegemonic considerations, and not by the dynamics of democratic processes, which are more conspicuous by their absence in China.

The Economic Dimension of Energy Transition

Nations differ in terms of their endowment of green resources, their dependence on the import or export of fossil fuels, the skill structure of their labour force, their capability to mobilise capital for investment, and the investment environment and ease of doing business. A favourable combination of these factors can enable a country to leapfrog to green energy.

Nature's endowment of a country with resources for shifting to green energy sources determines the pace of transition, particularly to solar, wind, and hydro. Solar energy requires large expanses of land and high radiation for most of the year. Countries with large deserts meet these requirements, but deserts pose their own challenges. The efficiency of solar panels decreases as their temperature increases, which occurs in deserts during periods of maximum radiation. Frequent dust storms can cover the panels with dust, effectively shutting them down. Part of the energy generated will be used for cooling and cleaning the panels. The most successful Mars mission used a nuclear battery on its *Perseverance* rover to avoid this problem, because Mars has frequent dust storms. However, its tiny helicopter, *Ingenuity*, did use solar panels for power and was completely shut down when its panels were covered with dust. *Perseverance* did lend a helping hand in shaking off some of the dust from *Ingenuity*'s panels, but the event confirmed the challenges posed by dust storms to solar energy generation.

Cold deserts like those in Tibet and in Lahaul-Spiti and Ladakh in India offer a good opportunity for solar power. The low temperatures enhance efficiency, and the lower incidence of dust storms reduces blackouts. Cloudy conditions are not frequent either. It has been found that cloud conditions and aerosols in Tibet reduce annual radiation by only 23 per cent, while on Norway's coasts this figure is almost 50 per cent.[6] It was found that in Lhasa, the annual irradiation was 7.6 GJ m^{-2}, which is 85 per cent of the corresponding annual irradiation at the top-of-atmosphere (TOA). Many other areas in China, such as Yunnan, Hainan, Western Inner Mongolia, and Xinjiang, offer this advantage. Similarly, the Gobi Desert in Mongolia, Atacama in Peru, the Great Basin in the US, and the Iranian desert spread over Iran, Afghanistan, and Pakistan offer similar potential of generating solar power. The requirement for a large area of land for solar power can be easily met in these cold deserts, as land utilisation tends to be low due to the extremely low annual precipitation in these areas, which discourages agriculture and even industrialisation.

A lack of natural endowment of mineral resources to manufacture equipment like solar panels and wind turbines is generally not a bottleneck, as there is an abundance of such resources around the world. The bottleneck was never the raw materials, but the processing facilities. China had created ample facilities, and their low prices led to the shutdown of processing facilities elsewhere. Once China had secured the market for itself, it hiked the price, holding the world market hostage to its manipulations. The spurt in demand and the increasingly hostile relations of Western democracies with China led to the demand for decoupling of such supply chains from China, with these critical minerals being the prime focus. In recent times, we have seen increased competition and lower prices of critical minerals in the world markets. For example, lithium prices have experienced a free fall from a record high of $81,360 per tonne in November 2022 to $20,782 per tonne in February 2024, reflecting a 67 per cent decrease year-on-year.[7] On 30 January 2024, the spot price was just over $13,000 per tonne—a fall of over 80 per cent.[8] China's virtual monopoly has been dented by the development of alternative sources. For example, Canada is becoming the main source for the US, replacing China. The price fall also included a component resulting from the steep fall in the demand for electric vehicles in China due to falling consumer confidence and household consumption in that country. Australia's Greenbushes Lithium mine—the world's largest—reported stockpiling of surplus production and indicated a cut in production if weak demand and prices persist.[9] India was exploring setting up a joint venture in Argentina for processing lithium, but the discovery of an estimated 5.9 billion tonnes of reserves in India upended all previous plans. This discovery could make India one of the largest lithium producers in the world. The prospects, though, come with a rider: The ore is hard rock, which requires significantly more water and electricity to process than brine-based lithium production in South America. To prevent India from becoming a rentier nation in this field, like some South American countries, only Indian nationals and their companies will be eligible for prospecting licences and mining leases, and they will have to process the mined material in India.[10]

The story appears to be developing along the same lines for another critical mineral: nickel. Its price crashed from a high of $50,000 per tonne in 2022 to $16,400 per tonne in February 2024. Although the demand has kept growing, there have been significant increases in supply from China and Indonesia, leading to a price fall, and the trend is likely to continue in the near future.[11] Another critical mineral, cobalt, appears to be on the same trajectory. Year-on-year prices fell 35.7 per cent in 2023, and the trend continues in 2024, with April prices being 16 per cent lower than a year ago. How quickly the markets are changing can be gauged from the fact that while there is an excess supply of cobalt at present, there was a deficit of 8,000 tonnes in 2021, and when production was ramped up, there was a surplus of 3,000 tonnes in 2022.[12]

Even copper has not escaped a beating in the market. Prices fell below $8,000 per tonne in October 2023. There was some recovery in 2024, but concerns about a supply glut remain. The International Copper Study Group has projected a surplus of 4,67,000 tonnes of copper in 2024, compared to a shortfall of 27,000 tonnes in 2023. Speculation about weakening demand continues, driven in part by the collapse of China's real estate market, which is a large consumer of copper, accounting for about 30 per cent of the total copper consumption of the country. On the other hand, demand for copper from the renewable energy and electric vehicle (EV) sectors has been increasing, although the fall in domestic EV sales in China raises questions about the sustainability of this demand in the near future. The oversupply of EVs in China is being dumped in other markets, resulting in a global fall in the price of EVs, which will also have a downward impact on copper prices.

Overall, it appears that critical minerals will not have any significant impact on any nation's transition towards renewable energy. A suitable mix of wind, solar, and hydro can take care of the differences in natural endowment, and all nations, big and small, rich and poor, currently have a great opportunity to transition to greener energy and contribute their part in slowing down climate change.

Technological and Production Capacity Dimension of Energy Transition

Countries vary widely in their technological prowess and their capability to translate technology into production at competitive prices. While the US and Europe used to be far ahead of China in technology, their failure to use technology to manufacture at competitive prices led to China becoming the factory of the world. The lower prices of Chinese solar modules were not merely the result of relatively lower wages in China; they were also due to two other factors that the West has been trying to emulate, but without the same level of success as China. The first was the economy of scale—the biggest contributor to China's monopoly in manufacturing. Its mega factories in solar panels and wind turbines could not be matched by any other country. The other factor was state subsidies, both direct and indirect, such as cheaper land, electricity, and water. In 2022, the subsidy for renewables in China was set at 3.87 billion yuan or $607 million, with 1.55 billion yuan going to wind farms, 2.28 billion yuan to solar power stations, and 39.24 million yuan to biomass power[13], and the effort has been increasing. At the annual session of China's legislature in early March, Prime Minister Li Qiang announced that the country will 'accelerate the construction of solar panel farms as well as wind and hydroelectric projects'. As its economy weakens, China plans to boost it by replacing the manufacture of clothing, furniture, and appliances with solar panels, electric cars, and lithium batteries, embarking on a two-decade programme to make China less dependent on fossil energy imports.[14] In the process, China has made the West dependent on it for purchasing renewable generation equipment, as the West followed the policy of subsidising the transition to green energy, irrespective of where the equipment was manufactured.

Belatedly, the West has realised the harm of purchasing, and thereby contributing to the economies of scale, of even the renewable generation equipment manufactured in China. To beat half-hearted Western measures, Chinese companies are now producing solar films that represent the bulk of the cost of solar panels and then shipping them to third countries for final assembly. The Biden administration had banned imports of materials and components made with forced labour in Xinjiang and has taken other protectionist measures under the Inflation Reduction Act to encourage manufacture in the US. In Europe, too, some governments have cut the share of imports from China to below 50 per cent, while others are considering following the US model of stiff protectionist policies to encourage domestic production.

This is again an example of how quickly the scenario changes for a country that holds a technological advantage but fails to convert it into a competitive manufacturing and trade model. Around 2010, the US and Germany had virtually monopolised the manufacture of solar modules. Seeing the opportunities in this field, China quickly offered state support and ramped up development and production at a much lower cost, throwing a challenge to the West by 2012. The Western companies could not compete and either went bankrupt or shifted their manufacturing base to China[15], and the rest is well-known history.

Similar is the story of onshore wind turbine nacelle assembly. China dominated the field in 2023 with 82 GW capacity, followed by Europe at 21.6 GW, the US at 13.6 GW, India at 11.5 GW, and Latin America at 6.2 GW.[16]

As of February 2024, China had the highest wind power capacity in the world at 3,28,970 MW, followed by the United States at 1,32,738 MW, Germany at 63,760 MW, and India at 40,070 MW.

Energy Transition: Profits, Policy, and Propaganda

There is a perception divide between the rich and developing nations regarding energy transition. While the former consider any environment-related expectations of change in economic behaviour as a potential threat to their high-consumption lifestyle, the latter view such expectations as a threat to their goal of becoming a high-income society. The corporate and academic world have also contributed substantially to this perception divide.

The environmental crusade is buried in the sounds of war drums, in the heaps of sponsored writing paraded as 'research' and in the boardrooms of governments and corporates, with the former doling out subsidies and the latter obfuscating profits with social responsibility. Then there are the activists masquerading as missionaries while making a career of it; they are the most damaging. Greta Thunberg, everybody's climate hero, interrupted her schooling at the age of fifteen to become a climate activist. At sixteen, she boarded a $4-million sailing yacht to attend the UN Climate Action Summit, where she thumped the lectern and screamed at diplomats, scholars, and professionals, 'How dare you?' A career in activism can be pursued without formal qualifications; one only needs a few traits: the art of finding a wealthy sponsor, a doomsday visage, and a dramatic display while exercising the power of rhetoric.

There may be educated activists out there sincerely concerned about global warming. Years of studies and research would have brought home to them a bitter truth that is not being addressed by the 'popular' activists. This truth is wholly in the domain of political incorrectness and has two faces:

- The rich refuse to consume less to save the planet.
- The poor refuse to remain poor to save the environment.[17]

Like Janus, anyone involved in the business of saving the planet—whether as a researcher, policymaker or activist—sees only one face at a time. For the ancient Romans, one face of Janus represented the 'beginning', while the other symbolised the 'end'. The former was the past, the latter the future. Janus had little to do with the present, which is dominated by fear and greed. Yet, we see the past and the future mostly through this prism of fear and greed. The fear of one section of humanity is due to the greed of another, and that has always been the cause of human violence, incorrect perceptions of an existential crisis, and hence, an inefficient response to it. Fear and greed enable Janus to transition us from the beginning towards the end, following the same path that brought us to the present existential crisis.

There are geological cycles of warm and ice ages. The last ice age finally ended about 11,000 years ago, and since then, the planet has been warming as it did in each warm age. If there were no humans, the warm age would still continue until all the polar and glacial ice melt, sea levels rise, and coastal areas are submerged. It is clear that humans are accelerating the process, not creating it. How much of it is human contribution lies at the heart of the debate. Most of the energy that humans use comes from one source that has been worshipped as the divine force sustaining life on earth: the Sun. Rama came from the lineage of the Sun. The Inca believed they were born from the Sun. The Pharaoh's Ra, the Mesopotamian's Shamash, the Sumerian's Utu, and the Celt's Lugh were all Sun gods. The only practical sources of energy that did not come from the Sun are geothermal energy and nuclear energy. All fossil fuels were once living matter sustained by the Sun.

The action of sunlight combines carbon and hydrogen in various proportions to give us 'fuels' that 'burn', a process of oxidation of both these elements that produces heat. High heat generates what we call 'light'. Thus, forests and crops produce 'fuel' for the hearth and for living beings, both animal and human. Animals do not have the concept of comfort and luxury. Humans require fuel for both; hence they have become a greater burden on the environment by extracting millions of years of deposited carbon and hydrogen and burning it quickly. The rich countries began craving comfort and luxury a few centuries earlier than poor countries and have, in increasing numbers, enjoyed it during the last century. Poor countries started much later and are now going at breakneck speed to make up for lost time. Both are trying to prevent the other from doing so.

The rich countries are thus promoting luxury tourism, where highly carbon-intensive travel dominates, and a luxury hotel guest's daily carbon footprint may exceed that of an entire group of villages in Africa. Meanwhile, the developing countries are promoting production and consumption of packaged products, where the packaging may have a higher carbon footprint than the contents, and more so when home delivered. The Global South is adding coal-based thermal power generation at a pace many times faster than during the pre-environmental activism era. The Global South is worried: Before there is a complete ban on additional coal power, they want to have enough existing firm power generation capacity. Coal power is one of the most obvious and time-tested sources of firm power. Meanwhile, the rich are resorting to symbolism when pushed by the activists. Replacing plastic straws with paper straws is a popular step. The latter are made with water-soluble polyvinyl (PVA) glue, similar to the commonly used white adhesives. The cheaper versions use fast-melt thermal glues that speed up the production process. The objection to plastic straws was that they end up in the oceans. That is where all this glue is ending up too, and we ingest some of it directly as we sip our drinks.

Forests are carbon sinks; true, but only up to a point. As the forest attains equilibrium, the net absorption becomes almost zero. The dead matter falls to the forest floor, decays, and releases methane—a gas more harmful for the environment than CO_2. In equilibrium, the carbon absorption becomes equal to carbon emission. Farmers are pilloried for burning agriculture residues and animal dung. Left to nature, these would decay and produce methane, and farmers' kitchens would use alternative fuels that emit more CO_2. Even if these wastes are converted to biofuels, their end product will still be CO_2. Farmers are not pilloried for growing rice, the flooded fields of which are major methane emitters. Nuclear energy is clean and green, yet it releases as heat the energy that was locked in radioactive atoms. Similarly, pumping out geothermal energy is also a net addition to the energy the Sun naturally sends to the Earth.

The real culprits are our fear and greed, and our insatiable craving for comfort and luxury. Ever-increasing human consumption is the real cause of environmental degradation; fossil fuels and plastics are only the visible symptoms. Until the countries of the world agree on a ceiling on each human's consumption level, the fight for sustainability will remain a charade. In the 19th century, Jean-Baptiste Say enunciated what has since been known as Say's Law: 'Supply creates its own demand.' John Maynard Keynes's ideas were formulated in another dictum known as Keynes' Law: 'Demand creates its own supply.' There is no contradiction between the two. Ouroboros, the mythological serpent of ancient Egypt and Greece, keeps eating its own tail while continuously regenerating itself. In the same way, demand and supply are points on an expanding spiral, chasing each other endlessly. In this eternal chase, humans, air, water, or even the earth do not matter; only fear and greed prevail.

Energy Security Dimension of Energy Transition

Until the recent past, energy security had a narrow meaning: safeguarding a country's access to fossil fuels, mainly coal, oil, and gas, to keep its economy supplied with enough energy for rapid growth. Future projections that showed that these sources of energy would last for a limited period due to increasingly rapid extraction led to the concept of sustainability of energy sources. This brought nuclear energy and renewables into sharp focus. Simultaneously, due to the high level of environmental degradation of land, water, and air caused by these fuels, the focus was on sustainability of the environment. The two drivers—sustainability of energy sources and sustainability of the environment—highlighted the need for energy transition. In the initial years of shifting to renewables, the cost of energy produced by solar radiation and wind was very high, and only the rich countries could afford to set up costly generation facilities and pay a higher price for energy. The same was the case with nuclear energy. The rich countries added a significant amount of nuclear generation, while the developing countries struggled with fuel availability and cost issues. The latter were concerned, and not without reason, that the high price of energy would retard their economic progress.

Gradually, as green energy became comparable in cost to fossil fuels, pressure increased on developing countries to speed up the transition to green energy. Yet, both solar and wind are infirm power that is ramped up and down by nature, and humans have little control over that. While the rich counties had their huge nuclear capacity to provide alternative firm power, developing countries still lag behind in using nuclear power as firm power due to reasons such as technology, fuel availability, and affordability. Let us take the case of China, which is the world leader in adding new nuclear generation capacity. In 2023, China had fifty-five working nuclear plants with a capacity of 53.3 GW, twenty-five new reactors were under construction, and more than seventy were in the planning stage. Yet, in 2023, nuclear power accounted for 5 per cent of China's total electricity generation, a figure that took fourteen years to reach, rising from 2 per cent. In India, the figure is a little more than 3 per cent. In the rich countries, nuclear generation accounts for a much higher proportion of total electricity generation:

Sweden has about 30 per cent, the US 18 per cent, and the UK more than 14 per cent. Germany was drawing more than 25 per cent of its energy from nuclear reactors until 2011 but has scaled down considerably since then. Even when these rich countries reduce nuclear generation, they can quickly bring the mothballed nuclear plants online in times of crisis. Germany did this in the first few months of the energy crisis caused by the Ukraine War, raising it to 6 per cent in 2022 and bringing it down to 1.4 per cent as LNG imports from non-Russian sources increased. During the crisis, Germany even revived some of its coal generation.

Thus, countries like China and India have to continue to rely on coal power to meet their need for firm power, as they will not have sufficient nuclear power to meet this need any time soon or even in the medium term. Both these countries are adding to their existing coal capacity. In 2022, China brought into operation 27.6 GW of coal generation and a whopping 47.4 GW in 2023. In 2022 alone, 106 GW of new coal-fired power was approved. Investment in coal mining went up from $70 billion in 2019 to $96 billion in 2022. China may not use all this thermal capacity. The capacity charge recently announced for new coal plants is an assurance that even if these plants lie idle, they will be paid the fixed capacity charge to cover the capital investment.[18] India produces 70 per cent of its power from coal and added 5.5 GW new capacity in 2023. Similar additions were made by other developing countries: Indonesia added 5.9 GW, Vietnam 2.6 GW, and Bangladesh 1.9 GW.[19]

Clearly, for reasons of energy security, developing countries regard coal generation as supplementary to renewable energy, rather than as an unwanted environmental burden. They will continue to do so until either they are enabled to quickly add nuclear capacity, or the cost of grid-level storage comes down so drastically that wind and solar generation become reliable sources of round-the-clock firm power.

Risks to Be Mitigated to Ensure a Transition with Energy Security

The International Energy Agency (IEA) defines energy security as the uninterrupted availability of energy sources at an affordable price,[20] as well as the relationship between the availability of natural resources for energy consumption and national security. The latter part shows the vulnerability of national security when natural resources are not available to provide uninterrupted energy at an affordable price. The risk factors for energy security in a fossil fuel environment are mainly related to price and transportation, both of which become uncertain in times of hostilities, whether involving physical violence or economic coercion. Energy transitions and the growth of cyber criminality are the new challenges to energy security. IEA has highlighted the fact that the diffused and decentralised nature of much renewable generation does raise the risk of cyberattacks, and many clean energy technologies rely on metals and minerals that are in short supply or whose production is dominated by a limited number of nations.

While most activists tend to favour the shift to renewables, there are dissenting voices too. Wind generation is a case in point where activists have raised issues ranging from risks to birds to noise for human beings. They have protested against harm to indigenous rights[21,22] and against the alleged deterioration of landscape aesthetics by windmills. For obvious reasons, these protests have remained confined to democracies, and no such protests have been noticed in totalitarian states like China. Even among democracies, the protests have been more in high-income countries, as the protestors are convinced that their governments can opt for other more expensive alternatives for energy transition. On the other hand, low-income countries face agitation against technologies that require large-scale acquisition of lands that sustain subsistence farming families or that cause serious visible damage to fragile ecosystems like hydro-projects in fragile mountains, and the courts have been on the side of the agitators. After the Kedarnath floods in June 2013, which killed more than 5,000 people and washed away entire settlements, the Supreme Court of India halted the approval of new hydroelectric projects in the state of Uttarakhand.[23] The court asked the government to justify each project from all aspects of ecology, including the biodiversity of the river basins. Ongoing and new projects could only be started after a hiatus of eight years.

How perceptions have changed during the last sixty years can be seen from one of the earliest large hydroelectric projects in India, the Bhakra Dam project. At that time, it was called a temple of modern India, and it led to the Green Revolution, rural prosperity in the states of Punjab and Haryana, and later in Rajasthan too. It provided food security to the rest of India, as the beneficiary states contributed large surpluses to support the rest of the country, and famines became a thing of the past. The Bhakra Dam is the source of the cheapest and cleanest electricity available to the states of Punjab, Haryana, and Himachal Pradesh. It provides canal irrigation to farmers who would have otherwise been dependent on bore wells using fossil-fuel electricity to pump out groundwater. In contrast, the construction of the Sardar Sarovar Dam in the state of Gujarat was delayed by more than fifteen years due to the agitation by the Narmada Bachao Andolan (NBA–Save the Narmada Movement). Because of the agitation, the World Bank withdrew from the project in 1993, and the Supreme Court had sided with the activists and had halted construction in May 1995. All the foreign investors also withdrew from the dam, and after this huge setback, which resulted in significant cost escalation, the Supreme Court allowed construction to resume in October 2000. Due to this delay, the original cost of the project escalated by a whopping 2,314 per cent, from Rs 3,530 crore to almost Rs 90,000 crore. Meanwhile, the agitators enjoyed publicity and luxurious foreign trips and awards. If a successful transition has to be made to green energy without hurting the economy, energy security, and national security, the democracies of the world will have to find a way to listen to the agitators without such disastrous consequences.

In addition to these risks, one of the biggest challenges to be mitigated during the transition to green energy is technological risk. The first concern is the lifecycle of new technology, as projections of its life span may turn out to be unreliable. Even more important is technological obsolescence much before the capital cost has been recovered. The earlier solar modules were not only more expensive but also had a much lower efficiency, and investors were allowed much higher tariffs by the regulators. Within a few years, the prices crashed and efficiency increased, allowing new projects to supply solar energy to distribution companies at prices that compete with fossil energy, putting a question mark over earlier investments. A great deal of money is going into grid-level battery storage, while there is optimism that hydrogen-based energy storage could soon be competitive with battery storage, thanks to the increase in efficiency and the decrease in the price of electrolysers. If that happens, as is likely by 2030, a lot of investment in battery manufacturing could be lost. Even if efforts are made to save battery manufacturers, the fact that hydrogen will have a much smaller environmental footprint than battery production and disposal at the end of their lifecycle may lead to pressure from activists to ban batteries. Similarly, if sometime in the future, graphene capacitor storage becomes feasible, it would hurt hydrogen, as the efficiency of capacitor storage could be higher than that of electrolysers. If none of the storage technologies being touted at present comes up to expectations, then the infirm power from solar and wind generators could again take a backseat, giving way to firm power from coal, gas, and nuclear reactors.

For transitioning to green energy, different sectors have their own requirements for transportation and distribution infrastructure. Hydrogen will require storage and distribution outlets. Batteries require fast-charging infrastructure, both at the grid and distribution levels. The time required to charge a battery is determined by its C-rate; 1C means it can be fully charged in one hour, while 0.25C means it would take four hours for a 0–100 per cent charge. A higher C-rate reduces battery life, while a lower C-rate increases charging time. Car owners would typically expect the topping up to take 30 minutes or less while they stop for coffee. A higher C-rate and shorter charging time mean charging at very high currents, which load the distribution system and heat up the batteries, resulting in fires and explosions, as has been repeatedly witnessed with electric vehicles in China. China's own Emergency Management Department reported that in the first quarter of 2023, an average of eight EVs caught fire every day—a 32 per cent increase over the previous period.[24] Some news outlets have tried to downplay that risk by reporting that more internal combustion (IC) vehicles catch fire than EVs. That, however, seems to be statistical jugglery, as the number of IC vehicles is much larger than that of EVs, and on a per vehicle basis, the probability of an EV catching fire is clearly much higher than that of IC vehicles. Moreover, EVs catch fire while charging or even when simply parked, while there is no corresponding issue with IC vehicles. While more research will be required to remove the smokescreen around the issue, some news does appear to cause uncertainty. In

July 2023, a ship carrying cars, including EVs, caught fire on board. It was reported that the fire, which started in an EV, caused one death and several injuries on board, and it took several days to extinguish it.[25] A report the next day put the total number of vehicles on board as 3,783, out of which 498 were EVs. A spokesperson of the International Maritime Organization (IMO) said that keeping in view the growing number of such incidents, the IMO is planning to revisit the issue of EV transport by ships and evaluate new measures for this purpose. A month later, it was reported that insurance premiums for shipping EVs may be revised, and systems onboard will be updated for handling EV fires. Such fires, called 'thermal runaway', start with the overheating of lithium-ion batteries, leading to an unstoppable increase in temperature. The fire-fighting systems on board are not designed for these much hotter fires.[26]

Hydrogen, a highly combustible gas, will present similar risks when stored on ground or in vehicles. Hydrogen has a flame speed of 3 metres per second, much higher than other inflammable gases, such as methane's 30 cm per second. When it burns with oxygen from the air, the temperature reaches 2,045 degrees Celsius, double the temperature at which most rocks melt. The saving grace is that hydrogen, being the lightest element, does not linger when there is a leak and dissipates upwards almost immediately. All this is not to say that countries should not transition to batteries and hydrogen; it only indicates the need for research to mitigate risk factors.

The Risk of Transition for Oil, Gas, and Coal Rentier States

While most of the other risks in the transition to green energy impacted democracies more than autocracies and dictatorships, this one will likely impact only the latter. A rentier state derives all or a substantial portion of its national revenue from the rent paid by foreigners, governments, individuals, or corporations for a nature's bounty within its borders. It has been said that 'rentier economies, trapped by effortless wealth, have no incentive to improve efficiency and are politically impeded … Rent is thus presented as a kind of curse, accounting for stunted development and political apathy—or democratic shortcomings, at the same time'.[27] With the 'unearned' wealth, the rentier state creates artificial employment opportunities and handouts to citizens to gain support and legitimacy. That gives the rulers political stability without democracy, as citizens get economic benefits in exchange for their loyalty.[28] As energy transition gathers momentum, the countries comprising the Gulf Cooperation Council (Bahrain, Kuwait, Oman, Qatar, Saudi Arabia, and the United Arab Emirates), which sit on 30 per cent of proven world crude oil and 22 per cent of global natural gas, will have to face international pressures in terms of reduced demand for oil and gas and increased expectations from the GCC countries that they reduce their greenhouse gas emissions.[29] As of 2023, 99 per cent of their domestic needs were met through oil and gas. These countries were by and large missing incentives, regulations, and an investment environment for green energy. Unless they give up their rentier mentality and bring about the required structural and institutional changes, they will face falling revenues and increased demand from the rest of the world that they invest in energy transition. Fortunately for the global environment, the GCC countries have started gearing up to meet the challenge of energy transition: Saudi Arabia has a target of 50 per cent renewable energy in its energy mix by 2030, UAE 44 per cent by 2050, Oman 30 per cent by 2030, Qatar 20 per cent by 2030, and Kuwait 15 per cent by 2030.[30] That raises a question for the West: Will

West Asia become a transition hub, and hence, remain a locus of energy geopolitics even after the transition?

In spite of this long list of impediments and risks on the path of the transition to green energy, it is remarkable that the world is moving towards the goal of substantially reducing greenhouse gas emissions and increasing the share of green sources in its energy mix. There may be hiccups, as happened temporarily when Russia invaded Ukraine, but the direction of the transition is unmistakable.

10

Energy Security: Concept and Reality

R.N. Prasher

Energy represents a conundrum for human survival. Energy consumption is linked to development, prosperity, health, and longevity; nations that have a high per capita consumption of energy are high on these indices too. Almost all of them are high on the democratic index also. Very few of them are high on the World Happiness Index though. So far, high energy consumption has led to degradation of the environment and the social fabric. Control over energy sources lies at the root of many geopolitical conflicts. Following the empowerment of their members by bodies such as the 1952 European Coal and Steel Community (ECSC) and the 1957 European Atomic Energy Community (Euratom), the Organization of the Petroleum Exporting Countries (OPEC) was created in 1960 as a symbol of the idea that control over an energy source can be weaponised and used as political power. Until that time, an optimal combination of GDP and population gave countries noteworthy weight in international relations. The 'Brundtland Report' had defined sustainable development as one where 'population size and growth are in harmony with the changing productive potential of the ecosystem'.[1] With OPEC, countries without a good-sized population and without much economic activity within their borders became international heavyweights. In a landmark 2016 paper, 'Do Renewable Energies Improve Energy Security in the Long Run?'[2], Emmanuel Hache had pointed out how 'Saudi Arabia and Norway make interesting examples when it comes to their disproportionate positioning with regards to their demographic or economic weight, through the sole presence of oil resources on their territory'. Energy was driving geopolitics, and its power was enough to keep the voices of environmental concern subdued.

By the late 1960s, the nations of the world were already worried about the environmental impact of energy, primarily coal, oil, and gas at that time, with some nuclear energy included. In 1968, Sweden took the initiative in the United Nations Economic and Social Council (ECOSOC) to promote the idea of a UN conference on the environment. ECOSOC passed a resolution in 1969, which was followed by the General Assembly Resolution 2398 of 1969. The idea fructified in the 1972 UN Conference on the Human Environment (UNCHE) in Stockholm, which, perhaps for the first time, brought a large part of the international community together to discuss the impact of human activities on our planet. The conference led to the establishment of the United Nations Environment Programme (UNEP), which remains the leading UN authority on the environment.

The conference provided a foretaste of how geopolitics will always overshadow environmental concerns. Although 114 nations participated in the preparatory work, the Soviet Union and the Warsaw Pact countries boycotted the conference, protesting the exclusion of East Germany, though even West Germany was excluded, as neither were members of the UN. Records of the UK, declassified in 2002, revealed, 'A secret group of developed nations conspired to limit the effectiveness of the UN's first conference on the environment.'[3]

Britain, the US, Germany, Italy, Belgium, the Netherlands, and France formed a cabal called the Brussels Group in July 1971—one year before the UN Conference began. According to declassified documents, the group was to remain informal and confidential, as an 'unofficial policymaking body'. Notes taken at the meetings of the group show that the members tried to ensure that the discussions at the UN Conference do not restrict trade, remain focussed on developed countries, 'and perhaps be less worried about making it a success for developing countries'. Britain and France had collaborated on the development of the supersonic airliner, the Anglo-French Concorde. Their narrow self-interests were revealed in one of the priority areas of the group: They wanted any control over sonic booms and pollution in the upper atmosphere to be left out of the scope of the conference and the UNEP.

Thus, geopolitics and geoeconomics have been at loggerheads with environmental concerns and the transition to cleaner sources of energy. As the thinking in the Brussels Group shows, these concerns have led to a concept of energy security, which has merged with the idea of national security. Hence, the transitions have been delayed until these ceased to be perceived as threats to national security. Developments in new technologies have resulted in transitions making economic sense and have opened one of the paths through the wall of resistance. Ironically, the fear that fossil fuels are not going to last and projections that oil will be over in forty years, while coal may last less than two centuries[4] fuelled research in alternatives that turned out to be cleaner sources. Cartels like OPEC+ unwittingly did their bit to accelerate such research when they repeatedly cut production to sustain high prices and caused global energy disruption, strengthening the walls of energy security. Yet, overall, the energy security game remains one in which the endowed producer nations and the economic powerhouses laid down the rules, and the poorer nations had to make sacrifices, not only of their bare necessities but also of their environment. A 2022 study found that 'the global energy security pattern coincides with the international geopolitical order. The countries with the "Best" energy security are found in Western Europe and North America while the countries with "Poor" or "Worse" energy security are located in Asia and the less developed regions of Africa'.[5]

The response to energy insecurity and the fear of being locked into asymmetric and dependency relationships has led to the evolution of resource nationalism. It is the tendency of people to demand—and of governments to assert control over—domestic natural resources. Although it applies to freshwater and marine resources too, its main application is in the field of fossil fuels—coal, oil, and gas—and includes control over transportation and storage facilities for these commodities. While this tendency in importing countries is understandable in terms of their energy security and has hampered the transition to cleaner energy, it has been displayed even by some resource-rich countries as well. Norway is a classic example. A 2022 paper raises the question, 'Most of the scholarship however focuses on security of supply, imports and enhanced domestic production, not on exports. How does exporting renewable energy resources affect sovereignty?'[6] It looks at Norway, a country which is already self-sufficient in renewables. In debates in that country, renewable expansion is perceived to weaken sovereignty, rather than strengthen it. Here, the asymmetric relationship is viewed as one with the powerful European Union (EU), which, by compelling member nations to completely switch over to renewables, is seen as wresting Norwegian sovereignty, engaging in green grabbing, and diluting local self-determination. Thus, resource nationalism can operate both in times of scarcity and in times of abundance of fossil fuels.

To penetrate these brick walls of the idea of energy security, the definitions have, over the years, incorporated more and more components, some of which are non-economic in nature and address human survival issues. Thus, the International Energy Agency (IEA) defines energy security as 'the uninterrupted availability of energy sources at an affordable price'.[7] Yet, to avoid difficult conflicts with transition goals, it divides them into two categories: long-term and short-term. Under the former, timely investments ensure energy supply 'in line with economic developments and environmental needs'. The short-term aspect may ignore these needs, as it focuses on 'the ability of the energy system to react promptly to sudden changes in the supply-demand balance'.

The harmonisation of energy transition with energy security has led to the development of the 4A's[8] of energy security: availability, accessibility, affordability, and acceptability. The Asia Pacific Energy Research Centre defines energy security as 'the ability of an economy to guarantee the availability of energy resource supply in a sustainable and timely manner with the energy price being at a level that will not adversely affect the performance of the economy'.[9] It consolidated the 4As into three categories:

- Physical energy security, the availability and accessibility of supply sources
- Economic energy security, the affordability of resource acquisition, and energy infrastructure development
- Environmental sustainability, the sustainable development and use of energy resources that 'meets the needs of the present without compromising the ability of future generations to meet their own needs'[10]

Thus, economic energy security provides a moral ground for delaying the transition until it becomes economically comfortable. The environmental sustainability aspect/part speaks to meeting 'the needs of the present'. These two compromises were seen in action in the aftermath of the European energy crisis in 2022, when Russia invaded Ukraine. Germany, which had previously mothballed its thermal and nuclear power generation, brought these facilities back online until an alternative of liquefied natural gas (LNG) to replace Russian piped compressed natural gas (CNG) could be made operational and enough gas storage could be constructed so that summer storage would enable comfortable winters. This was a grim reminder to those indulging in environmental hyper-activism: We live in a real world and governance is the art of the possible. Consider these two articles from the news agency Reuters:

- 2 November 2021: 'Germany to give 700 mln euros to help South Africa end coal use'[11]
- 4 October 2023: 'Germany approves bringing coal-fired plants back online this winter'[12]

Mothballed and even decommissioned coal-fired plants had been restarted 'temporarily' immediately after Russian gas supplies were disrupted. This was an energy transition in the opposite direction, as the government announced that it planned to burn more coal for a transitional period. A German press release dated 9 March 2023 stated, 'Coal remained the main energy source in electricity production in Germany in 2022: 8.4% more coal-generated electricity fed into the grid than in 2021. Photovoltaics provided almost as much electricity as natural gas: electricity production from natural gas down 11.3%, photovoltaics up 19.5%.'[13] The same had happened to nuclear plants. In 2022, German Chancellor Olaf Scholz announced that three nuclear plants would stay open temporarily. The plants were finally closed when LNG from alternative sources arrived to fill the newly created storage capacity. Yet, as the nuclear plants were finally being shut down, there were calls to let them remain operational from not only the opposition parties but even from Wolfgang Kubicki, deputy leader of the Free Democrats, a part of the ruling coalition. He said that Germany has the safest nuclear power plants worldwide and switching them off would be 'a dramatic mistake' with painful economic and ecological consequences.[14]

Let us imagine another scenario where China is able to take over Taiwan and assert its unquestioned control over the South China Sea bounded by its ten-dash line—the tenth dash having been added to include Taiwan. Let's say this happens long before 2060, the year in which Xi Jinping has committed China to becoming carbon neutral. We know that the pace of China's movement towards that goal is rather slow. While China has added huge capacity in solar and wind generation, it has been adding to its coal-based generation capacity also at a very rapid pace. In fact, in one year, China added more to its thermal capacity than the total added by the whole world. In 2023, China retired 4 GW of old thermal generation and added 50 GW of coal-fired electricity, thus increasing capacity by 46 GW, which is the same as the total coal-based generation in Japan. About 40 per cent of the 3,000 GW total power generation in China is still coal-based, and this figure will decline slowly due to feverish new capacity addition. To encourage investment in new coal capacity, China recently introduced capacity payments that minimise the investment risk of investors, as they are paid to cover the fixed cost, whether the plant runs or not.

The South China Sea is a critical trade route; 10 billion barrels of oil and oil products and 6.7 Tcf of LNG passed through it in 2023,[15] with much larger quantities lying unexplored beneath this body of water. If all these become sovereign assets of China much before it becomes carbon-neutral, it will be a big jolt to global goals of energy transition. China will not only use this oil and gas for its energy needs, its withdrawal as the world's largest importer of oil will send the market downward into a tailspin. Prices will fall, and China may itself offer cheap oil to capture market share, as it has done with manufactured products. Alternative forms of energy, such as solar, wind, and hydrogen, will again become too expensive, and hence, unattractive.

These scenarios go to show that energy security is multidimensional, with geopolitical, geoeconomic, nationalistic, and emotional parameters. Yet, there are two more dimensions of energy security: firstly, it can be achieved through a transition to domestic alternative sources of energy. Secondly, in all energy consumption systems, there is hidden demand elasticity that has the potential to decouple economic growth from energy use—higher growth can be achieved without increasing energy consumption through increased energy efficiency and energy conservation. These two areas are largely overlooked in the rush to transition to cleaner sources, particularly because, until we have scaled up cheap storage of renewable electricity from solar and wind sources, it is believed that this power is on a 'use it or lose it' basis. The Russian gas crisis in Europe led to the International Energy Agency (IEA) issuing 'A 10-Point Plan to Reduce the European Union's Reliance on Russian Natural Gas'.[16] It has three components for enhancing energy efficiency: the replacement of gas boilers with heat pumps, energy efficiency improvements in buildings, and thermostat adjustments by consumers. The first is expected to reduce gas use for heating by 2 bcm every year; the second will save another 2 bcm per year, in addition to lowering energy bills, increasing comfort, and boosting industrial competitiveness; and the third will save 10 bcm of gas every year for each one-degree Celsius change in thermostat. None of these technologies is new, and yet, Europe waited for Putin's depredations in Ukraine to motivate them enough to take these steps to increase their energy security. As we show in the chapter on hydrogen, the first automobile ran on hydrogen, before any ran on oil. Yet, we waited for two centuries for the idea of hydrogen cars to gain enough momentum to lead to commercial production. Economics did it. Geopolitics did it. Technology alone is a poor driver of change.

11

Hydrogen's Role in Energy Security

R.N. Prasher

Alternative green energies remain conceptual until economics makes sense. This has been particularly true with hydrogen, the cleanest alternative fuel that produces only water vapour as exhaust. Yet, hydrogen is one idea that has come full circle after more than two centuries. The first internal combustion engine (IC) was made by Isaac de Rivaz in 1804, and it used hydrogen as fuel. In 1806, he incorporated it in a vehicle that ran a short distance on hydrogen fuel. The concept of a fuel cell, which combines hydrogen and oxygen into water molecules and produces electricity during the process, was discovered by the Swiss scientist Christian Friedrich Schönbein as far back as 1838. Sir William Robert Grove, a scientist from Wales, created the Grove voltaic cell in 1842, the first fuel cell, which he called gas voltaic battery. A century later, in 1923, J.B.S. Haldane wrote, 'There will be great power stations where during windy weather the surplus power will be used for the electrolytic decomposition of water into oxygen and hydrogen.' In 1932, Francis Thomas Bacon, who descended from the family of Sir Francis Bacon and was an engineering professor at Trinity College, Cambridge, developed a fuel cell that was used in the

Apollo moon project, giving practical shape to the dreams of his predecessors in the field. US President Nixon welcomed Bacon to the White House with the words, 'Without you, Tom, we wouldn't have gotten to the Moon.'[1]

In 1977, J.O'M. Bockris coined the term 'hydrogen economy', which he defined as 'a system of industry, transportation, and household energy which depends on piped hydrogen as a fuel…'[2] His primary motive was to replace fossil fuels, which caused pollution and had to be transported from Middle Eastern sources. Moving into the third decade of the 21st century, we have rainbow colours of hydrogen types: green, made with renewable energy; yellow, made with nuclear energy; blue, produced using carbon capture and storage; turquoise, made through pyrolysis with carbon black as a byproduct; grey or brown, made by using natural gas or oil; and black, made from coal. Despite the long history of the idea and some practical uses, green hydrogen still remains a future goal, though we already have a few hydrogen-powered cars and electricity generation stations running on hydrogen. It has been called the Holy Grail of decarbonisation.[3]

Electrolysis is considered the leading green hydrogen-producing technology today. It produces highly purified hydrogen and works well in combination with renewable energy. It, therefore, holds brighter prospects than other types of hydrogen technology, such as those using nuclear energy or photocatalysis (technologies that are still at the laboratory stage). The electrolysis process relies on electrolysers, of which three types are currently in use: alkaline (ALK), proton exchange membrane (PEM), and solid oxide electrolyser cell (SOEC). PEM's higher reaction efficiency makes it well-suited to the volatility of wind and solar power. Globally, PEM technology is expected to commercialise rapidly. However, China is way behind in this technology. To secure PEM's future, China needs to replace imported components with domestic alternatives. SOEC recovers waste heat from high-temperature industrial processes, working well in conjunction with photothermal power systems. In China, the experience with SOEC electrolysers is currently limited to laboratory-scale demonstrations.

As of now, the world is dependent on coal, oil, and gas for a major part of its firm power needs. Renewables are infirm sources of power dependent on the vagaries of weather. The demand is highly variable over the course of twenty-four hours, and the balancing has to be achieved through a source of firm power. Supplies of oil and gas, to a very large extent, and coal, to some degree, are subject to geopolitics, and that affects the energy security of many nations. Any new international conflict sends jitters in the energy market, as we have seen recently at the start of the Ukraine War and again with the Gaza hostilities, though it appears that the world is gradually developing mechanisms to handle these shocks. Some nations and the European Union stand out[4] among those who are working feverishly to avoid becoming pawns on a geopolitical energy chessboard.

Japan

Japan formulated its Basic Hydrogen Strategy in 2017 and revised it in June 2023. It has the following components:[5]

- Originally, the aim of effectively developing hydrogen technology was to create a domestic hydrogen market ahead of the rest of the world. Given that the global hydrogen market is expected to generate $2.5 trillion per year in revenue and create 30 million jobs by 2050, the government has decided to update the strategy to not only develop the domestic market but also expand into overseas markets.
- The goals of green transformation (GX) are to realise stable energy supply, economic growth, enhanced international

industrial competitiveness, and decarbonisation. To seed the more than 150 trillion yen in GX-related investment, the Japanese government will provide upfront investment support of 20 trillion yen.

- This strategy aims at achieving an early hydrogen society to achieve carbon neutrality by 2050.
- The goals are sought to be achieved through enhancing Japan's competitiveness in the field and demonstrating a reliable safety strategy.
- Simultaneously covering ammonia, e-methane, and synthetic fuel (e-fuel), it aims to promote carbon neutrality by strategically proceeding with the development, demonstration, and introduction of technologies in view of the challenges, and a technology development timeline.

Following the S+3E (Safety, Energy Security, Economic Efficiency, and Environment) principles, Japan will enhance its presence in a global scenario where water electrolysis capacity is expected to reach 134 GW by 2030.

The European Union

In 2020, the EU issued the 'Hydrogen Strategy for a Climate-Neutral Europe'[6]. It recognises that hydrogen is essential to support the EU's commitment to achieving carbon neutrality by 2050, and at present, hydrogen represents a modest fraction of both the global and EU energy mix, with the majority still being produced from fossil fuels, which annually release up to 100 million tonnes of CO_2 in the EU. While in the past, interest in hydrogen has waxed and waned over several cycles, we have now reached a tipping point where new investments are coming into this sector regularly. The EU expects the share of hydrogen in Europe's energy mix to grow to 13–14 per cent by 2050. It predicts cumulative investments in renewable hydrogen in Europe to reach between 180 and 470 billion euros by 2050 and estimates that it could employ up to one million people, either directly or indirectly. The world market size of hydrogen in 2050 is estimated to be 630 billion euros, meeting 24 per cent of the world's energy demand by that year. However, at present, hydrogen is not competitive, and that is the major challenge to be overcome.

Twenty-six member states of the EU have signed the Hydrogen Initiative and 2x40 GW of electrolysers are planned to be set up by 2030, preferably next to large consuming industries. The EU's target is to produce up to 10 million tonnes of renewable hydrogen by 2030, by which time it is expected to become cost competitive. In the next phase, from 2030 to 2050, the EU's hydrogen industry is expected to reach a mature phase, with up to 25 per cent of all renewable energy being used for hydrogen production. This requires investment in electrolysers, creating and connecting solar and wind capacity to the electrolysers, investment in hydrogen transport distribution and storage, and setting up hydrogen refuelling stations. In May 2022, the European Commission published the REPowerEU plan, setting targets of 10 million tonnes of green hydrogen produced within the EU and the import of another 10 million tonnes.

To achieve economies of scale, the EU plans to simultaneously work on boosting the demand for hydrogen while scaling up production. This begins with replacing the use of fossil fuels in various carbon-intensive industrial processes, such as steel-making and in chemical industries. This step will substantially lower the greenhouse gas emissions of these industries and improve their global competitiveness. The other focus is on the transport sector, where hydrogen in fuel cells offers an alternative to batteries, the manufacture and scrapping of which leave a large environmental footprint. The strategy envisages repurposing the existing natural gas infrastructure for hydrogen transport to avoid stranded assets in pipelines. These, along with new pipelines, will form the 4,500-km European Hydrogen Backbone that will connect twenty-one European countries. Sixty-nine per cent of it will consist of repurposed natural gas lines, and the remaining will be new pipelines.

Germany

Germany adopted a National Hydrogen Strategy in 2020 and updated it on 26 July 2023. It is in consonance with the twin goals of achieving climate neutrality by 2045 and strengthening the energy security of the country. The latter became even more important after the traumatic effects of the disruption of gas supplies from Russia. The revised strategy states, 'The Russian war of aggression against Ukraine, which violates international law, and its effects on the global energy markets have more than clearly documented the problem of excessive dependence on energy imports from individual countries for Germany's security of energy supply.'[7] The nation, along with other similarly placed nations in Europe, had to build LNG infrastructure in record time, add storage capacity and fill it during the summer months with liquefied gas shipped from alternative sources. Meanwhile, as a stop-gap arrangement, Germany had to restart its coal and nuclear plants, which had been mothballed. Thus, for Germany and other European countries, the energy security promised by hydrogen is as important as its environmental promise. Federal Minister of Economic Affairs Robert Habeck summed up the goals as, 'Investing in hydrogen is an investment in our future—in climate protection, in qualified jobs, and in securing the energy supply.'[8]

Under the revised strategy, the domestic electrolyser capacity target for 2030 has been doubled to 10 GW. By that time, the hydrogen demand in the country is expected to be in the range of 95–130 TWh. More than half of it will have to be imported from Norway and Denmark through pipelines. The existing natural gas pipelines will be repurposed to avoid stranded assets in pipelines. By 2027/2028, a hydrogen start-up grid with more than 1,800 km of repurposed and newly built pipelines will be established as part of the 4,500-km European Hydrogen Backbone. By 2030, all major production, import, and storage centres will be connected to the relevant consumers.

By 2030, industry and transportation, with particular emphasis on heavy-duty commercial vehicles, will mainly use hydrogen, replacing fossil fuels. Hydrogen will be increasingly used by that year in aviation and shipping. The use of hydrogen for power generation will help with peak management by acting as a storage medium, generating hydrogen in surplus phases of renewable power generation.

It envisages limiting subsidies to green hydrogen only to encourage its dominance in the hydrogen mix. Simultaneously, in the transformation phase, other colours of hydrogen—primarily low-carbon hydrogen from waste or natural gas in combination with carbon capture and storage/sequestration (CCS)—will also be used until sufficient green hydrogen is available. Thus, in the ramp-up phase, low-carbon blue (from natural gas with CCS), turquoise (from methane pyrolysis), and orange hydrogen (from waste and residual materials) will also be promoted to a limited extent, but keeping in view the emissions in the upstream chain so that the ambitious greenhouse gas (GHG) emission limits are not compromised/disturbed.

The strategy includes the following elements:

- Green hydrogen will be the key element in Germany's energy transition.
- Production capacity and hydrogen demand will be simultaneously ramped up.
- The regulatory framework for transportation and distribution infrastructure of hydrogen will be developed

with coordination at the European level and, if possible, at the international level.

- German companies will be made competitive through R&D support to make Germany the leading provider of hydrogen technologies, from electrolysers to fuel cells, by 2030.
- International partnerships will be developed within Europe and even outside Europe with countries that have high potential for renewable energy to secure green hydrogen in the future.

The State Secretaries' Committee on Hydrogen is the top decision-making body. Below it is the National Hydrogen Council, an independent non-partisan body comprising twenty-five experts from the economy, science, and civil society. The council has set up working groups for R&D, production and import, transport, distribution and storage, and another for applications.

Spain

Pedro Sánchez, the prime minister of Spain, has plans to position the country as an important green hydrogen exporting nation of Europe. He says, 'Each kilogram of green hydrogen that replaces a fossil fuel will prevent nine kilograms of CO_2 being emitted into the atmosphere.' Spain's Ministry for Ecological Transition and the Demographic Challenge (MITECO) has designated green hydrogen as a 'country project'.

The country's 'Hydrogen Roadmap: A Commitment to Renewable Hydrogen', which provides a framework for developing renewable hydrogen, was approved by the Council of Ministers in October 2020. With this roadmap, Spain aims to achieve climate neutrality and 100 per cent renewable electricity by 2050, while also developing innovative industrial value chains that lead to a high-value-added green economy. It identifies the objectives to be achieved by 2030 in terms of installed capacity for both the industrial and transport sectors. Furthermore, it details the steps to ensure that hydrogen electrolysers are supplied with renewable energy.

The roadmap visualises the creation of hydrogen valleys or clusters where the production of green electricity, its transformation into hydrogen, and the consumption of that hydrogen are specially concentrated, giving economies of scale. These valleys will have associated pilot projects linked to the transport sector and off-grid energy systems. The huge potential of industries like oil refineries, fertilisers, and chemicals, which already use hydrogen from non-renewable sources, to transition to green hydrogen is sought to be fully harnessed, leading to decarbonisation of these high-carbon-footprint industries.

The prospect of using hydrogen for storage of energy has high potential to decarbonise the heat sector in both industry and residential segments. Spain hopes to give hydrogen an essential role in storing energy from 100 per cent renewable electricity by 2050. The roadmap is aligned with the EU's two strategies, the 2020 Hydrogen Strategy for a Climate-Neutral Europe and the 2021 Annual Sustainable Growth Strategy.

The strategy provides for Vision 2030 and Vision 2050. Vision 2030 envisions an installed capacity of 4 GW of electrolysers. In the industrial sector, 25 per cent of hydrogen is planned to transition to green hydrogen. In the transport sector, at least 150 buses, 5,000 other light and heavy vehicles, and two commercial train lines are planned to switch to green hydrogen. At five major ports and airports, green hydrogen-powered handling machinery will be installed, and 100 green hydrogen filling stations will be established. Spain has 13,000 km of gas pipelines, many of which will be repurposed to carry hydrogen. These and other milestones in the industrial, mobility, and power sectors will require an investment of 8,900 million euros by 2030.

Enagás, the Spanish energy company that operates the nation's transmission system as well as its gas grid is planning to set up a 32 MW electrolyser fed by a 150 MW solar plant and is also creating storage for 12 tonnes of green hydrogen. Green Hysland is developing a hydrogen ecosystem on the island of Mallorca, which will transform the island into the first hydrogen hub in southern Europe. Solar energy produced by the company on the island will be converted into 300 tonnes of green hydrogen per year and delivered to the local end-users in the tourism, transport, industry, and domestic energy sectors.

The United Kingdom

The UK Hydrogen Strategy was presented to the Parliament by the secretary of state for the Department of Business, Energy and Industrial Strategy in August 2021.[9] He said, 'developing a thriving low carbon hydrogen sector in the UK is a key plank of the government's plan to build back better with a cleaner, greener energy system … low carbon hydrogen has a critical role to play in our transition to net zero.' The strategy sets a goal of 5 GW of low carbon hydrogen production capacity by 2030—equivalent to the gas consumed by 3 million households in the UK. The document includes the £240 million Net Zero Hydrogen Fund and the UK Low Carbon Hydrogen Standard. It recognised that the UK had no low-carbon production of hydrogen, with most of the hydrogen produced and used in the UK being high-carbon, coming from fossil fuels with no carbon capture. Therefore, the goals were ambitious. The document highlights how the UK is collaborating with other leading hydrogen nations to develop low-carbon hydrogen to support the world's transition to net zero.

It is estimated that 250–460 TWh of hydrogen could be needed in the UK in 2050, making up to 35 per cent of its final energy consumption. The strategy document recognises not only the 'chicken and egg' problem of boosting supply and demand in tandem but also the fact that the UK is well-placed for both supply and demand to expand rapidly. From 1990 to 2019, it has reduced its power emissions by more than 70 per cent and has generated more electricity from offshore wind than any other country, and this capacity will be quadrupled to 40 GW by 2030. Based on this green electricity, the country has the potential to produce large quantities of green hydrogen. Simultaneously, the gas resources of the UK allow it to produce CCUS-enabled blue hydrogen, with lots of disused oil and gas fields in coastal locations as potential CO_2 storage sites. On the demand side, industrial clusters, from chemicals to food and drink, are exploring low carbon and green hydrogen to move towards net zero. The Industrial Decarbonisation Challenge provides up to £170 million, matched by £261 million from industry, for creating decarbonisation infrastructure, including CCUS and low-carbon hydrogen.

The document recognises the difficulties in making demand and supply projections for the future hydrogen market, but it sets a goal of 5 GW of low-carbon hydrogen by 2030. The challenges include lowering the cost of hydrogen to fossil-fuel levels, upscaling existing technologies, regulatory challenges, the need for new infrastructure, demand and supply coordination, and breaking the psychological barrier in first-of-a-kind investment.

China

On 23 March 2022, China's National Development and Reform Commission (NDRC) published the 'Medium and Long-term Plan for the Development of Hydrogen Energy Industry

(2021–2035)'. It states that hydrogen will play a key role in the development of China's energy sector, as well as in achieving the goals of carbon peaking by 2030 and carbon neutrality by 2060.

China is already the world's largest hydrogen producer, making 33 million tonnes every year. However, 60 per cent of this is black hydrogen, made from coal, while 25 per cent comes from natural gas, 14 per cent is an industrial byproduct or from other sources, and only 1 per cent is produced through electrolysis. According to the plan, by 2025, China will be producing between 1,00,000 and 2,00,000 tonnes of green hydrogen annually, with 1.3 GW of electrolysis capacity, generating between 3.3 and 6.7 TWh of energy. In the transport sector, the number of fuel cell electric vehicles will increase from 7,800 in 2022 to 50,000 by 2025.

China has been following the 1+N policy framework since 2022 to achieve the goal of emission peaking by 2030. The '1' refers to the overarching policy guidance and the 'N' refers to the action plans and policy measures for the sectors and industries crucial to achieving the emission peaking goal. Its goals are as follows:

- By 2025, energy consumption per unit of GDP will be lowered by 13.5 per cent, compared to the 2020 level; carbon dioxide (CO_2) emissions per unit of GDP will be lowered by 18 per cent from the 2020 level; and the share of non-fossil energy consumption will have reached around 20 per cent.
- By 2030, CO_2 emissions per unit of GDP will drop further and the share of non-fossil energy consumption will rise to 25 per cent. The installed capacity of wind and solar power will exceed 1,200 GW. CO_2 emissions will reach a peak, stabilise, and then decline.
- By 2060, energy efficiency will be at an advanced international level, and the share of non-fossil energy

consumption will be over 80 per cent, and China will be carbon neutral.

The high capacity in wind and solar power will propel China towards green hydrogen. With the Chinese government's support, the China Hydrogen Alliance (CHA) was launched in 2018, giving China a head start over other developed economies, where a systematic approach to hydrogen began in 2020. The CHA has set the goal of achieving 20 per cent share of hydrogen in China's energy demand by 2060. It has launched the Renewable Hydrogen 100 Initiative, which aims to increase the installed capacity of electrolysers to 100 GW by 2030, which will translate into a green hydrogen capacity of 7.7 million tonnes per year, according to a White Paper issued by the World Economic Forum.[10]

As has occurred with other components of China's economic growth, the country is now focussing on reducing the cost of electrolysers and renewable energy, which goes into the production of green hydrogen. At present, green hydrogen in China costs 3–5 times more per kg than black hydrogen made from coal. Carbon capture, utilisation, and storage (CCUS) is not well established there. The WEF White Paper states that although China has published standards for the entire hydrogen supply chain, there are gaps in technical standards for storage, transport, and refuelling; in this respect, China compares poorly with countries like the US and Japan.

Given the present geopolitical scenario with respect to investment in China, investment in the hydrogen sector will have to come mainly from domestic sources. China has faced one persistent problem across all sectors of its economy, from real estate to chips, electric vehicles to batteries, with lithium now joining the list: As the government starts giving subsidies to promote investment in any sector of the economy, too many investors join the fray, making unrealistic/wild demand projections. Soon, there is overcapacity, and if the commodity can be exported, China tries to dump it on foreign markets at absurdly low prices. Starting with the Trump administration, in 2018, this dumping led to protective measures by various countries, which have raised tariff and non-tariff barriers against cheap Chinese exports.

There is apprehension in some circles that this may happen to hydrogen as well. The cost of renewable electricity is a major part of green hydrogen production, and the electricity tariff in China is not market-determined but state-controlled. Thus, it will be possible for China to sell hydrogen to the world at a very low price by keeping the renewable electricity tariff artificially low by giving money to generators through alternative routes, such as capacity payments, which is already being implemented in the case of thermal power generation. An August 2023 report states that this is already happening in the hydrogen sector: 'China's provincial and municipal governments have jumped on the hydrogen bandwagon, rolling out plans to develop the industry after Beijing released its first ever national hydrogen strategy…'[11] As a result, production is likely to see strong growth, while development of infrastructure and demand growth may lag and face challenges, resulting in overcapacity. The over-enthusiastic local governments left the hydrogen strategy's target of 1,00,000 to 2,00,000 tonnes of green hydrogen by 2025, large as these may seem, far behind. Just the three provinces of Inner Mongolia, Qinghai, and Gansu—all high sunshine areas with low population densities, and hence, suitable for gigantic solar and wind farms—have set a combined target of 7,40,000 tonnes of green hydrogen by 2025. This is a clear scenario of oversupply, and it will deter any rational investor. Simultaneously, one of the factors endangering the Chinese economy's growth has been non-productive projects undertaken by local governments to boost GDP targets assigned by the Communist Party, resulting in unsustainable debt burden on the local governments, with some of them struggling to ward off defaults. It will be a pity if this push towards green hydrogen worsens this domestic situation as well as China's foreign trade relations when the nation tries to sell hydrogen to the world at an unrealistically low price.

The United States

The US released the draft of its US National Clean Hydrogen Strategy and Roadmap for public comments in September 2022 and it was finally published in June 2023.[12] It will be updated every three years. It follows the Infrastructure Investment and Jobs Act, signed by the president in November 2021, which authorises $62 billion for the US Department of Energy and includes $9.5 billion for clean hydrogen and for the Inflation Reduction Act, signed by him in August 2022. The latter provides additional policies and incentives for hydrogen, including a production tax credit to further boost the US's clean hydrogen market. The strategy focuses on investment and action in the near, mid-, and long-term to lay the foundation for broader clean hydrogen adoption, drive down cost, and upscale in a sustainable and holistic manner.

It is based on an assessment of hydrogen's potential contribution to national decarbonisation goals across various sectors of the economy over the next thirty years. The Department of Energy (DOE) issued a request for information on 15 February 2022, seeking feedback from stakeholders on the BIL Regional Clean Hydrogen Hub, electrolyser, and clean hydrogen manufacturing provisions, and the assessment includes this feedback. The key sectors identified for establishing a long-term role for hydrogen are refining, chemicals, iron and steel, freight and long-distance transport, buildings, and power generation and storage.

The supply strategy for hydrogen includes scaling up both hydrogen production from fossil fuels with CCS and through electrolysers using renewable electricity.

Risk reduction for pioneers is sought to be minimised through loan guarantees and R&D support, with enhanced international cooperation. Regulatory barriers that stymie investment will be eliminated, standards will be harmonised nationally, and efforts will be made to secure cooperation of other nations for international harmonisation. The strategy is dynamic and will keep the focus on four opportunity areas to increase momentum:

- Establishing and enabling industrial ports as hubs for production and use of hydrogen at scale.
- Using and repurposing existing gas infrastructure to accelerate new hydrogen supply.
- Simultaneously supporting land-based hydrogen transport infrastructure other than pipelines, such as fleets and corridors.
- Boosting shipping for international trade in hydrogen.

The roadmap envisages three phases or waves of hydrogen development:

The First Wave: The existing uses of fossil fuels that have few alternatives to hydrogen for decarbonisation will be targeted in all locations where hydrogen is accessible or can be made so. Existing ammonia plants, refineries, and industrial clusters present such an opportunity. Forklifts and material-handling equipment with limited geographical movement and frequent refuelling needs are already being brought into the hydrogen fold. In addition, transit buses and long-haul heavy vehicles represent other areas for a quick transition. Heavy machinery in mining, construction, and agriculture could substantially contribute to hydrogen demand in the first wave.

The Second Wave: Medium-duty trucks and regional ferries powered by fuel cells, and high-temperature heat requirements of certain chemical industries can be switched to hydrogen in the second phase. Ore-based steel production can profitably switch to green hydrogen, as it requires carbon-free reductants and high temperature. Power generation turbines can also switch, first to a mixture of hydrogen and natural gas, and later to pure hydrogen. Subsequently, scaled up fuel cells can come into play. In all these cases, stored hydrogen can serve a big role in management when consumption peaks. At present, such peak management is done through natural gas or nuclear power. Aviation fossil fuels are being replaced by biomass and waste-generated fuel, and hydrogen can supplement these.

The Third Wave: Some applications, like cement manufacturing, chemicals, and industrial heating at high temperatures, which were available earlier but could not be upscaled due to the higher cost of hydrogen, will become feasible in this phase due to lowered cost of hydrogen. By this time, scaled-up fuel cell technology at competitive prices will be available to replace diesel generators used for backup power for large single users, such as hospitals and data centres, as well as for microgrids. Hydrogen can be used in conjunction with methanol for rail transport, ships, and other maritime applications.

The strategy is explicitly flexible, and as technology and price factors become favourable, changes can be made to the timescale.

India

India issued the Green Hydrogen Policy in February 2022.[13] It aims at transition to green hydrogen (GH) and green ammonia (GA), particularly in the hard-to-abate sectors, to facilitate the achievement of India's net-zero targets. The policy defines GH/GA as 'produced by way of electrolysis of water using Renewable Energy (RE); including RE which has been banked and the hydrogen/ammonia produced from biomass'.[14] To encourage the transition, the policy provides several incentives, including:

- Waiver of inter-state transmission charges for a period of twenty-five years to the producers of GH/GA from projects commissioned before 30 June 2025.
- GH/GA can be manufactured using RE from a co-located renewable energy plant or sourced from remotely located renewable energy plants, whether set up by the same developer or a third party or RE procured from Power Exchange India Limited.
- GH/GA will be granted expedited clearance for open access to source RE.
- Banking will be permitted for thirty days for RE used to make green GH/GA, with capped banking charges.
- Transmission connectivity will be prioritised between GH/GA manufacturing units and the RE unit set up for this purpose.
- Land can be allotted in renewable energy parks for green GH/GA manufacturing units. New manufacturing zones will be established where GH/GA units can be set up.
- Manufacturers of GH/GA units will be allowed to set up storage facilities at ports for exports.
- RE consumed to produce GH/GA will count towards the Renewable Purchase Obligation (RPO) of the consuming entity. Any excess consumption over and above the RPO will count towards the RPO of the distribution company.
- Distribution licensees may procure and supply RE to the manufacturers of GH/GA, and the cost of energy supplied will be capped as determined by the Electricity Regulatory Commission.
- The Ministry of New and Renewable Energy (MNRE) will set up a single portal for granting all statutory

clearances and permissions for the manufacture, storage, and distribution of GH/GA in a time-bound manner.

In January 2023, MNRE issued the National Green Hydrogen Mission (NGHM),[15] which keeps in sight the twin national goals of India becoming energy independent by 2047 and achieving net zero by 2070, and the critical role of green hydrogen in achieving these goals. It recognises that the country's energy use doubled in the previous twenty years, and that 40 per cent of that energy has to be imported, costing $185 billion annually,[16] and that the energy requirement is likely to grow by at least 25 per cent (35 per cent, as estimated by the IEA)[17] by 2030. Domestic and imported energy transport across the country itself consumes a large amount of energy, and the transport by roads and railways is also time consuming. The National Green Hydrogen Mission statement highlights the fact that 'green hydrogen can enable utilization of domestically abundant renewable energy resources across regions, seasons, and sectors, feeding multiple usage streams, either as a fuel or as an industrial feedstock'.[18] It notes that 'the sensitivity of fossil fuels to geopolitical upheavals and the experience of supply chain disruptions due to COVID have accelerated the transition towards green fuels and feedstock'.[19] The mission views this as an opportunity for India to become a leading producer and exporter of green hydrogen and its derivatives.

It also recognises several challenges that have to be overcome: unfavourable cost economics, lack of harmonised standards and regulations, supply challenges, and capital-intensive enabling infrastructure. It is considered that, with recent technological advancements, a reduction in the cost of renewable energy and electrolysers, and aggressive national strategies of the world's major economies, these hurdles will be overcome, and green hydrogen will become cost-competitive for industrial, mobility, and other sectors of the economy.

In recent years, India has achieved some of the lowest long-term levelized costs for solar and wind power generation. To take advantage of it in producing competitive green hydrogen, the mission has been divided into two phases:

Phase I: The goal in the first phase is to increase demand by promoting utilisation of hydrogen in refineries, the fertiliser industry, and city gas sectors. Simultaneously, to boost supply, 'Make in India' will provide incentives for indigenisation of the value chain for the manufacture of electrolysers. Pilot projects will be taken up in steel production, long-haul heavy-duty mobility, and shipping to transition these hard-to-abate sectors to green hydrogen.

Phase II: During this phase, green hydrogen costs are likely to become competitive with fossil-fuel alternatives, and demand momentum will be built. This will allow accelerated growth of production. Pilot projects in railways and aviation can be taken up, and efforts will be made to penetrate all potential sectors to accelerate the decarbonisation of the economy.

While MNRE will have overall responsibility for coordination and implementation of the mission, the Ministry of Power (MoP) will be responsible for implementation of policies and development of the necessary power infrastructure in coordination with state governments, distribution companies, as well as creation of the regulatory framework. The Ministry of Petroleum and Natural Gas (MoPNG), the Ministry of Chemicals and Fertilisers, and the Ministry of Steel will encourage adoption of green hydrogen in their existing units, and new projects will be designed to maximise the usc of green hydrogen.

The Ministry of Road Transport and Highways will evolve regulations, standards, and codes to enable adoption of green hydrogen, initially for heavy and long-haul vehicles, and for creating the required retail network in conjunction with the Ministry of Petroleum and Natural Gas. The Ministry of Port, Shipping and Waterways (MoPSW) will facilitate adoption of hydrogen and its derivatives as fuel for ships, creation of storage facilities at ports, and refuelling facilities for marine vessels. This ministry will work towards making India a refuelling hub for green hydrogen and its derivatives. The Ministry of Railways will work on transitioning to green hydrogen for its operations and will develop regulations and standards for transporting green hydrogen by rail.

By 2030, global demand for green hydrogen is expected to reach around 100 MMT. If India achieves its potential of being among the lowest-cost sources, investments will flow into the country for production, and it is expected to produce 10 per cent of that demand. With a boost in domestic demand, this figure could be even higher. In this demand boost, the fertiliser industry is expected to play a big role. In 2020–21, India imported 18 MMT of urea, di-ammonium phosphate, and ammonia with foreign exchange worth $6 billion. With hydrogen availability, these fertilisers can be produced domestically. Competitive bidding is envisaged for establishing fertiliser plants based on GH/GA, and two plants are targeted by 2034–35.

The National Green Hydrogen Mission includes Strategic Interventions for Green Hydrogen Transition (SIGHT) for evolving and implementing specific incentive schemes and programmes. Initially, incentives will be provided for domestic manufacture of fertilisers and production of green hydrogen.

Skill development will be an important task/area in the transition to green hydrogen. In addition to equipping technical institutes to prepare a workforce with the necessary skills for the production and use of hydrogen, it will also be necessary to reskill the workforce currently working with polluting fuels, which are intended to be phased out and replaced by hydrogen.

The mission recognises various risks in this transition. The supply chain risks are sought to be countered by supply chain diversifications. The risk of water and land availability will be minimised by optimal location decisions and by creating land banks. Rigorous design and enforcement of safety standards will be ensured. Technological risk will be averted with funding of multiple R&D and pilot projects, and the creation of collaborative platforms for industry, academia, and startups.

Geopolitical Aspects of Transition to Hydrogen

The global hydrogen market revenue for 2023 is estimated at more than $242 billion and is expected to grow to more than $400 billion by 2030.[20] For comparison, the corresponding figures for CNG are $184 billion and $276 billion, respectively, showing how hydrogen has already surpassed CNG. More important than these figures is the fact that it is a general-purpose energy carrier that can be produced locally from solar and wind energy. Thus, it combines the advantages of local generation, portability, and energy storage, while being the ultimate zero-carbon emission fuel. Once it becomes a source of energy that is cheaper than fossil fuels, it will cause unimaginable disruption to geopolitics, which is held slave to the ownership of underground reserves in some nations. Countries like India, which have been almost totally dependent on oil and gas imports, may find that within a short period of time, this drain on their foreign reserves has stopped and their balance of payment situation has changed for the better. Although there may be some international trade in hydrogen, it is expected that the rule/focus will be domestic production.

As discussed in Chapter 5, a large number of factors are at play that disrupt geopolitics. Will hydrogen exacerbate or mitigate these disruptions? In 2022, 0.3 GW of hydrogen capacity was reported. By the end of 2023, it had jumped to 14 GW; China—chronically import-dependent for oil and gas—had half this amount. It has become a leading nation in the manufacture of electrolysers, with 61 per cent of the global capacity located there as of May 2024. As with everything else, here also China has overcapacity, as demand is yet to pick up to that level. Simultaneously, the world may need 5,000 GW of electrolysers. Many countries are in the process of setting up electrolyser manufacturing facilities, but it is almost certain that Chinese electrolysers will be cheaper. There will soon be complaints about state subsidies in China and the harm they cause to local industries in other countries. Then, punitive tariffs on Chinese electrolysers will not be far behind.

China had more than 750 GW of utility-scale solar and wind capacity at the end of March 2024, and that figure increases to 1,120 GW after including distributed solar. With all this green electricity, China can easily use the surplus electrolysers to make green hydrogen and tempt other countries to buy it rather than strain their grids for manufacturing hydrogen. It can set up manufacturing units for steel and fertilisers in the poorer countries of Asia, Africa, and Latin America, and use its own hydrogen, brought by hydrogen-powered ships, for such manufacturing.

Take the case of landlocked Nepal. Today, it is dependent on India for its fuel requirements, which are transported by road over difficult terrain, including high-altitude areas in the north of the country. China may transition it to a hydrogen economy, using the vast sunshine and windy areas of Tibet to generate green hydrogen and transporting it to Nepal through pipelines. Given the emerging surplus capacity in China, this hydrogen may be cheaper than fossil fuels. China would sell fuel cells to Nepal to generate electricity locally, create hydrogen storage there, and may provide cheap fertilisers produced with hydrogen, as well as support heavy transport running on hydrogen. The small, poor neighbour of India will be firmly in the dragon's embrace, almost cutting it off from India. In addition, when China's falling population will make it difficult to maintain the People's Liberation Army's present size, Nepal's Gurkha soldiers, with their formidable reputation on the battlefield, could come in handy for China. Nepal, the buffer between India and Tibet for centuries, will cease to be so, and the always open India–Nepal border may become a thing of the past. All this could happen because of China's lead on the lightest element on earth.

While hydrogen will provide energy security to almost all nations, there is a flipside too. Horrifying videos of the *Hindenburg* airship, which used hydrogen for lift, burning during landing in 1937, led to a complete ban on airships until helium became available. Even more than eight decades after the tragedy, airships have not been able to find a sizable place in the aviation sector. Hydrogen, when burning with an ample supply of air, has a flame temperature of 2,045 degrees Celsius, hotter than natural gas or methane. When burning, it consumes oxygen at eight times its weight, producing superheated water vapour. What's worse is that at such high temperatures, nitrogen in the air is converted to nitrogen oxides (NOx), a major air pollutant. Hydrogen flames are invisible and may escape detection at an early stage of fire. Its burning speed is higher than that of all other combustible matter, with a maximum speed exceeding 3 metres per second. Hence, the fire spreads very quickly. Storage systems must have weaker roofs so that the explosion goes vertically and does not spread laterally, which imposes a restriction on the pressure at which it can be stored.

All these combustion characteristics of hydrogen will make storage sites attractive to saboteurs and terrorists. It is true that even oil and gas storages are amenable to such attacks by drones and missiles, but the much higher temperature and faster spread of a hydrogen fire place it in a class apart.

The International Renewable Energy Agency (IRENA) has made projections about how hydrogen has the potential to redraw the energy map of the world.[21] Sub-Saharan Africa appears to be leading the pack in the technical potential for producing green hydrogen under $1.5/kg by 2050. It is closely followed by the Middle East and North Africa. The distant second places are taken by North America, Latin America, and Oceania. Asia is third in order, with Europe at the tail. If we see the night illumination satellite images, some of the darkest spots today have the potential of being the brightest ones in 2050. These projections come with significant caveats, the biggest of which is about the direction of the cost of production. There are considerable differences in this cost across regions, and the production and export potential will alter if these costs maintain the same relative levels or even out by 2050. While current energy exporters like Australia, Saudi Arabia, and the US may maintain their exports even in the hydrogen scenario, they may face stiffer competition from some importers of today, such as Chile, Morocco, and Namibia, which are likely to become exporters in the hydrogen era. What is certain is that many of today's fossil-fuel dominating countries face the prospect of stranded assets in the near future. Hydrogen is expected to become cheaper and is unlikely to generate as much revenue, even for countries that remain energy exporters after the transition.

The world's first oil well was drilled in 1859; since then, there have been no earthshaking changes in oil and gas production technologies. In the hydrogen era, rapid technological innovations are expected, and countries that excel in this area will reap huge benefits. China, however, has maintained a model where it has successfully adopted the technological innovations of other countries and has focussed on manufacture based on such innovations. IRENA expects this trend to continue in the hydrogen era, and China will continue to dominate the hydrogen sector on the basis of inventions that come from abroad.

Countries with vast pipeline infrastructure for natural gas may have an initial advantage, as these pipelines can be repurposed to carry hydrogen. Where these gas pipelines are serving industrial clusters, there will be no issue of location of industries. However, where the industrial centres are being served by coal, oil, or electricity brought from elsewhere, new pipelines will be required. Africa, South Asia, and Latin America have very few existing pipelines and will need more investment in hydrogen transmission infrastructure to take full advantage of the transition to a hydrogen economy. China, Europe, and North America, on the other hand, will have a head start because of existing gas transmission infrastructure.

All these disparities and differences across countries and regions will result in large-scale realignment of geopolitical equations across the globe. Since many of the projections are based on variables that cannot be fully foreseen at present, the uncertain world of geopolitics is likely to be even more uncertain during the coming decade, during which hydrogen will play an increasing role in geoeconomics and geopolitics.

Part III
The Practitioners

12

Geopolitical Impact of Disinformation

Manjula Prasher

During more than thirty-six years with the Indian Postal Service, I witnessed the transformation of technology for information-sharing, from the humble postcard, letters, leaflets, magazines, and books delivered by the postman and the cryptic telegram, and later, to the smartphone powered by artificial intelligence. In between, there were the radio, TV, pagers, and photocopiers. Political pamphlets delivered by hand had played a significant role from the earliest stages of democracy, bringing an egalitarian element to the political discourse. Thomas Paine's, 'Common Sense', a 47-page pamphlet written during 1775–1776 and published in January 1776, can be fairly called the seed of nationhood and democracy in America. Written persuasively, it exhorted people to break the shackles of colonial rule and form a representative government. It had a wider circulation and readership than any other printed material up to that time. But more than its influence on events in America, which was profound, as it helped trigger the American War of Independence from British rule, was its impact on the geopolitics of the nations across the Atlantic. Paine propounded that all humans are created equal, and hence the distinction between the king and the subjects is false. He used passages from the Bible to refute the divine right of kings. 'Common Sense' was translated into French and spurred the French against the monarchy, just as it had spurred the Americans against the British Crown rule. In France, he was a hero and was even elected to the French Assembly, where he played a leading role in drafting the French Constitution.[1]

The dissemination of 'Common Sense' and Paine's other pamphlet, 'The Declaration of the Rights of Man and of the Citizen', written in 1789 in defence of the French Revolution, found widespread readership on the African continent in the early 20th century and helped in starting anti-colonial movements in Africa. The Chartist movement in Britain in the 1830s and 1840s created another form of mass movement through a document; millions of signatures were obtained on a short petition demanding universal suffrage.[2] These examples show how opinions can contribute to the evolution of social and political movements across continents.

Democracies are rooted in diversity of opinions, tolerance of divergent opinions, deliberations and debate, and harmonisation of apparent contradictions in opinion. As a result, democratic ideals have continuously evolved, and anathemas of yesterday, like abolition of slavery or voting rights for women, have today become cornerstones of democracy. This resilience of democracy is nurtured by the free flow of information that facilitates formation of multiple opinions. This has become the dividing line between democracies and dictatorships. The former zealously safeguard the right of citizens to know, however unpleasant the information may be. The latter go to great lengths to keep their citizens oblivious of unpleasant happenings within the country and beyond the borders. Thomas Paine called the government a 'necessary evil'. Democratic constitutions compel governments to embrace the idea, happily or otherwise. Dictatorships, on the other hand, have large parts of state apparatus indulging in filtering the truth and blocking or supplanting it, as did the Bureaux of Propaganda in George Orwell's *Brave New World*. Similar was the charter for the Department of Agitation and Propaganda in the Soviet Union or the Central Propaganda Department of the Chinese Communist Party, giving them the monikers of the Iron Curtain and the Bamboo Curtain, respectively, behind which their citizens suffer the absence of information.

Information has two components: facts and opinions. Democratic propaganda is expected to keep the factual part of information value-neutral, and a free press is expected to play the hawk's eye in pointing out where facts are being filtered or doctored. Opinion is not value-neutral, but in democracies equal access to the means of dissemination would mean that all shades of opinion could circulate in the public domain. All of this did not bother dictators as long as facts and opinions were disseminated by individuals only through speeches and pamphlets. People could be barred from entering, arrested, and deported, and printed material could be seized at the borders and destroyed. Radio was the first means of information for the masses that did not respect national borders. During World War II, the Allied powers used the radio to keep the citizens in their countries and in the enemy territories informed of the events on the battlefields as well as political developments. The Axis powers—Fascist Germany, Italy, and Imperial Japan—also used the radio to boost the morale of their citizens with doctored stories and propaganda. Television remained confined to national boundaries for some time until satellite TV broke that barrier. However, satellite dishes could not be hidden as easily as radio antennas.

The internet was perceived as the biggest threat to dictators, but this hope was belied by the ease with which access could be controlled by local administrations. Even satellite phones did not help, as they could be easily detected when used, and they remain expensive and banned even in many democracies. Similarly, satellite terminals like VSAT or Elon Musk's Starlink cannot be operated without acquiescence of the state. Thus, the Chinese remain behind the Great Firewall that insulates them from the internet and its applications like Google, Facebook, and Twitter. They have to be content in their cocoon with corresponding Chinese applications like Weibo and WeChat, which are heavily patrolled by a two-million-strong cyber army, and it takes less than a minute for objectionable material to be removed.

The world would have continued to live with dictators keeping their citizens behind these firewalls, but they went a step further. The dictatorial regimes repurposed the means of information to hack into democracies' servers to steal technologies and citizens' data, and they did not stop at that. Disinformation became their tool of choice to sabotage democracies as artificial intelligence has enabled them considerably in this latent war. The means of disinformation have become so subtle that any amount of patrolling the internet, which is certainly frowned upon by freedom lovers, is time- and resource- consuming, and by the time the source is detected and blocked, it has already caused the intended harm and moved on. The geopolitical situation in the world and in democracies in particular has become bound with the issue of disinformation.

The Merriam-Webster dictionary defines disinformation as 'false information deliberately and often covertly spread (as by the planting of rumours) in order to influence public opinion or obscure the truth'. The ability of non-human Chatbots on the internet to simultaneously post the same information under different handles increases the credibility of the false information being spread. AI further assists in increasing this credibility by altering the form and language to make it appear that the posts are from unconnected humans. AI also assists in identifying the vulnerabilities of the individuals, as gleaned from their past choices and interactions on the internet. Then disinformation is tailor-made for each individual to optimally exploit those vulnerabilities.

A distinction is made between misinformation and disinformation: the former is false or inaccurate information—getting the facts wrong. The latter is false information that is deliberately intended to mislead—intentionally misstating the facts.[3] Misinformation may be inadvertent or due to a lack of correct information. Disinformation is intentional and targeted to help in achieving an outcome that cannot be achieved by transparently sharing information. When it is done by agents acting on behalf of a foreign country, its goal is usually to impact geopolitics by replacing military or economic warfare with information warfare. All the tactics of military war, such as concealment, subterfuge, and deception, are used in this information war.

An enemy can achieve the goal of impacting geopolitics through disinformation by several means:

- Creating an apparent alternative presence in the information space
- Sowing seeds of doubt about an ongoing discourse
- Promoting schism in the society
- Hurting the sense of national unity
- Partisan push in the democratic process

Creating an Apparent Alternative Presence in the Information Space

The alternative, apparently a legitimate democratic political discourse, can give a contorted direction to the discussion, which can fossilise into mistaken beliefs and force the hand of decision-makers. For example, China tries to harm India by creating direct threats to the border regions by establishing hostile border settlements and infrastructure, amassing forces and equipment, and aggressive displays at the border, accompanied by occasional calibrated hostilities. It is the only country that opposes India's case for a permanent seat on the Security Council and also opposes India's accession to the Nuclear Suppliers Group as well as uses its veto power to block India's initiative to designate certain individuals based in Pakistan as terrorists. It supplements these efforts by disinformation that China has no hegemonic goals through its controlled media in the country and abroad, its agents in the so-called India–China Friendship Association, and its Confucius institutes in various countries. The propaganda proclaims that China respects the sovereignty and integrity of all nations, while China protests vehemently when an Indian dignitary, including the prime minister, visits areas it claims as part of its territory. Although the Chinese narrative flies in the face of all facts, when repeated incessantly at every international forum, it becomes an alternative narrative.

Sowing the Seeds of Doubt about an Ongoing Discourse

The enemy can try to sow seeds of doubt about an ongoing discourse through disinformation, resulting in cynicism about its utility. This can result in indifference, disregard, and even dislike for the democratic process. This was on full display during the deliberations on the origin of COVID-19. While all evidence pointed to the fact that it originated in China and then spread to the rest of the world, by accident or by design, China created disinformation by blaming it on the rest of the world, falsely asserting that it came to China through imported seafood or US military personnel who had visited the country. In times of serious economic and social difficulties caused by the pandemic, China spread disinformation that while it was handling the epidemic effectively, democracies were failing at that. The world later saw the truth as democracies quickly returned to normal functioning and experienced an economic rebound, while China continued its lockdowns much longer, followed by a sudden opening up under pressure from agitations that threatened Xi Jinping and the Chinese Communist Party. The large number of deaths after the abrupt withdrawal of restrictions, estimated to be one and a half million, put paid to China's disinformation campaign. Yet, China persisted with its disinformation by issuing White Papers on why China has a democracy that works, and the US has one that doesn't.

Promoting Schism in Society

While the democratic process relies on harmonising divergent opinions into a middle path, disinformation can hinder this process by strengthening the feeling of victimisation in sub-groups, leading to the formation of extreme views and their fossilisation if sustained over time. This has the effect of creating a permanent schism in society, making it prone to internal conflict, and therefore, weak. While the Indian democracy permitted space to the communist ideology, which enabled the formation of communist governments in Kerala and West Bengal, the Soviet Union and later China, prompted the communists in India to take over the polity through the workers', students', and academics' organisations. The effort soon shifted from mere ideology that would be legitimate in a democracy to armed struggle against the state. Various shades of violent left-wing movements, including Naxalism and Maoism, penetrated the democracies of India and Nepal. In Nepal's case, they were successful in overthrowing the constitutional monarchy, which by itself cannot be faulted. But the entrenchment of communist ideology in that country and the disinformation spread by their ideologues on behalf of China and against India led to several years of difficult relations between Nepal and India. The influence of communism widened the schism between the northern and southern parts of the country and even threatened to split the country into a Chinese-influenced north and an India-influenced south. Deft handling by India over the years, along with a realisation by the Nepalese leaders of the pitfalls of throwing their lot with the Chinese Communists, has gradually restored Indo-Nepal relations to a semblance of normalcy.

In India, too, the communists lost their credibility in West Bengal and, to a large extent, in Kerala as well, due to the poor economic performance of these states, which have a large educated population. The absence of domestic employment opportunities led to the mass migration of both skilled and unskilled Keralites to Gulf countries, where they worked in semi-slave conditions to sustain their families back home. However, like in Nepal, communist ideas found deeper roots in the poorer, more backward states of India, creating a Maoist belt running through the forests and tribal areas of Nepal, Bihar, Jharkhand, Chhattisgarh, Odisha, and Andhra Pradesh. Again, thanks to the resilience of democracy, as elections were held regularly in these areas, even at the peak of extremism, the Maoists are now on their last legs with the pace of development picking up. Communism, which is born in poverty and sustains itself by perpetuating that poverty through disinformation about development, seems to be finally losing its roots in India.

We can mention here Pakistan's disinformation campaign against India, which is focussed on the large Muslim population and the people of Kashmir. The disinformation campaign and the two-nation theory, which was the basis for the creation of Pakistan, suffered a serious blow with the creation of Bangladesh. Yet, Pakistan, actively encouraged by China, continued with its disinformation campaign, particularly through bodies like the Organisation for Islamic Cooperation (OIC), where Pakistan-sponsored resolutions have been periodically passed on Indian Muslims and Kashmir. This had prolonged and deep-rooted consequences for India: Terrorists could commit atrocities in India with the assistance of a local support base created through such disinformation. Terrorism is, however, a double-edged weapon; Pakistan and China are reaping the harvest they had sowed. China's trillion-dollar investment in the China–Pakistan Economic Corridor (CPEC) is about to come undone due to repeated attacks on infrastructure and Chinese citizens. Pakistan's existence as a nation is increasingly being called into question, with events that bear a growing resemblance to those that led to the creation of Bangladesh.

Hurting the Sense of Pride in National Unity

All nations are diverse in some way or another, whether in linguistic, religious, ethnic, cultural diversity, or based on exclusive behavioural or cultural traits of sub-groups constituting the nation. These sub-groups believe in belonging to the nation because the traits that overlap are considered more vital for nationhood than those that are diverse. Neighbouring societies that have been interacting with each other over millennia develop overlaps and commonalities that bind them into a single nation, even as they hold fast to diverse and even conflicting traits. This is what has happened in India. The belief in being Indian has been nurtured by continuous and dense interaction between the people on this vast subcontinent, even though they remain linguistically, culturally, and ritually distinct. The emergence of faiths like Buddhism and Jainism, which denied many fundamental axioms of the predecessor faiths, did not undermine that belief in being part of one nation whose boundaries were recognised by all foreigners, despite the fact that it was divided into a large number of political entities. Invaders like the Greeks, Shakas, Kushans, Muslims, and Christian Europeans, and asylum seekers like the Jews and Zoroastrians, all talked about India when planning their invasions or seeking refuge. Most of them found the unifying factors in conformity with their culture and merged with the 'nation', while maintaining their distinct identity in non-overlapping areas. Yet, there were those who preached against accepting any substantive overlap whatsoever and remained part of the 'nation' from where they had come. These are the ones that become targets of disinformation.

Disinformation may not cause a rupture or schism but may weaken the idea of national unity. 'Us' and 'them' remain inseparable parts of joint families, neighbourhoods, towns, and cities, as long as these do not hurt the idea of nationhood. These usually promote competition, much like opposing teams on the sports field. The idea is to be better than 'them' without hurting them. Yet, any hint of 'us' and 'them' when talking about the nation damages the social fabric, and then hurting the 'other' becomes part of the game. The disinformation campaign seeks to exploit this vulnerability and uses it to create Trojan horses within the nation that may hurt national unity through spying, influence peddling, or physical, economic, or ideological sabotage. Portugal tried this for a considerable time with the local Christian population after Goa was liberated by the Indian forces, and Pakistan has been trying this with Indian Muslims. In both cases, over time, it became clear that India was intrinsically too cohesive to be broken by these efforts, particularly when those instigating the idea of 'otherness' became insignificant players on the geopolitical scene.

Partisan Push in the Democratic Process

Disinformation can play a partisan role in the democratic process, helping groups that are deemed favourable or weakening those who cannot be won over by threats, coercion, or inducements. This is the most talked about aspect of disinformation, and when detected at the time of important elections, it is labelled election meddling. Both Russia and China have been accused of doing this in the US and in some European countries. China, and to some extent the US, have been accused of meddling in Taiwan's elections. Elections in Latin America are frequently the focus of foreign meddling. China has often tried to influence elections in Australia through its large diaspora in that country. Comically, democracies are in no position to retaliate because there are no elections worth mentioning in Russia or China. All that the Western democracies can do is to influence the voters around the borders of countries like Russia and China to weaken the dictatorship's influence there and maintain a stronger foothold in the neighbourhood of the 'enemy', as is the case with Taiwan or Latin America.

The disinformation campaign for the purpose of election meddling has the potential of evolving into a war. The 2014 elections in Ukraine were, by proxy, 'contested' by both the US and Russia. The American side won the election, leading to the 'losing' Putin to annex Crimea and start the civil war in the eastern provinces of Ukraine, culminating in the 2022 invasion. As the war enters its fourth year, there is repeated talk of the use of nuclear weapons, showing how significant and dangerous the role of disinformation can be in elections and geopolitics.

Given the perils of disinformation for the victim nation, and at times, even for the aggressor, why do nations indulge in it? It is a low-cost alternative to an outright war; it is easy to deny and difficult for the other to retaliate. Maybe, it is the future of war. With AI, it could be more damaging to democracies than anything else dictators may do. Yet, the past has shown that ultimately democracies prevail—only the future will tell us how.

13

Produce in India, Feed the World

Sanjeev Chopra

Prime Minister Lal Bahadur Shastri's clarion call to the nation in 1965, 'Jai Jawan, Jai Kisan'[1], aptly sums up the intimate connection between national security and food security. A country must accord the highest priority to research, investments, training, and a regular review of both these crucial pillars: the jawan (the soldier) for defending the territory, and the kisan (the farmer) for ensuring that the land and water resources are put to optimal use for the country. The achievements in both sectors have to be acknowledged. In the last decade, India established the National War Memorial at India Gate to honour its soldiers, and the Krishi Karman Awards to recognise states with the highest improvement in food grain production. Jai Vigyan[2], the power of science, has been added to the slogan 'Jai Jawan, Jai Kisan', lending greater heft to the proposition. Food security is inextricably linked to energy security, and India, at present, is heavily dependent on energy imports. The Economic Survey 2023 includes a plan to make India energy independent by 2047. The study 'Pathways to Atmanirbhar Bharat' by the US Department of Energy's Lawrence Berkeley National Laboratory supports this timeline.[3]

This point was reiterated by India's National Security Advisor Ajit Doval[4] in his address at the 34th convocation of the Govind Ballabh Pant University of Agriculture and Technology (GBPAUT)[5], held in February 2023, explaining the intimate connection between national security and food security. He said that a nation which has to depend on food from an external source is not really sovereign, further adding, 'But in 75 years, India has ensured that not only it is self-sufficient in food grains but it is also in a position to export them to help other countries.'[6] This was significant in the context of some of the best irrigated lands being left behind in West Punjab in 1947. Doval explained, 'After partition, 22 million hectares of cultivable land went to Pakistan and many thought that India would not be able to feed its 35-crore population. Our population is now 135 crore, food grain production has increased to 315 million tonnes. We not only feed ourselves, but also export food grains.'[7] However, he also pointed out that the country must put in more efforts to increase farm productivity because China was producing more food grains than India, despite having a lesser amount of cultivable land. He added that no army can march on an empty stomach, and if the nation does not have a strong army, it will not be able to preserve its stock of food. Only nations which make policies conducive to both can achieve holistic success on all fronts.

The First and Foremost Task of a Sovereign

Contemporary history is replete with examples of nations which had strong armies with nuclear capabilities, but their political economy was fragile, as they could not take care of their food production. In fact, in the chapter 'The Starving Empire: Food and Politics in the USSR' in the 2023 book *Bread and Autocracy: Food, Politics, and Security in Putin's Russia*[8], it has been argued that Soviet (and Russian) history 'was a constant and ultimately failed struggle to overcome, adapt to, and survive the chronic and often acute food shortages that more than once escalated into widespread famines'[9]. The book also discusses the critical role of food shortages in the collapse of the Soviet Union. That such shortages can be overcome in just two decades is described vividly in the book: 'Russia, until the early 2000s a major importer of grain, is not only self-sufficient, but is the world's largest exporter ... The value of Russia's agricultural exports is larger than that of weapons, an industry for which it is globally renowned.' The recent disaffection in North Korea also stems from the fact that this nuclear-powered country is facing recurrent famines on account of its inability to address the issue of food shortage.

As such, the NSA's remarks are pertinent. Since time immemorial, the first task of a sovereign has been to ensure that the granary is full, and there is sufficient reserve for a difficult year.[10] A population's access to sufficient, safe, and nutritious food has been a core state interest since ancient times. In the Bible, Joseph rose to power after resolving Egypt's food shortages; in China, numerous Chinese emperors, including the fabled Ming dynasty, lost the 'Mandate of Heaven' or the right to rule, when they failed to address famines. The decline of the Sumerian and Harappan civilisations has also been attributed to their failure to produce adequate food for their populations. It was a common practice for the Romans to seize food from areas with ample resources, such as Egypt. Following the death of Cleopatra in 30 BCE, Egypt became vulnerable to depredation. Recurrent famines during the British rule over India posed a real threat to their legitimacy and rationale; famine conditions were a recurrent theme in the presidential addresses[11] at the annual sessions of the Indian National Congress at the turn of the century. The extravagant Coronation Durbar held in 1903[12], when large parts of the country were reeling under drought and famine, stirred nationalist sentiments. The three million deaths during the man-made Bengal Famine of 1943[13] marked the end of British legitimacy. In the 1950s and 1960s, at the height of the Cold War, the United States strategically decided to implement initiatives to increase food accessibility for its allies and potential allies, and India was also a beneficiary of the PL 480 programme. However, this also meant that India's foreign policy options were put to a severe test, which spurred us to move beyond the 'ship-to-mouth' existence.

The failure of the Mahalanobis model[14] to address issues of agriculture and livelihood led to massive price hikes and dependence on food imports from the US, Canada, and Australia. This trend was reversed by Lal Bahadur Shastri, who inducted Chidambaram Subramaniam[15] as the food and agriculture minister. This was the period when the green and white revolutions[16] took firm roots in India, setting India on a path of high growth in staples like wheat and rice, as well as milk. The green revolution package included high-yielding varieties of seeds, an adequate supply of credit and fertilisers, and most importantly, an assured procurement based on the Minimum Support Price (MSP)[17]. By the mid-seventies, India had become self-sufficient in wheat and rice, but problems of malnutrition, stunting, and lack of a balanced diet remained. As incomes grew and diets changed, there was an increase in the demand for protein-rich foods—milk, eggs, and dairy products, as well as pulses and oilseeds. Even though the production of pulses has grown substantially, we will need to continue importing these commodities in the foreseeable future.

Food Security in the Global Discourse

The 1974 World Food Conference[18], and even more significantly the 1996 World Food Summit[19] in Rome[20] in

November 1996, drew high-level political attention to the issues of chronic hunger and malnutrition. An important outcome of the summit was the adoption of the Rome Declaration on World Food Security, which reaffirmed the right of everyone to have access to sufficient, safe, and nutritious food. The declaration also recognised that poverty eradication is essential to improving access to food. This is what paved the way for the Millennium Development Goals (MDGs) and the Sustainable Development Goals (SDGs) by the UN to which every member country, including India, is a signatory. This was also the first successful attempt at establishing a universally accepted definition and norm for 'food security'. The conference agreed that 'food security, at the individual, household, national, regional and global levels [is achieved] when all people, at all times, have physical and economic access to sufficient, safe and nutritious food that meets their dietary needs and food preferences for a healthy and active life'.[21] With this definition, it became clear that 'food insecurity is multidimensional, and affects people at the global, regional, national, sub-national, and household levels. It presents itself in various forms, such as chronic, acute, and transient'.[22] Member states agreed to 'pledge their political will and (their) common and national commitment to achieving food security of all and to an ongoing effort to eradicate hunger in all countries, with an immediate view of reducing the number of undernourished people to half their present level no later than 2015'.[23] This was accepted by the United Nations—first in the MDGs, then the SDGs[24], and now in the development agenda of the SDGs from 2015–30.

The 2008 Economic Meltdown

The salience of food security in the overall security paradigm was reinforced during the 2008 economic meltdown.[25] It also highlighted the vulnerability of nations with regard to food security due to currency fluctuations and arbitrary restrictions on the export of agricultural commodities, including staples. It became clear that securing a sufficient stock of food was perhaps the most important task of the sovereign authority. The distance between civilisation and chaos is just nine meals.[26]

The 2008 crisis saw two distinct responses, both of which were initially at odds with each other, but later reconciled over a series of conferences organised under the auspices of the FAO, in conjunction with the World Food Programme (WFP)[27] and the International Fund for Agricultural Development (IFAD)[28]—the three Rome-based organisations dealing with these issues. The two approaches have been described as:

- Addressing the root causes with improvements in production and technology, including research and innovation; incentives for private investment; sound natural resource management related to soils, biodiversity, and water; and coordinated engagement for climate change adaptation and mitigation
- Responding to and preventing food emergencies through sound trade, bioenergy, and grain reserves policies and prevention of excessive speculation in food markets

Both these approaches were led by India and China. Since both nations had large populations, had suffered famines in the past few decades, and were very keen to ensure that their citizens would have adequate insurance against food vulnerability, they were in agreement regarding the public stockholding of food as an exception to the World Trade Organization (WTO) norms.

However, while China (as a state) was keen on acquiring lands in Africa, Central Asia, and Latin America to insulate itself from the global price volatility by securing its own resources—such as equipment, seeds, fertilisers, and manpower—and bringing the entire produce back to China, India's approach was quite the opposite.

India offered a partnership to Africa[29] to develop its own food security, in the sense that the first right to the produce would belong to the host country, and any surplus (if and when it happens) could be traded globally for better returns to both stakeholders. India was not acquiring land; it was facilitating production and global trading after meeting the food security requirements of the host country.[30]

Agriculture Outsourcing

The first internal paper for the Ministry of Agriculture and Farmers' Welfare was assigned to me in September 2010, titled 'Agriculture Outsourcing: Possibility, Prospects and Policy Options for India'.[31] The immediate context was the 'land rush', which saw over 20 million hectares of land being acquired by states and investment firms (many backed by sovereign wealth funds) in the four-year period between 2006 and 2010, with the trend gaining momentum after the 2008 global meltdown, which was aggravated by disruptions in the word food trade.

With respect to food security, the lead interventions were made by China, Japan, Korea, and Malaysia in East Asia, apart from Bahrain, Jordan, Kuwait, Qatar, Saudi Arabia, and the UAE in the Middle East. These predominantly rich economies were worried about the tightening food markets and sought to outsource their domestic food production by gaining access and/or control over farms and agricultural lands. The second school of thought was that financial returns stemmed from the recent trends of high world food prices and low land prices in many parts of the world. The financial meltdown led investors such as BlackRock and Morgan Stanley to acquire large tracts of land, including in Ukraine. The speed with which this was progressing raised alarm bells:

Was it neo-imperialism? In any case, the US Department of State took note of Chinese interventions, from food as a national security perspective to Beijing's desire to secure nutrition for its massive population, which may be a primary motive for some actions that others consider aggressive, such as the purchase of land in Africa and investment in agriculture and fisheries around the world, and that Chinese engagement may fundamentally alter the global food regime.

This was the context in which the Union Ministry of Agriculture and Farmers' Welfare sought the views of the Indian Institute of Foreign Trade (IIFT)[32], the Manohar Parrikar Institute for Defence Studies and Analyses (IDSA),[33] and the Research and Information System for Developing Countries (RIS)[34]. The three knowledge organisations (with IIFT as the lead) were assigned the task of preparing a document for interministerial consultation. Shri U.S. Bhatia, who had just relinquished his charge as India's ambassador to the World Trade Organization (WTO), was chosen to be the lead author of the study. He stated in his report, 'Given the increasing volatility in international prices of food crops in recent years, it is essential that we explore more stable international opportunities for meeting our food needs. Therefore, offshore agriculture investments emerge as a necessary concomitant to India's policy framework for addressing food security. As only a small proportion of food production is internationally traded, a large country like India cannot depend on food imports to meet any shortages or deficits.'[35] He concluded, 'The Ministry of Agriculture will obviously need to play the nodal role in the initiative … Given the importance of the matter, the Ministry of Agriculture may consider establishing dedicated divisions for Africa and Latin America. These divisions will maintain data on land availability and their agro-climatic conditions and continuously monitor the developments in host country policies, particularly those relating to land acquisitions, seed laws, import of capital equipment, re-export policies, etc. This would enable the ministry to develop a country-wise matrix with identified variables that would assess the opportunities, risks, and stability that would support potential Indian investors.'[36]

Responsible Investments in Agriculture

However, the global outcry against transborder land transactions led to FAO convening a series of meetings on Responsible Investment in Agriculture and Food Systems.[37] By this time, the Ministry of Agriculture and Farmers' Welfare, in consultation with the ministries of external affairs, commerce, fertilisers, and defence, took the view that while India may extend support to entrepreneurs who may wish to invest in lands abroad, as a nation, India will refrain from this. This was the position taken by me[38] at the FAO conference: The first rights over the produce from the land, water, and natural resources belonged to the local population. Land could be used for growing commercial crops only after the local and regional food security had been assured. Thus, a region should divert its productive areas to cotton or tobacco only if there is an institutional mechanism in place to provide food security. China was also compelled to agree to this, but has now taken up internal agriculture outsourcing, that is, leveraging technology, financial and human resources from across the country to bring hitherto uncultivated or single-crop lands into round-the-year crop cultivation cycles. Perhaps this is what the NSA had in mind when he challenged the agriculture scientists to devise appropriate packages for the large tracts of land where production and productivity is far below the national norms.

When I was with the Ministry of Agriculture and Farmers' Welfare, India legislated the National Food Security Act

(NFSA) 2013 (two years before the commitment of 2015), with both the political dispensations—the Congress-led UPA and the BJP-led NDA—voting in favour, even though some BJP MPs did raise issues[39] with regard to the implementation criterion. The NFSA provides highly subsidised food grains to up to 75 per cent of the rural population and 50 per cent of the urban population. Although the Constitution of India does not have any explicit provision regarding the right to food, the fundamental right to life, enshrined in Article 21 of the Constitution, may be interpreted to include the right to live with human dignity, and this would include the right to food and other basic necessities. In India, 'food security' at the household level is being addressed through the Public Distribution System (PDS) and the Targeted Public Distribution System (TPDS). The act is also gender-sensitive; the ration card is issued to the eldest woman of the household, aged 18 years or above. The total allocation for the current fiscal under this head is Rs 2.05 lakh crore, and the coverage extends to over 80 crore individuals. This is also aligned with the United Nations General Assembly's Sustainable Development Goal 2.

Food Security in Times of Crisis

When the COVID-19 outbreak took place in 2020, the government launched the Pradhan Mantri Garib Kalyan Anna Yojana (PMGKAY)[40] to provide each person covered under the National Food Security Act 2013 with an additional 5 kg grains (wheat or rice). This has now been extended for another five years from 1 January 2024. What is even more significant is the fact that this benefit of free rations can be availed through portability by any migrant labour or beneficiary under the One Nation One Ration Card (ONORC) plan from nearly 5 lakh ration shops across the country.

One major realisation in the aftermath of COVID-19 was that countries with a resilient food security ecosystem—from pre-production to post-harvest management and last-mile delivery to households through the extensive network of the PDS—were able to face the situation with greater fortitude compared to those that were dependent on imports. COVID-19 made countries, from the continental-sized Australia[41] to well-developed economies like the UK[42] and Singapore[43], realise that they had to build agriculture systems on which they could depend, even during emergencies. This is the context in which the UK decided to reduce its very high dependence on food imports and Australia decided to focus on making the hinterland of each major city—Brisbane, Melbourne, and Sydney—as well as each province 'self-dependent' on critical staples. Meanwhile, Singapore has committed to the 30/30 and 50/40 pledges. The island nation aims to produce at least 30 per cent of its food domestically by 2030, and 50 per cent by 2040.

The lessons for India were that dependence on fertiliser imports[44] had to be brought down to the bare minimum by innovative mechanisms like fertigation, soluble fertilisers, and aerial spraying through drones. Green hydrogen and ammonia produced domestically in India can help improve fertiliser security by reducing the country's dependence on imported raw materials and limiting emissions from fertiliser manufacturing.[45] India imports 56 per cent of its edible oil requirements, and most of it is subsidised for the consumer by the state governments.[46]

The situation with regard to pulses is better: the import component is less than 15 per cent and the fillip to the production of pulses and oilseeds had to be taken up on a war footing. The expression 'war footing' becomes important in the context of the interconnectedness between food security and national security.

Large countries like India, and for that matter China, cannot afford to depend either on global aid or trade for meeting their domestic requirements of food, since if either of the countries enters the word market to buy or sell major commodities like wheat, rice, pulses, oilseeds, and sugar, the price volatility is very high on account of the sheer volumes. On the other hand, if a country like Singapore, or for that matter Nepal or Mauritius, were to purchase their entire supplies, there would be just a 'delta difference' to the world prices.

COVID-19 also made it clear that while chips, computers, fabrics, machine tools, design, and a host of other services can be globalised, food can be outsourced only at great peril. Therefore, there is a 'significant reversal' of the outsourcing model that was tried out in the first and second decades of this century. The second major lesson from COVID-19 was that while combating a global pandemic required global cooperation, national-level strategies, and regional-level rollouts, the actual task of mitigation and amelioration fell on the shoulders of local authorities—hospitals, emergency services, police, school systems, and municipalities. These services were responsible for preparing a coordinated strategy to ensure that the virus was contained.

The Time Lag between Crisis and Mitigation Strategy

There is always a time lag between an emergency and the response to it. Thus, when COVID-19 began its spread from China to the rest of the world in a matter of weeks, it took time for a coordinated strategy, whether it was travel-related protocol, medical kits for prevention and cure, vaccination regime, oxygen cylinders, or a robust chain to supply critical staples to the most vulnerable sections of society across the world. From the World Health Organization (WHO)[47] to the United Nations, and the Bill & Melinda Gates Foundation (BMGF)[48], the response was quick, sharp, and focussed because deaths were being reported on an hourly basis, and there was a demand for immediate action by the media and civic society, and the political leaders rose to the challenge because it stared them in the face.

However, the major difference between a 'black swan' event like COVID-19, with a litany of deaths confronting us, and the response to a long-term crisis like climate change is comparatively lackadaisical. This challenge—perhaps even more consequential than COVID—has not received the quick and rapid response commensurate with its gravitas. The issue of climate change has been in the 'present continuous' ever since the rise of the Industrial Revolution, and it is now growing at a pace that is causing alarm among decision-makers and leaders from across the world. Therefore, the Intergovernmental Panel on Climate Change (IPCC) was established as the UN body for assessing the science related to climate change. It was created by the United Nations Environment Programme (UNEP) and the World Meteorological Organization (WMO) in 1988 to provide political leaders with periodic scientific assessments concerning climate change, its implications and risks, as well as to propose adaptation and mitigation strategies. The IPCC has been at the forefront of advising governments, corporations, and civil society about two possible strategies to arrest climate change: these involve transitions in the way we meet our energy and food requirements. Yet, the strategies for both transitions must ensure that the process does not disrupt our energy and food security. While the oil crises have occupied centre stage in the discourse on strategic thought—from sea lanes of communication (SLOC)[49] to alternative fuel sources—not enough attention has been paid to how we produce what we eat.

Alternative Fuels and Alternative Proteins

This is where India has the real potential to emerge as a thought leader with an actionable agenda on two of the most important transitions that the world has to make, alternative fuels and alternative proteins, especially the latter. While much has been written about alternative fuels, and India has assumed a leadership role in the International Solar Alliance[50], this chapter will focus on alternative proteins and India's potential to become the world leader in the research, production, and value chains for alternative proteins, which is also in keeping with the concepts of Ahimsa[51] and sustainability. This also fits well into the discussion paper 'Produce in India: Feed the World,'[52] which talks about strategies for leveraging the mosaic of agriculture production in India. These include everything from organic farming by default[53] to natural and regenerative farming[54] by marginal farmers;[55] conventional farming by small farmers; capital-intensive production by medium and small farmers; horticulturists engaged in high-value agriculture (HVA)[56] of fruits, nuts, vegetables, and flowers; dairy farmers who have made India the world's largest milk-producing nation; and last but not least, biotechnology-driven companies that produce alternative protein options, such as vegetarian meats. Each of these production systems has its own ecosystem in terms of livelihoods, fertiliser use, marketing, and returns to farmers. They can all work in conjunction with each other because, as things stand today, the 110–115 MT of wheat and 125–130 MT[57] of rice cannot be produced by organic methods alone. In the case of the first two (organic and natural farming), the effort must focus on ensuring that producers get the best and most remunerative prices so that production systems are sustained and villages, especially those along the borders, are not abandoned, as in the case of the higher reaches of Uttarakhand.

But the real challenge and opportunity, one in which India can assume global leadership, as it has done in the case of IT, is in the arena of biotechnology. As Shri Atal Bihari Vajpayee put it so succinctly, while IT (information technology) stands for 'India Today', BT (biotechnology) stands for 'Bharat Tomorrow'.

Given that India is perhaps one of the few countries in the world where vegetarian food has an established and growing market, it is important to understand the growing global market for vegan and vegetarian foods, not only from the perspective of ethical concerns related to animal cruelty and human health issues but also from an environmental standpoint. The damage caused to rainforests in the Amazon, along with CO_2 emissions from cattle, has become a significant part of the discourse on environment and climate change. In a recent discourse titled 'Barbecue Earth'[58], hosted by the Carnegie Endowment for International Peace[59], a major share of global warming and climate change has been attributed to 'meat as a commodity'. However, such is the pressure exerted by industrial meat producers and ranchers of the Americas on the UN that any discussion on what meat production does to the planet is put on the backburner. Meat and livestock rearing creates an enormous, unnecessary demand for energy, water, crop inputs, land, and other resources. Currently, more than one-third of the global grain supply is fed to animals. Therefore, reducing animal agriculture and increasing the production of alternative proteins is a path towards improved food security and public health.

Biotech to the Fore?

Much like the silicon chip, the on-the-horizon technology for changing the way we have imagined our food systems is biotechnology. In our quest for alternative and sustainable proteins, it offers a large potential market with many spin-offs or catalysing connections to other fields of advanced manufacturing, where IT, robotics, plant genetics, and food technologies will also play equally important roles. India must look at the global export market. It is the second largest (buffalo) beef exporter in the world.[60] When global trends are showing a significant increase towards veganism[61] and vegetarian meats, should India be breaking its own path or follow the trend?

Beijing is well-positioned to benefit from a protein transition. It has drawn up a five-year plan dedicated to research and production augmentation.[62] Can India beat China in this new paradigm shift? The fact is that in the first round of agriculture outsourcing, China had performed much better than us—and it was not because of us, but rather the large outcry against the 'land grab' that finally led the FAO to change its position. It should also be clear to us that whether it is the FAO or UNESCO, all countries try to present their positions in the language of universal public good! In this round, the government has still not fully played an active role, neither has the industry envisaged its true potential, and academia has not provided us with a holistic picture that captures the entire value chain, including its possible impact on incomes and livelihoods of those engaged in this sector.

Although we live in an interconnected world, food security is the key responsibility of the sovereign, and every nation and region within a nation must strive to utilise the available land and water resources to achieve it. Second, publicly funded national agriculture and research systems[63] must address issues relating to climate vulnerability and invest in crops that will adapt to the new conditions. Third, newer techniques, such as micro irrigation, in conjunction with drones and satellite imagery, have to be deployed to preserve water and nano-fertilisers to ensure the optimal use of resources. Fourth, given the new temperature control techniques or the extensive use of central heating and air conditioning, diets must reflect a corresponding change. In other words, the shift from red meat to white meat (poultry and fish) and the reduced use of dairy products can also mark a significant change in the agricultural production pattern. Then there is the plant-based sector, which aims to meet consumer demand for new product variations, with opportunities for standalone products, new formats, technologies, and the latest innovations.

The India plant-based meat market[64] is characterised by the presence of many local, regional, and global vendors. The key players operating in this market include ITC, GoodDot, Evo Foods, Mister Veg, Blue Tribe, Greenest Foods, Vezlay, Wakao, Imagine Meats, Veggie Champ, GoodDO—The Vegan Eatery, PlantMade, and other prominent players. This is where a new strategic partnership between the food processing industry, academia, biotechnology, health industries, food departments, and regulatory agencies like the Food Safety and Standards Authority of India (FSSAI) should work more closely to ensure that—just as in the case of the International Solar Alliance—the new protein and nutrition alliance should be led by India. This, coupled with investments in micro irrigation to enhance the productivity of large tracts of land, especially in the 112 aspirational districts[65], will go a long way in making India not only food secure but also helping it in its quest to lead the world towards a healthier environment and lifestyle.

Let vigyan and anusandhan join forces with the jawans and the kisans, and let us leverage our technologies, institutions, polices, as well as our traditions of robust entrepreneurship to 'Produce in India, Feed the World'.

14

Regenerating India through Inclusive, Sustainable Growth

Rabindra Nath Sen

A group of people on a ship, cut off from the rest of the universe, is a powerful metaphor; the group will survive or perish with the ship. Swami Vivekananda used the ship metaphor for our nation: 'If there are holes in this national ship, this society of ours, we are its children, let us go and stop the holes. Let us gladly do it with our hearts' blood; and if we cannot, then let us die. We will make a plug of our brains and put them into the ship, but condemn it never.'[1] Another visionary, R. Buckminster Fuller, usually called Bucky, used the phrase 'Spaceship Earth' in his 1983 book *Grunch of Giants* to describe humans as the passengers and crew aboard this large ship who had to work together to keep the planet functioning properly.[2] It appears that the passengers and crew have not managed the ship very rationally during the last century and it has developed many holes that Vivekananda was worried about.

What leaks out of the holes in Spaceship Earth is LIFE. This four-letter word, the definition of which has eluded scientists so far, is what distinguishes our home planet not only from other planets and their moons in our solar system but also from all the other planets in the universe that we know about, even as we search for signs of life beyond Earth. Here, on Earth, we have tried to improve the standard of living of people, as envisaged by Bucky: 'I do know that technologically humanity now has the opportunity, for the first time in its history, to operate our planet in such a manner as to support and accommodate all humanity at a substantially more advanced standard of living than any humans have ever experienced.'[3] On this journey of economic development, we abandoned the thoughts of Vivekananda, who spoke of a holistic rejuvenation of the masses—physical without abandoning the spiritual—giving us the motto, 'Elevation of the masses without injuring their religion.'

India's Prime Minister Shri Narendra Modi brought the issue of life once again into focus when on 1 November 2021 at COP 26 in Glasgow he introduced the concept of LiFE movement. In a stirring speech, he said, 'I came with a concern for the humanity. I came as a representative of a culture that gave the message of "Sarve Bhavantu Sukhinah", which means "Happiness for all".' He invoked the Vedic mantra सं गच्छध्वं संवदध्वं सं वो मनांसि जानताम्।[4] (saṃ gacchadhvaṃ saṃ vadadhvaṃ saṃ vo manāṃsi jānātām), which means, 'Let's move together … let's all interact together … and everyone's minds should also be one.'[5] Then,. he introduced the concept of LiFE: 'Today, the world admits that lifestyle has a big role in climate change. So, I propose before you a One-Word Movement. This One-Word, in the context of climate, can become the basic foundation of One World. This word is—LIFE ... L, I, F, E, which means Lifestyle For Environment.'[6] He elaborated on the need for a mass movement towards an environmentally conscious lifestyle, shifting away from mindless and destructive consumption towards mindful and deliberate utilisation.

Following up on the concept, on 5 June 2022 he launched the global initiative 'Lifestyle for the Environment—LiFE Movement'. He stated the goal of the movement was a lifestyle that is in tune with our planet and does not harm it, describing the followers of this lifestyle as 'pro-planet people'. He stated, 'Mission LiFE borrows from the past, operates in the present and focuses on the future. Reduce, Reuse and Recycle are the concepts woven into our life.'[7] The online launch was attended by many dignitaries who lauded the initiative. Bill Gates congratulated the PM 'for taking a lead on this global initiative of citizen action to promote pro-climate behaviours'. Achim Steiner, UNDP global head, said, 'Countries like India are serving as kinetic energy behind the decisive climate action on the world stage.' India, the only living ancient civilisation, the country with the largest population and the largest democracy in the world seems to be finally getting into position as the captain of Spaceship Earth.

Let us discuss the action initiated by the Government of India to realise Swami Vivekananda's dream of India's regeneration through inclusive growth. Three months after Finance Minister Nirmala Sitharaman's announcement in the Union Budget 2023–24, the Ministry of Environment, Forest and Climate Change (MoEFCC) readied the draft contours for rolling out India's first Green Credit Programme (GCP). 'The idea is to create a market-based mechanism for undertaking environment-friendly activities by providing additional incentives in the form of green credits. A monetary value will be put for each green credit depending on the activity for which it has been earned,' a senior environment ministry official, who wished to remain anonymous, told the *Print*.[8]

The environment ministry has identified eight select activities under the Environment (Protection) Act for which green credit can be earned. These include tree plantation; water conservation; water harvesting and water use efficiency/savings; promoting natural and regenerative agricultural practices; waste management; air pollution reduction; mangrove conservation and restoration; Ecomark-based green credits; and construction of buildings and other infrastructure using sustainable technologies and materials.

This initiative is part of the Prime Minister's Mission LiFE, which serves as a guideline for India's policy formulation. Green credits are an instrument notified by the MoEFCC on 26 June 2023. They aim to incentivise ordinary consumers to voluntarily take environmentally positive actions and make sustainable choices to reduce their individual carbon, water, and waste footprints, to move towards the Nationally Determined Contributions (NDCs) under the Paris Agreement. The vision is that if hundreds of millions of ordinary people voluntarily make sustainable choices, then India will experience a 'supply push' from its ongoing large renewable energy investment programme and a 'demand pull' from the new green credits concept, encouraging citizens to voluntarily demand various technologies, such as EVs, rooftop solar, and water harvesting, while seeking methods to reduce their carbon footprint, like using energy-efficient appliances and not sending kitchen waste to landfills. Together, these two forces will create momentum to achieve India's net-zero goals faster. The recent announcement regarding green credits is not happening today because there is an affordability constraint for most people to 'go green' from the demand side.

A key success criterion of Mission LiFE should be that customers will not have to pay extra to live a sustainable lifestyle; otherwise, this programme cannot be called 'voluntary'. Given today's clean technology pricing structures and limited availability of retail loan facilities for the same, it is largely still easier to afford 'conventional' or non-green products, which are polluting and non-energy efficient, than to acquire clean and green technologies. Therefore, today it is cheaper from a consumer's point of view (not society's point of view) to be non-sustainable rather than sustainable, as we understand from the recent notification. This is what green credits are hoping to address, by making it easier to 'go green' and removing, or at least mitigating, the 'green surcharge', while rewarding those who participate in this MoEFCC endeavour of green credits.

The housing and sustainable buildings sector is one of the most important and potentially impactful entry points to test this new instrument. A sustainable building serves as a vehicle to deliver several sustainability interventions simultaneously (energy, water, waste, and plantation), while delivering immediate benefits to consumers. Clean energy technologies are a good example. The upfront cost is high, which creates a barrier to entry, and affordable loans are rarely available to retail consumers. However, once the technology is somehow accessed, the lifetime operating costs are much lower than conventional solutions, through savings on energy bills, water bills, and avoided petrol/diesel payments by using electric vehicles (EVs), etc.

The other consideration for why housing is an ideal test for this instrument is that customers should be using a 'bundle' of sustainable/green technologies simultaneously to do their part for Mission LiFE. Examples of items to include in the green 'bundle', apart from the sustainable materials used in the building envelope, are super-efficient fans and other domestic appliances, LEDs, rooftop solar systems, passive cooling building structures, water-saving fixtures, rainwater harvesting, grey water recycling, electric mobility options connecting to shared public transport, solar charging stations, recycling and waste segregation, circular economy, on-site biodigesters, etc.

After returning from Ayodhya on 22 January 2024, Prime Minister Narendra Modi said he had decided to begin a new scheme to help people set up solar panels in their homes. The decision, he indicated, was inspired by the realisation that all devotees of the world get energy from the light of the Suryavanshi Lord Sri Ram. He said that the first decision he made after returning from Ayodhya was that his government would launch the Pradhanmantri Suryodaya Yojana (PSY), with the goal of installing rooftop solar panels on one crore houses. To address the affordability of rooftop solar units, Union Minister Anurag Thakur announced on 29 February 2024 the approval of the PM Surya Ghar: Muft Bijli Yojana as part of PSY. Under this scheme by the Ministry of New and Renewable Energy (MNRE), 45 GW of renewable energy will be produced. One crore households could avail of 300 units of free electricity and an annual income of Rs 15,000. This would not have been a difficult choice for the government, considering the prime minister's aversion to freebies—or 'revdis', as he calls them—being doled out by many states, a large and harmful part of which is free electricity provided by many states to low-income groups. Given the abundance of sunlight in India, the government is better off providing poor households with solar panels instead of the free electricity that many states have been offering. This may be the logic behind the PM Surya Ghar: Muft Bijli Yojana.

The Centre wants to spend Rs 75,000 as 'central financial assistance' to help a poor household acquire solar panels. The plan is to subsidise household rooftop solar panel setups for up to 2–3 kw capacity. This should allow for 200–300 kWh (or 'units') of power to be generated every month. The figure of 200–300 kWh of monthly power is significant because it is the amount of power that various state governments are currently fully subsidising—giving it away for free.

A solar rooftop installation of 2 kWh will not come cheap, though. The government estimates that such a unit would cost Rs 1 lakh; it will provide a 60 per cent direct subsidy. The remaining 40 per cent, or about Rs 40,000, will have to be borne by the consumer. The government will also offer loans with interest rates pegged at a relatively cheap 7 per cent per annum (at present rates) to bridge the gap for consumers. Moreover, beneficiaries can sell the surplus electricity via net metering, which will be installed by the distribution companies (DISCOMs) that manage the grids.

All these features are designed to make the scheme appealing. But whether it is appealing enough for people to not be swayed by the free electricity giveaway is still uncertain. Battling free handouts is not easy; after all, once given, it's nearly impossible—and politically suicidal—to undo them. That is another reason why the Centre has chosen this scheme instead of just fighting the 'revdi culture' through narrative alone.

The solar scheme also offers states that have already given free electricity handouts a way out. For instance, today, the Karnataka government provides free power of up to 200 units to nearly one crore households. Even if 10–20 per cent of these homes were to move to the Surya Ghar setups, it would reduce the loads on the grid as well as on the state exchequer. If the financing part of the scheme works well and a large number of households install enough capacity to pay off their loans with the excess power they generate, the PM Surya Ghar initiative may, in the coming years, defeat one of the most ruinous freebies being doled out by state governments: free electricity.

The additional 45 GW of power generated locally through rooftop solar (RTS) under the PM Surya Ghar initiative will be best utilised if consumed locally. This will substantially reduce the Aggregate Technical and Commercial (AT&C) losses and lead to a reduction in overall transmission and distribution (T&D) costs associated with taking power from the generating point to the rural consumption centres. To achieve this, we will need to focus on massive micro/macro industrialisation, which will enable local production of goods and services, making them available to the local population at an affordable cost, while also generating employment. It can be seen that rural India is on the path to growth, and this is being accelerated through various government interventions, one of which is rural electrification, the latest being through PM Surya Ghar. This initiative will ensure the availability of 24x7, 300 kWh power to the majority of households at an affordable cost, or even at zero cost.

The Household Consumption Expenditure Survey (HCES) 2022–23 was released in February 2024.[9] It showed that household spending increased 2.6 times in rural areas and 2.5 times in urban areas since the last survey, in which non-food items had risen more than food items. The gap between urban and rural household consumption has narrowed: In 2022–23, the average monthly per capita expenditure in rural areas was Rs 3,773, compared with Rs 6,459 in urban areas. The gap between urban and rural consumption narrowed to 1.71 times in 2022–23, down from 1.8 times in 2011–12. In 2004–05, urban consumption was almost double that of rural consumption.

Presently most of the rural demand, including the present increase in demand for goods and services, is mainly sourced from outside. Now, with additional support through the PM Surya Ghar scheme, which provides affordable and surplus power to rural households, the time has come to ignite rural growth by establishing micro- and mini-industries to meet the increased demand and catalyse a surge in overall demand at rural households. This will improve the standard of living, create additional employment opportunities, and stimulate India's growth through their participation.

With the consistent efforts of the Government of India, we are on the right path to addressing Swami Vivekananda's dream of the masses rising and enjoying economic growth without losing their spirituality. To carry forward this process of national rejuvenation, we will have to generate employment opportunities through small and micro industries after studying the consumption pattern of today and the near future, so that necessities like cereals, bread, biscuits, etc., can be produced locally, without sourcing from outside. In addition, we may study the present agriculture production and new developments that can be converted into value-added products for consumption both in rural and urban areas. To develop facilities in small towns that are on par with those available in cities, we may lay fibre-optic cables to ensure high-speed internet penetration so that back-office work can be sourced from them at a competitive cost. The availability of quality education and penetration of high-speed internet will uplift the education quality and availability of qualified manpower.

The government may encourage NGOs and startups to develop and showcase them, aiming to multiply them across the country at a competitive cost. This will make India a torchbearer for both developing and developed nations, with a strong and intellectually competent workforce capable of leading the new world where every individual will be self-sufficient. This will take India and the world to a new era of civil harmony and growth by restoring their lost individuality without diminishing their national pride and innate spiritual nature.

15

Geopolitics and Global Energy Security with Special Reference to India

Dr Brij Behari Dave

Like a grand chessboard, geopolitics orchestrates the intricate dance between nations, where power, security, and economic gains intersect. Imagine a global theatre, its curtains drawn by geography, revealing a stage where nation-states vie for dominance. Rudolf Kjellén, intellectual cartographer and political scientist, had coined the term geopolitics in 1905. His work served as a compass, guiding us through the labyrinth of international affairs; his canvas was the interplay of geographical, historical, economic, and social forces shaping a nation's destiny.

Picture this: rivers as ancient scribes, etching borders; mountains as silent sentinels, guarding secrets; forests whispering tales of resilience; lakes mirroring epochs. These natural boundaries, once sacrosanct, framed geopolitical landscapes. But then, seismic shifts took place: the Soviet Union crumbled, and the market ascended—an economic Prometheus unshackled. International relations scholar Francis Fukuyama, in a bold stroke, declared the 'End of History'. Yet history, ever the phoenix, rekindled. Enter the rebirth of geopolitical studies—a phoenix rising from the ashes of the 1990s. Now, geopolitics adapts to an interconnected world. It's no longer a zero-sum game: It's a symphony of relative gains and shared destinies. Our compass oscillates. Political control over territory reverberates across continents. Strategic petroleum reserves, akin to vaults of sovereignty, guard against volatility. Efficiency, the alchemist's elixir, transforms scarcity into abundance.

Today, geopolitics isn't static; it's a dynamic discourse among international actors. The chessboard rearranges, alliances shift, and cooperation beckons. As the curtain rises, we navigate the currents—a saga of power, resilience, and ever-evolving human drama. Now the concept was adjusted to the international economic and political integration that had taken place and included how political control over a territory influences power and political and economic outcomes through factors, mechanisms, and institutions in the international economic and political system.[1] Modern geopolitics became concerned with the political discourse among international actors, driven by the factors that determine the political and economic importance of a country's geographic location. 'Relative gains matter, but so (also) joint gains from possible cooperation.'[2]

Geoeconomics and geostrategy are integral parts of geopolitics. Geoeconomics describes and analyses the distribution of resources in and between states, focusing on industrial capacity, technological, scientific, and administrative competence and capacity, finance, and the flows of trade across global economic spaces. Geopolitics is very much a geoeconomic phenomenon and vice versa. Any state's control of a given territory is in the end a question of 'economic gain': how to finance the costs and how to gain an optimal share of the values created or transmitted in/on that territory. Geostrategy has mostly been used as a military concept. It describes plans for obtaining physical control of certain areas, or the capability to deny control to others, irrespective of prevailing geopolitical and geoeconomic structures. Together, they presuppose intentionality and are thus not natural phenomena.

Energy is one of the most valuable businesses in the world, worth trillions of dollars a year. It is the centrepiece of most discussions about climate change because it is associated with around 80 per cent of human-made greenhouse gas emissions. As nations compete for it, energy has also been a fuel for geopolitical conflict, and today, competition for resources lurks beneath the Russia–Ukraine War and even the Israel–Hamas crisis.

Before the war, Ukraine was the conduit through which Russia supplied Europe with 40 per cent of its gas. The gas was transported under a 2019 agreement between Russia and Ukraine, which expired at the end of 2024. Russia invaded Ukraine within forty-eight hours of the mothballing of the Nord Stream 2 pipeline that it had built, bypassing Ukraine to supply Europe. Subsequently, both Nord Stream 1 and 2 were mysteriously damaged in blasts. Russia has since occupied approximately 20 per cent of Ukraine's territory, including regions most richly endowed with natural resources like gas, coal, iron ore, and lithium.

When the Russian gas taps were turned off, Europe turned to other markets, such as the U.S. and the Middle East, including Israel. The competition for Israel's natural gas reserves did not trigger the conflict, but it lingers as an underlying factor. Israel recently entered the global natural gas export market. In 2022, after Russia invaded Ukraine, Israel signed an MoU with Egypt and the European Union to export natural gas from its Tamar gas field, the closest of three offshore gas projects to Gaza. Although the planned EastMed pipeline to Europe never made it past negotiations with Turkey and lost support from the US, exports to Egypt were now to be liquefied there and sent to Europe to meet its needs to diversify from Russia. This offered a massive cash windfall for Israel. Hamas, Hezbollah, and Iran, however, took a dim view. Exports from Tamar were halted two days after Hamas's terrorist attack on Israel on 7 October 2023 amidst security concerns. They have recently restarted, though production at Israel's other major gas field, Leviathan, may yet be affected. Another gas field, Karish, is located in territory that, as recently as 2022, had been disputed by Lebanon and over which Hezbollah had threatened to 'act'.

Past conflicts over natural gas and energy security concerns offer lessons. In 2014, when Russia annexed Crimea, the European Commission noted that every unit of natural gas saved equals 2.6 units that EU member states need no longer buy from Russia. By 2022, it didn't have a choice. It expressed its policy as 'energy efficiency first' and mandated gas and electricity reductions while simultaneously making billions in market incentives available.

This chapter assesses the issues related to the Indian energy sector through a geopolitical and energy security lens, focusing on energy access and economic drivers that have helped shape these lenses historically and their impact on the future. The energy needs of the Indian economy and the policy drivers linking them are of increasing relevance to global energy producers and consumers seeking to understand their impact on the energy markets worldwide. Indian imports of fossil and non-fossil fuels have always impacted markets and policies. The Indian energy economy is also in the midst of an energy transition, with an increasing share of renewables that has significant ramifications for global energy markets and the politics of climate obligations and just transition. The confluence of these issues is shaping energy markets and will be critical for future researchers in the energy domain to study and understand.

India's Energy Security

India, as a country, represents one of the last of the large high-growth fossil fuel energy markets with the potential to grow over the coming decades. The low per capita energy consumption in

India (currently about 0.6 tonnes of oil equivalent [toe], which is half of the Asian average and a third of the global average) (see Figure 15.1) is a cause for concern for everyone in the country, economists and politicians alike, and they are frantically looking for an alternate source of energy which is in abundance, climate-friendly, and available at an affordable price across the nation. We are facing an exceptionally adverse situation as far as energy availability is concerned, arousing an urgent need to invent new sources of renewable energy at 'affordable prices' to support our growth story, which is an immense success in a world fraught with recession, near-recession or very depressed GDP growth in most countries, as opposed to India's growth engine heating up and expected to continue for at least two decades at a rate nearing 8 per cent per annum.

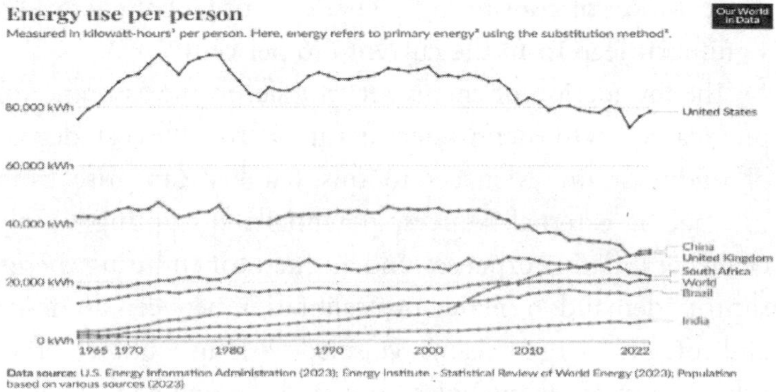

Figure 15.1 Energy Use Per Person.
Source: US Energy Information Administration (2023), Energy Institute

India's economic juggernaut has been thundering forward at a rapid pace for several years. This phenomenal growth, fuelled by a burgeoning young population (approximately 1.4 billion with an average age of 29) and a growing per capita income slated for a high trajectory, necessitates a commensurate escalation in energy resources. This rising demand presents a unique challenge. In 1991, when India embarked on economic liberalisation, merchandise trade accounted for a mere 14.1 per cent of a US $270 billion GDP. By 2020, this figure had ballooned to 24.4 per cent of a US $2.6 trillion GDP.[3] Globalisation has enmeshed India within the intricate web of the global economy, fostering a deep economic interdependence. Notably, petroleum products have been a significant driver of this export growth—a curious fact considering India imports nearly 80 per cent of its crude oil requirements. The reliance on fossil fuels extends beyond oil, with imports of coal and gas also exhibiting a steep upward trend over the past decade. OPEC's 2023 World Oil Outlook paints a stark picture: India's primary energy demand is projected to nearly double to a staggering 38.5 million barrels of oil equivalent per day (mboe/d) by 2045. This insatiable demand will propel India to a position of consuming 10 per cent of global energy—a significant leap from the current 6.6 per cent.

The foundation of energy security lies in the assurance of physical access to energy reservoirs at a reasonable cost, devoid of undue strain. Menaces to this stability can arise from internal or external sources, potentially disrupting supply chains or inflating expenses. India's quest for enduring energy security demands a meticulous calibration between domestic and foreign energy streams, coupled with an embrace of an eclectic mix of technologies. This multifaceted strategy aims to mitigate risks and foster resilience.

Yet, the calculus does not end there. Affordability emerges as another pivotal facet in India's energy security paradigm. Energy outlays must not weigh disproportionately on the shoulders of the less affluent strata of society. Hence, the government must meticulously engineer a 'prudent energy amalgam', encompassing a diverse array of domestic, imported, and regionally exchanged resources. This discerning curation process not only dampens the volatility of prices but also ensures accessibility to energy at equitable rates.

India's burgeoning economic aspirations may necessitate a concomitant augmentation of energy reservoirs. However, navigating this terrain mandates a nuanced equilibrium: ensuring energy security via diversification of sources and technologies, all the while safeguarding affordability for the nation's most vulnerable segments.

Demand-Supply Gap

Immediate energy security hinges on the agility of the energy infrastructure to swiftly adapt to abrupt shifts in the supply-demand equilibrium. Discrepancies between demand and supply signify a heightened reliance on imports, thereby escalating the financial burden on the nation's economy.

Coal, Oil, and Gas

Demand for coal is rising every year; domestic production is also increasing, but the demand-supply gap is also growing, as we can see in Figures 15.2, 15.3, and 15.4 (for coal, oil, and gas, respectively), causing an increase in 'import dependence' to meet domestic needs.

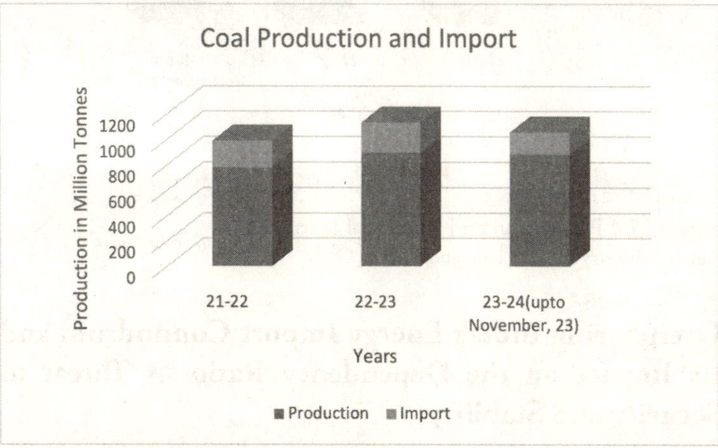

Figure 15.2 Coal Production and Import.
Source: Ministry of Coal, India

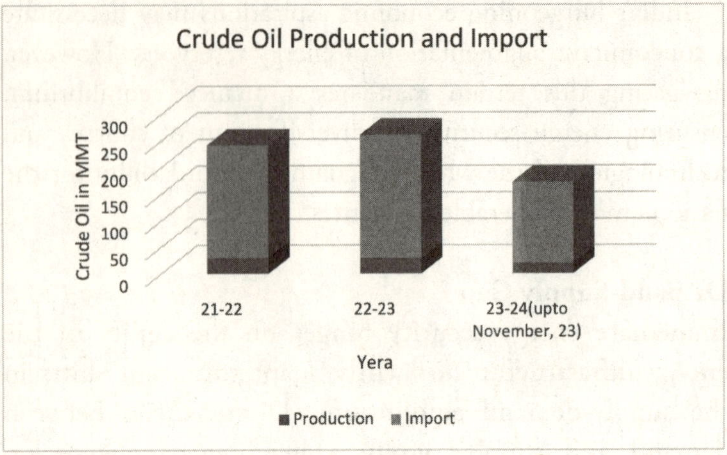

Figure 15.3 Crude Oil Production and Import.
Source: Snapshot of India's Oil and Gas Data Monthly Ready Reckoner, November 2023, Petroleum Planning and Analysis Cell

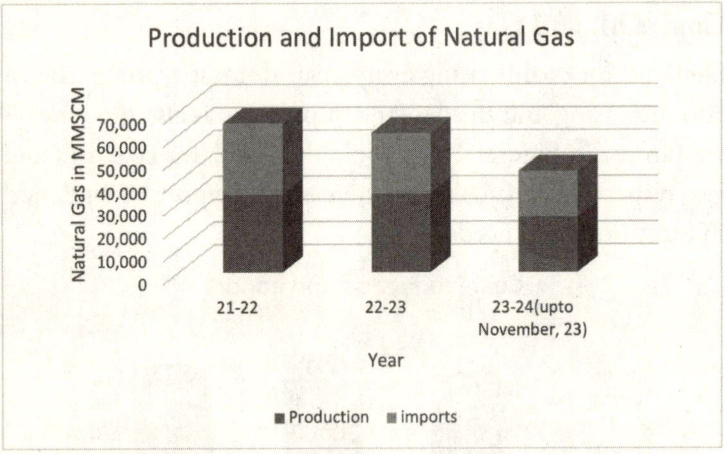

Figure 15.4 Production and Import of Natural Gas.
Source: Ministry of Petroleum and Natural Gas[4]

Deciphering India's Energy Import Conundrum and Its Impact on the Dependency Ratio: A Threat to Security and Stability

A critical aspect of ensuring energy security involves meticulously calibrating the nation's import requirements with its export and tax-derived revenue. As the following illustrations depict, India exhibits a concerning overreliance on imported crude oil, followed by natural gas and coal. These indicators present a concerning picture, highlighting the Indian economy's vulnerability to the twin threats of rising energy prices and supply insecurity.

The widening demand-supply gap for energy fuels has precipitated a steep rise in import dependence, reaching a precarious 71 per cent for crude oil. This stark reality exposes India's ever-increasing reliance on external actors to satiate its thirst for crude oil. Such a scenario raises a multitude of concerns:

- Unreliable supply: The nation's energy security hinges on the whims of other countries, potentially jeopardising the regularity and consistency of crucial energy supplies.
- Price vulnerability: India becomes susceptible to the dictates of exporting nations regarding energy fuel prices. This susceptibility exposes the nation to the unpredictable fluctuations of the international energy market.
- Financial strain: The exorbitant cost of these large-scale energy imports creates a significant financial burden on the Indian economy. This burden, in turn, has a ripple effect, impacting domestic energy prices and potentially hindering economic growth.

In essence, India's current energy import trajectory presents a multifaceted challenge to its long-term energy security and economic stability. Addressing this challenge necessitates a multi-pronged approach, potentially encompassing strategies to diversify energy sources to reduce dependence on a few countries and volatile markets; boost domestic energy production through exploration and exploitation of indigenous resources; and embrace energy-efficiency measures to minimise overall energy consumption.

By implementing such a comprehensive strategy, India can strive towards a future of energy independence and economic resilience.

The Quest for Energy Dominance

- The finite and uneven distribution of energy resources worldwide has engendered fierce competition among nations vying for access to these invaluable assets. This competition frequently ignites geopolitical tensions, conflicts, and even wars. A quintessential example is the Gulf War of the 1990s when Iraq's annexation of Kuwait was spurred by its thirst for accessing the abundant oil reserves of the latter.
- The Heartland Theory posited by Halford Mackinder and the Rimland Theory advocated by Nicholas Spykman underscore the pivotal significance of gaining control over resource-endowed regions for a country to assert and extend its influence or hegemony globally. In this vein, nations endowed with oil, gas, and other energy resources enjoy a distinct advantage over resource-deficient counterparts in terms of power projection and influence.
- Securing a dependable supply chain of energy resources is imperative for any nation aiming to safeguard its national interests, including energy security and industrial development. This necessity significantly influences a country's decisions in its bilateral and multilateral relationships, shaping its diplomatic and strategic manoeuvres on the global stage.

Considering the data presented above, it becomes apparent that India must rely substantially on imports from other nations to meet its energy demands, as our domestic reserves and production fall short of fulfilling these requirements. Consequently, it becomes imperative to assess our total reserves of coal, oil, and gas relative to our production levels to estimate approximately how long our reserves can sustain our current rate of consumption, which is poised to escalate with time. As previously discussed, our per capita energy consumption lags behind that of more developed nations. However, with sustained economic growth projected in the forthcoming decades, the energy demand is anticipated to surge accordingly.

Production-to-Reserve Ratio

Coal

India possesses 107,727 million metric tonnes (MMt) of proven coal reserves as of 2016, ranking fifth globally and constituting approximately 9 per cent of the world's total coal reserves, estimated at 1,139,471 million metric tonnes (MMt). This figure translates to proven reserves equivalent to 111.5 times India's annual coal consumption. According to the British Petroleum Statistical Review of World Energy, India's current coal reserves are projected to last for approximately 207 years. However, as outlined in the Integrated Energy Policy of 2006, at the current consumption rate, these proven coal reserves are forecasted to remain for only 80 years. Furthermore, if domestic coal production maintains a growth rate of 5 per cent annually, the entirety of extractable coal reserves would be depleted within 45 years. This scenario raises profound concerns regarding energy security, given coal's pivotal role as the backbone of India's energy sector. Compounded by escalating import reliance, this situation presents a formidable energy security challenge that demands immediate attention. Nonetheless, the minister of Mines has articulated ambitions for India to achieve self-sufficiency in coal production by 2026, thereby mitigating dependence on coal imports.

Oil

Table 15.1 shows the position of crude oil reserves and production in India:

Table 15.1: Crude Oil Reserves and Production

	Barrels	Global Rank
Oil Reserves	4,728,790,000	24th
Oil Production per Day	1,016,371	20th
Oil Consumption per Day	4,443,000	3rd
Daily Deficit	(-) 3,426,629	
Oil Imports	4,255,300	
Oil Exports	5	
Net Imports	4,255,295	

(Data shown is for 2016, which is the latest year with complete data in all categories. Source: https://www.worldometers.info/oil/india-oil/)

As of 1 April 2022, India boasts 651.77 mt of proven oil reserves[5], representing approximately 0.2 per cent of the global oil reserves estimated at 244 billion tonnes. This indicates that India's proven reserves are equivalent to 4.78 times its annual oil consumption. Consequently, in the absence of imports, the nation would have less than 5 years of oil supply left, considering current consumption levels and excluding unproven reserves.

The stark reality of this low reserves-to-production ratio underscores the urgent need to ramp up domestic exploration and development endeavours. It is imperative to embark on initiatives aimed at discovering new fields and augmenting the country's reserves base. This proactive approach is essential to bolstering India's energy security and mitigating the risks associated with over-reliance on imports.

Table 15.2 and Figure 15.5 show the energy mix by fuel type:

Table 15.2: India's Total Installed Capacity by Source (GW)

Source	As of May 2023	Percentage of Energy Mix
Coal	205.235	49.13
Lignite	6.620	1.60
Gas	24.824	6.00
Diesel	0.589	0.14
Hydro	46.850	11.22
Nuclear	6.780	1.62
Renewables	125.692	30.20
Total	417.66	100

Source: https://powermin.gov.in/en/content/power-sector-glance-all-india

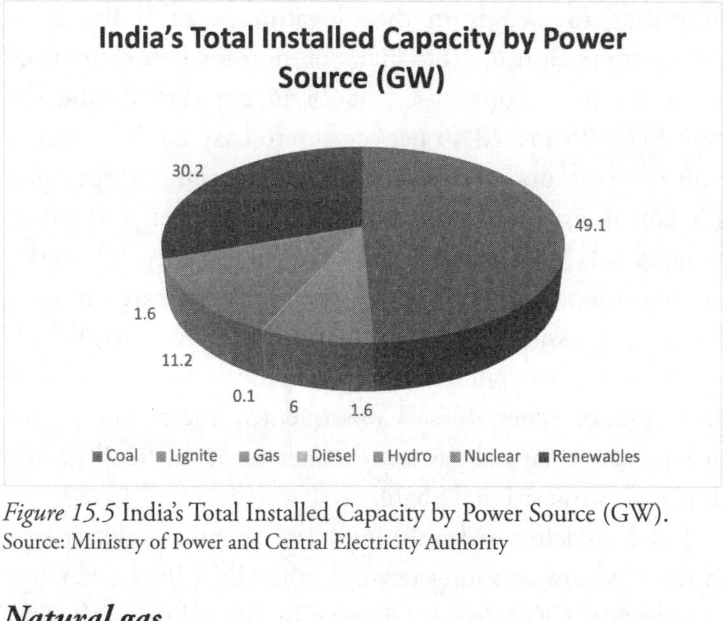

Figure 15.5 India's Total Installed Capacity by Power Source (GW).
Source: Ministry of Power and Central Electricity Authority

Natural gas

Natural gas demand has been increasing continuously over the years. To keep up with demand, the production of natural gas has also been stepped up. Even with increased production, it is expected that the natural gas supply will fall short of the projected demand. It is predicted that with the current production rate for natural gas, domestic reserves will last for twenty-two years from 2017.

Renewable energy

The Indian power sector employs a wide range of fuel sources, including traditional sources such as coal, oil, and gas, as discussed above, alongside environmentally sustainable sources such as solar, wind, biomass, industrial waste, and both large and small hydro plants.

India's power sector is presently dominated by fossil fuels, yet the nation harbours ambitious aspirations to significantly elevate the proportion of renewable and nuclear energy. According to data from the Government of India's Press Information Bureau, the share of non-fossil fuel in total electricity production stood at 25.44 per cent during the year 2022–23 and 22.45 per cent up to May 2023.[6] Diligent endeavours are underway to curtail the escalation of greenhouse gas emissions and lessen dependence on energy imports, concurrently bolstering India's energy security. However, the transition from coal to renewables is anticipated to span decades, necessitating the continued flexibility of fossil-fuel-based energy to stabilise the grid amidst the intermittent operation of renewables. Consequently, India will persist in relying on natural gas and cleaner forms of fossil energy during this transitional phase.

India has delineated ambitious targets for renewable energy in the medium and long term. At the UN Climate Change Conference (COP 26) in Glasgow in 2021, Prime Minister Narendra Modi unveiled Panchamrit or the five-point agenda to combat climate change. The targets articulated at COP 26 encompass achieving a non-fossil energy capacity of 500 GW by 2030, fulfilling 50 per cent of our energy requirements through renewable energy by 2030, slashing total projected carbon emissions by one billion tonnes from now until 2030, reducing the carbon intensity of the economy by 45 per cent by 2030 over the 2005 levels, and attaining the target of net-zero emissions by 2070.

As of 31 May 2023, data from India's Ministry of New and Renewable Energy indicates that the nation's installed renewable energy capacity reached 179 GW, with solar and wind contributing 67 GW and 43 GW, respectively. The remainder comprises small hydro, biomass, and other sources. However, the gap between India's installed renewable energy capacity and actual electricity production from non-fossil fuel sources persists due to the intermittent nature of renewable energy sources, such as wind and solar. Table 15.3 shows the energy mix of renewable energy in India.

Table 15.3: Renewable Energy Mix by Source (GW)

Source	As of May 2023	Target for 2030
Wind Power	42.86	140
Solar Power	67.07	280
Biomass Power	10.24	10
Small Hydro	4.94	70
Waste-to-Energy	0.55	(No target)
Total	125.69	500

Source: Indian Central Electricity Authority

Liquefied natural gas

India stands as the twelfth-largest consumer[7] and seventh-largest importer[8] of liquefied natural gas (LNG) globally. Despite constituting 5.1 per cent of India's energy mix in 2022,[9] the Indian government aims to elevate the share of liquefied natural gas in the national energy mix to 15 per cent by 2030, facilitating the transition to renewable energy.

India and the United States

In November 2020, the Indian government issued a public procurement order under the 'Make in India' initiative to promote domestic production of goods and services. While the order grants preference to Indian suppliers in government tenders, there remain opportunities for US companies in India. Overall, the US's share of India's energy-related equipment and commodities market exhibits growth potential. US companies, particularly, stand to benefit from opportunities in higher-value manufactured goods within power utilities. Since 2017, with support from both governments, the United States has emerged as a significant energy source for India, with US oil and gas export value to India reaching $12.5 billion in 2022.

Bilateral energy commodities and equipment trade between the US and India soared to $18.5 billion in 2022, from $14 billion in 2021. This growth is propelled by various factors, including India's escalating energy demand and its steadfast commitment to clean energy collaboration.

Indeed, it would be remiss not to highlight the advancements in other renewable energy sectors, particularly in the realm of green hydrogen, where India is swiftly emerging as a prominent player in the green hydrogen economy. The government has spearheaded several initiatives to catalyse the growth of this sector. Notably, in 2022, the government inaugurated the National Hydrogen Mission, with the ambitious target of achieving a green hydrogen capacity of 5 million tonnes per annum by 2030. This presents a ripe opportunity for US companies to engage in technology collaborations with Indian counterparts seeking to venture into the green hydrogen sector.

Furthermore, the natural gas infrastructure sector is poised to offer lucrative prospects in the forthcoming years, particularly as India embarks on the construction of new LNG terminals, expands pipelines across the nation, and fortifies city gas distribution infrastructure to encompass piped city gas for buildings and compressed natural gas dispensers for transportation. Additionally, LNG dispensing units and virtual pipelines in the form of cryogenic containers present supplementary opportunities for US companies. The burgeoning demand for new entrants in the fuel retailing business to invest in dispensing technologies for alternative fuels signifies a promising avenue for LNG, biofuels, and hydrogen technologies. Consequently, Western companies stand to benefit from these growing opportunities within India's evolving energy landscape.

Accessibility to Clean Energy

A critical energy security concern for Indian households is the lack of provision of clean energy. While electricity reached most households in India by 2019, approximately 660 million Indians still lacked access to modern or clean cooking solutions in 2020. They rely entirely on traditional biomass for cooking, which causes around 8,00,000 premature deaths in India every year due to household air pollution.[10] These deaths primarily involve women and children. There are various government schemes like PAHAL (Pratyaksh Hanstantrit Labh) and PMUY (Pradhan Mantri Ujjwala Yojana), which had a target of providing subsidised LPG connections to 80 million households by 2020 but had reached 102.7 million as of 1 March 2024. A survey reveals that these people still use biomass for cooking because, despite the LPG subsidy, biomatter is abundantly available at no or minimal cost for a significant number of households, especially in rural India.

The Challenges of Smart Grid

The transmission and distribution of electricity is associated with huge losses in production, distribution, and utilisation. Production and distribution are the two sectors in the country's power sector that constitute the 'weakest link' in the entire value chain and need wide-ranging reforms at all levels. The International Energy Agency (IEA) estimates that modernising and expanding the grid will require monumental efforts, equivalent to the creation of a new global grid.

Challenges in the Transmission Sector

India boasts an extensive network of transmission lines responsible for carrying electricity from power plants to distribution substations. Among these, two significant corridors stand out: firstly, the North–South Corridor, spanning 2,000 kilometres, facilitating the transmission of electricity from the northern states to the southern states; secondly, the East–West Corridor, extending over 3,400 kilometres, facilitating the flow of electricity from the eastern states to the western states.

Despite recent strides towards achieving universal electricity access, India grapples with numerous hurdles in power transmission, adversely affecting the efficiency, reliability, and overall robustness of its electricity distribution infrastructure. These challenges encompass a range of issues:

- Inadequate infrastructure: A significant portion of India's transmission infrastructure is antiquated and in dire need of upgrades or replacements. Ageing infrastructure demands frequent and extensive maintenance to uphold its reliability, thereby escalating maintenance costs for power utilities. Furthermore, the lag in the adoption of state-of-the-art and smart technologies by power utilities—particularly state-owned entities—contribute to less efficient grid operations.

- Land acquisition and right-of-way issues: Constructing new transmission lines often entails navigating complex land acquisition processes, which frequently encounter delays and disputes. Instances of public protests and environmental apprehensions have arisen in various parts of India, particularly when transmission lines traverse ecologically sensitive areas, and there is a lack of adequate consultation with affected local communities.
- Overloading and congestion: The increasing power demand and insufficient expansion of transmission infrastructure have resulted in overloading and congestion within India's power transmission network. Overloaded lines occasionally precipitate grid instability and heighten the risk of blackouts. Congested transmission infrastructure exacerbates electricity losses and poses ongoing threats to the integrity of equipment, such as power lines, transformers, and switching gear.
- Operational and maintenance challenges: Effective maintenance and operation of transmission assets are indispensable for ensuring grid reliability. However, inadequate maintenance practices and operational lapses by power utilities have contributed to technical failures and disruptions in power supply. Notably, the widespread power outage in July 2012, impacting approximately 700 million people across eight states, was attributed to disturbances in the northern grid, prompting a mandate for all utilities to adopt stringent grid management practices.

Challenges in the Distribution Sector

India's distribution sector plays a crucial role in the conveyance of electricity from power plants to consumers, with two primary categories of distribution companies: State Electricity Boards (SEBs), which are government-owned entities operating in most Indian states; and private distribution companies, exemplified by Tata Power Company Ltd, the nation's largest private sector power utility, boasting an installed generation capacity exceeding 13,735 MW.

However, the country contends with several challenges in power distribution, hindering the effective and reliable delivery of electricity to end consumers. These challenges, some interrelated, include:

- High Aggregate Technical and Commercial (AT&C) losses: AT&C losses, encompassing technical and commercial losses during transmission and distribution, including theft, billing inefficiencies, and non-payment, impose significant financial strain on power utilities. AT&C losses exceed 30 per cent, undermining revenue collection.
- Inadequate last-mile connectivity: Certain regions, particularly rural and remote areas, face limited access to the power distribution network, impeding the provision of reliable electricity to households and businesses. Border states like Arunachal Pradesh and Jammu and Kashmir rank poorly in rural power availability, with vast swathes remaining unelectrified despite purported claims of 100 per cent rural electrification.
- Overload of distribution infrastructure: Some distribution networks struggle to accommodate escalating load demand, resulting in the overloading of transformers, substations, and distribution lines, culminating in frequent power outages and voltage fluctuations.

- Inaccurate metering and billing: Deficient metering and billing systems contribute to revenue losses for distribution companies, stemming from faulty meters, billing inaccuracies, and suboptimal collection processes, undermining financial viability.
- Voltage fluctuations and power quality: Voltage fluctuations, poor power quality, and recurrent voltage surges impair the performance of electrical appliances and machinery. Inconsistent power supply compromises industrial productivity and consumer satisfaction.

Addressing Distribution Challenges

Addressing these multifaceted challenges is imperative for enhancing the efficiency, reliability, and sustainability of India's power distribution network, thereby ensuring equitable access to electricity for all segments of society.

To achieve this, the adoption of a modernised electrical grid, known as a smart grid, has emerged as a transformative solution. Leveraging analogue or electronic information and communication technologies, smart grids automate data collection and enable proactive response mechanisms based on real-time insights into the behaviours of both suppliers and consumers. Over the past decade, society's increasing digitalisation and reliance on power have underscored the pressing need for innovative network topologies, monitoring tools, and environmentally friendly energy sources. Forecasts indicate a quadrupling of demand over the next two decades, intensifying the imperative for novel solutions. However, the proliferation of renewable energies, with their inherent intermittency, imposes considerable strain on power networks. Consequently, the success of the clean energy transition hinges on a fundamental overhaul of power systems, with a heightened emphasis on digitalisation across all grid domains—from generation and transmission to distribution and end-use.

Digitalisation holds the key to addressing demand growth, decarbonisation challenges, and enhancing grid resilience. Digital solutions empower utilities to address these challenges effectively. By enabling efficient fault detection and faster restoration times, digital technologies mitigate the costs and disruptions associated with outages. Moreover, they optimise maintenance practices, prolonging the lifespan of grid assets and deferring substantial investments in grid expansion. The World Economic Forum has estimated that an investment of about $21 trillion in grid upgrades by 2050 will be required to achieve a net-zero trajectory globally.[11]

Despite the transformative potential of smart grid implementation, global investments in grid infrastructure fall short of the levels required to achieve net-zero emissions globally. Annual investments in grids must more than double by 2030, with a significant portion allocated to distribution grids for expansion, reinforcement, and digitalisation. While challenges to scaling up investment persist, smart grid implementation yields substantial benefits across various domains.

Digitally enabled demand response can significantly reduce the curtailment of variable renewable energy systems, boosting system efficiency and reducing costs for customers. Furthermore, advanced supply and demand forecasting facilitate integrated energy planning and enhance the visibility and flexibility of electricity demand, further supporting decarbonisation efforts.

Moreover, digital technologies play a pivotal role in extending decentralised, clean energy access to remote or underserved communities. By enabling more efficient mini-grids and community assets, digital solutions facilitate energy access and usage optimisation. Additionally, technologies like smart inverters enhance electricity delivery management, minimise service interruptions during peak demand, and maximise electricity utilisation during low-demand periods.

Furthermore, digital technologies offer a strategic approach to managing growing demand and electrification while avoiding unnecessary grid expansion investments. With the rising demand for space cooling, particularly in emerging markets and developing economies, digital electricity distribution systems provide granular visibility, ensuring grid stability, affordability, and resilience against localised outages.

In essence, the widespread adoption of digital technologies in power systems is pivotal for realising a sustainable, resilient, and efficient energy future, capable of meeting the evolving demands of society while advancing decarbonisation objectives.

How Do the US, China, and India Ensure Energy Security and Protect Their Interests through Geopolitics?

In the intricate tapestry of international relations, energy policies often become threads woven into the broader narrative. The revelation that funding legislation before the US Congress seeks to block China from purchasing oil from the Strategic Petroleum Reserve (SPR) adds another layer to the complex dance between economic interests and geopolitical tensions. Fuelling this move is a bipartisan determination to establish a hard line on China—a sentiment that seems to be one of the few unifying forces in the polarised halls of Capitol Hill.

Amid the backdrop of escalating competition with the Chinese government, numerous bills have been introduced, each vying to address the multifaceted challenge posed by the emerging global powerhouse. The focal point of this legislation, however, revolves around the SPR, a strategic asset with a history intertwined with both political and economic landscapes. In 2022, the decision of then president Joe Biden to sell 180 million barrels of SPR oil as a remedy for soaring gasoline prices following Russia's invasion of Ukraine set the stage for the current controversy. The subsequent sale of a million barrels to UNIPEC America, a Houston-based arm of China's Sinopec, stirred the pot further.

This move is not unprecedented; even under President Donald Trump, in 2017, SPR oil found its way to PetroChina International, a subsidiary of the Chinese state oil company PetroChina Company Limited. However, the latest attempt to curb such transactions signals a renewed robustness, reflecting an evolving stance on the interplay between economic cooperation and strategic rivalry. The SPR, currently holding over 360 million barrels of oil, is approaching historic lows due to the sales in 2022. While the desire to secure domestic oil resources is understandable, the question remains whether such restrictive measures are a pragmatic response or merely a symbolic gesture. Last July, the Democratic-controlled Senate passed a bill to ban SPR oil exports to China, a move criticised by some for its potential to create an illusion of problem-solving with minimal political impact. Beyond the legislative nuances lies the broader issue of US–China energy relations. In 2022, US oil companies sold a substantial 83 million barrels of oil to China, underscoring the interconnectedness of the two economies.

While navigating this delicate geopolitical landscape, it becomes imperative to assess the potential ramifications of these legislative decisions on economic ties, global energy markets, and the overall stability of international relations. As the 1,050-page funding bill awaits the House vote, followed by the Senate's subsequent consideration and potential implementation, it underscores the intricate tango of diplomacy and strategy. Striking a balance between safeguarding national interests and fostering global cooperation will be the key to ensuring a harmonious dance in the world of energy politics. The coming days will unveil whether this legislative move is a masterstroke or a potentially discordant note in the symphony of international relations.

Changes to India's Foreign Policy

Geopolitical considerations hold significant sway not only for India but for all nations. In response to the escalating energy demands and climate imperatives, India's foreign policy has undergone notable shifts, aimed at safeguarding national interests and ensuring energy security:

- Discounted Russian oil: India capitalised on discounted Russian crude oil offers following the Russia–Ukraine conflict, diversifying its energy trade partners. Russia emerged as India's largest oil importer, constituting approximately 40 per cent of its crude imports. Despite criticism from Western countries, India's strategic approach prioritises securing cheaper oil to meet national demand from various sources.
- Exploration of new transport corridors: India and Russia explored new transport routes like the Northern Sea Route (NSR) and the Eastern Maritime Corridor (EMC), aiming to bolster connectivity between Vladivostok and Chennai. Additionally, India agreed to train its seafarers in Polar and Arctic waters at the Russian Maritime Training Institute in Vladivostok.
- Development of Chabahar port: India invested in the development of Chabahar port in Iran, facilitating access to oil-rich Iran, Afghanistan, and Central Asian countries, bypassing Pakistan.
- International Solar Alliance (ISA): Founded by India in 2015, ISA serves as a collaborative platform to accelerate the deployment of solar energy technologies, thereby

enhancing energy access, security, and transition in member countries.

- Global Biofuels Alliance (GBA): Launched during the G20 Summit in New Delhi in 2023, India spearheaded the Global Biofuels Alliance, aiming to bolster biofuels' share in the energy mix through knowledge-sharing, R&D investments in waste-to-energy, and technical cooperation.
- Green Hydrogen alliances: India and Saudi Arabia signed a Memorandum of Understanding (MoU) to develop a green hydrogen supply chain, promoting collaboration in green hydrogen production and resilient supply chain development for renewable energy materials.

These strategic initiatives underscore India's proactive stance in embracing sustainable energy solutions, fostering international cooperation, and mitigating geopolitical risks to ensure long-term energy security and environmental sustainability.

Challenges for India

High import dependence for crude oil

India's oil import dependency has remained high in recent years, with figures reaching 84.4 per cent in 2020–21, 85 per cent in 2019–20, and 83.8 per cent in 2018–19. Moreover, the Persian Gulf countries have consistently accounted for approximately 60 per cent of India's crude imports over the past fifteen years.

Furthermore, Russia emerged as India's foremost oil-sourcing country in 2023. However, this development presents its own set of challenges, particularly concerning potential disruptions in the supply chain and the deepening relationship between Russia and China. The evolving geopolitical dynamics, coupled with sanctions imposed by

Western nations on Russia, pose significant threats to India's energy security interests.

In essence, while India has diversified its oil import sources to some extent, reliance on particular regions and countries exposes it to vulnerabilities stemming from geopolitical tensions and disruptions in global supply chains. Mitigating these risks necessitates a comprehensive strategy that encompasses diversification efforts, diplomatic engagement, and proactive measures to safeguard energy security interests.

Nuclear Suppliers Group

India's nuclear energy generation faces considerable challenges due to limited domestic reserves of uranium, amounting to only about 2 per cent of the world's total uranium reserves. As a result, India relies heavily on imports of nuclear fuel and technology to sustain its nuclear power programme.

Additionally, India's aspirations to join the Nuclear Suppliers Group (NSG) have been impeded by China, which has posed obstacles and raised objections. China's opposition to India's NSG membership, often citing concerns related to Pakistan and India's non-signatory status to the Nuclear Non-Proliferation Treaty (NPT), significantly hampers India's energy interests. China has conditioned India's NSG membership on resolving issues related to its relationship with Pakistan and adhering to NPT norms.

India's pursuit of the NSG membership is primarily driven by the need to access foreign-sourced nuclear material and advanced technology to bolster its nuclear energy capabilities. However, China's resistance to India's inclusion in the NSG complicates India's efforts to secure necessary resources and technologies for its nuclear energy sector, highlighting the geopolitical challenges that impact India's energy security objectives.

Lack of domestic reserves of critical minerals

India faces notable challenges in securing adequate supplies of critical minerals fundamental to its industrial development and transition towards greener technologies. India's shortage of domestic reserves, especially of critical minerals like lithium and cobalt, necessitates reliance on international sources, complicating its industrial and environmental agendas. The issue is exacerbated by the complexity of global supply chains and the political instability in mineral-rich regions such as Africa. Notably, China's dominance in the production and processing of approximately 90 per cent of these critical minerals presents a significant strategic challenge. This dominance subjects India, along with the rest of the world, to potential supply vulnerabilities and geopolitical pressures. Further complicating the scenario, specific countries hold significant shares of the global reserves of these minerals. For example, the Democratic Republic of Congo is the leading holder of cobalt reserves, accounting for roughly 70 per cent of the total global reserves. This centralisation of mineral reserves introduces additional risks of supply disruption due to geopolitical or economic instability within these nations. Additionally, the ongoing Russia–Ukraine conflict has introduced further uncertainties in the global supply chains for critical minerals. Russia's role as a significant producer of nickel, palladium, titanium sponge, and scandium, along with Ukraine's status as a major producer of titanium, means that the conflict has direct implications for the availability of these essential materials. This situation threatens the stability of supply chains that industries around the world, including India, depend upon for their raw materials, impacting sectors ranging from electronics to renewable energy technologies.

High comparative costs of renewable energy

- While renewable energy sources may appear to be cheaper, some hidden and indirect costs make them far less financially attractive.
- Given the intermittent nature of sources like solar and wind, energy storage solutions, such as batteries, become crucial.
- While the initial costs of renewable installations might seem competitive, the associated storage costs can be significant, especially when we factor in the lifespan and efficiency of current battery technologies. This is particularly relevant when comparing the continuous power generation capabilities of fossil fuel plants to the on-and-off nature of renewables.
- At our present juncture in the energy transition, fossil fuels continue to dominate, constituting approximately 80 per cent of the global energy economy. These fuels play a pivotal role in powering our societies, including essential sectors like transportation and food production. Natural gas is key, particularly for industry, heating, and power. Replacing it with low-carbon, minimally polluting energy generation will take decades, huge investments, and immense volumes of resources.
- Over the past two decades, a staggering $6 trillion has been invested globally in clean energy, and an additional $3 trillion has been allocated to grid infrastructure. Despite these substantial investments, we find ourselves far from achieving full electrification. Currently, only approximately 20 per cent of global energy consumption is in the form of electricity. For electrification to be a solution for either decarbonisation or energy security, it will need to scale up by orders of magnitude. First, electricity will need to be green, which would require an increase of at

least three to four times in renewable energy capacity. Then electricity will need to replace/displace the other 80 per cent of the energy supply, which would require at least another four to five times increase from a higher base as well as substantial innovation in technology.

- The transition to renewable energy sources (RES) is indeed a critical aspect of the global energy shift. However, according to the International Energy Agency (IEA), grids are the 'weak link' for the energy transition. Already, projects equivalent to five times the volume of all wind and solar capacity added in 2022 are stuck in the queue for grid connections. Even if this current gridlock is addressed, the IEA projects the need to add or refurbish 80 million kilometres of grids by 2040—the equivalent of the entire existing global grid or enough power lines to wrap around the earth approximately 2,000 times.
- Upgrading the grid is an incremental solution, but it does not solve the main issue: the majority of energy is squandered in losses related to extracting and converting (10 per cent), generating (50 per cent), and carrying and distributing (10 per cent). A substantial amount of these losses is in the form of waste heat, which occurs when energy is generated far from the point of use, utilising technologies (using conventional fuels like gas and even 'low-carbon' fuels like nuclear) that generate as much heat as electricity but cannot or do not use it. Many of these losses can be avoided by decentralising energy generation, bringing it closer to the point of use, and limiting or eliminating transmission and distribution losses. This would achieve a step change in the efficiency of supply.
- Even more energy is lost at the time of use. Buildings, industries, and transportation account for 70 per cent of energy consumption. Buildings can waste up to one-third of their energy simply due to inadequate mechanical and

electrical infrastructure, such as lighting, air conditioning, and controls. This issue can be resolved by upgrading the equipment and using the savings to offset the costs. Industry is less electrified than commercial or residential buildings, but it may make significant changes in the way it consumes heat by recovering, storing, and recycling it. Despite some electrification, transportation remains primarily an oil-dependent industry, with 'well-to-wheel' losses of up to 75 per cent. Electrification and low-carbon transportation fuels are becoming more cost-effective.

- We need a revolution in efficiency. Simply investing more, whether in renewable energy or transmission grids, will not achieve the green energy revolution, especially when they are plugged into an inefficient system. At the same time, we need to do more with less. Energy efficiency is the largest, fastest, and cheapest source of greenhouse gas emission reductions, cost reductions, productivity gains, resilience, and energy security.
- If we become more efficient, we may only need a fraction of the energy we are using and competing for, and the challenges of achieving the green energy revolution cost-effectively, as well as ensuring security of supply, may not be insurmountable after all.

2070 Carbon-neutrality as a Challenge

- There are numerous hurdles in India's target for carbon neutrality by 2070.
- First, it would require about $10 trillion in investment, and given the constraints in climate finance mobilisation, it seems an arduous task.
- Secondly, phasing out coal completely is difficult, given the requirements of industries and the slow progress in the addition of renewable energy. Also, the intermittent nature of renewables makes coal a viable option.

- It also requires innovation and collaboration in the desired technologies to meet the target in the long run.

The Way Forward

India must secure its energy interests through the following measures:

- Strategic Petroleum Reserves (SPR): All oil-importing member countries of the International Energy Agency (IEA) must hold emergency oil stocks equivalent to at least 90 days of net oil imports. With the help of imported oil, India has been building its strategic petroleum reserves at Vishakhapatnam, Mangalore, and Padur. It should also consider having strategic reserves of coal as well as natural gas.
- Strategic autonomy: India must proactively exercise its strategic autonomy in the maintenance of bilateral and multilateral relations to secure the national interests of the country in the energy sector. Therefore, it must maintain its healthy relations with the Middle East, Russia as well as the USA for diversification of risks associated with supply chain management of energy resources and critical minerals supply. The three-year India–Australia Critical Minerals Investment Partnership and the purchase of discounted Russian oil in this context are the right measures.
- Critical minerals partnerships: India's membership in the Minerals Security Partnership, along with state-owned joint venture KABIL's agreement with Argentina to tap the critical minerals, are much-needed initiatives towards a reliable and efficient critical minerals supply chain. Such opportunities must be leveraged well by the Indian government and investors.
- Commercial mining of critical minerals: The rising demand for critical minerals for green energy transition and the inadequate, slow progress in the exploration

and production of potential domestic reserves of critical minerals have driven India's amendments in the Mine and Minerals (Development and Regulation) Act 1957, to boost commercial mining of select critical minerals in the country. Private participation in the mining of critical minerals, with increased investments in R&D, is imperative.

- Deep ocean exploration: India must ensure a robust implementation of crucial policies such as the Deep Ocean Mission, O-SMART, and Samudrayaan Mission (Matsya 6000) to explore, tap, and exploit the polymetallic nodules and other energy resources to fulfil the increasing energy demands of the country.
- Geospatial energy mapping: The Geospatial Energy Map of India launched by ISRO and NITI Aayog (2021) attempts to identify and locate all primary and secondary sources of energy and their transportation/transmission networks to provide a comprehensive view of energy production and distribution in the country. It should be used effectively by the private sector and other stakeholders in the research and development of energy resources.
- Loss in transmission, use, and smart grid formation: The biggest and dirtiest secret of the energy market is that most of it is lost in generating, transmitting, distributing, and using it. Solving this problem would be revolutionary, reducing competition for resources that contribute to conflict as well as climate change.

Conclusion

Energy dynamics and geopolitical stratagems are irrevocably entwined. The advent of remarkable energy reservoirs, such as shale gas in the USA and significant lithium deposits in India, alongside breakthroughs in correlative technologies, have positioned the energy sector at the zenith of diplomatic discourse. Such treasured resources and the innovation surrounding them are destined to continue shaping the tapestry of international relations and foreign policy well into the foreseeable future. As a nascent player on this global stage, India is at a critical juncture. It must execute a strategy of meticulous deliberation, optimising its international engagements—whether bilateral, regional, or multilateral—to harness the utmost benefit from its energy agreements and liaisons. The inception of the International Energy Agency (IEA) was a direct consequence of the 1973–1974 oil embargo, underscoring the precarious nature of energy security. While maintaining a vigil on energy security remains its cornerstone, the contemporary IEA has evolved to embrace a more expansive remit. This includes a dedicated focus on mitigating climate change and advancing decarbonisation efforts, enhancing energy accessibility and efficiency, fostering investment and innovation in renewable sources, and ensuring the provision of reliable, affordable, and sustainable energy for the global populace. Through the examination of notable works, such as those by Austvik, Panwar, Dwivedi, and others cited within the bibliography, this discourse has excavated the intricate relationship between energy security and geopolitical manoeuvring. It elucidates the pivotal role energy plays in not only fuelling the engines of nations but also in scripting the dynamics of international alliances and rivalries.

16

Sustainability in Agriculture through Energy Transition

Ajit Balaji Joshi

The environmental sustainability of the farming community is inseparably linked to the energy sustainability of agriculture. The agriculture sector is so intertwined with urban settlements in a country like India, and the size of the farming community represents such a high percentage of the population, that it is meaningless to discuss energy sustainability and energy security without simultaneously ensuring such sustainability and security for the agriculture sector. Since it impinges on the food security of the nation also, sustainable agriculture is vital for our national security, both through energy security as well as food security.

The Food and Agriculture Organization (FAO) defines Sustainable Agriculture and Rural Development (SARD) as: '[T]he management and conservation of the natural resource base, and the orientation of technological and institutional change in such a manner as to ensure the attainment and continued satisfaction of the human needs for present and future generations. Such sustainable development (in agriculture, forestry and fisheries sectors) conserves land, water, plant and animal genetic resources, is environmentally non-degrading, technically appropriate, economically viable and socially acceptable.'[1]

With that definition in mind, FAO has laid down the following goals for SARD:

- Improve food security by ensuring an appropriate and sustainable balance between self-sufficiency and self-reliance
- Promote employment and income generation in rural areas, particularly focusing on poverty alleviation
- Conserve natural resources and protect the environment[2]

Sustainability and energy transition are critical in the agriculture sector, both from the input (energy) and output (greenhouse gases) perspectives. The food and agriculture sector consumes 30 per cent of the total energy consumption in the world for production, transport, and processing. The distribution of energy across these three activities varies widely with the development level of the countries. In low-GDP countries, cooking takes a higher share of the energy, while in high-GDP countries, processing, transport, and distribution consumes more energy.[3] (see Figure 16.1)

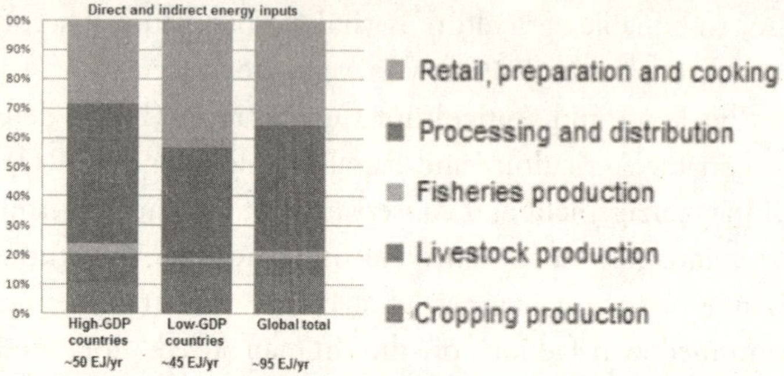

Figure 16.1 Indicative Shares of Final Energy Consumption for High- and Low-GDP Countries and the Global Total.[4]
Source: Food and Agriculture Organization

A study of the food sector in the US has revealed that it takes three calories of energy, which is primarily from fossil fuels, to produce one calorie of food energy in the US, but for grain-fed beef, thirty-five calories are required for each calorie of beef. Of the total energy, around 32 per cent is consumed in home refrigeration and preparation, 21 per cent in agricultural production, 14 per cent in transport, and 7 per cent in packaging (see Figure 16.2).[5] Food packaging and fertilisers have a 40 per cent share in petrochemical products.

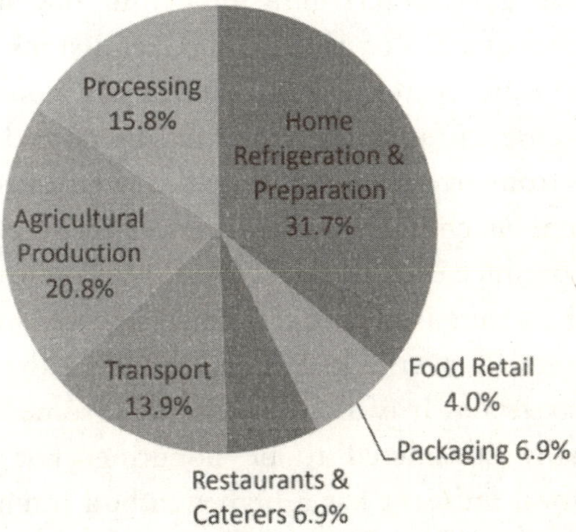

Figure 16.2 Energy Spent Related to Food Production in the US.
Source: University of Michigan, Center for Sustainable Systems

The import content of food consumption in high-income countries has been increasing. The UK's reliance on imported food has grown, with more cereals, dairy, fruit, meat, starchy roots, sugar, and vegetables being imported in 2019 compared to 1986. By 2023, nearly half of the UK's food was imported from overseas, with the share of some food groups, such as fruit and vegetables, reaching as high as 78 per cent.[6]

As less developed countries like India increase their per capita GDP, the energy spent on non-agricultural production will move towards the US level. We have seen this happen in the case of China, where the energy consumption of the food manufacturing industry increased from 28.8 million tonnes of standard coal equivalent (tce) in 2010 to 74.3 million tce in 2019, that is 250 per cent in just nine years.[7] As nations become richer, not only does per capita food consumption go up, the consumption of processed and packaged foods grows even faster, with a corresponding rapid rise in energy consumption in the food sector.

The scenario is equally dismal with regard to greenhouse gas (GHG) emissions from the agriculture sector. One-quarter of global GHG emissions are from the agriculture sector[8], with the leading contributions being from nitrous oxide from fertilisers and manure, methane from rice production, and carbon dioxide from agricultural machinery. Within the sector, livestock and fisheries produce even more GHGs than crop production. Due to the strong influence of farmers' lobbies worldwide, this is generally overlooked and kept out of the ambit of carbon taxes. Yet, it is more intense than some industries traditionally considered to be polluting. For example, China's food industry has a higher carbon intensity than more than two-thirds of manufacturing industries, such as construction, manufacture of fabricated metals, and production of machinery and equipment.

Agriculture is the largest consumer of freshwater, taking up 70 per cent of another increasingly scarce commodity. It also shifts land use away from forests and woodlands. Half of the world's habitable land is used for agriculture. The biomass of livestock maintained by humans outweighs that of wild mammals by a ratio of 15:1, and the biomass of poultry is three times that of wild birds. The GHG emissions from producing one kilogram of beef are almost 100 kg, while those from producing one kilogram of rice—a crop that is considered high in methane—are less than 5 kg.[9] Growing one kilogram of cereals (other than rice) or fruits and vegetables in India produces less than one kilogram of GHGs, compared to the 45 kg of GHGs emitted from producing one kilogram of mutton.[10] This shows that the environmental load of the agriculture sector is also related to food habits and consumption choices can increase or decrease GHG emissions. Again, as a society becomes more affluent, its per capita consumption of animal-based food goes up substantially. In China, between 2010 and 2020, per capita beef consumption went up by 35 per cent.[11]

The Future of Mankind Lies in Sustainability and Energy Transition in Agriculture

The global population is expected to increase by 2 billion in the next thirty years.[12] The average human will have more disposable income at that time, with the poorer areas of Africa, Asia, and Latin America gradually moving up the prosperity ladder. Agriculture will provide not only more essential food but also luxury food items and even biofuels for the 9.7 billion people in 2050. If, meanwhile, agriculture is not transitioned to cleaner energy and made sustainable, it will seriously affect climate change efforts. Many large population countries, including China and India and regions like sub-Saharan Africa, are expected to reach carbon neutrality much after 2050. It will be futile to expect the governments of these countries to put their food security on the backburner and give precedence to climate change. The poor in these countries have seen how the West, and even China, polluted the planet to feed their economies. The dilemma for the world will be dominated by two simple truths: one, the rich refuse to consume less to save the planet; two, the poor refuse to remain poor to save the environment.[13] It is the food and agriculture sector that will bear the responsibility of saving humanity from hunger and ecological disaster without discomforting either the rich or the poor.

The difficult task before the food and agriculture sector is one that will require action on three fronts: land, water, and energy. All three will need to focus on two transformations: the transition to optimisation and the transition to alternative technologies. In addition, food choices will need a closer look to optimise nutrition using a minimum of these three resources.

Land and Water Use Optimisation and Alternative Technologies

Already having appropriated a disproportionately large area of land on Earth for agriculture and allied activities, there is simply no room for further expansion. In fact, there is a clamour for giving areas back to nature through the movement called 'rewilding', which is defined as 'the process of rebuilding, following major human disturbance, a natural ecosystem by restoring natural processes and the complete or near complete food web at all trophic levels as a self-sustaining and resilient ecosystem with biota that would have been present had the disturbance not occurred'.[14]

Although rewilding is an ambitious concept that is not likely to find widespread acceptance, not expanding cultivated lands by repurposing forest and wildlife areas is itself a goal that continues to recede. Between 1985 and 2022, Brazil converted 87.6 million hectares of forests to agriculture and allied activities, with most of it going to pasture. However, agriculture has also taken a significant portion (11 per cent) of the natural forests, which have seen a reduction from 581.6 million hectares to 494.1 million hectares in this period.[15] A large part of the deforested land used for agriculture was soy farming, spurred by its rising demand as feed for pigs in China, where pork is a popular staple. However, Brazilian farmers seem to be waking up to the issue. The rate of deforestation has decreased slightly in recent times, even though the area for soy farming has increased. This has been made possible by regenerating depleted ranches to compensate for the expanding agriculture frontier.[16]

India's problem is not about producing food for export as much as it is about feeding the largest population of any nation in the world. Most of the low-income families are in rural areas, and they are dependent on subsistence agriculture or on meagre income from marginal farms. Though in the initial phase of its economic development—as everywhere else in the world—agriculture in India subsidised industrial growth through cheap food and low wages, it has kept the rural marginal farmers poor. Now, the stage has come where the vociferous farmers are demanding a guaranteed Minimum Support Price (MSP) for all crops. In many cases, these prices happen to be above the market price, and the difference becomes a state subsidy to the agriculture sector, which is recouped through direct and indirect taxes from the manufacturing and service sectors. This pattern is likely to continue for a long time, as has happened in the developed world, where the secondary and tertiary sectors of the economy subsidise agriculture to sustain production and support farmers' households. However, a closer look may show chinks in subsidy calculations because businesses factor the cost of capital into the total factor cost of production, whereas this is not being counted when calculating the cost of production in agriculture. Land has become expensive all over the country, particularly in the food-bowl states, and adding the cost of capital will raise the price of food so high that it will require an immediate sharp upward revision of wages. That will make Indian industries suffer further, as they have already been reeling under the pressure of low prices of Chinese products. By this argument, agriculture may still be subsidising the growth of secondary and tertiary sectors of the Indian economy.

It need not be like that. Agriculture can and should be sustainable without subsidies by optimising land use, crop diversification, improved marketing, and use of commercial principles. In India, virtually all cultivable land is used for agriculture and allied activities. Therefore, for agricultural growth, raising productivity per unit of land is the main driver of growth. The World Bank states that for this purpose, increasing yields, diversification to higher value crops, and developing value chains to reduce marketing cost will help increase farmers' incomes from the same plot of land. The rate of growth in yield has slowed compared to the momentum of the Green Revolution days, and innovation is required to sustain this growth rate. Water conservation through watershed management can help convert a single irrigated crop area into two irrigated crop areas and transform rainfed agriculture into irrigated agriculture. But this is not without side-effects. Intensive irrigation displaces millets, several pulses, and oilseeds. It has been observed in Haryana, Rajasthan, Chhattisgarh, and Odisha that wherever the canal system reaches, these crops are replaced by environmentally harmful water-intensive crops like rice.

Around 48 per cent of India's farmlands dedicated to food crops and 68 per cent dedicated to non-food crops are said to be rainfed. In practice, however, pump sets, mostly running on subsidised or free electricity, are being used to provide some, if not excessive, irrigation to many of these areas. If an area is intensively irrigated, it is futile to try to persuade farmers to grow millets, oilseeds, and most pulses, as the high moisture levels in neighbouring fields will adversely affect the health of these crops. Unless the water allowance for the entire area is reduced, introduction of these crops that are beneficial for a balanced and nutritious diet and have high profit margins for farmers because of low input costs, will face serious challenges. A national land-use strategy should ensure that high water usage/intensity, whether due to cheap canal water or cheap electricity for pump sets, is reduced to facilitate the reintroduction of these crops.

Energy Optimisation and Transition in Indian Agriculture

Energy use in Indian agriculture is highly wasteful. Most of the tractors are based on old diesel technology and are used beyond their efficient lifespan. Trailers used in conjunction with these tractors are fabricated in small local workshops and add to the inefficiency. Other farm machinery like harvesters and threshers are also frequently made locally, further adding to energy inefficiency. The worst offenders are the motors used in pump sets. As the water table decreases, the motors have to be replaced with higher horsepower motors. Farmers usually adopt the cheaper alternative of upscaling the motors locally. Since these motors burn out faster, the winding is replaced locally, which adds load without improving efficiency. This results in frequent burnout of distribution transformers, imposing additional cost on the distribution company. Considering that there are 22 million agriculture pumps in India consuming about 20 per cent of the country's total energy consumption, the inefficient pumps constitute a huge burden on the power distribution system. In 2016, the Indian government's Bureau of Energy Efficiency launched the Energy Efficient Agriculture Pump Programme under the Demand Side Management (AgDSM)[17] scheme. These energy-efficient star-labelled pump sets save 30 to 40 per cent energy. The AgDSM has other components to improve energy, such as enhancing energy efficiency in aquaculture through the use of energy-efficient aerators and providing training and extension support. The programme for energy efficiency in the integrated cold-chain sector aims to reduce losses occurring during transit, which can be as high as 18 per cent for fruit and 13 per cent for vegetables. The India Cooling Action Plan was launched in March 2019 to provide energy-efficient design specifications and good practices in agriculture operations, post-harvest management, and packing operations.

Energy transition in agriculture is aimed at generating electricity through solar energy in farms. The Decentralised Renewable Energy (DRE) Programme plays an integral part in pushing the nation towards carbon neutrality. While India has expanded its large-scale solar energy projects across the country, this programme focuses on steering renewable energy towards farm-level generation, integrated with the national grid. This will provide low-cost clean energy to the farmers and enhance the grid's stability. This programme has components both for the rural domestic sector as well as for agriculture. The PM-Surya Ghar: Muft Bijli Yojana is aimed at providing 300 units of free electricity to 10 million rural households through rooftop solar equipment. This will help achieve the target of 100 GW solar generation by 2026, of which 70 GW had been achieved by September 2023. The programme will be coupled with the use of artificial intelligence in the distribution network to predict real-time energy demand and accordingly manage the power generation system.

For facilitating on-farm generation through solar panels, KUSUM (Kisan Urja Suraksha evam Utthan Mahabhiyan) scheme was launched in 2018. One of its components, A-Kusum, co-locates solar panels with the crops—a technique known as agrivoltaics. The panels are elevated 2 to 3 metres above the ground to allow crop growth below. Coupled with drip irrigation and water harvesting, this method has the additional advantage of better groundwater retention.

Bloomberg Philanthropies and India Climate Collaborative have launched India Agrivoltaics Alliance, which will give a boost to this programme.[18]

India's NITI Aayog envisions the transformation of Indian agriculture from agroindustry to agroecology, which will increase farm productivity while enhancing sustainability and resilience to climate change.[19] Energy transition is already playing a significant role in helping achieve that goal.

17

India's Journey for Sustainable Energy: A Beacon on the Global Stage

Vivek Kumar Dewangan

India is one of the world's fastest-growing economies, benefitting from its diverse business environment and vast consumer base. Supported by strong macroeconomic fundamentals, robust domestic demand, fiscal discipline, high saving rates and demographic trends, India has emerged as the fifth-largest economy globally. With an estimated Gross Domestic Product (GDP) of more than $3.5 trillion, generated by a population of over 1.4 billion, India ranks among the highest population-based economies in the world.

The energy sector plays a crucial role in India's economic growth, accounting for a significant portion of its GDP. India is the world's third-largest energy consumer. The country's industrialisation and urbanisation continue to place substantial demands on its energy sector. While fossil fuels still dominate the energy mix, there is a notable shift towards renewables like solar and wind power. Dependence on fossil fuels poses several risks related to energy security, global market volatility, resource scarcity, and environmental degradation.

A sustainable economy requires energy for economic growth and development worldwide, especially in the light of climate change. Energy plays a vital role in a country's economic and social development. In recent decades, many countries have faced extreme risks due to volatile oil prices, geopolitical tensions, wars, and severe weather. To achieve long-term energy security, countries must lessen their dependence on imported energy sources (oil, gas, coal, etc.) and more productively utilise their indigenous natural energy resources. Energy security is a critical aspect of a nation's development and stability, and for a country as populous and rapidly growing as India, it is of paramount importance. With a burgeoning economy and a large population to sustain, the country faces unique challenges and opportunities in ensuring reliable access to energy resources. As it aims to become a global economic power, a steady energy supply is essential to develop sustainable infrastructure, human skills, and technological abilities.

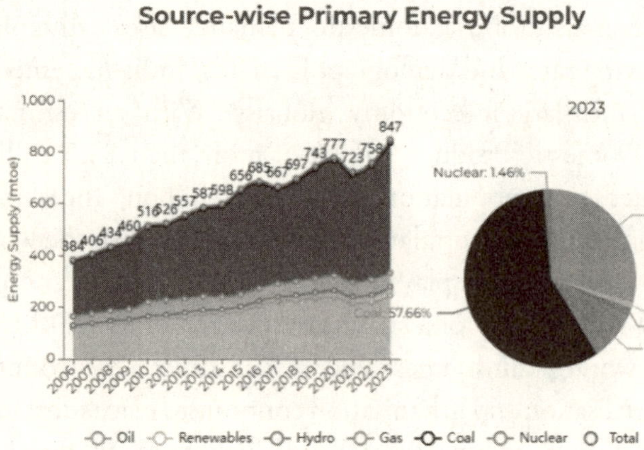

Figure 17.1 Current State of India's Energy Sector with Source-wise Primary Energy Supply, https://iced.niti.gov.in/energy

India is the world's third-largest energy-consuming country, thanks to rising incomes and improving standards of living.

Energy use has doubled since 2000, with most of the demand still being met by coal, oil, and gas. On a per capita basis, India's energy use and emissions are half of the Asian average and a third of the global average. In terms of emissions, the energy sector accounts for about 76 per cent of total emissions, followed by the agriculture sector, which is about 13 per cent. The electricity sector is the largest contributor to the Indian energy sector and accounts for about half of the sector's energy emissions.

India is one of the largest producers and consumers of electricity in the world, with a total installed capacity of 428 GW by the end of 2023. The country's electricity peak demand has been increasing consistently in recent times and touched an all-time high of 250 GW on 30 May 2024. Its renewable energy (RE) capacity stands at around 181 GW, comprising roughly 43 per cent of the total installed capacity. In line with the 'Panchamrit' target of achieving 500 GW of non-fossil fuel-based energy by 2030, the country's installed capacity is likely to reach 777 GW, involving an addition of 312 GW in non-fossil capacity over the current level of 188 GW. In the financial year 2022–23, the total power generation reached 1,624 billion units (BU), marking an 8.87 per cent growth compared to the previous year. Non-fossil fuel power generation as a whole stood at 418 BU, reflecting a growth rate of 10.9 per cent compared to the previous year. During the current FY 2023–24, the total power generation had already reached 1,301 BU by December 2023. With the growing energy demand, the 20th Electric Power Survey (EPS) has projected that peak electricity demand will reach 335 GW by 2030, and the electrical energy requirement during the FY 2029–30 is estimated to be about 2,280 BU. All these indicate the huge growth of the Indian electricity sector.

Key Challenges in India's Energy Security

Despite efforts to diversify the energy mix, India remains heavily dependent on imported fossil fuels, exposing the country to vulnerabilities in global markets and supply chains. As of today, India meets nearly 85 per cent of its crude oil requirements and about one-fifth of its coal supplies through imports. Oil products and imported coal are mainly used in the transport and electricity sectors. India's oil products contribute 95 per cent of the final energy used in the transport sector, with natural gas, biofuels, etc., comprising the remaining portion. The Indian transport sector has grown by 50 per cent since 2010 and now accounts for 20 per cent of the country's final energy use. In terms of energy consumption, the transport sector is the second-biggest contributor to the country's overall energy use, after the industries sector. Hence, India's energy security remains closely tied/linked to global fossil fuel markets, highlighting the need for continued vigilance and adaptability in the face of changing geopolitical realities.

Another major challenge in India's and the world's energy landscape is the risk associated with the climate change crisis. Climate risk and sustainable finance are key focus areas for regulators, national and supranational authorities across the world, and driving collaborative efforts is critical. The UN Intergovernmental Panel on Climate Change (IPCC) Report of August 2021 highlighted the changes being observed in the Earth's climate in every region across the entire climate system. The report states that emissions of greenhouse gases from human activities are responsible for approximately 1.1 degree Celsius of warming from 1850–1900 and finds that, averaged over the next twenty years, global temperatures are expected to reach or exceed 1.5 degrees Celsius of warming. Between 1901 and 2018, India's average temperature rose by 0.7 degree Celsius, primarily led by an increase in greenhouse gas (GHG) emissions. This rapid growth in GHG emissions has been driven by multiple factors, such as high population growth rates, increasing levels of industrialisation and urbanisation. The increase in average temperatures has already affected the livelihood of millions of people, with more frequent sporadic climatic events, such as cloudbursts, flash floods, prolonged droughts, etc., becoming the norm.

India's Commitment to the World for Sustainable Growth

India has been placed in a sweet spot to address both the above-mentioned challenges: phasing out fossil fuel dependency and mitigating emission-related climate concerns. The Indian Government has put several policies and targets in place to support its contribution to reducing global emissions. These efforts are outlined in India's pledges made at recent and past COP events:

Paris Agreement (2015)

India is a signatory to the Paris Agreement (COP 21), which aims to limit global warming to well below 2 degrees Celsius above pre-industrial levels, with an aspiration to limit the temperature increase to 1.5 degrees Celsius. As part of this agreement, India has made the following commitments:

- To reduce emissions intensity with respect to GDP by 33–35 per cent below 2005 levels by 2030
- To achieve about 40 per cent of installed electricity capacity from renewable energy resources by 2030

It is noteworthy to mention that India has already achieved both these targets well ahead of the committed time—the first one eleven years ahead and the second one nine years ahead.

COP 26 (2021)

India's COP 26 'Panchamrit' commitments include:

- Reaching 500 GW of non-fossil installed electricity capacity by 2030
- Sourcing 50 per cent of its energy requirements from renewable energy by 2030
- Reducing total projected carbon emissions by one billion tonnes from now until 2030
- Reducing the carbon intensity of the economy by 45 per cent by 2030, compared to 2005 levels
- Achieving the target of net-zero emissions by 2070

COP 28 (2023)

India's engagements at COP 28 in Dubai represented a comprehensive and proactive approach to tackle climate change, with the LeadIT Summit 2023 being hosted by India and Sweden. Some of the key commitments and endeavours of our country at COP 28 include:

- The launch of key initiatives, including LeadIT 2.0 for industry transition, and the Green Credits Programme to incentivise pro-environment actions
- Efforts to enhance its global climate action through initiatives like the International Solar Alliance (ISA), the Coalition for Disaster Resilient Infrastructure (CDRI), LeadIT, Infrastructure for Resilient Island States (IRIS), and the Big Cat Alliance, complementing its domestic efforts

COP 29 (2024)1

1. Climate finance gap: The amount was increased from the earlier \$100 billion to \$300 billion every year. India, however, asked for setting the annual goal at \$1.3 trillion.

2. Government-to government carbon market was finalised. India hopes to operationalise its carbon trading market by 2027.
3. India raised the issue of climate-related trade barriers. It was decided to discuss this issue in future.
4. India stressed the need for unrestricted access to green technologies by removing IPR restrictions.

Reform Initiatives Taken by the Indian Government

India has demonstrated a firm commitment to achieving the ambitious energy transition goals announced by Prime Minister Narendra Modi at COP 26 in Glasgow in 2021. In a significant step towards sustainability, the Indian government has taken many key initiatives aimed at ushering in a green energy revolution:

National Solar Mission and National Wind-Solar Hybrid Policy

The National Solar Mission (NSM) is an important programme of the Government of India to promote solar energy and address energy security and climate change challenges. It is part of the National Action Plan on Climate Change (NAPCC), representing India's contribution to global efforts in combating climate change.

Additionally, the Ministry of New and Renewable Energy (MNRE) issued the National Wind-Solar Hybrid Policy in May 2018 to promote large grid-connected wind-solar photovoltaic (PV) hybrid systems. The policy aims to optimise the utilisation of wind and solar resources, enhance grid stability, and encourage technological innovations in renewable energy. The Central Electricity Authority (CEA) and the Central Electricity Regulatory Commission (CERC) will formulate necessary standards and regulations to support wind-solar hybrid systems.

Rooftop solar programme

With an objective to achieve 40 GW of rooftop solar (RTS) capacity in the country, the Government of India launched the Rooftop Solar Programme Phase II on 8 March 2019. The programme envisaged the installation of 4,000 MW of RTS capacity in the residential sector by providing central financial assistance and incentives to distribution companies (DISCOMs) for achieving additional RTS capacity in a year, over and above the installed capacity of the previous year. A provision of total central financial support of Rs 11,814 crore, including service charges to the implementing agencies, has been made under the programme, which was initially scheduled for completion by 2022 but has since been extended until 31 March 2026. In the same direction, the Pradhan Mantri Surya Ghar: Muft Bijli Yojana (PMSGMBY) was launched in February 2024, aiming to install rooftop solar power systems in 10 million households across the country with an outlay of Rs 75,021 crore. The PMSGMBY is going to be a game-changer, as the subsidy amount for 1–2 kW category has been substantially enhanced to Rs 30,000 for 1 kW and Rs 60,000 for 2 kW capacity. The subsidy for 3kW and above capacity has been capped at Rs 78,000.

The Pradhan Mantri Kisan Urja Suraksha evam Utthaan Mahabhiyan (PM-KUSUM)

This scheme was launched with the aim of solarising agricultural pumps for over 3.5 million farmers, comprising three components: decentralised solar power plants, standalone solar pumps, and the solarisation of existing grid-connected pumps. As of 30 June 2023, 113.08 MW of solar power plants and 2.44 lakh solarised pumps have been installed, resulting in a significant reduction in CO_2 emissions and diesel consumption. Recent amendments extend the scheme until 31 March 2026, introduce feeder-level solarisation, and waive penalties for solar power generators with shortfalls.

National Green Hydrogen Mission

This mission was launched by the government in 2022, with the intended objectives of making India a leading producer and supplier of green hydrogen in the world; creating export opportunities for green hydrogen and its derivatives; reducing dependence on imported fossil fuels and feedstock; developing indigenous manufacturing capabilities; attracting investment and business opportunities for the industry; creating employment opportunities and fostering economic development; and supporting R&D projects. In the Union Budget 2023–24, the National Green Hydrogen Mission has been allocated an outlay of Rs 19,700 crore, which is expected to play a significant role in helping India achieve its annual production target of 5 MMT (million metric tonnes) of green hydrogen by 2030.

Focus on energy storage

Expanding India's renewable energy capacity requires flexible generation to maintain grid balance. Energy storage systems, notably pumped-hydro storage systems and battery energy storage systems (BESS), address challenges posed by intermittent generation and peak demand misalignment. The government issued a National Framework for Promoting Energy Storage Systems in August 2023 to encourage the adoption of energy storage for ensuring an environmentally sustainable and financially viable power sector. The Union Cabinet has approved a Viability Gap Funding (VGF) scheme for developing 4,000 MWh of Battery Energy Storage Systems (BESS) by 2030–31. This scheme offers up to 40 per cent of the capital cost as VGF, amounting to an initial outlay of Rs 9,400 crore. This move is a significant pro-environment step and is expected to reduce the cost of battery storage and enhance viability. Aimed at harnessing renewable energy like solar and wind power, the scheme targets a Levelised Cost of Storage (LCoS) ranging from Rs 5.50 to 6.60 per kWh, ensuring clean, reliable, and affordable electricity. The minister of power has also proposed a production-linked incentive (PLI) scheme for grid-scale batteries to bolster capacity and encourage ongoing investment.

Initiatives for the clean transport sector

As a part of the National Electric Mobility Mission Plan 2020 (NEMMP), the government had introduced FAME Phase I with a fund allocation of Rs 529 crore and FAME Phase II with a budgetary support of Rs 10,000 crore. In 2021, the government approved the PLI scheme with a budgetary outlay of Rs 25,938 crore to support domestic manufacturing of vehicles and electric vehicles (EVs). The government later approved another PLI scheme for manufacturing advanced chemistry cell (ACC) batteries with a capital outlay of Rs 18,100 crore. The GST was also reduced from 12 per cent to 5 per cent on EVs and from 18 per cent to 5 per cent on chargers, along with providing green license plates and road tax waivers. In addition, the Ministry of Road Transport and Highways (MoRTH) issued a notification advising states to waive road tax on EVs.

Carbon credit mechanism

The government has introduced the Carbon Credit Trading Scheme 2023 to reduce greenhouse gas emissions. Industries will now have carbon emissions targets, replacing previous energy-efficiency goals. A National Steering Committee and Bureau of Energy Efficiency will oversee procedures and issue carbon credit certificates. Trading will occur through a secure registry, regulated by the Central Electricity Regulatory

Commission. Obligated entities can earn or purchase carbon credits to meet targets or face penalties for non-compliance.

Energy-efficient measures undertaken

The Perform, Achieve and Trade (PAT) scheme, under the National Mission for Enhanced Energy Efficiency, mandates energy-intensive industries to set and achieve energy-efficiency targets. Industries implementing energy-saving measures earn energy saving certificates (ESCerts) for traded incentives. Many other schemes implemented by the government help in increasing energy efficiency, including the Standards and Labelling (S&L) programme, Unnat Jyoti by Affordable LEDs for All (UJALA), Street Lighting National Programme (SLNP), Building Energy Efficiency Programme (BEEP), and Agricultural and Municipal Demand Side Management programmes.

Some of the other key steps taken by the government include allowing 100 per cent FDI under the automatic route, waiver of inter-state transmission charges for the sale of solar and wind projects, setting a commissioning deadline of 30 June 2025, declaring the trajectory for Renewable Purchase Obligation (RPO) by 2029–30, setting up ultra-mega renewable energy parks, implementing the CPSU Scheme Phase II, laying new transmission lines and creating substation capacity under the Green Energy Corridor scheme, establishing standard tariff-based competitive bidding (TBCB) guidelines for photovoltaic and wind projects, and launching the Green Term Ahead Market to facilitate the sale of renewable energy power through exchanges.

Rural Electrification Corporation's efforts in the country's power sector reforms: Past and future

Ensuring energy access by 2030 is one of the major outcomes envisaged under the SDG 7 goals adopted by the United Nations. Energy deprivation has a detrimental effect on people's well-being. Apart from reducing economic opportunities for employment, energy poverty leads to poor social outcomes in the health and education sectors. Lack of energy access impacts the vulnerable sections of the society most. The Government of India, through its various flagship electrification schemes, has brought about a profound improvement in the quality of life for people, even in the farthest areas of the nation.

Village electrification story

Until 2014, 18,374 census villages in India lacked electricity access. On 15 August 2015, from the ramparts of Red Fort, Prime Minister Modi declared a resolve to electrify the remaining unelectrified villages across the country within a time span of 1,000 days. It was a mammoth task to be completed within a challenging timeline under the Deen Dayal Upadhyaya Gram Jyoti Yojana (DDUGJY). After months of perseverance by the power sector, on 28 April 2018, with the lighting of the first electric bulb in Leisang, a small village nestled in the rocky mountains of Manipur, India achieved the historic milestone of 100 per cent village electrification.

The story of this electrification is not merely one of numbers, but of grit, toil, and overcoming insurmountable odds. The final leg of rural electrification involved the toughest terrains—deserts, mountain ranges, rivers, and areas affected by Left-wing extremism. Taking electricity to the darkest corners of a country as huge and diverse as India was a task of epic proportions.

Almost two-thirds of India's population resides in rural areas. However, with increasing access to basic amenities and the transforming face of rural India, the lines between rural and urban areas are progressively blurring. Modern amenities, including the use of electrical appliances, television, and mobile phones, are no longer limited to urban areas. Children no longer depend on daylight to study. With a sustained focus on the development of our hinterland, villages are increasingly getting connected to the mainstream.

Household electrification story

The success of DDUGJY paved the way for the rollout of an ambitious household electrification scheme, the Pradhan Mantri Sahaj Bijli Har Ghar Yojana (SAUBHAGYA), which aimed to electrify every home. The prime minister called upon all stakeholders to channelise their energies towards the electrification of each and every household in the country within a challenging timeframe of eighteen months. The scheme had a total outlay of Rs 16,320 crore. The International Energy Agency (IEA) described India's village electrification programme as a success story and highlighted it as a bright spot for energy access in its report 'Energy Access Outlook 2017'. SAUBHAGYA is the story of a nation's journey; a journey that transformed the lives of millions of Indians; a challenge of epic proportions that was overcome by a nation in just a few months, bringing to life the world's largest household electrification drive.

An achievement of such magnitude could not have been possible without the support and relentless efforts of a team that worked as a cohesive unit. From the onset, we were faced with the challenge of identifying unelectrified households across the country. We had to be pragmatic in our approach. We utilised a more than 150-year-old backbone of our country's communication network: the Department of Post. A survey was conducted through it to determine the number of unelectrified households. Sankhya, a web portal and mobile app, was specifically developed for this survey to provide real-time analysis and formulate a prudent strategy.

The implementation of SAUBHAGYA showcased exemplary cooperative federalism, as both the State and Central governments collaborated seamlessly. Fifty-six DISCOMs worked tirelessly, organising camps at the village level to ensure electricity connections for every willing household. Special 'Saubhagya raths' were deployed to raise awareness and identify unregistered households. A 24x7 control room addressed queries and grievances, facilitating speedy resolutions. Stand-alone solar photovoltaic (PV)-based systems were installed in areas with scattered households. This effort resulted in universal electrification by 31 March 2019, propelling India towards accelerated development.

As the nodal agency for the DDUGJY and SAUBHAGYA schemes, the Rural Electrification Corporation (REC) has played an instrumental role in realising the dream of a power-sufficient India and ensuring last-mile connectivity to every Indian. REC is also one of the nodal agencies for the Revamped Distribution Sector Scheme (RDSS). We are sure that it will be augmenting the efforts of the Government of India in ensuring quality and reliable power supply for all.

REC's efforts in the country's energy transition journey: The path ahead

The transition to clean and green energy requires large investments. Various promising estimates have been made for fund requirements to achieve the net-zero targets set by the country. According to the report 'Investment Sizing India's 2070 Net-Zero Target' by the Council on Energy, Environment and Water (CEEW), India would need cumulative investments of $10.1 trillion to achieve net-zero emissions by 2070, with $8.4 trillion required to transform India's power sector. The World Economic Forum, in its report 'Mission 2070: A Green New Deal for a Net-Zero India', estimates a $15-trillion investment opportunity, which includes $6 trillion for energy transition. Additionally, the National Electricity Plan projects a significant fund requirement of Rs 33.60 lakh crore by 2032 for expanding the generation sector, with renewable energy playing a dominant role. All these indicate that REC has an important role to play as a major financier of the country's energy sector.

REC is relentlessly engaged in supporting green energy projects of various technologies through project financing. This includes options like solar, wind, and hybrid, as well as promising upcoming technologies like green hydrogen, green ammonia, and e-mobility. Our unwavering goal is to make low-cost funds readily available, driving India's ambitious target of 500 GW of non-fossil fuel-based capacity by 2030. The key highlights are:

- REC has positioned itself as a leader in driving India's energy transition and targets to attain a green finance loan portfolio of Rs 3 lakh crore by the FY 2030.
- During the FY 2024–2025, REC has already sanctioned around Rs 1,25,000 crore for RE projects covering solar, wind, hybrid, pumped storage plants (PSPs), green hydrogen, green ammonia, as well as e-mobility.
- REC had hosted the Green Finance Summit in July 2023 on the sidelines of India's G20 presidency and signed MoUs worth Rs 2.86 lakh crore with various developers of green projects.
- It has played a pivotal role in strengthening of the country's transmission and distribution (T&D) system. The T&D segment accounts for 53 per cent of the company's total loan book of Rs 4.97 lakh crore.
- In addition, REC has been financing e-buses since 2019 and has already sanctioned more than 10,000 e-buses. During the FY 2023–2024, it sanctioned projects worth Rs 6,630 crore for 5,150 e-buses, along

with charging infrastructure in Maharashtra, a 100 e-bus project in Bihar, and a repayment term loan (RTL) of Rs 495 crore for 500 e-buses in Hyderabad.

- REC has also been appointed as the overall programme implementation agency for the rooftop solar initiative PM Surya Ghar: Muft Bijli Yojana, which will further intensify its commitment towards fulfilling the country's green energy transition.

India's pursuit of energy security intersects with intricate geopolitical dynamics in the Indian Ocean Region and worldwide. Navigating these challenges necessitates strategic investments in infrastructure, diplomatic engagements, and the adoption of renewable energy. Balancing economic needs, environmental considerations, and geopolitical realities is key for India to ensure its energy future while fostering global stability and sustainability. As India progresses towards a cleaner, greener future with universal energy access and enhanced quality of life for its citizens, REC, as a financier, will intensify its efforts to achieve these goals, as it has done in the past.

18

Addressing Imperatives of India's Energy Security

Gurdeep Singh

India is at the juncture of a momentous transformation, aspiring to enter the golden phase of Amrit Kaal and create a landmark in its history by becoming a developed economy by 2047. The nation aims to become one of the top three economies and is poised to reach the target of a $5-trillion economy within the next few years. India's economy experienced robust growth of 8.2 per cent in 2023–24,[1] surpassing the International Monetary Fund's growth projections for India and maintaining its status as the world's fastest-growing major economy. The energy sector's significance is naturally on the rise, given its pivotal role in the country's growth strategy. Amidst the escalating energy demands, India is steadfastly expanding its energy capacity to meet these growing demands while ensuring affordable energy access to all citizens.

Energy Security Landscape

Recent global crises have fundamentally reshaped the world's outlook on the future of energy. Disruptions caused by successive events, including the COVID-19 pandemic, supply chain disruptions during the recovery phase, and armed conflicts, have created substantial imbalances between the global energy demand and the capacity to meet it. This has prompted a comprehensive reassessment of how energy security, transition, and affordability can collaboratively propel global growth and prosperity. Energy security concerns seem to have taken—hopefully temporarily—precedence over the priorities of achieving clean and affordable energy on a global scale, and this situation calls for a localised agenda to address the 'energy trilemma' of security, sustainability, and affordability.

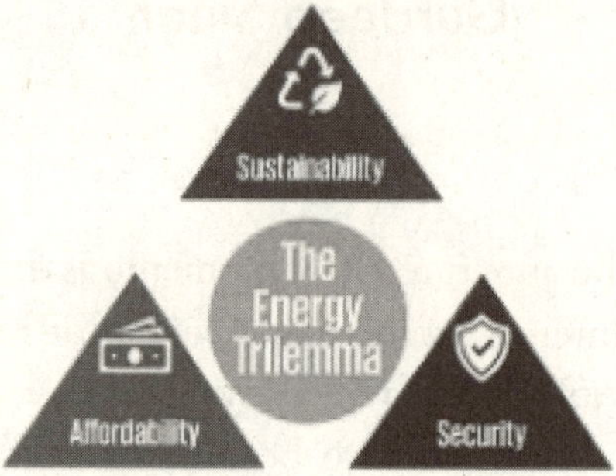

Figure 18.1 The Energy Trilemma[2]

In this context, it is important to note that India's substantial coal reserves provide a dependable source of energy that is not susceptible to geopolitical uncertainties, and it has the potential to minimise the impact of global events on energy prices and supply chains, ensuring a more resilient and secure energy infrastructure. India has limited energy resources of oil and gas, and it heavily depends on imports to meet its growing energy demands. Coal has been a cornerstone of India's energy sector for decades, contributing significantly to the country's industrial growth and electricity generation and is the key to India's energy security strategy.

According to NITI Aayog, India's energy demand is projected to more than double by the year 2047, serving as a crucial catalyst for future economic growth.[3] The primary energy demand, largely driven by urbanisation, is predominantly attributed to the industry and transport sectors. The 'Make in India' initiative and the associated increase in domestic manufacturing will propel demand for raw materials from the steel, cement, and iron industries, among others. The staggering levels of energy demand pose a formidable challenge for India, prompting the nation to double down on coal. Coal production surged from 893.19 million tonnes in 2022–23 to 997.83 million tonnes in 2023–24, marking a growth of 11.71 per cent.[4] According to the Ministry of Coal, it is poised to touch 1 billion tonnes soon.[5]

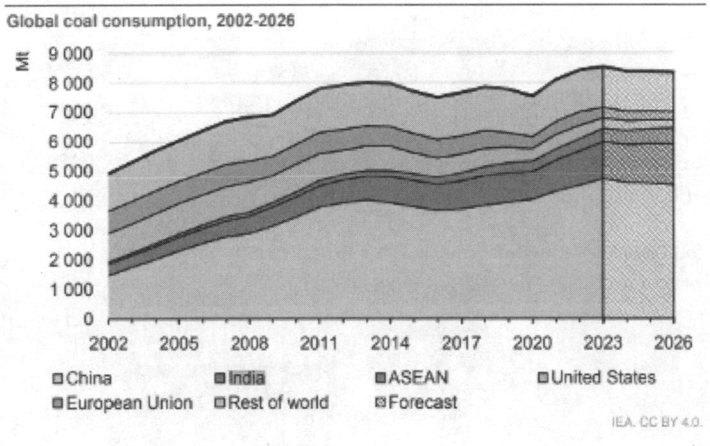

Figure 18.2 India Energy Security Scenarios (2047), NITI Aayog.
Source: IEA Coal 2023

Historically, coal has played a crucial role in India's energy sector, fulfilling 55 per cent of the country's energy needs and more than 75 per cent of its electricity needs. Given India's abundant reserves of coal and limited availability of natural gas, dependence on coal-fired plants remains substantial, further accentuating their significance. Electricity generated by coal-based power plants increased by a phenomenal 10 per cent between 2021 and 2023. Furthermore, India's current installed coal capacity of 215 GW is set to expand, with around 80 GW of new capacity in the pipeline. New coal mines are required to be opened in the future to meet the energy and coal demand. Also, there would be significant coal demand for projected adoption of clean coal technologies, such as coal gasification, coal liquefaction, etc.

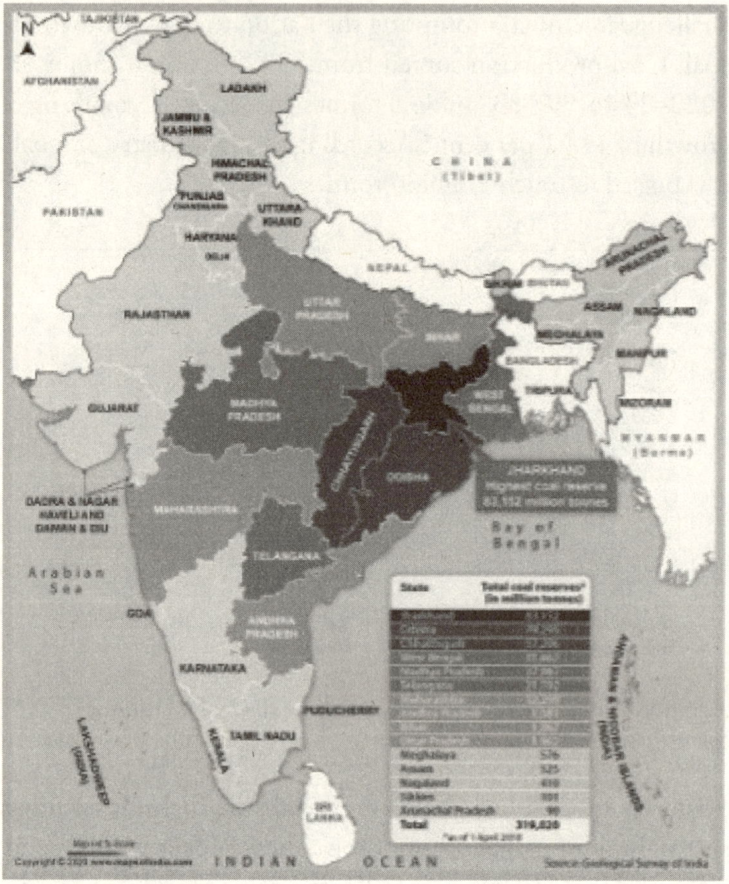

Figure 18.3 Coal Reserve
Source: Maps of India

Importance of Coal for the Indian Economy

The coal sector is intricately linked not only with various industries but also with the communities residing in proximity to coal mining and utilisation. This intricate connection has resulted in a significant economic and social dependence/reliance on the coal sector, impacting livelihoods, infrastructure, environmental conditions, state revenues, and the overall quality of life in these regions. Coal mining serves as a significant source of large-scale employment opportunities. The majority of this employment is concentrated in states known for coal production, including Jharkhand, Odisha, Chhattisgarh, West Bengal, Madhya Pradesh, Telangana, and Tamil Nadu.

Coal mining serves as a catalyst for economic stimulation in local communities, directly impacting the coal sector and indirectly influencing other industries by generating employment opportunities. The establishment of mines in an area contributes to local development, fostering enhancements in infrastructure, such as road networks and water supply systems. This presence facilitates improved accessibility to health and education services for the local population. Educational initiatives provided by mining companies, along with skill development for employees, present additional positive outcomes.

Further, India's railway sector, logistics, and iron, steel, aluminium, and cement industries are among several industries that depend on India's domestic coal. It is estimated that the Indian Railways derives more than 47 per cent of its freight revenue from coal and uses this income to subsidise passenger fares.[6] Considering the importance of rail transport, particularly for the poorer segments of the population, any reduction in fare subsidies will impact the underprivileged section of society. In addition, Indian Railways employs around 1.3 million people. Any reduction in the transportation of coal will also impact such employment opportunities. Furthermore, there are considerable secondary employment opportunities in both the formal and informal sectors.

India's Power Sector in the Epoch of Transformation

India's energy landscape is undergoing a transformative shift, driven by a strong commitment to sustainability, renewable energy, and enhanced energy access. The country's ambitious targets, as articulated by Prime Minister Narendra Modi at the COP 26 Summit, outline a clear trajectory towards achieving 50 per cent non-fossil fuel-based generation capacity by 2030 and net-zero emissions by 2070.

Despite comprising more than 17.7 per cent of the global population, India's carbon emissions account for only 4 per cent. Nevertheless, the country is steadfastly prioritising the development of environmentally sustainable energy sources to enrich its energy mix and achieve net-zero emissions by 2070. The power sector in India has undergone a remarkable transformation over the past nine years, marked by significant advancements, such as an increase in power generation capacity, expanded electricity access, and a pronounced focus on renewable energy sources.

Currently, India holds the fourth position globally in terms of renewable energy installed capacity, with 43 per cent of the installed electricity capacity derived from non-fossil-fuel sources. The solar energy installed capacity in India has witnessed a staggering growth, increasing more than twenty times in the last decade.

The country already has numerous policy measures in place to accelerate the shift to cleaner and more efficient technologies. Some of the major policy initiatives by the Indian government, such as lower tax rates, transmission waivers, binding agreements, capital subsidies, 100 per cent FDI, green corridors, Renewable Purchase Obligations (RPOs), must-run status for renewables, and ultra-mega renewable parks, etc., coupled with strong national targets, have helped make renewables cost-competitive and created huge demand for them.

India has also made substantial progress in the adoption of biofuels, with ethanol blending in petrol escalating from 1.5

per cent a decade ago to surpassing 12 per cent by 2023. The nation is committed to achieving a target of blending 20 per cent ethanol with petrol by 2025.

The commitment to power generation and universal electrification has played a pivotal role in India's transformative journey. A significant milestone in this endeavour is the successful implementation of the Pradhan Mantri Sahaj Bijli Har Ghar Yojana (SAUBHAGYA) initiative, achieving universal household electrification. Since its inception on 25 September 2017, this initiative has successfully provided electricity connections to 2.86 crore unelectrified households in both rural and urban areas. The result is evident in the increased power availability in rural areas, which has risen from approximately 12 hours per day in 2014 to 22.5 hours per day currently, while urban areas enjoy nearly uninterrupted power supply, with almost 24-hour availability.

The Deen Dayal Upadhyaya Gram Jyoti Yojana (DDUGJY) was launched in 2014 to improve the quality and reliability of power supply in rural areas. This programme achieved a commendable feat on 28 April 2018 by electrifying 18,374 previously unelectrified villages and strengthening the distribution network to ensure that electricity reaches every corner of rural India.

Government initiatives promoting energy efficiency, such as the Unnat Jyoti by Affordable LEDs for All (UJALA) scheme, have yielded remarkable outcomes. The procurement cost of LED bulbs witnessed a drastic reduction of almost 90 per cent between 2014 and 2019, decreasing from Rs 310 to Rs 39.90. The distribution of over 36.86 crore LED bulbs under this scheme has not only contributed to lowered electricity costs for households but has also fostered domestic manufacturing of LED bulbs, aligning with the 'Make in India' campaign.

Over the last decade, India has successfully added more than 1.8 lakh circuit kilometres of transmission lines, effectively connecting the entire country to a single grid operating on one frequency. The integration of smart grids, advanced metering infrastructure, and demand response mechanisms has significantly strengthened grid stability, empowering consumers to actively manage their energy consumption. This concerted effort reflects India's commitment to achieving a robust and inclusive power infrastructure.

India's commitment to solar energy is evolving into a nationwide movement, evidenced by the recent launch of a significant initiative, the Pradhan Mantri Surya Ghar: Muft Bijli Yojana for solar rooftop installation in one crore houses. This scheme aims to empower one crore families to achieve energy self-sufficiency, with arrangements being made to feed surplus electricity generated in their homes directly into the grid. This initiative presents a substantial investment opportunity across the solar value chain, with the potential for significant impact in a country like India.

To enhance the efficiency of power distribution, the government has implemented initiatives like the Revamped Distribution Sector Scheme (RDSS). This scheme showed promising results, with aggregate technical and commercial (AT&C) losses down to 15.41 per cent in the FY 2022–23. In addition, the government's endorsement of domestic manufacturing in the solar energy sector, under the broader goal of Atmanirbhar Bharat (self-reliant India), is evident through policies like the Production Linked Incentive (PLI) scheme, Basic Customs Duty (BCD), and the Approved List of Module Manufacturers (ALMM). These policies incentivise the growth of the sector, addressing the heavy dependence of the Indian solar sector on imports.

India is also making rapid strides in green hydrogen, with the implementation of the National Green Hydrogen Mission positioning the country to become a hub for hydrogen production and export.

NTPC: A Catalyst for Ensuring Energy Security in India

As the country's largest thermal power generator, the National Thermal Power Corporation (NTPC) stands at the forefront of driving innovative initiatives to facilitate the energy transition in India. The company has made significant progress in the renewable energy sector, including green hydrogen, carbon capture, and nuclear power. Simultaneously, it is enhancing the flexibility of its units and working towards reducing emissions.

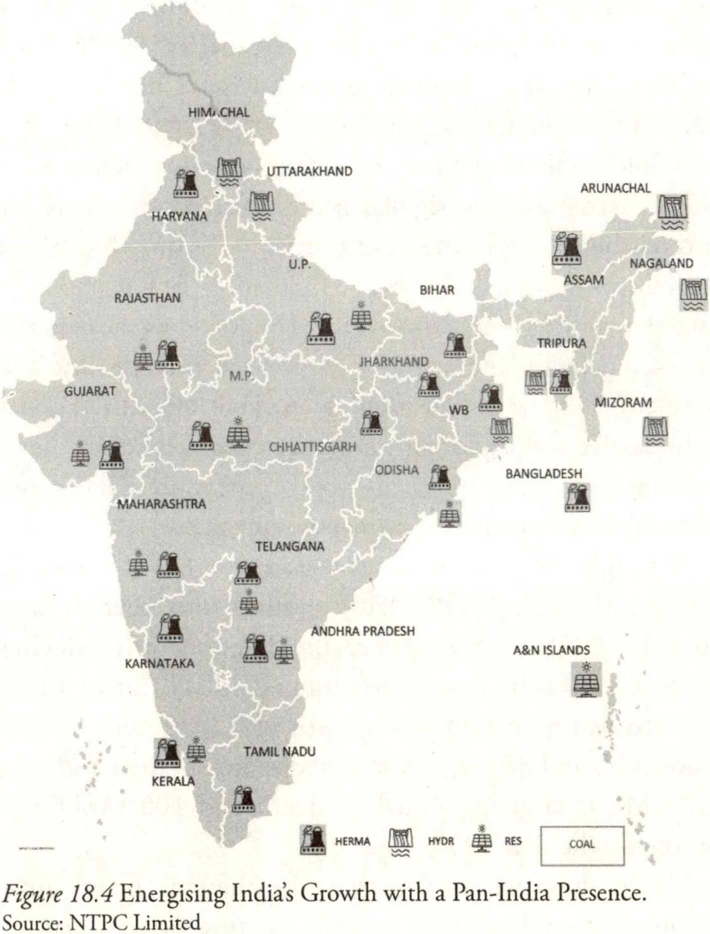

Figure 18.4 Energising India's Growth with a Pan-India Presence.
Source: NTPC Limited

NTPC is also diversifying its energy sources, emphasising a balanced mix of cost-effective thermal power and cleaner renewable energy to meet the growing demand. With an installed capacity exceeding 75 GW, NTPC aims to evolve into India's largest integrated power company, targeting a capacity of 130 GW with a diversified fuel mix, and generating 600 billion units by 2032.

It has adopted an aggressive stance towards renewable energy, including ventures into green hydrogen. NTPC envisions nearly 45–50 per cent of its capacity coming from non-fossil fuels by 2030, with a medium-term target of achieving 60 GW of renewable capacity by 2032—a commitment also reflected in its Energy Compact goals submitted to the United Nations.

While embracing the transition towards renewables, NTPC recognises the significance of coal power plants for grid reliability, employment, and social inclusion. Through its flexibility measures, NTPC is also facilitating the integration of variable renewable energy into the grid by providing the required flexible operation and ancillary services for grid stability. The company is actively transitioning to more efficient thermal technologies and exploring innovative energy solutions, such as biomass co-firing, green hydrogen production, and waste recycling based on circular economy principles.

Through its coal mining subsidiary, NTPC Mining Limited (NML), NTPC has ventured into coal mining operations. NML has surpassed the milestone of producing its maiden 100 million metric tonnes (MMT) of coal and has recorded a year-on-year growth of 77 per cent in coal production and 88 per cent in coal dispatch in the FY 2022–23. NML is targeting a coal production of 100 MMT per annum by the year 2030.

NTPC has plans to convert its thermal plants into chemical complexes for carbon capture and alternate fuel production. This will help avoid premature closures and reduce dependency on imported fossil fuels. The commitment to emission mitigation includes implementing flue-gas desulphurisation systems and DeNOx combustion modifications. NTPC is also delving into the potential of nuclear power, including advanced and modular reactors, to advance its sustainability goals.

Furthermore, the adoption of carbon capture and utilisation (CCU), along with the development of downstream chemical industries based on CO_2 captured from thermal power plants, represents promising steps in addressing challenges and offers significant employment opportunities. The viability of carbon capture for both existing and new coal power plants, coupled with incentives for commercial-scale green hydrogen production, will play a crucial role in accelerating the transition towards a more sustainable energy landscape.

As a key player in India's energy landscape, NTPC has undertaken several initiatives to promote the sustainable use of coal, aligning with the broader goal of balancing economic development with environmental stewardship. Some of these notable initiatives include:

Biomass co-firing

In 2017, NTPC initiated the Blue Sky initiative, introducing biomass co-firing in coal-fired power plants, starting with NTPC Dadri. The primary goal was to address the challenge of stubble burning while concurrently mitigating CO_2 emissions from coal-fired power plants by partially substituting coal with biomass. Cumulatively, NTPC has placed orders for 45 lakh tonnes of biomass, encompassing both short- and long-term agreements for twenty-one stations. The company has achieved biomass co-firing ranging from 5–10 per cent using non-torrefied biomass pellets and is actively working towards increasing the biomass co-firing ratio to 20 per cent and beyond, without significant modifications, by utilising torrefied biomass pellets.

In addition, NTPC is in the exploration phase of implementing 100 per cent biomass firing in coal-based power plants with minimal modifications. The company is investigating the feasibility of obtaining year-round pellets from sustainable agroforestry practices. These pellets, derived from stubble and husk, are utilised in most of the coal-fired power plants nationwide. This innovative approach not only reduces coal consumption and carbon emissions but also discourages the harmful practice of burning crop residue. Moreover, it generates economic value from agricultural waste. NTPC's pioneering method leverages existing infrastructure in coal-based power plants to contribute significantly to the renewable energy sector.

Waste-to-fuel

Aligned with the Government of India's Swachh Bharat Mission and its commitment to green energy, through its subsidiary NTPC Vidyut Vyapar Nigam Limited (NVVN), NTPC has initiated various projects in the waste-to-energy sector. These endeavours aim to contribute to a pollution-free environment, promoting the health and welfare of the people. In Varanasi, a thermal gasification-based waste-to-energy (WtE) plant with a demonstration scale of 24 tonnes per day (TPD) has been successfully commissioned. Additionally, NTPC has established a waste-to-charcoal project in Varanasi, with a capacity of 600 TPD, highlighting the organisation's commitment to sustainable waste management.

Expanding its efforts, NTPC is in the process of setting up a 900 TPD waste-to-coal plant in Astauli village, Greater Noida, along with a 400 TPD plant in Bhopal and a 200 TPD facility in Hubballi. The charcoal produced from these ventures will be efficiently utilised for co-firing at NTPC's coal-fired power plants. This strategic approach not only addresses the escalating waste generation challenge but also mitigates the strain on limited landfill space, offering an effective means of solid waste management.

Carbon capture and utilisation

Carbon capture and utilisation (CCU) from flue gas represents a promising avenue for the decarbonisation of coal-based plants. The captured CO_2 holds the potential to be used in the production of green chemicals. To illustrate this, the captured CO_2 can undergo catalytic hydrogenation, utilising green hydrogen to synthesise methanol. This methanol, in turn, serves as an alternative fuel in the transport and aviation sectors, contributing to emissions reduction while also substantially lowering reliance on imports. Another application of captured CO_2 involves the production of green ammonia and urea. Additionally, both methanol and ammonia produced can be directly utilised in boilers, thereby reducing the need for input coal and minimising CO_2 emissions. To capture and convert CO_2 from waste flue gases into hydrocarbons like methanol and ethanol, NTPC is actively engaged in setting up carbon capture and utilisation (CCU) projects. This innovative approach not only produces clean fuel but also sequesters carbon, effectively addressing two critical challenges—reducing carbon in the atmosphere and producing clean fuel—simultaneously. The 10 TPD CO_2-to-methanol project aims to capture CO_2 from existing thermal plants and utilise it to produce valuable products such as methanol. The CO_2 capture block was commissioned in August 2022. Work is ongoing for the indigenisation of catalysts and reactors for the conversion of the CO_2-to-methanol plant. NTPC is also setting up a 10 TPD 4G ethanol synthesis plant in Lara, Chhattisgarh.

Currently, space for CCU is being allocated in all new thermal plants planned by NTPC. After the successful implementation of CCU technology in new plants, the technology can be extended to existing coal-based power plants to reduce emissions after considering techno-economic viability of the proposed installation and any site-specific issues, such as space availability for installation, etc.

The economic feasibility of CO_2 utilisation routes is crucial for its industrial application. Presently, green methanol and 4G ethanol costs are comparatively higher than production from conventional methods. However, the cost of green chemicals will significantly reduce when green hydrogen—which constitutes approximately 75–85 per cent of the overall green chemical cost—becomes available at a cost-competitive price. Further, incentives in the form of carbon credits can help in developing a sustainable value chain for green chemicals. The green chemicals produced using carbon capture can be utilised in the transport sector (as a replacement for petrol/diesel), the energy sector (in diesel generator sets, boilers, fuel for gas turbines, heater modules, etc.), and blended with LPG. These applications can reduce CO_2 emissions, particulate matter, etc., thereby providing an accelerated path towards a circular economy.

Conclusion

Energy transition and decarbonisation are the need of hour to meet the global climate targets. However, for a developing country like India, where per capita energy consumption is a fraction of the global average, ensuring energy security, sustainability, and affordability is an equally important aspect. Meeting the energy needs of the underserved population, improving safe and sustainable energy access for the poorest and most vulnerable groups is the first and foremost consideration in India. Balancing the need for economic development, job creation, and reliable energy supply with environmental considerations is a complex challenge. In view of the above and considering the challenges of the Indian scenario, it is crucial to emphasise that energy security is of paramount importance for India, and renewable capacity addition alone will not be enough to ensure reliability, sustainability, and affordability in the future.

The role of coal in ensuring India's energy security is undeniable, given its historical prominence and the current energy landscape. As India strives to meet the rising energy demand, achieve the objectives of net zero, and fulfil its nationally determined contributions (NDCs), coal continues to be a critical component of the energy mix. India's massive investments in infrastructure, exemplified by initiatives like the National Infrastructure Pipeline (NIP) and the PM GatiShakti National Master Plan (PMGS-NMP), further underline the importance of a robust energy sector, wherein coal stands as a dependable source.

The resilience and adaptability of coal, coupled with advancements in pollution control technologies, carbon capture and utilisation, and coal gasification, showcase its potential to contribute to a more sustainable energy future. Decarbonising fossil-fuel-based plants becomes an equally important aspect for achieving the COP 26 commitments as well as meeting India's electricity demand in the future. There is a wide assumption that there must be an end to the use of coal to achieve the net-zero emission (NZE) targets. However, the addition of renewable capacity to the grid does not necessarily/essentially mean closure of fossil-fuel-based plants. Fossil-fuel plants are not competing with renewable generators; instead, they are facilitating the integration of variable renewable energy into the grid by offering the necessary flexible operation and ancillary services to ensure grid stability.

While acknowledging the imperative to diversify the energy portfolio and embrace cleaner alternatives, it is crucial to recognise the ongoing efforts to make coal utilisation more efficient and environmentally friendly. As the nation's leading electricity generator, NTPC has played a pivotal role in driving innovation and implementing initiatives that align with India's energy security goals. The company's commitment to renewable energy, green hydrogen, carbon capture, and exploration of nuclear power exemplify a holistic approach towards a diversified and sustainable energy landscape.

In navigating the path forward, it is crucial for India to leverage the potential of emerging technologies, enhance research and development in cleaner coal utilisation, and continue exploring alternative energy sources. A comprehensive and inclusive energy strategy, which recognises the multifaceted nature of India's energy landscape, will be instrumental in ensuring not only energy security but also sustainable and responsible energy practices for the benefit of the nation and the global environment. As India stands at the crossroads of its energy transition, the role of coal remains pivotal, albeit evolving, in the pursuit of a resilient and sustainable energy future.

19

The Role of the Bhakra Nangal Project in Providing Food, Water, and Energy Security in Northern India

Manoj Tripathi and Charanpreet Singh

Water, a scarce natural resource, is fundamental to life, livelihood, food security, and sustainable development. India has more than 17 per cent of the world's population, but only 4 per cent of the world's renewable water resources and 2.4 per cent of the world's land area. There are further limitations on utilisable quantities of water due to its uneven distribution over time and space. In addition, there are challenges of frequent floods and droughts in different parts of the country. With a growing population, rising needs of a fast-developing nation, and the expected impacts of climate change, the availability of utilisable water will be under further strain in the future, increasing the possibility of deepening water conflicts among various user groups. Storage and multipurpose projects like Bhakra and Pong help address the issues of temporal and spatial distribution of water in an efficient manner.

After India's Independence, most of the irrigated area of the northwestern part of undivided India went to Pakistan, and food grain shortages, which began after World War II, became very acute. In the 1950s, India had to start importing food grains. This situation was further aggravated by the wars of 1962 and 1965 with neighbouring countries. The failure of monsoon in 1965 and 1966 forced India to substantially increase the import of food grains. Reliable irrigation provided by the Bhakra and Nangal Dam projects of the Bhakra Beas Management Board (BBMB) led to a massive increase in the production of food grains in Punjab and Haryana as well as increase in productivity, which became much higher than the rest of the country. The Bhakra Nangal Project has been a major source of the green revolution in this part of the region. In addition, it is also a source of drinking water for many major towns in the states of Punjab, Haryana, Chandigarh, Rajasthan, and Delhi. Furthermore, this project provides cheap green energy to the northern states of the country.

The Scenario before the Bhakra Nangal Project

Southwest Punjab and the adjoining areas of Rajasthan had suffered from many devastating famines due to severe drought until India's Independence. Records speak of Emperor Akbar ordaining in 1568 that 'this jungle (Hisar district in Punjab) in which subsistence is obtained with thirst, be converted into a place of comfort'.[1] Something was perhaps done, but obviously, that did not stop famines from recurring. The arrival of the British and their rule did not make much difference to this part of India, at least with regard to droughts and famines. The Government of India appointed three successive famine commissions in the last three decades of the 19th century to report on the dimensions of the droughts, their causes, and the relief for the affected people. Detailed codes for providing relief were drawn up. However, Hisar district featured repeatedly in famine distress records. The district gazettes of Hisar states that the first such event for which authentic accounts existed relates to the year 1783. Many thousands died as a result.

Similar accounts are narrated about the famines of 1860–61, 1868–69, 1876–78, 1899–1900, 1918, 1929–30, 1932–33, and 1938–40. Likewise, accounts are available in the district gazetteers relating to the other districts of Punjab (for example, Ferozepur and Amritsar) and Rajputana (for example, Sri Ganganagar). The Report of the Famine Commission (1860–61) described the famine tract south of the Sutlej (particularly Ambala, Patiala, and Bhatinda) as follows:

'It is black, wretched, and without water, a mere sterile land. The wells are so deep that artificial irrigation from them is impossible; the water is so brackish and impure which none save natives of the tract can drink it with impunity; rains are scanty and precarious; vegetation is represented by a few stunted thorn bushes, or a temporary crop of grass, scattered over the great parched plains.'[2] The reports of the Famine Commission trace the history of past famines from 1769. Since the 1870s, with the standardisation of rain gauge networks and the availability of the India Meteorological Department (IMD)'s records, the documentation of droughts was placed on a sound footing. Unfortunately, it appears that a fatalistic view was adopted by the administration, which believed that droughts and famines would be unavoidable and all that could be done was to save human lives to whatever extent possible. It is, however, noted that even then, many voices were raised in favour of drought-proofing these regions. Some follow-up actions, such as providing canal irrigation in Punjab and Bikaner followed, but such steps were missing from the region we are concerned with here. It was almost at the dawn of Independence that this long-overdue action was initiated. It is indeed ironic that this part of India had to suffer for such a long period due to the loss of agricultural production and the consequent famines.

The total extent of cultivable area in post-Partition Punjab (excluding Shimla and Kangra districts) in the early 1950s was around 8.5 million hectares (ha). The net area sown was around 6.6 million ha. The net irrigated area was about 43 per cent. There were problems with the type and quality of irrigation provided. The canal-irrigated area accounted for just one-fourth of the net area sown, and tubewells had yet to appear in any significant manner. There was neither electricity nor diesel oil for running the pumps. Well irrigation, which accounted for a third of the irrigated area, was practiced with the aid of bullock-driven Persian wheels or water buckets lifted with camel power. The intensity of irrigation and water allowances were very low. In the absence of storage, the canal system was dependent on the flow of the river. In most years, during the non-monsoon months, the delivery at the canal heads dwindled. In drought years, it became impossible to deliver the 'authorised' full supply discharge, with the problem sometimes extending into even the rainy season. The delivery of water was unsteady and unreliable. Thus, even with the 'available irrigation', agriculture and food production remained a gamble dependent on rain.

The people of southwest Punjab resorted to the cultivation of millets like jwar and bajra for food grains, as the scarcity of water reduced the productivity of wheat. While undivided Punjab ranked as the granary of India because of its canal system, after Partition, Punjab became deficient in food grains, as most of the irrigated areas and important canal systems of undivided Punjab went to Pakistan.

The Scenario after the Bhakra Nangal Project

The Partition in 1947 resulted in India receiving only 20 per cent of the canal system of undivided Punjab, despite having 50 per cent of the population, as only the Upper Bari Doab Canal between the Ravi and the Beas (1859) and the Sirhind Canal in southern Punjab (1872) came to India's share. The Bhakra Nangal Project was taken up as a joint venture between the states of Punjab and Rajasthan immediately after Independence. Its construction began in 1948 and was completed in 1963.

The Bhakra Dam, a 225.55-metre-high, 518.16-metre-long concrete gravity dam, is located on the Sutlej River in the foothills of the western Himalayas/lower Shiwaliks in Himachal Pradesh, a northern state of India. It is a multipurpose hydroelectric project. The Gobind Sagar Reservoir, created by the construction of the Bhakra Dam, has a gross storage capacity of 9,867.86 MCM (million cubic metres), live storage of 7,436.03 MCM, and dead storage capacity of 2,431.83 MCM. It is one of the largest reservoirs in India. The average annual energy generated from two powerhouses located on the left and right banks of the Bhakra Dam is about 5,600 million units (MU).

Benefits from the Project

- Immense contribution to the economy through an increase in agricultural and farm production.
- A study commissioned by the World Bank, published in 2008, shows the following impact on different crops with and without the Bhakra Dam:

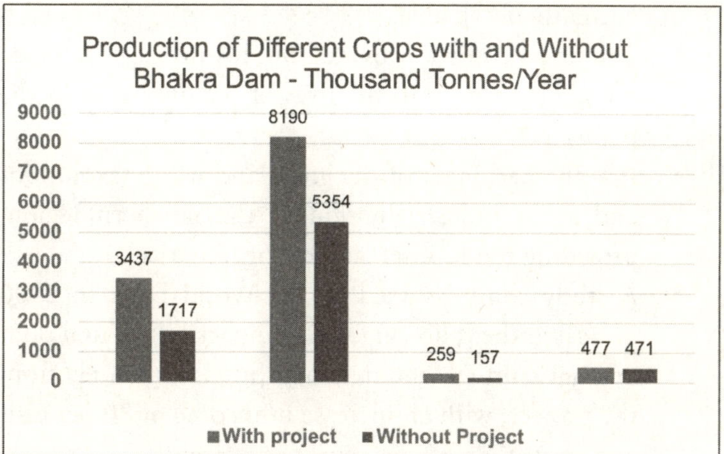

Figures 19.1 Production of Different Crops with and without Bhakra Dam[3]

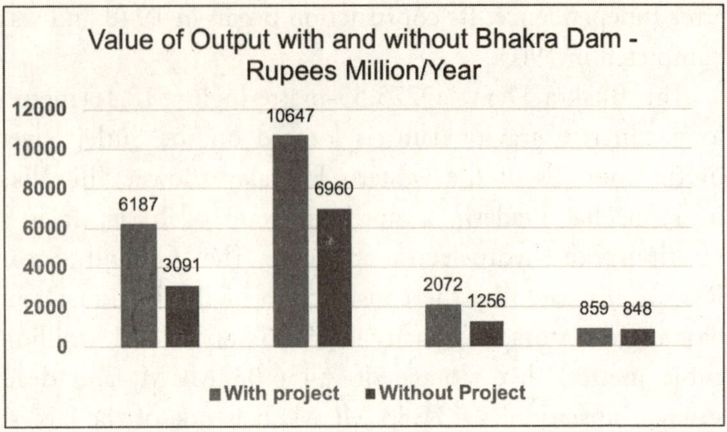

Figure 19.2 Value of Output with and without Bhakra Dam

The study indicates:

- Without the Bhakra Dam, the production of rice would have been about half of what was being produced in 1979–80 with Bhakra.
- The production of wheat would have been between 54 percent and 65 per cent of the currently produced quantity.
- The total value of these four major crops would have been between 52 per cent and 61 per cent of the value currently obtainable.
- The flood control provided by this project has made a huge difference in the lives of people living in the plains.
- It is the harbinger of the green and white revolutions and rapid industrialisation in the northern region, providing food, water, and energy security.
- A study commissioned by the World Bank in 2006 indicated the following social impacts: The rural poor and agricultural labourers benefitted immensely from the project, with an increase in income of 80 per cent and more than 60 per cent, respectively.

- Millions of very poor seasonal migrants from Bihar and the urban poor benefitted from lower food prices.
- Urban areas also benefitted indirectly, resulting in urban poverty reduction.

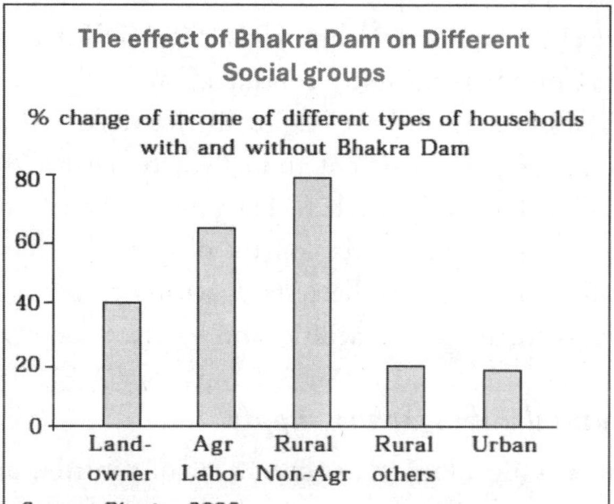

Source: Bhatia, 2005.

Figure 19.3 Effect of the Bhakra Dam on Different Social Groups[4]

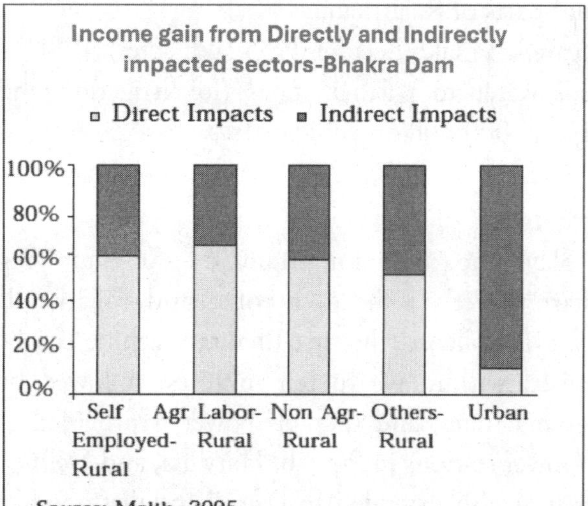

Source: Malik, 2005.

Figure 19.4 Income Gain due to the Bhakra Dam[5]

Annual food grain production

The growth rate of food grain production between 1960–61 and 1978–79, on an all-India basis, was 2.77 per cent, but it varied from state to state. Punjab and Haryana led with average growth rates of 8 per cent and 5.3 per cent per year, respectively. Jawaharlal Nehru University (JNU) and the Planning Commission jointly conducted an analysis of growth at the district level. Forty-eight districts recorded a high growth rate of over 4 per cent annually between 1962–65 and 1971–74. Punjab, Rajasthan, Haryana, and western Uttar Pradesh accounted for three-fourths of these districts. Similarly, milk production in these states witnessed a huge increase due to better irrigation facilities and water availability.

Irrigation and drinking water supply

- The Bhakra Nangal Project has been a major contributor to the green revolution in this region.
- In addition, it is also a source of drinking water to all major towns in the states of Punjab, Haryana, Chandigarh, Delhi, and parts of Rajasthan.
- Area irrigated: 54 lakh hectares (135 lakh acres).
- Supply of water to partner states (for irrigation and drinking): 34,000 million cubic metres.

Hydel power

- Bhakra plays the most important role in supplying 'black start power' in the event of a grid collapse. If there is a grid collapse, the first Bhakra machine can be synchronised within five to ten minutes, followed by the other machines, and start-up power is provided to thermal power stations in Punjab, Haryana, and Delhi.
- The supply is also extended to crucial installations like railways tractions, airports, and hospitals.

- Power generated by the Bhakra left bank powerhouse, which consists of five units, is 630 MW.
- Power generated by the Bhakra right bank powerhouse, which also consists of five units, is 785 MW.
- The total installed capacity of the Bhakra Project is 1,415 MW.
- The average annual energy generated from the powerhouses of Bhakra is about 5,600 MU.

Flood control

- Flooding is the single-largest natural calamity for humanity.
- The Bhakra Dam has largely eliminated the occurrence of floods in the plains of the Sutlej River.
- Floods of more than six lakh cusecs can be absorbed in the Gobind Sagar Reservoir by careful planning in advance if accurate predictions about heavy rainfall in the catchment area are available. The Bhakra Dam has also eliminated the occurrence of famines of yore in the region.
- The water of the Sutlej, which earlier was going to waste in the Arabian Sea and causing floods during monsoons, became a boon for agricultural and industrial development after the Bhakra Dam came up.
- The people in areas influenced by the dam are harvesting the fruits of the hard labour of thousands of known and unknown workmen, technicians, and engineers.
- The BBMB palys an important role in averting shortfall in water availability as well as sudden heavy discharges resulting in flood. Careful assessment of inflow of water in various periods of the year, based on inputs from the Indian Meteorological Department about rain and snow in catchment area and of water requirement for crops based on rainfall in the command area, have to be made. In case of an error in either of these assessments, more water may be

released in anticipation of high inflow and then there will be shortfall if inflow is below expectations. On the other hand, if less water is discharged anticipating low inflow and then high inflow takes place, water crosses the danger mark of the dam and has to be discharged in a short time through spillways. This causes wastage of precious water as well as creates floods downstream. Regular meetings of the technical committee take these critical decisions and in the long period of the dam's existence, mismatch has occurred only twice, in 2008 and 2023, with disastrous floods.

Pisciculture

- The Bhakra and Beas reservoirs are important sources for raising fish in the region. A large quantity of high-quality fish, approximately 314.58 MT, worth around Rs 399.76 lakh, is harvested every year from the Bhakra reservoir. Presently, thirty-four fishermen cooperatives, with a membership of 6,191 fishermen, are engaged in fishing activities. The Himachal Pradesh Fisheries Department has acknowledged the contribution of Bhakra reservoir as a classic example of large reservoirs contributing to job generation and the production of premium/high-quality animal protein, i.e., fish.

Rural electrification

- In 1951, only forty-two out of 11,947 villages in Punjab had electricity. With the help of power generation from Bhakra, Punjab and Haryana were the first states in India to provide electricity to every village.

Industrial development

- With the help of reliable and low-cost power generation from the Bhakra Beas Management Board's projects, the region also witnessed large-scale industrialisation, which had a tremendous impact on the local economy.

- The National Fertilisers Limited factory at Nangal is a direct result of the power generation by Bhakra. Agriculture-based industries have also flourished in the command area of the Bhakra Project. Large industrial towns were subsequently developed in Ludhiana and Jalandhar in Punjab, and Panipat and Faridabad in Haryana.

Water security from the Bhakra reservoir

The levels and inflows of the Bhakra reservoir in recent years are given below, which show that, in general, there has not been much variation in the inflows of the reservoir during the lean seasons compared to the average value. The average inflows during the depletion period are 4.76 million-acre feet (MAF). Thus, no shrinkage of the water level has been experienced, especially during the lean season.

Year	Level on 21 Sep. (Start of Lean Season)	Level on ending 20 May (End of Lean Season)	Inflows of Depletion period in MAF (lean season)
2010-11	1681.10	1573.97	5.853
2011-12	1680.51	1541.04	4.631
2012-13	1655.83	1559.15	4.691
2013-14	1678.19	1575.56	4.672
2014-15	1678.34	1598.23	4.687
2015-16	1676.72	1561.88	4.330
2016-17	1650.38	1539.71	4.659

Year	Level on 21 Sep. (Start of Lean Season)	Level on ending 20 May (End of Lean Season)	Inflows of Depletion period in MAF (lean season)
2017-18	1668.78	1501.36	3.907
2018-19	1651.25	1615.88	5.776
2019-20	1675.34	1563.80	5.014
2020-21	1659.61	1512.52	4.144
2021-22	1642.67	1559.40	4.997
2022-23	1667.90	1558.64	4.424

Figure 19.5 Levels and Inflows of the Bhakra Reservoir

Multipurpose projects like the Bhakra Dam provide benefits for a longer duration and have more far-reaching impacts and benefits compared to a number of small projects with similar installed capacities. The Bhakra Nangal Project provides affordable access to clean water for drinking, agriculture, industry, and household use, addressing India's serious water resource problem. Trends suggest that India is expected to become 'water scarce' by 2050. Water, along with food and energy, forms a critical part of the 'new security agenda', which redefines the understanding of security as a basis for policy responses and long-term planning. Multipurpose storage projects provide immense benefits, and storage projects like Bhakra can turn flood- and drought-prone areas into food bowls of the country.

20

India's Energy Security: The Road Ahead

Dip Kishore Sen

India stands at a unique crossroads today. On the one hand, the economy is poised to grow at more than 7 per cent annually for a prolonged period[1], which demands huge power consumption; on the other hand, India must switch to cleaner sources of power generation to honour its commitment to reducing its carbon footprint to ultimately achieve the national goal of net-zero emissions by 2070. Growth in GDP is directly correlated with energy consumption, which increases emissions of methane (CH_4), carbon dioxide (CO_2), and other greenhouse gases (GHGs), thus accelerating global warming and climate change. Hence, a developing nation like ours (which has been a late entrant in the industrial revolution) not only has to ensure its energy security but is also burdened with a moral obligation to strike a delicate balance between growth and emission mitigation—for the greater good of the entire world.

Global Warming: A Reality

When former US Vice President Al Gore produced the documentary 'An Inconvenient Truth' to highlight the dire consequences of global warming, its release in 2006 created quite a stir globally. In fact, it ended up winning two Academy Awards, in addition to garnering multiple international accolades and recognitions. But at that time, many had dismissed it as gross fearmongering. However, less than two decades later, the reality of climate change has started to bite. Twenty twenty-three marked a milestone year, witnessing temperatures consistently exceeding the 1850–1900 pre-industrial levels. Extreme weather events have become more frequent, compelling governments worldwide to huddle up and devise strategies to combat this clear and present danger.

There is no room for debate that much of the global warming today has been a result of large-scale industrialisation and the rampant use of fossil fuels. Governments are presently faced with a unique trilemma of balancing energy security with adherence to environmentally sustainable practices while keeping in mind the affordability factor in terms of pricing power, so that socioeconomic disparities do not worsen.

Governments today agree that global warming is irreversible. Thus, their efforts are now directed towards slowing it down and mitigating its impact as much as possible. It is no longer enough to reduce emissions; there is an urgent need to reverse them as well. At the COP 28 climate talks in Dubai, held in December 2023, more than 130 countries pledged to protect the environment and committed to achieving the following targets by 2030:

- Reduce greenhouse gas emissions: Cut emissions by 43 per cent compared to 2019 levels. Further, reduce methane emissions by at least 30 per cent from 2022 levels, as methane is more damaging than CO_2 due to its ability to deplete the ozone layer.
- Enable a 3x scale-up of renewable energy (RE) capacity to a minimum of 11,000 GW.

- Double the efficiency levels of existing generating assets from 2 per cent to 4 per cent.

Work in Progress

Aligned with the 2030 targets, a lot of work is happening worldwide. The larger focus is on switching to clean energy sources, which has fast-tracked the scaling up of renewable energy (RE) capacity. However, the intermittent nature of RE, due to its dependence on natural forces, remains a challenge. This is forcing both governments and private sectors to opt for hybrid projects to ensure round-the-clock (RTC) availability of power. This makes it imperative to invest in enhancing battery and storage capacity. Green hydrogen, as a clean energy source, is rapidly gaining traction worldwide. In parallel, biofuels and sustainable aviation fuel (SAF) are seen as holding great promise as alternative fuels with low carbon content. Going forward, electric power will drive the transportation sector. The blending of biofuels is also likely to pick up, although there remains a question mark over the sustainability of biofuel use, as its production competes directly with the food chain—unless the raw material is switched to agricultural waste.

Having said that, the necessary innovations or technological breakthroughs are still a few years away, and new technologies will take time to mature and attain scale, which will ultimately pave the way for a complete switch to cleaner sources of power. Until then, a premium has to be paid for facilitating the transition, because clean energy sources have yet to become cost competitive. The onus is on the governments to allocate substantial resources to make this transition happen.

Meanwhile, the systematic retirement of old and inefficient thermal power plants that use fossil fuels, along with the implementation of flue-gas desulphurisation (FGD), will need to be done urgently to reduce impact on the climate.

Countries' Level of Preparedness

Countries are putting up a fight against climate change. However, they are adopting different strategies and are in different phases of this fight; their actions are mostly determined by their level of economic development. Europe has taken the lead, and climate change has been on its radar for more than a decade. The governments there have been allocating substantial resources to clean energy initiatives. Those countries have also made good progress in tapping offshore wind energy, so much so that subsidy is no longer needed for it. The USA has been relatively slow compared to Europe. However, the Inflation Reduction Act (IRA) of 2022 has generously allocated resources to put the economy on a path towards meeting its global climate change commitments. Heavy subsidies are being offered to businesses, households, and even sub-national governments when they make investments aimed at reducing emissions and switching to clean energy. China, which produces about 30 per cent of total global emissions (more than the emissions from the US, the European Union, and India combined), has pledged to reduce emissions by 65 per cent from its 2005 level by 2030 and achieve carbon neutrality by 2060.[2] The countries in the Middle East are working towards making oil and gas less carbon-intensive, in addition to investing heavily in solar energy, green hydrogen, blue hydrogen, blue ammonia, and carbon capture projects. Biofuels, especially bioethanol, have been a part of Brazil's national energy policies for nearly half a century. South Korea is actively pursuing a switch from renewable energy to nuclear energy. However, African countries have made little progress on the clean energy front, except to some extent with geothermal energy (i.e., utilising the Earth's natural heat energy stored beneath the surface to generate electricity or provide direct heating), because of the inherent geological advantages, particularly along the East African Rift System, which extends from the Red Sea down to Mozambique. Countries like Kenya, Ethiopia, Tanzania, Djibouti, and Uganda are actively exploring and harnessing geothermal energy resources. In their transition journey, African nations will need active support from the developed world, which must help them in ensuring a unified fight to combat global warming.

Where Does India Stand?

India's energy consumption has more than doubled since 2000, driven by a growing population, industrialisation, urbanisation, and rising aspiration levels. It currently stands at around 1 Gtoe (gigatonne of oil equivalent) per annum. Over 90 per cent of India's energy needs are met by three fuels:

- Coal (46 per cent) has underpinned the expansion of electricity generation and industry, and remains the largest single fuel in the energy mix.
- Oil (24 per cent) consumption and imports have grown rapidly on account of rising vehicle ownership and road transport use.
- Biomass (21 per cent), primarily fuelwood, makes up a declining share of the energy mix but is still widely used as a cooking fuel. Despite recent success in expanding coverage of LPG in rural areas, 660 million Indians have not fully switched to modern, clean cooking fuels or technologies.

The balance 9 per cent of the energy requirement is met by natural gas, hydro, nuclear, and renewable energy sources.

Near-universal household access to electricity was achieved in 2019. However, energy use on a per-capita basis remains well under half the global average, and there are widespread differences in energy use, as well as in the quality of service, across states and between rural and urban areas. The affordability and reliability of energy supply are key concerns for India's consumers.

Any developing economy thrives on electricity consumption. For India, while the current peak demand for electricity is around 205 GW, the National Electricity Plan 2022–32 projects a peak demand of 277.2 GW by 2026–27 and 366.4 GW in 2031–32. India's present installed capacity stands at 442 GW, within which fossil fuels account for 56 per cent, while RE sources (including hydel power) account for 42 per cent. The plan aims to enhance non-fossil-based capacity to 57.4 per cent by 2026–27 and to 68.4 per cent by 2031–32.[3] Having said that, since RE sources like solar or wind power cannot ensure stable supplies, the baseload of India's power demand (i.e., the minimum amount of power the electrical grid requires at any given time) continues to be provided by coal-fired power plants.[4] Internationally, many developed nations are gradually phasing out their coal-based power generation capacity. For example, 60 per cent of electricity generation in the USA is from fossil fuels (43.1 per cent from natural gas, with the share of coal reduced to 16.2 per cent), while the remaining 40 per cent comes from nuclear power (18.6 per cent) and RE sources (21.4 per cent).[5] However, India's reliance on conventional fuels is unlikely to go away anytime soon.

India has the 5th largest GDP (after the USA, China, Germany, and Japan), but India's per capita CO_2 emissions (2.13 tonnes) is significantly lower than the global average (4.66 tonnes). All the developed countries emit even higher CO_2 per capita: USA (14.3 tonnes), China (8.37 tonnes), Germany (7.05 tonnes), and Japan (7.95 tonnes).[6] Hence, even if India's energy consumption rises as it progresses towards becoming a developed nation, the per capita CO_2 emissions figure will still be lower than that of developed countries.

Of the two non-coal fossil fuels, namely oil and gas, oil is much more carbon intensive. To produce the same amount of energy, 33 per cent more CO_2 is generated from oil compared to gas. Thus, natural gas, a cleaner source, will remain in demand as a transitional bridging fuel, and priority capital will be spent on gas production as well as on setting up the distribution infrastructure. The demand for crude will be increasingly driven by crude-to-chemicals projects, as India's per capita consumption of petrochemical products is still much lower than that in developed nations. However, for both these non-coal fossil fuels, India is largely dependent on imports. India imports around 85 per cent of its crude oil requirements and around 45 per cent of its natural gas needs. This makes India particularly vulnerable to supply disruptions and price volatility in the global energy market. As a safeguard, strategic petroleum reserves (SPRs) are being built across various locations to enhance energy security in case of supply disruptions or emergencies. A more lasting solution would be to identify hydrocarbon reserves within the country. The government intends to increase the exploration acreage to 0.5 million sq. km by 2025 and 1 million sq. km by 2030. The 99 per cent reduction in no-go areas, or places where exploration activity was previously prohibited, has freed up 0.91 million sq. km for hydrocarbon exploration. Additionally, the government is setting up a National Data Repository (NDR) so that large companies can participate in energy exploration in India's sedimentary basins. Work is also underway to create a cloud-based artificial intelligence/ machine learning (AI/ML)-powered NDR 2.0.[7]

Constantly changing geopolitics has proved to be a stumbling block for setting up transnational gas pipelines.

For India, as many as three such pipeline schemes (Myanmar–Bangladesh–India, Iran–Pakistan–India, and Turkmenistan–Afghanistan–Pakistan–India) did not materialise. Now, the focus has shifted to obtaining gas in liquefied natural gas (LNG) form, which also allows the flexibility to change supplier sources, unlike the pipeline mode, where buyers are stuck with a single supplier, giving the latter an undue advantage.

At the COP 26 summit in Glasgow, held in 2021, India made a commitment to achieve net-zero emissions by 2070. It has also set a target to harness 50 per cent of its energy requirement from RE sources and reduce carbon emissions by 1 billion tonnes, both by 2030.

From the present 191 GW installed capacity of non-fossil fuel-based power, India aims to scale it up to 500 GW by 2030. Within this, 485 GW is expected to come from RE sources, up from today's capacity of 180 GW.[8] Although this implies a more than 2.5x increase in RE capacity and may seem somewhat ambitious, these are achievable targets. India enjoys a geographical advantage that needs to be exploited. With nearly 300 sunny days every year, India's solar energy potential is huge. There is already substantial solar power generation capacity (more than 75 GW). In addition, 50 solar parks, with an aggregate capacity of 37.49 GW, have been approved. In addition, the Pradhan Mantri Suryodaya Yojana[9] aims to enhance the adoption of solar power usage at the household level. With a targeted installation of 10 crore solar rooftops on houses, which will reduce electricity bills of poor middle-class families, this plan intends to increase the grid-connected solar rooftop capacity from the present 11 GW to 40 GW. India's installed wind energy capacity currently stands at 45 GW. With a coastline of more than 7,600 km, there is great potential to tap offshore wind generation. An offshore target of 30 GW by 2030 has been set, and potential sites have been identified.

Clean Energy: The Building Blocks

Storage: The issue of intermittency of RE sources makes it imperative to explore storage solutions.[10] Energy transition cannot happen unless the storage problem is solved. By making use of storage systems such as battery energy storage system (BESS), pumped hydro storage (PHS), hydrogen energy storage system (HESS), and compressed air energy storage (CAES), the excess RE generated during peak production can be stored for later use. This will also be key to enhancing grid stability. However, India's perception of energy storage needs to be expanded from assets that enable round-the-clock supply of RE to assets that can provide various grid services. Widening the use of energy storage technologies requires a favourable policy and regulatory framework, financial support, and personnel training. Storage solutions are bound to be costly initially, but over time, they promise substantial returns. With increased R&D on these solutions and as economies of scale come into play, the cost of storage is expected to come down and become commercially viable. Until then, government support in the form of fiscal incentives would be helpful.

Green hydrogen: Globally, hydrogen has emerged as a major part of the fuel mix used by industries like steel, refineries, fertilisers, etc. For its decarbonisation initiatives, India is primarily relying on green hydrogen and has announced the ambitious National Green Hydrogen Mission in January 2023, aiming to become a global leader in the production, utilisation, and export of green hydrogen. India has proactively started putting in place policies such as free transmission, open access, and non-applicability of cross-subsidy surcharges on RE required for producing green hydrogen. In the first phase of the mission, the focus is on replacing grey hydrogen used in oil refining and grey ammonia used in fertiliser manufacturing for domestic use. In addition, a production-linked incentive (PLI) scheme for electrolyser manufacturing has been announced, which has received an overwhelming response, reflecting the growing interest in green hydrogen. Given the abundance of available land and natural resources like sunlight and wind, India has the potential to emerge as a global supplier of green hydrogen and green ammonia. Already, the EU member states, Japan, and South Korea have shown interest in sourcing green hydrogen and green ammonia supplies from India. According to the International Energy Agency (IEA), green hydrogen and other low-carbon technologies can potentially create a USD 80-billion market in India by 2030.

Solar components: Solar energy forms a significant part of India's transition to green energy. However, a 2.5-3x increase in solar energy capacity requires massive import of solar modules from China. Given the growing volatility in geopolitics, India must reduce this dependency. Presently, India has almost no capacity in solar materials, except for solar modules and cells. Its capacities for manufacturing solar wafer, polysilicon (the raw material for solar wafer production), and ancillary materials are very limited, thus the heavy dependence on imports. Even the main equipment that manufactures solar modules and upstream materials are non-existent in India and need to be imported from either Europe or China.[11] PLI and SPECS (Scheme for Promotion of Manufacturing of Electronic Components and Semiconductors) are expected to play a key role in bolstering the domestic manufacturing ecosystem for solar energy.[12] Already, private developers have envisaged several mega projects for producing polysilicon, which is required for solar power cells and semiconductors.

Nuclear Energy: Nuclear energy is also part of India's energy mix, although its share is not even 2 per cent of the total. While it is considered the best option for clean energy, currently the public sector dominates this field. India has private companies involved in the construction and manufacturing of machine parts for nuclear power plants, but no private company owns or operates a nuclear power plant at present. The world is witnessing a growing trend of small-capacity atomic power plants, popularly called small modular reactors (SMRs),[13] which offer unique features such as modularity, scalability, a small footprint, and improved safety. These reactors are seen as a potential solution for repurposing of retiring coal-based thermal power stations.

India can encourage private sector participation for the development of SMRs. However, the raw material uranium is in short supply in India, and we need to depend on the import of natural uranium from France, Canada, Russia, Kazakhstan, and Uzbekistan. This calls for large-scale mineral prospecting within India. Another alternative is nuclear fusion technology, which does not depend on nuclear fuel. However, making fusion technology viable at a commercial scale will take some more time. Funding for the R&D of nuclear fusion technology may speed up its commercial deployment.

Energy efficiency: Improving energy efficiency across sectors like industry, transportation, and buildings is a crucial part of India's energy policy. Initiatives such as the Perform, Achieve, and Trade (PAT) scheme have been implemented to promote energy efficiency in industries. While India continues to rely on coal for a significant portion of its energy needs, there are efforts to increase the efficiency of coal-based power plants and explore cleaner technologies such as carbon capture and storage (CCS).

The Missing Link

To ensure that India does not become energy deficient, the Nation Electricity Plan targets the following additional generation capacity by 2032:

- Coal/Lignite : 49 GW
- Nuclear : 13 GW
- Hydro : 16 GW
- Solar : 310 GW
- Wind : 82 GW

The bulk is expected to come from RE sources.

While there is clarity on the way forward, the Indian government would need to address a couple of issues to make this green transition a reality:

- Adopting advanced technologies and innovations prevalent in developed nations to enhance energy efficiency, reduce emissions, and optimise resource utilisation calls for substantial investments in R&D, skill development, and technology transfer.
- Transition to clean and green energy has to be made affordable for the masses.

Everything will ultimately boil down to how the finances needed for this transition get mobilised. As per IEA projections, India will need an average annual investment of USD 160 billion across its energy economy between now and 2030 to be on target for its ultimate net-zero emissions goal by 2070. This is a huge amount, keeping in mind that the budget outlay for the entire infrastructure sector for 2024–25 stood at around USD 135 billion. This can be immensely challenging when access to low-cost global funds is virtually unavailable. The Indian government would need to leverage its diplomatic goodwill to scout for and secure long-term funds. In addition, it would need to incentivise the private sector (both domestic and foreign) to play an active role for this transition to unfold successfully—whether it is through collaboration on R&D, skilling, investing in setting up green-tech manufacturing units, or even financing. To make mass adoption of clean energy technology a reality, our policymakers should ensure the availability of soft loans and other fiscal incentives for both manufacturers and users of such technology and also allow for accelerated depreciation of these assets.

To counter climate change at the international level, some progress has already been made in setting up early warning systems, building climate-resilient infrastructure, and working on ecosystem restoration. However, much more needs to be done if we are serious about leaving a liveable planet for future generations. India, by virtue of its growing stature as an economic force, enjoys clout and can influence global policymakers. This was evident in the way the Indian government took the lead in setting up the International Solar Alliance in 2015. Now is the time for India to appeal to all countries to jointly establish an international institutional mechanism that brings together governments, the corporate sector, and leading scientific minds to seamlessly collaborate on technology R&D towards clean and green energy, as well as cost optimisation. Additionally, India should also propose the creation of dedicated multinational vehicles that can finance the laggards to help them catch up.

Part IV
The Dream

21

Technology: The End of Geopolitics

Harry Dhaul

As the year 2060 unfolds, I descend from the latest model of the interstellar spaceship, *The Voyager*, and my eyes eagerly absorb the sight of an unfamiliar yet captivating landscape on Earth.

Stretching out before me, the world unveils a panorama transformed beyond recognition. Across the horizon, biodomes punctuate the scenery, their sleek structures glistening under the soft glow of the sun. Within these domes, a marvel of innovation unfolds as high-speed, high-yield crops flourish in meticulously controlled environments. The days of anxiously waiting for a bountiful harvest are past; instead, these crops mature with astonishing speed, their lifecycle condensed to a mere ten days. This remarkable feat ensures a steady stream of produce—a lifeline to sustain humanity's ever-growing needs. The once vast expanses of traditional agricultural fields have gracefully yielded to the supremacy of these futuristic bubbles, marking a groundbreaking revolution in food production and land use. This has had a profound impact on the geopolitics of the world.

These revolutionary changes in the process of producing food, along with the radical transformations in energy generation that have been achieved in the past two decades, have ushered in a new epoch of human history. Gone are the days when striving for profit at any cost was the bedrock upon which human society was built, when numerous and continuous conflicts for domination of fossil fuels and freshwater were the norm, and when people with control over large quantities of natural resources were the privileged.

Human society has now evolved and collectively strives for peace, sustainability, co-dependence, and cooperation while the powerplay of geopolitics—the attempt to achieve hegemony on world affairs by competing nations—is a relic of the past.

This metamorphosis of thought is also reflected in the natural landscape across the globe, with the previously large urban agglomerations now receding and greenery beginning to dominate these landscapes. Futuristic and environment-friendly systems of housing and industry dot the planet, while rivers, streams, and waterfalls flow wondrously. Large forests, marine sanctuaries, and wildlife corridors have emerged once again, and crop lands and grasslands have become carbon sinks.

The dance between the Earth and the sun, marked by the celestial mechanics of a seventy-eight-year cycle/wiggle, had ushered in severely damaging climatic patterns just two decades ago, altering the speed of winds and intensifying the jet streams, leading to temperatures escalating in the summers and plummeting in the winters. Humanity then stood at the precipice of this climatic metamorphosis, facing the brunt of extreme weather conditions—a testament to the inevitable forces of climate change. This pushed the human race into an extended 'Age of Conflict', with each nation vying for the last available natural resource and habitable land. Yet, it is within this crucible of environmental, social, and economic upheaval that a silver lining emerged, postponing the impending doom faced by the human race indefinitely and halting the geopolitical conflicts centred around the race to acquire control over fossil fuels and minerals for economic profit—dreams of the rich but the means of the poor.

Ironically, the catalyst for such a transformational change in the way humans behave and exist, and that silver lining for humanity, emerged from the wastelands and deserts, which had increased significantly due to the extreme climate crisis. This is because beneath the scorching gaze of the sun, these neglected lands now stand as colossal reservoirs of solar energy. Through the ingenuity of advanced technologies, the relentless heat of the desert sun is no longer a foe to be endured but a valuable resource to be harnessed.

During the day, intricate systems beneath the desert harvest, capture, and store this abundant energy, like a treasure awaiting to be discovered. And when darkness descends upon the land, this stored energy is unleashed, coursing through intricate networks of heat exchange systems, illuminating the night sky, powering essential functions, and warming the hearts of those who call this planet home. With humankind no longer reliant on sprawling solar farms, towering wind turbines, or daunting dams, nature itself now stands as the ultimate solution, offering its boundless energy with open arms. This has rendered the social debate between the haves and the have-nots irrelevant.

Across these vast expanses of wastelands and deserts, previously overlooked and forsaken, now lies the key to human prosperity. Here, amidst the unforgiving terrain, lies a wealth far greater than any oil well could offer: the inexhaustible abundance of natural energy. Once-thriving urban centres, symbols of humanity's conquest over nature, now fade into the tapestry of memory. In their place, communities thrive in harmony with the Earth, drawing sustenance directly from its energy reserves. Energy, once a centralised force dictating the ebb and flow of daily life, now flows freely and democratically, as each individual and community becomes a beacon of self-sufficiency. Blessed with digital connectivity and technological transformation, the reason for living in concrete urban jungles has become a relic of history.

The concentration of power is no longer confined to the elite or the privileged few, as the arsenal of cutting-edge technologies now stands within reach of every individual, irrespective of borders or boundaries. Gone are the days where influence was synonymous with the control of oil fields or the mastery of a comprehensive energy supply chain. Instead, enterprise has metamorphosed into a realm characterised by the decentralisation of energy generation, thereby eliminating concentrated centres of energy and power.

These tides of change have reshaped not only the physical world but also the geopolitical tapestry of nations. Where once oil-exporting nations reigned as economic titans, their dominance now wanes as the curtains fall on the era of fossil-fuel-based industries. The concept of an oil-based economy is dead. In a profound shift, every individual has become a steward of the Earth's resources, tapping into the boundless reservoirs of solar energy that lie above and beneath the surface. The notion of an economy shackled to the whims of oil is consigned to the annals of history, replaced by a paradigm where nations prosper in harmony with nature's bounty. The concept of exploitation has given way to a more equitable and sustainable system, where the needs of all are taken into account. Nature has reclaimed its role as the primary provider for humankind, heralding a future where the lines between survival and harmony are erased.

The once-unchallenged dominion of the few, built upon the bedrock of fossil-fuel monopolies and the orchestration of colossal transportation systems spanning continents, has now collapsed. As the sun, that radiant celestial entity, emerges as the quintessential source of inexhaustible energy, the traditional bastions of control find themselves grappling with a new reality—a reality where the supremacy of sustainability supersedes the tyranny of scarcity, and the power and geopolitics surrounding control and manipulation are relegated to the past.

As nations pivot towards these new renewable energy sources, all those who hold the reins of solar and wind energy find themselves at the forefront of this new era. No longer shackled by the volatility of oil markets, these nations now wield influence that transcends borders, shaping the destinies of nations and continents alike. With so many of them, the need to compete or dominate is vanishing, creating true energy democracies.

In this new epoch, the sun, wind, and soil stand not as passive observers but as active collaborators in the grand symphony of human progress. Together, they herald the dawn of a new age—a world where the forces of nature converge to power our collective journey towards a brighter tomorrow.

This monumental transition has not only redrawn the contours of power but has also vanquished the spectre of conflict and conquest that had long haunted humanity. War as a concept has become outdated. The geopolitical era of constant conflict between the haves and the have-nots has finally been put to rest. The old systems, built on the pillars of exploitation and greed, have crumbled, making way for a new age of cooperation and mutual benefit. Wars, once fuelled by the insatiable thirst for control over dwindling resources, acquisition for greater profits, and competition for geopolitical hegemony, now appear as relics of a bygone time, rendered obsolete in the face of an abundance of energy—a testament to the indomitable power of unity, the boundless realms of science, and the unwavering spirit of exploration.

The spectre of conflict has been exorcised, replaced by the radiant dawn of collaboration and coexistence. In this new age, every individual, regardless of origin or affiliation, finds himself endowed with a boundless capability to tap into the celestial reservoirs for his sustenance and progress.

As information now flows seamlessly across borders, the age-old game of exploitation for profit has become obsolete. The notion of perpetually upgrading the so-called poor to the middle class, so they can feed the machine of capitalism, no longer holds sway. With the democratisation of knowledge, brought about by this information age, the barely concealed profit-driven exploitation has come to an end. The once opaque system of competition and greed has been laid bare, revealing its inherent injustices and inefficiencies.

The once mighty global economy, built on intricate financial systems and digital currencies, has crumbled under the weight of its own complexity. The era of credit cards, stock markets, cryptocurrencies, and online transactions has now become a distant memory. What has emerged from the ashes is a revival of an ancient practice: the barter system. Back in the early days of human civilisation, when coins and paper money were yet to be invented, people exchanged goods directly. If you had an abundance of wheat and needed a new pair of shoes, you would find someone willing to trade their leather craftsmanship for your grain. This simple system of swapping goods formed the backbone of early economies.

As the intricate supply chains that once spanned continents collapsed due to environmental catastrophes, resource scarcity, and geopolitical upheavals, people found themselves isolated, disconnected from the global marketplace. Further, the relentless march of automation, artificial intelligence, and decentralised systems disrupted traditional economic hierarchies. In this new reality, the barter system reemerged as a lifeline. Farmers swapped produce, artisans exchanged skills, and communities supported one another. The simplicity of bartering transcended borders and reminded humanity of its shared vulnerability.

Land ownership, too, lost its allure. Urban sprawl and environmental crises forced us to rethink our relationship with the Earth. A movement has emerged, advocating for communal living, vertical gardens, and sustainable habitats. Virtual reality has also helped this cause by offering vistas more captivating than any acre of land. Why own a backyard when you can explore enchanted forests or build virtually changing digital cities? The concept of 'ownership' has now shifted from physical to virtual.

In this era where innovation knows no bounds, the once-familiar sight of bustling airliners etching their trails across the skies, congested roads and heavy traffic have become a thing of the past. Instead, there emerges a revolutionary mode of travel, powered not by the roar of jet engines but by the Earth's own electromagnetic pulse. These bespoke conveyances, tailored to individual whims and desires, herald a new age of personal anti-gravity exploration and unfettered mobility. No longer beholden to the constraints of mass transit or the confines of overcrowded airports, travellers now find themselves liberated from the shackles of conventional transportation.

Jetpacks, once confined to science fiction, are now a reality. So are anti-gravity pods—sleek capsules that reduce the effects of gravity through vacuum technology and, suspended in mid-air, allow passengers to glide silently from point A to point B, having evolved from Maglev technology. These hybrid vehicles seamlessly transition from road to air, bypassing congestion and obstacles. The oceans and rivers, too, are no longer barriers, as water-based drones glide effortlessly, delivering goods and monitoring marine ecosystems. These aquatic couriers crisscross the globe, connecting coastal cities and remote islands for on-demand physical travel by all.

Through ingenious processes, sunlight is harnessed and transmuted into the lifeblood of these forms of modern transportation: ammonia and hydrogen. With each revolution of the wheels and each journey embarked upon, the reliance on antiquated fossil fuels dwindles, replaced by the promise of a cleaner, greener future.

Water scarcity, which led to multiple conflicts just three decades ago, is no longer an insurmountable challenge. Humans now harness water from the very air they breathe, ensuring a sustainable and abundant supply. Water recycling has reached unprecedented levels, ensuring that every precious drop is reclaimed and reused. Contaminants, pathogens, and even trace chemicals, are all removed from water, rendering it safe for reuse. Every flush, every shower, and every industrial discharge contributes to a closed-loop water cycle, while communities embrace decentralised water recycling. Buildings, neighbourhoods, and cities all have their own water treatment and recycling facilities, and coastal regions rely on desalination plants where solar-powered reverse osmosis systems convert seawater into freshwater.

As the natural aquifers, lost to the age of urbanisation, have been replenished and purified, the rivers and lakes killed through pollution are now revived and flow freely without emitting the stench of human greed. The 'water wars' have now become obsolete. Streams and rivulets are no longer diverted to cater to agricultural and energy needs; they are now left alone in their pristine and natural forms. The geopolitics of water is dead, as water is harvested from the air wherever required.

Plastics, once ubiquitous and persistent, have also met their demise through the tireless collaboration of scientists, engineers, and environmentalists who have developed ingenious methods to accelerate their degradation, creating vibrant ecosystems. New materials have emerged—biodegradable polymers, plant-based plastics, and sustainable composites—which have now completely replaced plastics.

Commerce, energy, minerals, transportation, industry, and even the most basic sustenance of food and water, which were all wielded as weapons to stoke the flames of strife and discord among nations in the past, have now been transformed into sacred threads that weave the fabric of global unity and collaboration, binding humanity in a shared journey towards prosperity and enlightenment. The reliance on artificial constructs for survival has diminished and in this symphony of transformation, the once-elusive dream of peace and abundance has now found its crescendo, resonating across the expanse of time and space with the harmonious rhythm of a world finally awakened to its fullest potential.

This paradigm shift is characterised by a collective recognition that the Earth's resources are finite, and that the earlier trajectory of unchecked consumption was unsustainable. The once-mighty machine of profit-driven capitalism has been replaced by a world awakening to the fact that there can be no long-term prosperity without a healthy planet. This seismic shift in the collective human narrative is attributed not just to a change in ideology but to a fundamental alteration in the very dynamics of our planet and its relationship with the cosmos.

The geopolitical game of the human race has been put to rest; it is no longer the dreams of the rich and means of the poor. The notion that there is nothing left to conquer, no treasure worth the turmoil, also marks the advent of this new epoch of global harmony. Human society now resembles the utopia of Sat Yuga, as described in Hindu scriptures, where nobody locked their house doors because there was nothing to steal, given the abundance. I am not sure whether this was due to a reduction in population or other social engineering, but I'm finally able to see humanity achieve the ultimate goal of peace across the planet. It is almost as though humanity has stumbled upon the elusive philosopher's stone, transmuting the base lead of its past conflicts and disparities into the gleaming gold of shared prosperity.

This new experience of human society, where desires are no longer tethered to the scarcity of resources, unfurls a tapestry of life so divergent from the epochs overshadowed by strife and supremacy that my arduous journey through the cosmos seems but a fleeting moment in the vast expanse of time. I finally witness the demise of geopolitics as we knew it at the turn of the century.

Notes

Preface

1 'Why geopolitics is a game of chess: Strategy, power, and the ultimate checkmate', *ET Edge Insights*, 18 January 2024. https://etedge-insights.com/featured-insights/geopolitics-and-strategy/why-geopolitics-is-a-game-of-chess-strategy-power-and-the-ultimate-checkmate/.

Chapter 2: Geopolitical Implications of Lopsided Natural Resource Endowment

1 Richard Auty, *Sustaining Development in Mineral Economies: The Resource Curse Thesis*, Routledge, 1993.
2 Vladimir Lenin, *Imperialism, the Highest Stage of Capitalism*, 1917, Ch. 8, 'Parasitism and Decay of Capitalism'.
3 Alexis de Tocqueville, *Democracy in America* (J.P. Mayer [ed.]), New York: Harper Perennial, 1988.
4 Michael Levin, 'Botswana's Success: Good Governance, Good Policies, and Good Luck'. https://documents1.worldbank.org/curated/en/304221468001788072/930107812_201408253094647/additional/634310PUB0Yes0061512B09780821387450.pdf.
5 Ibid.
6 Ibid.
7 Ibid.
8 https://archive.uneca.org/stories/botswana-shining-beacon-hope-fight-against-corruption-africa.

Chapter 3: Ensuring India's Energy Security and Transition to Green Energy in the Face of Geopolitical Upheavals

1 Indian Power Sector: An Update, Ministry of Power, 10 July 2017. https://pib.gov.in/PressReleasePage.aspx?PRID=1495026.

2 Status of power generation and power supply position in the country, Ministry of Power, 19 December 2023. https://pib.gov.in/PressReleaseIframePage.aspx?PRID=1988262.

3 Transmission Overview as of 31 January 2024, Ministry of Power. https://powermin.gov.in/en/content/overview-0.

4 Make in India not only for India but for the world, Ministry of Power, 7 March 2024. https://pib.gov.in/PressReleasePage.aspx?PRID=2012135.

5 https://economictimes.indiatimes.com/industry/energy/power/peak-power-demand-likely-to-cross-400gw-by-2030-r-k-singh/articleshow/106990885.cms?from=mdr.

6 Make in India not only for India but for the world, Ministry of Power, 7 March 2024. https://pib.gov.in/PressReleasePage.aspx?PRID=2012135.

7 'Renewable Energy Sources Can Meet 90% Global Supply by 2050: RK Singh', NDTV News, 31 October 2023. https://www.ndtv.com/india-news/renewable-energy-sources-can-meet-90-global-supply-by-2050-power-minister-rk-singh-4530850.

8 UNDP Climate Promise. https://climatepromise.undp.org/what-we-do/where-we-work/india.

9 https://www.irena.org/News/pressreleases/2022/Jan/India-and-IRENA-Strengthen-Ties-as-Country-Plans-Major-Renewables-and-Hydrogen-Push

10 World Energy Outlook 2023, International Energy Agency (IEA), October 2023. https://www.iea.org/reports/world-energy-outlook-2023.

11 IEA holds training week to boost energy efficiency policy action in India,18 December 2023. https://www.iea.org/news/iea-holds-training-week-to-boost-energy-efficiency-policy-action-in-india.

12 Impact of Energy Efficiency Measures for the Year 2022–23, Study by Deloitte Touche Tohmatsu India LLP for the Bureau of Energy Efficiency, Ministry of Power, Government of India, December 2023. https://beeindia.gov.in/sites/default/files/publications/files/Impact%20Assessment%202022-23_%20FINAL%20Report.pdf.

13 Green hydrogen for Decarbonising Asia's Industrial Giants: Analyzing H2 Electrolyzer Market Opportunity in Key Industrial Applications, Asia Society Policy Institute, 2024. https://asiasociety.org/sites/default/files/2024-04/ASPI_GreenHydrogen_2.pdf.

Chapter 4: Challenges of Renewable Energy Integration and Energy Transition

1 https://unfccc.int/sites/default/files/NDC/2022-06/INDIA%20 INDC%20TO%20UNFCCC.pdf.
2 https://cea.nic.in/wp-content/uploads/ps___lf/2022/11/20th_EPS____ Report___Final___16.11.2022.pdf.
3 https://cea.nic.in/wp-content/uploads/irp/2023/05/NEP_2022_32_ FINAL_GAZETTE-1.pdf.
4 https://cea.nic.in/wp-content/uploads/comm_ transmission/2024/11/MoM_24_NCT.pdf at p.20.
5 https://pib.gov.in/PressReleasePage.aspx?PRID=1992732.
6 https://pib.gov.in/PressReleasePage.aspx?PRID=2058735.
7 https://www.niti.gov.in/sites/default/files/2024-07/Domestic%20 Manufacturing%20Capacity%20%26%20Potential%20Cyber%20 Secuirty%20Challanges%20in%20Wind%20Sector%20and%20 Way%20Forward.
8 https://ciire.in/pdf/Final-Digital-Version-of-Global-champions-for-advancing-renewable-energy-innovation-and-manufacturing.pdf
9 https://mnre.gov.in/en/production-linked-incentive-pli.
10 https://pib.gov.in/PressReleaseIframePage.aspx?PRID=2094992.
11 https://www.energetica-india.net/news/127-gw-of-re-projects-under-construction-89-gw-in-tendering-stage-mos-power-shripad-naik.

Chapter 5: Facets of Geopolitical Disruption

1 https://www.theguardian.com/world/2024/feb/29/troops-ukraine-risk-provoking-nuclear-war-vladimir-putin-tells-nato.
2 'Macron's Ukraine troop talk shakes up NATO allies', Reuters, 28 February 2024. https://www.reuters.com/world/europe/macrons-ukraine-troop-talk-shakes-up-nato-allies-2024-02-27/.
3 'Ukraine war briefing: Macron says don't be "cowards" as he digs in over ground troops remark', *The Guardian*, 6 March2024. https://www.theguardian.com/world/2024/mar/06/ukraine-war-briefing-macron-says-dont-be-cowards-as-he-digs-in-over-ground-troop-s.
4 'Brexit: Labour will seek re-write of deal, Starmer says', BBC, 18 September 2023. https://www.bbc.com/news/uk-66839501.
5 'Natural selection in chip industry: 10,000 chip companies closed in China in the past two years', *DigiTimes Asia*, 9 May 2023. https://www.digitimes.com/news/a20230509PD206/china-ic-design-distribution-investment-bankruptcy.html.

6 '"It is Desolate": China's Glut of Unused Car Factories', the *New York Times*, 23 April 2024. https://www.nytimes.com/2024/04/23/business/china-auto-factories-price-cuts.html.
7 'Cyber attack shuts down U.S. fuel pipeline "jugular", Biden briefed', Reuters, 8 May 2021. https://www.reuters.com/technology/colonial-pipeline-halts-all-pipeline-operations-after-cybersecurity-attack-2021-05-08/.
8 'US fuel pipeline hackers "didn't mean to create problems"', BBC, 11 May 2021. https://www.bbc.com/news/business-57050690.
9 'China's cyber army is invading critical US services', the *Washington Post*, 11 December 2023. https://www.washingtonpost.com/technology/2023/12/11/china-hacking-hawaii-pacific-taiwan-conflict/.
10 'Chinese Government Poses "Broad and Unrelenting" Threat to U.S. Critical Infrastructure, FBI Director Says', FBI, 18 April 2024. https://www.fbi.gov/news/stories/chinese-government-poses-broad-and-unrelenting-threat-to-u-s-critical-infrastructure-fbi-director-says.
11 'China Wants Your Data—And May Already Have It', National Public Radio, 24 February 2021. https://www.npr.org/2021/02/24/969532277/china-wants-your-data-and-may-already-have-it.
12 https://edition.cnn.com/2024/09/04/asia/philippines-alice-guo-fugitive-arrested-intl-hnk/index.html.
13 'US warns space companies about foreign spying', Reuters, 18 August 2023. https://www.reuters.com/world/us/us-warns-space-companies-about-foreign-spying-2023-08-18/.
14 'FBI Director Wray warns of Chinese hacking, espionage threats against American companies', *The Hill*, 7 July 2020. https://thehill.com/policy/cybersecurity/506250-fbi-director-wray-warns-of-chinese-hacking-espionage-threats-against/.
15 'The global chip shortage is starting to have major real-world consequences', CNBC, 7 May 2021. https://www.cnbc.com/2021/05/07/chip-shortage-is-starting-to-have-major-real-world-consequences.html.
16 'Romney, colleagues introduce bipartisan bill to counter national security risks of economic entanglement with China', Mitt Romney, US Senator from Utah, 21 March 2024. https://www.romney.senate.gov/romney-colleagues-introduce-bipartisan-bill-to-counter-national-security-risks-of-economic-entanglement-with-china.
17 https://ec.europa.eu/commission/presscorner/detail/en/speech_23_2063.

18 Amit Shah, 'By saying no to RCEP, PM Narendra Modi has kept India first', *The Economic Times*, 13 November 2019. https://economictimes.indiatimes.com/news/economy/foreign-trade/view-by-saying-no-to-rcep-pm-modi-has-kept-india-first/articleshow/72028437.cms?from=mdr.

19 'Regionalization vs. globalization: what is the future direction of trade?', 15 July 2021. https://www.weforum.org/agenda/2021/07/regionalization-globalization-future-direction-trade/.

20 'Iran, Hamas, and Islamic Jihad: A marriage of convenience', European Council on Foreign Relations, 18 December 2023. https://ecfr.eu/article/iran-hamas-and-islamic-jihad-a-marriage-of-convenience/.

21 https://www.nato.int/60years/doc/5-Soviet-Union-s-request-to-join%20NATO/Soviet%20request%20English.pdf.

22 'Russia's request for membership of the Council of Europe', Parliamentary Assembly, Opinion 193 (1996). https://assembly.coe.int/nw/xml/xref/xref-xml2html-en.asp?fileid=13932&lang=en.

23 'Is Huntington's "Clash of Civilisations" a self-fulfilled prophecy?', E-International Relations, 29 January 2020. https://www.e-ir.info/2020/01/29/is-huntingtons-clash-of-civilizations-a-self-fulfilled-prophecy/.

24 'Poland fears "major incident" as thousands of migrants mass at Belarusian border', Radio Free Europe/Radio Liberty, 8 November 2021. https://www.rferl.org/a/belarus-migrants-poland-border-incident/31551118.html.

25 'Finland pushing back "weaponised migration" on Russia border', France24, 23 November 2023. https://www.france24.com/en/live-news/20231123-finland-pushing-back-weaponised-migration-on-russia-border.

26 'China wants food. Brazil pays the price', *The Atlantic*, 15 February 2020. https://www.theatlantic.com/international/archive/2020/02/china-brazil-amazon-environment-pork/606601/.

27 'Reassessing Indonesia's nickel downstreaming policy', East Asia Forum, 14 October 2023. https://eastasiaforum.org/2023/10/14/reassessing-indonesias-nickel-downstreaming-policy.

28 'Indonesia's nickel bounty sows discord, enables Chinese control', United States Institute of Peace, 21 March 2024. https://www.usip.org/publications/2024/03/indonesias-nickel-bounty-sows-discord-enables-chinese-control.

29 'Indonesia proposes critical minerals trade deal with US', Reuters, 7 September 2023. https://www.reuters.com/business/indonesia-proposes-critical-minerals-trade-deal-with-us-2023-09-07/.

30 'Volatile global LNG market: Impact on India', Institute for Energy Economics and Financial Analysis, 12 February 2024. https://ieefa.org/resources/volatile-global-lng-market-impact-india.

Chapter 6: China: The Great Disruptor of the Global Geopolitical Order

1 'Xi Jinping's misguided plan to escape economic stagnation', *The Economist*, 4 April 2024. https://www.economist.com/leaders/2024/04/04/xi-jinpings-misguided-plan-to-escape-economic-stagnation.

2 'China has over 600 million poor with USD 140 monthly income: Premier Li', *The Times of India*, 28 May 2020. https://timesofindia.indiatimes.com/china-has-over-600-million-poor-with-usd-140-monthly-income-premier-li/articleshow/76074863.cms.

3 'Mao Zedong's "Art of the 1962 War": Perception of Opportunity versus Perception of Threat', Manekshaw Paper, No. 76, 2018. https://www.claws.in/static/MP76_Mao-Zedong%E2%80%99s-Art-of-the-1962-War-Perception-of-Opportunity-Versus-Perception-of-Threat.pdf.

4 'Chairman Mao's Road to War and Salvation in 1962', United Service Institution of India. https://www.usiofindia.org/publication-journal/chairman-maos-road-to-war-and-salvation-in-1962.html.

5 Ibid.

6 Ibid.

7 Neville Maxwell, *India's China War*, Jaico Publishing House, Bombay, 1970.

8 Bertil Lintner, *China's India War: Collision Course on the Roof of the World*, Oxford University Press, 2018.

9 Neville Maxwell, 'Jawaharlal Nehru: Of Pride and Principles', Foreign Affairs, April 1974, Vol. 52, No. 3, pp. 633–643.

10 'Relations between the Chinese Communist Regime and the USSR: Their Present Character and Probable Future Courses', Central Intelligence Agency, 10 September 1952. https://www.cia.gov/readingroom/docs/DOC_0001086032.pdf.

11 Charles Kraus, 'How Stalin Elevated the Chinese Communist Party to Power in Xinjiang in 1949', Wilson Centre, 11 May 2018. https://www.wilsoncenter.org/blog-post/how-stalin-elevated-the-chinese-communist-party-to-power-xinjiang-1949.

12 Austin Jersild, 'Sharing the Bomb among Friends: The Dilemmas of Sino-Soviet Strategic Cooperation', Wilson Centre. https://www.wilsoncenter.org/publication/sharing-the-bomb-among-friends-the-dilemmas-sino-soviet-strategic-cooperation.

13 Ivo Daalder, 'Xi is fixated on ending China's century of humiliation', Politico, 12 April 2003. https://www.politico.eu/article/xi-is-fixated-on-ending-chinas-century-of-humiliation/.

14 Andrew Osborn and Andrey Ostroukh, 'Putin rues Soviet collapse as demise of "historical Russia"', Reuters, 12 December 2021. https://www.reuters.com/world/europe/putin-rues-soviet-collapse-demise-historical-russia-2021-12-12/.

15 'The leaders of China and Russia have finished talks. Here are some takeaways', NPR, 22 March 2023.

16 'Vladimir Putin's Pomp-Filled China Trip Underscores the Limits of Western Pressure', *TIME*, 17 May 2024. https://time.com/6979248/putin-russia-xi-china-western-pressure-analysis/.

17 'US accuses China of backing Russia's invasion of Ukraine: Beijing is "picking a side" and can't claim to be neutral any more', Politico, 24 April 2024. https://www.politico.eu/article/us-accuses-china-backing-russias-invasion-of-ukraine/.

18 'For the first time, NATO accuses China of supplying Russia's attacks on Ukraine: The statement was a major departure for the alliance, which until 2019 never officially mentioned China as a concern', *The New York Times*, 10 July 2024. https://www.nytimes.com/2024/07/10/us/politics/nato-china-russia-ukraine.html.

19 Philipp Ivanov, 'Together and Apart: The Conundrum of the China–Russia Partnership', Asia Society Policy Institute, 11 October 2023. https://asiasociety.org/policy-institute/together-and-apart-conundrum-china-russia-partnership.

20 R.N. Prasher, 'Xi Jinping salivates as Russia bleeds', *Daily World*, Chandigarh.https://epaper.dailyworld.in/Details.aspx?id=102710&boxid=78273&uid=&dat=2023-05-15.

21 'Yi Fuxian, Critic of China's Birth Policy, Returns as an Invited Guest', *The New York Times*, 23 March 2016. https://www.nytimes.com/2016/03/24/world/asia/china-yi-fuxian-boao-family-planning.html.

22 'China's President Pledges No Militarization in Disputed Islands', *The Wall Street Journal*, 25 September 2015. https://www.wsj.com/articles/china-completes-runway-on-artificial-island-in-south-china-sea-1443184818.

23 Michael Bristow, 'China encroaching along Nepal border', BBC News, 8 February 2022. https://www.bbc.com/news/world-asia-60288007.

24 Ryo Nemoto, Rieko Miki, '5 Chinese missiles land in Japan's EEZ: defense chief', *Nikkei Asia*, 4 August 2022. https://asia.nikkei.com/Politics/International-relations/Taiwan-tensions/5-Chinese-missiles-land-in-Japan-s-EEZ-defense-chief.

25 'Japan accuses China of pushing territorial claims during pandemic', Al Jazeera, 14 July 2020. https://www.aljazeera.com/news/2020/7/14/japan-accuses-china-of-pushing-territorial-claims-during-pandemic.

26 Rebecca Ratcliffe, 'Why the rusting wreck of a second world war ship is so important to China', The Guardian, 30 October 2023. https://www.theguardian.com/world/2023/oct/30/sierra-madre-phillippines-ship-china-blockade.

27 David Vergun, 'New EDCA sites named in the Philippines', U.S. Department of Defense, 3 April 2023. https://www.defense.gov/News/News-Stories/Article/Article/3350297/new-edca-sites-named-in-the-philippines/.

28 Kiki Siregar, 'What the remote Natuna Islands reveal about Indonesia's stance on China', CNA, 5 August 2023. https://www.channelnewsasia.com/asia/indonesia-china-natuna-islands-tensions-south-china-sea-geopolitics-3676876.

29 'Malaysia rejects new China map claiming entire South China Sea', Al Jazeera, 31 August 2023. https://www.aljazeera.com/news/2023/8/31/malaysia-rejects-new-china-map-claiming-entire-south-china-sea.

30 Maria Siow, 'Malaysia keeps eye on "status quo", Beijing trade ties with quiet approach in South China Sea', *South China Morning Post*, 28 February 2024. https://www.scmp.com/week-asia/politics/article/3253487/malaysia-keeps-eye-status-quo-beijing-trade-ties-quiet-approach-south-china-sea.

31 Bama Andika Putra, 'Brunei silent claims in the South China Sea: a case for the theory of trade expectations', *Cogent Social Sciences*, Vol. 10, 2024 – Issue 1. https://www.tandfonline.com/doi/full/10.1080/23311886.2024.2317533.

32 Sufrizul Husseini, 'Why Brunei is hedging between the U.S. and China', United State Institute of Peace, 26 October 2023. https://www.usip.org/publications/2023/10/why-brunei-hedging-between-us-and-china.

33 'China, Vietnam speed up developments in South China Sea as territorial disputes intensify', NHK World, Japan, 25

December 2023. https://www3.nhk.or.jp/nhkworld/en/news/backstories/2920/.

34 R.N. Prasher, 'You give me Siberia, I will give you Crimea', 27 January 2023. https://kreately.in/you-give-me-siberia-i-will-give-you-crimea/.

35 Daniel Goma Pinilla, 'Border Disputes between China and North Korea', *China Perspectives*, March–April 2004. https://journals.openedition.org/chinaperspectives/806.

36 'China is redefining its borders with its neighbors, including Russia', *Le Monde*, 4 September 2023. https://www.lemonde.fr/en/international/article/2023/09/04/china-is-redefining-its-borders-with-its-neighbors-including-russia_6122600_4.html.

37 'South China Sea, Analysis', U.S. Energy Information Administration (EIA), 21 March 2024. https://www.eia.gov/international/analysis/regions-of-interest/South_China_Sea.

38 Sumanta Bhattacharya, 'Can India's Necklace of Diamonds Strategy Defeat China's String of Pearls?', ResearchGate, July 2022. https://www.researchgate.net/publication/362124651_Can_India's_Necklace_of_Diamonds_Strategy_Defeat_the_China's_String_of_Pearls.

39 Simon Denyer and Luna Lin, 'China sends its top actors and directors back to socialism school', *The Washington Post*, 1 December 2017. https://www.washingtonpost.com/news/worldviews/wp/2017/12/01/china-sends-its-top-actors-and-directors-sent-back-to-socialism-school/.

40 Nectar Gan, 'All aboard Xi Jinping's train of thought as city decorates subway carriage with propaganda', *South China Morning Post*, 3 July 2018. https://www.scmp.com/news/china/policies-politics/article/2153582/all-aboard-chinas-propaganda-express-xi-jinpings-new.

Chapter 7: Geopolitics: Russia

1 V.A. Kolosov, M.V. Zotova, and N.L. Turov (all from the Institute of Geography, Russian Academy of Sciences, Moscow, Russia), 'Geopolitics and Political Geography in Russia: Global Context and National Characteristics', *Regional Research of Russia*, 2022, Vol. 12, No. 1, pp. 80–95. https://link.springer.com/content/pdf/10.1134/S2079970522020046.pdf.

2 'In Ukraine war, China is helping tilt momentum in Russia's favor, top U.S. spy says', NBC News, 3 May 2024. https://www.nbcnews.com/politics/national-security/china-helping-russia-momentum-ukraine-war-top-us-spy-rcna150437.

3 'The South China Sea, a fault line in China–Russia relations?', ISEAS, 13 October 2020. https://www.iseas.edu.sg/media/commentaries/the-south-china-sea-a-fault-line-in-china-russia-relations/.
4 Franck Billé, Grégory Delaplace, Caroline Humphrey, eds., *Frontier Encounters: Knowledge and Practice at the Russian, Chinese and Mongolian Border*, Open Book Publishers, 2012.
5 Vedica Kant, *If I die here, who will remember me: India and the First World War*, Roli Books, 2014.
6 'Making Britain: Discover how South Asians shaped the nation, 1870–1950', First World War (1914–1918). https://www5.open.ac.uk/research-projects/making-britain/content/first-world-war-1914-1918.
7 Hemen Ray, 'Changing Soviet Views on Mahatma Gandhi', *The Journal of Asian Studies*, Nov. 1969, Vol. 29, No. 1, pp. 85–106. https://www.jstor.org/stable/pdf/2942525.pdf.
8 Ibid.
9 Jane Degras, ed., *The Communist International*, z919–z943, II, Oxford, I960, pp. 5I9 and 544–45.
10 Rashmi-Sudha Puri, 'Gandhi and the Second World War', *The Indian Journal of Political Science*, Jan–March 1977, Vol. 38, No. 1, pp. 30–53. https://www.jstor.org/stable/41854773.
11 Nandan Unnikrishnan, '1971: When Delhi and Moscow came together', Observer Research Foundation (ORF), 16 August 2021. https://www.orfonline.org/research/1971-when-delhi-and-moscow-came-together.
12 'India–Russia Defence Cooperation', Indian Embassy, Moscow, 5 May 2024. https://indianembassy-moscow.gov.in/india-russia-defence-cooperation.php.
13 BrahMos Aerospace Website: https://www.brahmos.com/content.php?id=1.
14 Matt Pottinger, 'China Has Crossed Biden's Red Line on Ukraine', Foundation for Defense of Democracies (FDD), 30 April 2024. https://www.fdd.org/analysis/op_eds/2024/04/30/china-has-crossed-bidens-red-line-on-ukraine/.
15 Yulia Gorbunova, 'The Revolving Door of Persecution in Crimea', Human Rights Watch, 7 September 2021. https://www.hrw.org/news/2021/09/07/revolving-door-persecution-crimea.

Chapter 8: Iran: Geopolitics in the Persian Gulf

1 Colin Turner, *Islam without Allah? The Rise of Religious Externalism in Safavid Iran*, Curzon Press, 2000, p. 84.

2 Chelsi Mueller, *The Origins of the Arab–Iranian Conflict: Nationalism and Sovereignty in the Gulf between the World Wars*, Cambridge University Press, 2020, Ch. 4 'Reza Shah's Persian Gulf Policy', 1925–1941, pp. 110–111.

3 R.N. Prasher, 'It is an eternal war', *Daily World*, Chandigarh, 6 November 2023. https://epaper.dailyworld.in/Details.aspx?id=123179&boxid=78086&uid=&dat=2023-11-06.

4 Georgina Mccartney and Arathy Somasekhar, 'Oil tankers continue Red Sea movements despite Houthi attacks', Reuters, 9 January 2024. https://www.reuters.com/markets/commodities/oil-tankers-continue-red-sea-movements-despite-houthi-attacks-2024-01-09/.

5 Ray Takeyh (CFR expert), 'Drone Strike Risks Dangerous U.S.–Iran Escalation', Council on Foreign Relations (CFR), 29 January 2024.

6 David S. Cloud and Ken Thomas, 'Iran-backed Militia Suspected of Strike on U.S. Troops Says It Will Suspend Attacks', *The Wall Street Journal*, 30 January 2024.

7 Bruno Reynaud de Sousa, 'Beating the (White) House: How a "Rogue" Iran Broke Free from the "Axis of Evil" and Became an Antifragile State' in *The Geopolitics of Iran*, Francis José B.S. Leandro, Carlos Branco, Flavius Caba-Maria (eds.), Palgrave Macmillan, 2021, p. 117.

8 Ibid.

Chapter 9: The Promise, Perils, and Pitfalls of Energy Transition

1 'Al Gore: These are the skills climate leaders must build now', World Economic Forum, 2 February 2022. https://www.weforum.org/stories/2022/02/al-gore-climate-policy-leadership-skills-climate-change/.

2 Adnan Z. Amin, 'A New World: The Geopolitics of the Energy Transformation', 2019, published by the Global Commission on the Geopolitics of Energy Transformation, p. 6. https://www.irena.org/-/media/files/irena/agency/publication/2019/jan/global_commission_geopolitics_new_world_2019.pdf.

3 Ibid.

4 Ibid., p. 8.

5 Zeynep Clulow and David M. Reiner, 'Democracy, economic development and low-carbon energy: When and why does democratization promote energy transition?', Energy Policy Research Group, University of Cambridge, 2022. https://www.jstor.org/stable/resrep46907.

6 Nuozhen Gelsor et al., 'Solar Energy on the Tibetan Plateau: Atmospheric Influences', *Solar Energy*, Volume 173, October 2018, pp. 984–992. https://www.sciencedirect.com/science/article/abs/pii/S0038092X1830793X.
7 Jennifer L., 'Why Lithium Prices Are Plunging and What to Expect', Carbon Credits, 8 February 2024. https://carboncredits.com/why-lithium-prices-are-plunging-and-what-to-expect/.
8 'Lithium Prices in Free Fall: Implications for Clean Energy Transitions in the Private Sector', Bradley Intelligence Report, 1 February 2024. https://www.bradley.com/insights/publications/2024/02/lithium-prices-in-free-fall-implications-for-clean-energy-transition-in-the-private-sector.
9 'Lithium prices will likely drop further on surplus output', *The Hindu*, 12 January 2024. https://www.thehindubusinessline.com/markets/commodities/lithium-prices-likely-to-drop-further-on-surplus-output/article67731781.ece.
10 'India's lithium industry: Potentials and pitfalls', Observer Research Foundation (ORF), 10 August 2023. https://www.orfonline.org/expert-speak/indias-lithium-industry-potentials-and-pitfalls.
11 'Nickel Prices Expected to Drop Further in 2024', Metal Miner, 27 March 2024. https://oilprice.com/Metals/Commodities/Nickel-Prices-Expected-to-Drop-Further-in-2024.html.
12 'Oversupply, low prices for cobalt to persist in 2024 as demand slips', S&P Global, 27 December 2023. https://www.spglobal.com/commodityinsights/es/market-insights/latest-news/metals/122723-oversupply-low-prices-for-cobalt-to-persist-in-2024-as-demand-slips.
13 'China sets 2022 renewable power subsidy at $607 million', Reuters, 16 November 2021. https://www.reuters.com/business/energy/china-sets-2022-renewable-power-subsidy-607-mln-2021-11-16/.
14 'How China Came to Dominate the World in Solar Energy', *The New York Times*, 7 March 2024. https://www.nytimes.com/2024/03/07/business/china-solar-energy-exports.html.
15 'China breaks West's solar monopoly', Gulf News, 15 September 2018. https://gulfnews.com/business/analysis/china-breaks-west39s-solar-monopoly-1.1026961.
16 'Global Wind Report 2023', Global Wind Energy Council. https://gwec.net/globalwindreport2023.
17 R.N. Prasher, 'Net Zero: Myth, Reality or Escapism', *Daily World*, Chandigarh, 26 February 2024. https://epaper.dailyworld.in/Details.aspx?id=139136&boxid=78162&uid=&dat=2024-02-26.

18 'China's new coal plants set to become a costly second fiddle to renewable', Reuters, 23 March 2023. https://www.reuters.com/business/energy/chinas-new-coal-plants-set-become-costly-second-fiddle-renewables-2023-03-22/.

19 'China sharply increases capacity of newly-launched coal-fired TPPs', Global Energy, 9 February 2024. https://globalenergyprize.org/en/2024/02/09/china-sharply-increases-capacity-of-newly-launched-coal-fired-tpps.

20 'Energy security in energy transitions', World Energy Outlook 2022, International Energy Agency. https://www.iea.org/reports/world-energy-outlook-2022/energy-security-in-energy-transitions.

21 Greta Thunberg and Norwegian activists stand firm against wind farm on Sami reindeer herding land: The activists say a transition to green energy shouldn't come at the expense of the rights of indigenous people,' Euronews, 12 October 2023. https://www.euronews.com/green/2023/10/12/greta-thunberg-and-norwegian-activists-stand-firm-against-wind-farm-on-sami-reindeer-herdi.

22 'Norway agrees to compensate Indigenous people over land for Europe's largest onshore wind farm: The wind farm fought against by Greta Thunberg will keep operating with compensation paid to Sami reindeer herders', Euronews, 7 March 2024. https://www.euronews.com/green/2024/03/07/sami-activists-backed-by-greta-thunberg-reach-deal-to-save-reindeer-farming-from-giant-win.

23 'Did hydel projects have a role in Uttarakhand disaster? asks Supreme Court', *Down to Earth*, 14 August 2013. https://www.downtoearth.org.in/environment/did-hydel-projects-have-a-role-in-uttarakhand-disaster-asks-supreme-court-41911.

24 'Failure of EVs in China calls for more research', *Qatar Tribune*, 15 March 2024. https://www.qatar-tribune.com/article/113062/business/failure-of-evs-in-china-calls-for-more-research.

25 'Ship carrying nearly 3,000 cars ablaze off Dutch coast, crew member dead', Reuters, 27 July 2023. https://www.reuters.com/world/europe/one-dead-cargo-ship-fire-electric-car-suspected-source-dutch-coastguard-2023-07-26/.

26 'Ocean shippers playing catch up to electric vehicle fire risk', Reuters, 28 July 2023. https://www.reuters.com/business/autos-transportation/ocean-shippers-playing-catch-up-electric-vehicle-fire-risk-2023-07-27/.

27 Anaïs Özyavuz, Dorothée Schmid, 'Persistence and Evolutions of the Rentier State Model in Gulf Countries', Note de l'Ifri, April 2015. https://www.ifri.org/sites/default/files/migrated_files/documents/atoms/files/rentier-state-final.pdf.

28 Hugo Toledo, 'The political economy of emiratization in the UAE', *Journal of Economic Studies*, 18 January 2013. https://doi.org/10.1108/01443581311283493.

29 Aisha Al-Sarihi, Judith A. Cherni, 'Political economy of renewable energy transition in rentier states: The case of Oman', E*nvironmental Policy and Governance*, Volume 33, Issue 4, August 2023, pp. 423–439. https://doi.org/10.1002/eet.2041.

30 Héla Miniaoui, 'Challenges of GCC investment in the energy transition', The Forum: ERF Policy Portal, 26 December 2023. https://theforum.erf.org.eg/2023/12/25/challenges-of-gcc-investment-in-the-energy-transition.

Chapter 10: Energy Security: Concept and Reality

1 'Report of the World Commission on Environment and Development: Our Common Future', 1.3: Sustainable development. https://sustainabledevelopment.un.org/content/documents/5987our-common-future.pdf.

2 Emmanuel Hache, 'Do Renewable Energies Improve Energy Security in the Long Run?', *International Economics*, Vol. 156, 2018, pp. 127–135. https://c.coek.info/pdf-do-renewable-energies-improve-energy-security-in-the-long-run-.html.

3 Mick Hamer, 'Plot to undermine global pollution controls revealed', *New Scientist*, 2 January 2002. https://www.newscientist.com/article/dn1734-plot-to-undermine-global-pollution-controls-revealed/.

4 *A Quest for Energy Security in the 21st Century: Resources and Constraints*, Asia Pacific Energy Research Centre, Institute of Energy Economics, Japan, 2007. https://aperc.or.jp/file/2010/9/26/APERC_2007_A_Quest_for_Energy_Security.pdf.

5 Getao Hu, Jun Yang, and Jun Li, 'The Dynamic Evolution of Global Energy Security and Geopolitical Games: 1995-2019', *International Journal of Environmental Research and Public Health*, 2022, 19(21), 14584. https://doi.org/10.3390/ijerph192114584.

6 Susanne Therese Hansen, Espen Moe, 'Renewable energy expansion or the preservation of national energy sovereignty? Norwegian renewable energy policy meets resource nationalism', *Political Geography*, Vol. 99,

November 2022, 102760. https://www.sciencedirect.com/science/article/pii/S0962629822001743?via%3Dihub.

7 IEA Glossary. https://www.iea.org/glossary.

8 *A Quest for Energy Security in the 21st Century: Resources and Constraints*, Asia Pacific Energy Research Centre, Institute of Energy Economics, Japan, 2007. https://aperc.or.jp/file/2010/9/26/APERC_2007_A_Quest_for_Energy_Security.pdf.

9 Ibid.

10 UNESCO World Heritage Convention, Glossary. https://whc.unesco.org/en/glossary/375#:~:text=Sustainable%20development%20is%20development%20that,and%20Development%20%E2%80%93%20Rio%201992).

11 'Germany to give 700 mln euros to help South Africa end coal use', Reuters, 2 November 2021. https://www.reuters.com/business/environment/germany-give-700-mln-euros-help-south-africa-end-coal-use-2021-11-02/.

12 'Germany approves bringing coal-fired power plants back online this winter', Reuters, 4 October 2023. https://www.reuters.com/business/energy/germany-approves-bringing-coal-fired-power-plants-back-online-this-winter-2023-10-04/.

13 'Electricity production in 2022: coal accounted for a third, wind power for a quarter', Destatis, 9 March 2023. https://www.destatis.de/EN/Press/2023/03/PE23_090_43312.html.

14 'German government rejects new call to delay nuclear shutdown', Associated Press, 12 April 2023. https://apnews.com/article/germany-nuclear-power-plants-shut-down-5ce6958e25374bbbe1dd80cbfbc2398a.

15 South China Sea, Overview, U.S. Energy Information Administration (EIA), 21 March 2024. https://www.eia.gov/international/analysis/regions-of-interest/South_China_Sea.

16 'A 10-Point Plan to Reduce the European Union's Reliance on Russian Natural Gas', IEA, 3 March 2022. https://iea.blob.core.windows.net/assets/1af70a5f-9059-47b4-a2dd-1b47991 8f3cb/A10-PointPlantoReducetheEuropeanUnionsRelianceonRussianNaturalGas.pdf.

Chapter 11: Hydrogen's Role in Energy Security

1 'The Brits Who Bolstered the Moon Landings', BBC Archive. https://www.bbc.co.uk/archive/the-brits-who-bolstered-the-moon-landings/zfcrscw.

2 J.O'M Bockris, 'The Hydrogen Economy', *Environmental Chemistry* 1977, Springer, Boston, MA. https://doi.org/10.1007/978-1-4615-6921-3_17.

3 'Green Hydrogen: The Holy Grail of Decarbonisation? An Analysis of the Technical and Geopolitical Implications of the Future Hydrogen Economy', Rossana Scita, Pier Paolo Raimondi and Michel Noussan, Fondazione Eni Enrico Mattei, Milan (FEEM), Working Paper No. 013.2020. https://www.econstor.eu/bitstream/10419/228789/1/ndl2020-013.pdf.

4 Ibid.

5 'Overview of Basic Hydrogen Strategy', Agency for Natural Resources and Energy, June 2023. https://www.meti.go.jp/shingikai/enecho/shoene_shinene/suiso_seisaku/pdf/20230606_4.pdf.

6 'Communication from the Commission to the European Parliament, the Council, the European Economic and Social Committee and the Committee of the Regions: A hydrogen strategy for a climate-neutral Europe', COM/2020/301 final, Brussels, 8 July 2020. https://eur-lex.europa.eu/legal-content/EN/TXT/?uri=CELEX:52020DC0301.

7 'National Hydrogen Strategy Update – NHS 2023', Federal Ministry for Economic Affairs and Climate Action (BMWK), Public Relations, Berlin, July 2023, p. 2.

8 'Energy from climate-friendly gas', National Hydrogen Strategy, The Federal Government. https://www.bundesregierung.de/breg-en/news/hydrogen-technology-2204238.

9 UK Hydrogen Strategy, presented to Parliament by the Secretary of State for Business, Energy & Industrial Strategy, August 2021. https://assets.publishing.service.gov.uk/media/64c7e8bad8b1a70011b05e38/UK-Hydrogen-Strategy_web.pdf.

10 'Green Hydrogen in China: A Roadmap for Progress', World Economic Forum, White Papers, June 2023 (in collaboration with Accenture and China Hydrogen Alliance). https://www.weforum.org/publications/green-hydrogen-in-china-a-roadmap-for-progress/.

11 'Climate change: China's hydrogen sector faces overcapacity risk as ambitious production plans outstrip demand, say analysts', *South China Morning Post*, 21 August 2023. https://www.scmp.com/business/china-business/article/3231703/climate-change-chinas-hydrogen-sector-faces-overcapacity-risk-ambitious-production-plans-outstrip.

12 U.S National Clean Hydrogen Strategy and Roadmap, June 2023. https://www.hydrogen.energy.gov/docs/hydrogenprogramlibraries/pdfs/us-national-clean-hydrogen-strategy-roadmap.pdf.

13 Green Hydrogen Policy, Government of India, Ministry of Power, 17 February 2022. https://powermin.gov.in/sites/default/files/Green_Hydrogen_Policy.pdf.

14 'Harnessing Green Hydrogen: Opportunities for Deep Decarbonisation in India', NITI Aayog, June 2022. https://www.niti.gov.in/sites/default/files/2022-06/Harnessing_Green_Hydrogen_V21_DIGITAL_29062022.pdf.

15 National Green Hydrogen Mission, Government of India, Ministry of New and Renewable Energy, January 2023. https://cdnbbsr.s3waas.gov.in/s3716e1b8c6cd17b771da77391355749f3/uploads/2023/01/2023011390.pdf.

16 'Green Hydrogen: Enabling Measures Roadmap for Adoption in India', World Economic Forum (WEF), Insight Report, January 2024, p.4. https://www3.weforum.org/docs/WEF_Green_Hydrogen_Enabling_Measures_Roadmap_for_Adoption_in_India_2024.pdf.

17 Ibid.

18 National Green Hydrogen Mission, Government of India, Ministry of New and Renewable Energy, January 2023. https://cdnbbsr.s3waas.gov.in/s3716e1b8c6cd17b771da77391355749f3/uploads/2023/01/2023011390.pdf.

19 Ibid.

20 'Hydrogen Markets', Markets and Markets, July 2023. https://www.marketsandmarkets.com/Market-Reports/hydrogen-market-132975342.html.

21 'Geopolitics of the Energy Transformation: The Hydrogen Factor', International Renewable Energy Agency (IRENA), 2022. Fig. 3.4, p. 45 https://www.irena.org/-/media/Files/IRENA/Agency/Publication/2022/Jan/IRENA_Geopolitics_Hydrogen_2022.pdf?rev=1cfe49eee979409686f101ce24ffd71a.

Chapter 12: Geopolitical Impact of Disinformation

1 'What was Paine's role in the French Revolution?', The Thomas Paine National Historical Association. https://thomaspaine.org/pages/resources/what-was-paine-s-role-in-the-french-revolution.html.

2 Malcolm Chase, 'What did Chartism Petition for? Mass Petitions in the British Movement for Democracy', *Social Science History*, Vol. 43, No. 3, Special Issue: 'The Transformation of Petitioning' (fall 2019), pp. 531–551. https://www.jstor.org/stable/26753195.

3 'Misinformation and disinformation', American Psychological Association. https://www.apa.org/topics/journalism-facts/misinformation-disinformation.

Chapter 13: Produce in India, Feed the World

1 This clarion call was given by Lal Bahadur Shastri in his tribute to the Indian soldiers for having won the 1965 war with Pakistan and to the Indian farmers for their efforts in making India food secure.

2 Jal Vigyan was added by Prime Minister Atal Bihari Vajpayee. Prime Minister Narendra Modi added Anusandhan (research) to this slogan.

3 'India Can Achieve Energy Independence by 2047 through Clean Technology: Study', News from Berkeley Lab, 14 March 2023. https://newscenter.lbl.gov/2023/03/14/india-energy-independence-by-204720.

4 Formerly in the Indian Police Services, he currently heads the NSA with the rank of a cabinet minister.

5 Govind Ballabh Pant University of Agriculture and Technology was the first agricultural university established in India on the pattern of the land-grant universities of USA.

6 'Food security important for national security, need to increase farm productivity: NSA Doval', ANI, 16 February 2023. https://www.aninews.in/news/national/general-news/food-security-important-for-national-security-need-to-increase-farm-productivity-nsa-doval20230216203118/.

7 'Doval awarded honorary D Litt degree by GB Pant University', Awaz–The Voice, 16 February 2023. https://www.awazthevoice.in/india-news/doval-awarded-honorary-d-litt-degree-by-gb-pant-university-19518.html#:~:text=National%20Security%20Advisor%20(NSA)%20Ajit,34th%20convocation%20of%20the%20University.

8 Janetta Azarieva, Yitzhak M. Brudny, and Eugene Finkel, *Bread and Autocracy: Food, Politics, and Security in Putin's Russia*, Oxford University Press, 2023. https://academic.oup.com/book/46739/chapter-abstract/413267913?redirectedFrom=fulltext.

9 Ibid.

10 Kautilya in the *Arthashastra*.

11 The extravagance was critiqued by S.N. Banerjea in 1902, Lalmohan Ghosh in 1903, Henry Cotton (former chief secretary of Bengal) in 1904, as well as by Gopal Krishna Gokhale in 1905.

12 The second durbar, held in 1903, marked the succession of Edward VII. On the orders of King Edward VII, it was attended by the Duke of Connaught. However, India was going through a massive famine during this period.

13 The Bengal famine of 1943 was one of the worst disasters in twentieth-century South Asia. It was devastating in terms of its scale, causing three million deaths, and occurred during the World War II, when India was under British rule.

14 The Mahalanobis Plan was India's second five-year plan (1956–61), proposed by Professor Prasanta Chandra Mahalanobis. This plan gave priority to investment goods, as they were crucial for India's further economic growth. The plan explored the allocation of investment between the different sectors of the economy.

15 Chidambaram Subramaniam has been credited with giving topmost priority to research and extension in agriculture. He, along with M.S. Swaminathan and B. Sivaraman, then agriculture secretary, put India on the path to self-sufficiency in food grains.

16 The white revolution refers to the Anand pattern of milk-producing cooperative societies. Farmers received technical inputs and an assured price for their milk.

17 The Union Government of India announced the MSP under the leadership of Lal Bahadur Shastri in 1965 to give the farmers a positive incentive to produce more food, and to protect the farmers from the market risk of being unable to find a buyer for their produce.

18 The first World Food Conference was held in Rome in 1974 (5–16 November) by the United Nations under the auspices of the UN Food and Agriculture Organization (FAO), in the wake of the devastating famine in Bangladesh in the preceding two years. It led to the Universal Declaration on the Eradication of Hunger and Malnutrition. Governments attending the World Food Conference proclaimed that 'every man, woman and child has the inalienable right to be free from hunger and malnutrition in order to develop their physical and mental faculties'.

19 Rome Declaration on World Food Security and the World Food Summit Plan of Action, World Food Summit, 13–17 November 1996, Rome, Italy.

20 Rome is the headquarters of the triad of food and agriculture-related organizations: Food and Agriculture Organization (FAO), International Fund for Agricultural Development (IFAD), and World Food Programme (WFP).

21 'Chapter 2. Food security: concepts and measurement', Food and Agriculture Organization. https://www.fao.org/4/y4671e/y4671e06.htm#fnB30.

22 'Hunger: A National Security Threat', United Nations, UN Chronicle, 11 June 2012. https://www.un.org/en/chronicle/article/hunger-national-security-threat.

23 'Progress Insufficient to Meet 1996 World Food Summit Target of Halving Number of Hungry by 2015, FAO Report States', United Nations. https://press.un.org/en/1998/19981123.sag19.html.

24 Unlike the MDGs, which primarily targeted developing countries, the SDGs are applicable to all countries, including developed ones. This universal commitment promotes global cooperation and acknowledges that sustainable development is a shared responsibility.

25 The 2007–08 financial crisis, or the global financial crisis (GFC), was the most severe worldwide economic crisis since the Great Depression. This was caused by predatory lending in the form of subprime mortgages targeting low-income homebuyers, excessive risk-taking by global financial institutions, a continuous buildup of toxic assets within banks, and the bursting of the United States' housing bubble, culminating in a 'perfect storm' that led to the Great Recession.

26 In 1906, Alfred Henry Lewis stated, 'There are only nine meals between mankind and anarchy.' Since then, his observation has been echoed by people as disparate as Robert Heinlein and Leon Trotsky. The key here is that, unlike all other commodities, food is the one essential that cannot be postponed.

27 World Food Programme (WFP), an organization established in 1961 by the United Nations to help alleviate world hunger. It received the Nobel Peace Prize for its efforts and accomplishments in 2020.

28 The International Fund for Agricultural Development (IFAD) is an international organisation whose objective is to improve agricultural development and livelihoods in developing countries.

29 The Federation of Indian Chambers of Commerce & Industry (FICCI) had prepared the base document for the India–Africa partnership on agriculture. I also made a presentation on this at the EXIM Bank head office in Mumbai.

30 The discussion paper of the Ministry of Agriculture submitted to the office of the National Security Agency, February 2011 (International Cooperation Division of the Ministry of Agriculture, Krishi Bhawan, New Delhi).

31 This was done with the backing of the then agriculture minister, Sharad Pawar, and the agriculture secretary, P.K. Basu.

32 The Indian Institute of Foreign Trade is a business school in India. Established in 1963, it works as an autonomous institute under the Ministry of Commerce and Industry.

33 The Manohar Parrikar Institute for Defence Studies and Analyses, New Delhi, is India's foremost think tank for advanced research in international relations, especially defence, strategic and security issues, and providing training to civilian, military, and paramilitary officers of the Indian government.

34 Research and Information System for Developing Countries (RIS) is a New Delhi-based autonomous policy research institute that specialises in issues related to international economic development, trade, investment, and technology. RIS is envisioned as a forum for fostering effective policy dialogue and capacity-building among developing countries on global and regional economic issues. It is supported by the Ministry of External Affairs.

35 'NAFED, IFFCO, ICAR can fix India's food security by going global', India Century, 23 September 2022. https://www.indiancentury.in/2022/09/23/nafed-iffco-icar-can-fix-indias-food-security-by-going-global/.

36 Ibid.

37 The CFS Principles for Responsible Investment in Agriculture and Food Systems—known as RAI—acknowledge that the starting point for defining how responsible investment in agriculture and food systems can contribute to food security and nutrition is the recognition and respect for human rights. They are a set of ten principles that apply to all types and sizes of agricultural investment, including fisheries, forests, and livestock. They address all stakeholders and apply to all stages of the value chain. As a soft law instrument, they are globally applicable and include actions to address a range of environmental, social, and economic issues. As the RAI principles were developed through a multi-stakeholder process, they already have wide buy-in. All CFS stakeholders are asked to collaborate, network, and identify joint activities to promote the use of the RAI Principles at the local, national, and regional levels. http://www.fao.org/3/a-au866e.pdf.

38 I attended this meeting in my capacity as the joint secretary, international cooperation of the Ministry of Agriculture and Farmers' Welfare.

39 The point being made was that this would depress the real value of the farm produce of the marginal famer.

40 Pradhan Mantri Garib Kalyan Anna Yojana is a food security welfare scheme that was announced by the Government of India on 26 March 2020 during the COVID-19 pandemic in India. The programme is operated by the Department of Food and Public Distribution under the Ministry of Consumer Affairs, Food and Public Distribution.

41 'Climate resilient agricultural development and food security', Australian Government, Department of Foreign Affairs and Trade. https://www.dfat.gov.au/development/topics/development-issues/climate-resilient-agricultural-development-food-security.

42 Food Security, Seventh Report of Session 2022–23, UK Parliament. https://publications.parliament.uk/pa/cm5803/cmselect/cmenvfru/622/report.html.

43 The island nation is working towards '30 by 30' to build up its agri-food industry's capability and capacity to sustainably produce 30 per cent of its nutritional needs by 2030. https://www.sfa.gov.sg/food-for-thought/article/detail/a-sustainable-food-system-for-singapore-and-beyond.

44 India's fertiliser requirement is around 43.5 million tonnes per year. India is dependent on imports for muriate of potash and imports nearly 5 million tonnes of phosphate rock, 2.5 million tonnes of phosphoric acid, and 3 million tonnes of diammonium phosphate (DAP) annually.

45 Anuraag Nallapaneni and Shaifali Sood, 'Green Hydrogen Adoption in Fertilizer Manufacturing: Opportunities and Challenges', WRI India, 14 March 2023. https://wri-india.org/blog/green-hydrogen-adoption-fertilizer-manufacturing-opportunities-and-challenges.

46 Radheshyam Yadav, 'Deep Dive. Will India be self-reliant in edible oil production by 2030?' *The Hindu BusinessLine*, 14 November 2022.

47 The WHO is the nodal agency identified by the UN to harness multilateral and country-wise strategies to address COVID-19.

48 Based in Seattle, Washington, the Bill & Melinda Gates Foundation was launched in 2000 and is reported to be the second largest charitable foundation in the world. It played a crucial role in the production and distribution of vaccines during COVID-19.

49 Sea lanes of communication (SLOC) is a term describing the primary maritime routes between ports used for trade, logistics, and naval forces. It is generally used in reference to naval operations to ensure that SLOCs are open or closed, such as in times of war.

50 The International Solar Alliance is an India-led alliance of more than 120 signatory countries, most being sunshine countries that lie either completely or partly between the Tropic of Cancer and the Tropic of Capricorn.

51 Ahimsa is the ancient Indic principle of nonviolence that applies to actions towards all living beings. It is a key virtue in Indian religions like Jainism, Buddhism, Hinduism, and Sikhism.

52 This was also the title for the group report by participants of phase V at the Lal Bahadur Shastri National Academy of Administration (LBSNAA) in November 2014.

53 See Sujata Gaonkar's article 'Organic by default!' on LinkedIn.

54 Regenerative agriculture is a farming method that focuses on improving soil health, which can lead to more productive and profitable farms. Healthy soil can produce more food and nutrition, store more carbon, and increase biodiversity. It can also support other ecosystems through natural processes like water drainage and pollination.

55 A farmer with less than one hectare (2.5 acres) is called a marginal farmer.

56 For over a decade, horticulture production at 352 MT (2022–23) has exceeded cereal production in weight, volume, and value.

57 Advance estimations, reported by *The Financial Express.*

58 'Barbecue Earth' is a six-part narrative podcast about meat. But it's not about the best way to grill a delicious steak. It's about meat as a commodity, a powerful industry, and a major reason why our planet is overheating. Join Heewon Park and Noah Gordon of the Carnegie Endowment for International Peace offer on a world tour of meat's global impacts. They look at a farmer's revolt in the Netherlands, cattle laundering in Brazil, lab-grown meat in California, the United Nations' reluctance to talk about what meat production does to the planet, and much more.

59 The Carnegie Endowment for International Peace is a nonpartisan international affairs think tank headquartered in Washington, D.C., with operations in Europe, South and East Asia, the Middle East, and the United States.

60 'India Emerges as Second Largest Beef Exporter in the World', The Wire, 5 March 2024. https://thewire.in/trade/who-are-the-biggest-exporters-of-beef-in-the-world/?mid_related_new.

61 Veganism is the practice of abstaining from the use of animal products—particularly in diet—and an associated philosophy that rejects the commodity status of animals. A person who follows the diet or philosophy is known as a vegan.

62 Based on the podcasts of the Carnegie Endowment for International Peace.

63 In India, the National Agricultural Research, Education and Extension System (NAREES), including the state agricultural universities and Krishi Vigyan Kendras, are organised under the auspices of ICAR (Indian Council of Agricultural Research).

64 The India plant-based meat market was worth USD 38.2 million in 2021 and is further projected to reach USD 836.2 million by 2028, at a CAGR of 54.7 per cent during 2022–2028 (forecast period). The growth of this market can be primarily attributed to the rising demand for plant-based meat products driven by high meat consumption, coupled with the growing vegan and flexitarian population. Moreover, favourable marketing and innovative growth strategies are being adopted by the market players. Such factors promise bright prospects for the growth of the Indian plant-based meat products market over the forecast period. (Blueweave Consulting).

65 Aspirational districts, as identified by NITI Aayog, for special focus on some key sectors: livelihoods, education, health, and water resources infrastructure. Typically, these are districts with rainfed agriculture.

Chapter 14: Regenerating India through Inclusive, Sustainable Growth

1 'Swami Vivekananda and Nation Building', Press Information Bureau, Government of India, 11 January 2015. https://pib.gov.in/newsite/PrintRelease.aspx?relid=114520.

2 'What is Spaceship Earth?', R. Buckminster Fuller Collection, Stanford University Libraries. https://exhibits.stanford.edu/bucky/feature/what-is-spaceship-earth.

3 Ibid.

4 *Ṛgveda*, Maṇḍala 10, Sukta 191, Rik 2.

5 'National Statement by Prime Minister Shri Narendra Modi at COP 26 Summit in Glasgow', Ministry of External Affairs, Government of India, 2 November 2021. https://www.mea.gov.in/Speeches-Statements.htm?dtl/34466/National+Statement+by+Prime+Minister+Shri+Narendra+Modi+at+COP26+Summit+in+Glasgow.

6 Ibid.

7 'PM launches global initiative "Lifestyle for the Environment–LiFE Movement"', Press Information Bureau, Government of India, 5 June 2022. https://www.pib.gov.in/PressReleaseIframePage.aspx?PRID=1831349.

8 'Go green, earn green: India's 1st Green Credit scheme to reward eco-friendly actions by individuals, industries', *The Print*, 1 May 2023.

9 Household Consumption Expenditure Survey: 2022–23, Fact Sheet. Ministry of Statistics and Programme Implementation, Government of India. https://www.mospi.gov.in/sites/default/files/publication_reports/Factsheet_HCES_2022-23.pdf.

Chapter 15: Geopolitics and Global Energy Security with Special Reference to India

1 Agnew and Corbridge, 1989.

2 Victor, Jaffe and Hayes, 2006: 5. https://www.academia.edu/36243674/Concepts_of_Geopolitics_and_Energy_Security.

3 World Bank, 2022.

4 https://ppac.gov.in/uploads/whatsnew/1702638638_MRR_November%202023.pdf.

5 https://www.mospi.gov.in/sites/default/files/publication_reports/Energy_Statistics_2023/Chapter%201-Reserves%20and%20Potential%20for%20Generation.pdf.

6 'More than one-fourth of total electricity production during year 2022–23 from non-fossil fuels: Union Minister for Power and New & Renewable Energy', Press Information Bureau, 1 August 2023. https://pib.gov.in/PressReleaseIframePage.aspx?PRID=1944696#:~:text=The%20Union%20Minister%20for%20New,25.44%25%20and%2022.45%25%20respectively.

7 https://www.eia.gov/international/overview/country/IND.

8 https://oec.world/en/profile/bilateral-product/petroleum-gas/reporter/ind.

9 https://www.iea.org/countries/india/natural-gas.

10 Health Effects Institute, 2020.

11 https://www.weforum.org/stories/2025/01/grid-flexibility-for-resilient-equitable-digital-energy-future/.

Chapter 16: Sustainability in Agriculture through Energy Transition

1 'Energy for Sustainable Agriculture and Rural Development and Food Security in Africa', Chapter 2 in *Future Energy Requirements for Africa's Agriculture*, Food and Agriculture Organization of the United Nations, Rome, 1995. https://www.fao.org/3/V9766E/v9766e03.htm.

2 Ibid.

3 '"Energy-Smart" Food for People and Climate', Issue Paper, Food and Agriculture Organization of the United Nations, 2011. https://www.fao.org/4/i2454e/i2454e00.pdf.

4 Ibid.
5 'Eating sustainably: Energy and food production', University of Michigan, Centre for Sustainable Systems. https://sustainability.emory.edu/wp-content/uploads/2018/02/InfoSheet-Energy26FoodProduction.pdf.
6 'Health Effects of Climate Change (HECC) in the UK: 2023 Report', Ch. 9: 'Climate Change and Food Supply', UK Health Security Agency. https://assets.publishing.service.gov.uk/media/659ff76ee96df5000df844c3/HECC-report-2023-chapter-9-food-supply.pdf.
7 Boqiang Lin, Chunxu Guan, 'Assessing consumption-based carbon footprint of China's food industry in global supply chain', *Sustainable Production and Consumption*, Volume 35, January 2023, pp. 365–375. https://www.sciencedirect.com/science/article/abs/pii/S2352550922003086.
8 Hannah Ritchie, 'Food production is responsible for one-quarter of the world's greenhouse gas emissions', Our World in Data, 6 November 2019. https://ourworldindata.org/food-ghg-emissions.
9 Hannah Ritchie, Pablo Rosado and Max Roser, 'Environmental Impacts of Food Production', Our World in Data. https://ourworldindata.org/environmental-impacts-of-food.
10 Sylvia H. Vetter, et al., 'Greenhouse gas emissions from agricultural food production to supply Indian diets: Implications for climate change mitigation', Agric Ecosyst Environ. 16 January 2017, 237: 234–241. Available at https://www.ncbi.nlm.nih.gov/pmc/articles/PMC5268357/.
11 OECD-FAO Agriculture Outlook 2021–2030, Ch. 6 – Meat. https://www.oecd.org/en/publications/2021/07/oecd-fao-agricultural-outlook-2021-2030_31d65f37.html.
12 'Peace, Dignity and Equality on a Healthy Planet', Global Issues: Population, United Nations. https://www.un.org/en/global-issues/population.
13 R.N. Prasher, 'Net Zero: Myth, Reality or Escapism?', *Daily World*, Chandigarh, 26 February 2024. https://epaper.dailyworld.in/Details.aspx?id=139136&boxid=78162&uid=&dat=2024-02-26.
14 Steve Carver, et al, 'Guiding Principles for Rewilding', *Conservation Biology*, Volume 35, Issue 6, 16 March 2021, pp. 1882–1893. https://conbio.onlinelibrary.wiley.com/doi/10.1111/cobi.13730.
15 Letycla Bond, 'Brazil loses a quarter of natural forest in nearly forty years: A new survey mentions the advance of farming', Agencia

Brasil, 20 October 2023. https://agenciabrasil.ebc.com.br/en/geral/noticia/2023-10/brazil-loses-quarter-natural-forests-nearly-40-years.

16 Fabio Taixeira, 'Can Brazil's farmers grow more soy without deforestation?', Context, Thomson Reuters Foundation, 4 October 2023. https://www.context.news/nature/can-brazils-farmers-grow-more-soy-without-deforestation.

17 Agriculture Demand Side Management Programme, Bureau of Energy Efficiency, Ministry of Power, Government of India. https://beeindia.gov.in/en/programmesdemand-side-management/agricultural-demand-side-management-programmeagdsm.

18 Deepak Gupta and Subrahmanyam Pulipaka, 'India's next agriculture revolution can happen under solar panels', *The Economic Times*, 29 November 2023. https://energy.economictimes.indiatimes.com/news/renewable/indias-next-agriculture-revolution-can-happen-under-solar-panels/105601323.

19 'A new paradigm for Indian agriculture: From agroindustry to agroecology', NITI Aayog, 2022. https://www.niti.gov.in/sites/default/files/2023-03/A-New-Paradigm-for-Indian-Agriculture-from-Agroindustry-to-Agroecology.pdf.

Chapter 17: India's Journey for Sustainable Energy: A Beacon on the Global Stage

1 https://www.icicidirect.com/research/equity/finace/india-in-cop-2029.

Chapter 18: Addressing Imperatives of India's Energy Security

1 'GDP growth at 8.4% in 3rd quarter, fastest in 1.5 years', *The Times of India*, 1 March 2024. https://timesofindia.indiatimes.com/business/india-business/indias-gdp-grows-at-84-in-3rd-quarter-fastest-in-15-years/articleshow/108118441.cms.

2 https://www.eprmagazine.com/news/kpmg-enters-in-indias-flagship-energy-conclave/.

3 'India Energy Security Scenarios 2047', Niti Aayog. https://iess2047.gov.in/#?inputs=1-1-1-1-1-1-1-1-1-1-1-1-1-1-1-1-1-1-1-1-1-1-1-1-1-1-1-1-1-1-1-1-1-1-1-1-1-1-1-1-1-1-1-1-1-1. https://solarquarter.com/2024/04/12/indias-energy-demand-to-more-than-double-by-2047-strategies-for-efficiency-and-sustainability-discussed-at-ficci-roundtable/.

4 https://coal.gov.in/en/major-statistics/production-and-supplies.

5 S. Anand, 'India on track to hit 1 billion tonne in coal production, registers 11% increase: Pralhad Joshi', ETEnergyWorld, 26 January

2024. https://energy.economictimes.indiatimes.com/news/coal/india-on-track-to-hit-1-billion-tonne-in-coal-production-registers-11-increase-pralhad-joshi/107160163.

6 Y. Bhargava, 'Coal is railways' cash cow—why India's climate goals pose risk for transporter', The Print, 21 June 2023. https://theprint.in/india/governance/coal-is-railways-cash-cow-why-indias-climate-goals-pose-risk-for-transporter/1634060/.

Chapter 19: The Role of the Bhakra Nangal Project in Providing Food, Water, and Energy Security in Northern India

1 https://www.cbip.org/ISRM-2022/images/7-8%20April%2022%20Rishikesh/Data/Session%203/7%20%20Sh.%20C.P.%20Singh.pdf.

2 Ibid.

3 https://bbmb.gov.in/writereaddata/Portal/GeneralDocument/48_1_paper.pdf.

4 Bhatia, 2005.

5 Malik, 2005.

Chapter 20: India's Energy Security: The Road Ahead

1 'Strong reforms over last 10 years lays foundation of solid growth over next decade: Jefferies', *The Economic Times*, 22 February 2024. https://economictimes.indiatimes.com/news/economy/indicators/strong-reforms-over-last-10-years-lays-foundation-of-solid-growth-over-next-decade-jefferies/articleshow/107912063.cms?from=mdr.

2 'China promised climate action. Its emissions topped US, EU, India combined', Al Jazeera, 30 August 2023. https://www.aljazeera.com/economy/2023/8/30/chinas-coal-habit-clouds-climate-fight-as-emissions-top-us-eu-combined#:~:text=China%20produces%20about%2030%20percent,entire%20rest%20of%20the%20world.

3 'Renewable energy as an integral part of India's energy security: A critical appraisal', ET Energy World, 31 August 2023. https://energy.economictimes.indiatimes.com/news/renewable/renewable-energy-as-an-integral-part-of-indias-energy-security-a-critical-appraisal/103235396#:~:text=By%20relying%20on%20a%20diverse,security%20while%20reducing%20carbon%20emissions.

4 'Thermal capacity addition gains pace in FY24 amid high power demand projections', *Mint*, 27 March 2024. https://www.livemint.com/industry/energy/thermal-capacity-addition-gains-pace-in-fy24-amid-high-power-demand-projections-11711540796063.html.

5 'What is U.S. electricity generation by energy source?', US Energy Information Administration. https://www.eia.gov/tools/faqs/faq.php?id=427&t=3.
6 Per capita CO_2 emissions, Our World in Data. https://ourworldindata.org/grapher/co-emissions-per-capita#all-charts.
7 'Despite challenges, India's plans for energy sector are ambitious. It needs proper execution', *Business Today Magazine*, 19 February 2023. https://www.businesstoday.in/magazine/industry/story/despite-challenges-indias-plans-for-energy-sector-are-ambitious-it-needs-proper-execution-369010-2023-02-05.
8 'Committed to achieve 50 pc of renewable power sources ahead of 2030, says official', *The Economic Times*, 12 January 2024. https://economictimes.indiatimes.com/industry/renewables/committed-to-achieve-50-pc-of-renewable-power-sources-ahead-of-2030-says-official/articleshow/106759405.cms?from=mdr.
9 'PM Modi announces solar roof-top scheme for one crore households', *The Hindu*, 23 January 2024. https://www.thehindu.com/news/national/pm-modi-promises-one-crore-rooftop-solar-households/article67766221.ece.
10 'Renewable energy as an integral part of India's energy security: A critical appraisal', ET Energy World, 31 August 2023. https://energy.economictimes.indiatimes.com/news/renewable/renewable-energy-as-an-integral-part-of-indias-energy-security-a-critical-appraisal/103235396#:~:text=By%20relying%20on%20a%20diverse,security%20while%20reducing%20carbon%20emissions.
11 'India's energy security: Key challenges and the way forward', ET Energy World, 24 April 2023. https://energy.economictimes.indiatimes.com/news/renewable/indias-energy-security-key-challenges-and-the-way-forward/99737657#:~:text=India%20requires%20to%20resort%20to,to%20its%20net%2Dzero%20target.
12 '21 companies bid for electrolyzer incentives in India', PV Magazine, 19 December 2023. https://www.pv-magazine-india.com/2023/12/19/21-companies-bid-for-electrolyzer-incentives-in-india/.
13 'Government is working on new technologies such as Small Nuclear Reactors to make clean energy transition', Department of Atomic Energy, 6 December 2023. https://pib.gov.in/PressReleaseIframePage.aspx?PRID=1982958#:~:text=Small%20Modular%20Reactors%20(SMR)%20is,commitment%20to%20Clean%20Energy%20transition.

Bibliography

Aggarwal, Prachi. *China's Energy Security: The Journey from Self-Sufficiency to Global Investor*. Palgrave Macmillan, 2022.

Alden, Chris and Alvaro Mendez. *China and Latin America Development, Agency and Geopolitics*. Bloomsbury Academic, 2023.

Amineh, M. Parvizi and Yang Guang. *Secure Oil and Alternative Energy: The Geopolitics of Energy Paths of China and the European Union*. Brill, 2012.

Austvik, Ole Gunnar and Carolina Lembo. 'EU–Russian Gas Trade and the Shortcomings of International Law'. In *Journal of World Trade* 51, no. 4 (2017): 645–674.

———. 'Concepts of Geopolitics and Energy Security'. In *IAEE Energy Forum*. International Association for Energy Economics, 2018.

———. 'The Energy Union and Security-of-Gas-Supply'. In *Energy Policy*. Vol. 96: 372–382. London: Elsevier Science, 2016.

Boudellal, Méziane. *Power-to-Gas: Renewable Hydrogen Economy for the Energy Transition*. De Gruyter, 2023.

Boute, Anatole. *Energy Dependence and Supply Security: Energy Law in the New Geopolitical Reality*. Oxford University Press, 2023.

Chen, Shaofeng. *Approach to Energy Security: An International Comparative Perspective*. Palgrave Macmillan, 2023.

Chitadze, Nika (ed.). *The Russia–Ukraine War and Its Consequences on the Geopolitics of the World.* IGI Global, 2023.

Considine, Jennfer I; Douglas Cooke, Geoffrey Wood, Sylvain Cote, and Abdullah Aldayel. *A Research Agenda for Energy Politics.* 2023. https://www.elgaronline.com/edcollchap/book/9781789901764/book-part-9781789901764-10.xml.

Curtis, Simon and Ian Klause. *The Belt and Road City: Geopolitics, Urbanisation, and China's Search for a New International Order*. Yale University Press, 2024.

Dugin, Aleksandr. *Foundations of Geopolitics: The Geopolitical Future of Russia*. Arktogeja Publication (Russian): 1997. English translation 2022.

Dwivedi, Aadarsh. 'Energy Security in India'. 2022. https://www.researchgate.net/publication/361865085_Energy_Security_In_India.

Eder, Thomas Stephan. *China–Russia Relations in Central Asia: Energy Policy, Beijing's New Assertiveness and 21st Century Geopolitics.* Wiesbaden: Springer Fachmedien, 2014.

Fukuyama, Francis. *The End of History and the Last Man.* New York: The Free Press,1992.

Fuller, Graham E. *The Center of the Universe: The Geopolitics of Iran.* Westview Press, 1991.

Geopolitics of the Energy Transformation: The Hydrogen Factor. International Renewable Energy Agency (IRENA), 2022.

Goel, Malti and Gautam Sen (eds.). *Climate Action and Hydrogen Economy: Technologies Shaping the Energy Transition.* Climate Change Research Institute. Springer Nature, 2024.

Green Hydrogen in Power Systems. Edited by Vahid Vahidinasab, Behnam Mohammadi-Ivatloo, Jeng Shiun Lim. Switzerland: Springer Nature, 2024.

Heiduk, Felix. *Asian Geopolitics and the US–China Rivalry.* Routledge, 2022.

Kandpal, Vinay, Anshuman Jaswal, Ernesto D.R. Santibanez Gonzalez, and Naveen Agarwal. *Sustainable Energy Transition: Circular Economy and Sustainable Financing for Environmental, Social and Governance (ESG) Practices*. Switzerland: Springer Nature, 2024.

Kjellén, Rudolf. *Stormakterna: Konturer Kring Samtidens Storpolitik*. Stockholm: Hugo Gebers Förlag, 1905.

Krishnan, Ananth and Stanly Johny. *The Comrades and the Mullahs: China, Afghanistan and the New Asian Geopolitics*. India: HarperCollins, 2022.

Kumar, Sudarshan, Avinash K. Agarwal, Bhupendra Khandelwal, and Paramvir Singh. *Ammonia and Hydrogen for Green Energy Transition*. Springer, 2024.

Leandro, Francisco José B.S., Carlos Branco, and Flavius Caba-Maria (eds.). *The Geopolitics of Iran*. Palgrave Macmillan, 2021.

Li, Lingqun. *China's Policy towards the South China Sea: When Geopolitics Meets the Law of the Sea*. Routledge, 2018.

Madlovics, Bálint and Bálint Magyar (eds.). *Ukraine's Patronal Democracy and the Russian Invasion: The Russia–Ukraine War, Volume One. Russia's Imperial Endeavor and Its Geopolitical Consequences: The Russia–Ukraine War, Volume Two*. Central European University Press, 2023.

Markey, S. Daniel. *China's Western Horizon: Beijing and the New Geopolitics of Eurasia*. Oxford University Press, 2020.

Mirsaeedi-Farahani, Shabnam. *Energy Sector Diversification in Iran: Evolving Strategies and Interests in the Electricity Sector*. Wiesbaden: Springer Fachmedien, 2015.

Nwokolo, Samuel Chukwujindu, Anthony Umunnakwe Obiwulu, and Paul C. Okonkwo. *Africa's Propensity for a Net Zero Energy Transition*. Taylor & Francis, 2024.

Nyga-Łukaszewska, Honorata. *Economics of Energy Security: Perspectives of Natural Gas Exporters*. Routledge, 2023.

Panwar, Kuldeep, Govind Kumar, and Alok Semwal. 'Role of Smart Grid Connection in Renewable Energy Sources'. In *IJFANS*, 2012. https://www.ijfans.org/uploads/paper/6d8f94d29228f924de4aef64644bfc30.pdf.

Rowen, Ian. *One China, Many Taiwans: The Geopolitics of Cross-Strait Tourism*. Cornell University Press, 2022.

Roychoudhury, Jitendra. 'Geopolitics and Energy Security Issues in India'. In *A Research Agenda for Energy Politics*. 2023: 21–33. https://www.researchgate.net/publication/370253635_Geopolitics_and_energy_security_issues_in_India.

Shayan, Fatemeh. *The Gas Troika on the European Gas Market: Russa, Iran and Qatar*. De Gruyter, 2023.

Sourgens, Frédéric Gilles and Leonardo Sempertegui. *Principles of International Energy Transition Law: Law as an Instrument of Development in the 21st Century*. Oxford University Press, 2023.

The War in Ukraine: Russia's Ruptured Relations with the West. Geopolitics, Supply Chains and Power Dynamics in 2023. Economist Intelligence Unit, 2023.

Van de Voorde, Marcel (ed.). *Hydrogen Production and Energy Transition*, Volume I. De Gruyter, 2021.

———. *Hydrogen Storage for Sustainability*, Volume II. De Gruyter, 2021.

———. *Utilization of Hydrogen for Sustainable Energy and Fuels*, Volume III. De Gruyter, 2021.

Victor, David G., Amy M. Jaffe, and Mark H. Hayes. *Natural Gas and Geopolitics: From 1970 to 2040*. New York: Cambridge University Press, 2006.

Wastnidge, Edward and Simon Mabon. *Saudi Arabia and Iran: The Struggle to Shape the Middle East*. Manchester University Press, 2022.

Wong, Pak Nung. *Techno-Geopolitics US–China Tech War and the Practice of Digital Statecraft*. Routledge, 2022.

About the Editor and Contributors

Nitin Gadkari

Shri Nitin Gadkari is a senior minister in the Union Cabinet for the Ministry of Road Transport and Highways and has earned accolades worldwide for the transformation of this sector over the last decade. His model of rural connectivity in Maharashtra, where he served as minister for the Public Works Department, was adopted by the Government of India and led to the Pradhan Mantri Gram Sadak Yojana (PMGSY). As an agriculture enthusiast, he has promoted water management, solar energy projects, and the use of modern technology and management tools in agriculture, biofuels, and non-conventional sources of energy. A postgraduate in commerce, he holds a law degree and a diploma in business management. He started his political career as a student leader. He believes in and works towards transforming the Indian economy into one with some of the lowest logistics costs to make India more competitive in international trade.

Suresh Prabhakar Prabhu

Shri Suresh Prabhakar Prabhu is the chancellor of Rishihood University and visiting professor at the London School of Economics. He has been a member of the Indian Parliament for six terms and has held ten different portfolios in the Union Cabinet, including industry, power, environment and forests, railways, civil aviation, commerce, and fertilisers and chemicals. The French Institute of International Relations

(IFRI), Berlin, has conferred an honorary doctorate on him. He is a renowned chartered accountant, a law graduate, a banker, and a cooperator. He has been the Indian prime minister's sherpa to the G8 and G20, playing a crucial role in shaping the Indian agenda for these summits.

Raj Kumar Singh

Shri Raj Kumar Singh is a former Indian Administrative Service (IAS) officer who held the post of Union home secretary. He was subsequently elected a member of Parliament for two terms from 2014 to 2024. He was Union minister of state, holding independent charge of the Ministry of Power and the Ministry of New and Renewable Energy. He also held charge as minister of state for skill development and entrepreneurship. Later, from 2021 to 2024, he served as a cabinet minister. He holds a degree in law and has also studied at the Delft University of Technology, Netherlands. He brought about remarkable changes in India's power sector, particularly in terms of round-the-clock availability of power, energy security, and energy transition. He has taken a firm stand that while ensuring India's energy security, coal-based generation will not be completely abandoned at this juncture.

Ghanshyam Prasad

Shri Ghanshyam Prasad, chairperson of the Central Electricity Authority and ex-officio secretary to the Government of India, is also an ex-officio member of the Central Electricity Regulatory Commission. He is president of the Central Board of Irrigation and Power and holds key positions in many bodies within the power sector, including the Nuclear Power Corporation of India. He is an electrical engineering graduate from Banaras Hindu University and holds a master's degree in energy and environment management from IIT

Delhi. He has represented India in joint working groups with Nepal, Bangladesh, Myanmar, and Australia. He is passionate about promoting renewable energy.

R.N. Prasher (Editor)

R.N. Prasher is a retired IAS officer of the 1975 batch with extensive experience in the water and power sectors. He served as the principal secretary of Haryana's irrigation and power departments and was a member of the Bhakra Beas Management Board. Prasher has been an outspoken advocate for the suspension of the 1960 Indus Water Treaty between India and Pakistan, arguing that water-scarce India could utilize the water currently flowing into the sea as permitted by the treaty.

After his retirement, he served as the principal advisor to the chief minister of Haryana, overseeing inter-state water disputes across various forums, including the Supreme Court of India. He later became the chairman of the Haryana Electricity Regulatory Commission. Prasher is also a regular contributor to Chandigarh's *Daily World*, where he writes a weekly editorial. He has published over 230 articles, primarily focused on geopolitics.

A passionate traveller, he frequently drives solo in the high Himalayas, gaining valuable insights into the challenges and potential of the region's rivers for India.

Radha Krishna Mathur

Shri Radha Krishna Mathur was the first lieutenant governor of the Union Territory of Ladakh. A former member of the IAS, he was the chief secretary of Tripura and held important positions in the Government of India, such as secretary of defence production, secretary of defence, and secretary of small and medium enterprises. Later, he served as the chief information commissioner of India. He is an alumnus of the Indian Institute of Technology Kanpur (IITK), where he received his bachelor's degree in mechanical engineering, and IIT Delhi, where he obtained his master's degree. In addition, he holds an MBA degree from the International Centre for Promotion of Enterprises (ICPE), Ljubljana, Slovenia. His vast experience in the Indian defence establishment and as lieutenant governor of a territory that shares a long and active border with China is reflected in the chapter on the geopolitics of China.

Manjula Prasher

Mrs Manjula Prasher is a former secretary to the Government of India, Department of Posts. She subsequently worked as the central information commissioner. Her long administrative experience has given her a deep understanding of how the freedom to access and disseminate information can be turned on its head and misused for partisan purposes, and how disinformation can be countered.

Sanjeev Chopra

Shri Sanjeev Chopra, a former IAS officer who headed the prestigious Lal Bahadur Shastri National Academy of Administration, has decades of administrative experience, including many years in the Government of India's Ministry of Agriculture and Farmers' Welfare. He is a fellow of the United Services Institution of India and the Royal Asiatic Society of Great Britain and Ireland. His book *We the People of the States of Bharat* has remained immensely popular and has been translated into many Indian languages. He is a distinguished professor of public policy at UPES and of history and public policy at Swami Rama Himalayan University. He is on the academic council of the National Centre for Good Governance and on the academic and research advisory council of the National Institute of Disaster Management.

Rabindra Nath Sen

Shri Rabindra Nath Sen is former chairman of the West Bengal Electricity Regulatory Commission and the Damodar Valley Corporation. He has been the managing director of NTPC-ALSTOM and the CEO of NTPC-SAIL Power Company Limited (NSPCL), where he brought about a turnaround at the Bhilai plant. He is a mechanical engineering graduate and holds a master's degree in business administration. He has participated in power sector events in Asia, Europe, and America and has published many papers. He is the editor of *Energy Konnect*, a bimonthly publication for the power sector.

Brij Behari Dave

Dr Brij Behari Dave, a former civil servant of the Indian Postal Service, holds a master's degree in organic chemistry, postgraduate diplomas in forestry as well as in management and public administration, and a doctoral degree. He has thirty-nine years of experience working with both state governments and the Government of India. He is an avid researcher and has published twenty-eight papers in Indian and international journals.

Ajit Balaji Joshi

Shri Ajit Balaji Joshi has wide-ranging interests, from Marathi literature to information technology, and is known for turning around financially weak organisations. As an IAS officer, he has served in many districts and departments of Haryana and is currently looking after the agriculture department in Punjab. His career has been marked by many innovations, including schools for children of brick-kiln workers, building parks in villages, a 24/7 call centre to help distressed college students during the COVID years, and a programme for doorstep delivery of nutritious food to the economically disadvantaged at affordable prices. He guided Haryana's urban development body out of the red zone by facilitating a phenomenal increase in its revenue.

Vivek Kumar Dewangan

Shri Vivek Kumar Dewangan, an IAS officer, is currently the chairman and managing director (CMD) of India's Rural Electrification Corporation Limited (REC). He is an electronics engineer with a postgraduate degree in optoelectronics and optical communication from IIT Delhi. He has held various assignments in the Government of India, including in the ministries of power, petroleum and natural gas, law, commerce, agriculture, rural development, and finance. In addition to his role at REC, he is the chairman of REC Power Development and Consultancy Limited (RECPDCL).

Gurdeep Singh

Shri Gurdeep Singh, CMD of the behemoth National Thermal Power Corporation (NTPC), is an electrical engineer and has undergone international courses at Saïd Business School-University of Oxford (UK), Harvard Kennedy School-Harvard University (USA), Darden School of Business-University of Virginia (USA), and Civil Service College (Singapore). He is a member of the International Energy Agency's high-level advisory group on coal in the global net-zero transition and also a member of the Clean Energy Ministerial H2I advisory group. He served as co-chair of the taskforce on energy and resource efficiency at the B20 Italy 2021.

Manoj Tripathi

Shri Manoj Tripathi, former chairman of the Bhakra Beas Management Board (BBMB), is a graduate in mechanical engineering and also holds an MBA in finance. He is a member of the Central Power Engineering Services and has twenty-eight years of experience, primarily in the hydropower sector. He has been involved with hydro projects in India as well as in Bhutan and Nepal.

Charanpreet Singh

Shri Charanpreet Singh is a civil engineer with a bachelor's degree (gold medal) from REC (now NIT) Jalandhar and an ME (Structures) with honours from TIET Patiala. He joined the Punjab irrigation department as an SDO in 1999 and was subsequently deputed to the Bhakra Beas Management Board (BBMB), where he served for over 24 years. His expertise encompasses design, technical solutions for hydro structures, analysis of dam instrumental data, sedimentation studies, and silt management. He ensured the safe operation and timely maintenance of the Bhakra and Nangal dams and the Nangal Hydel Channel and successfully executed special repairs on hydro structures exceeding 65 years of age. His contributions to the water management of the Bhakra and Pong reservoirs were crucial in meeting the water and power demands of BBMB partner states.

Dip Kishore Sen

Shri Dip Kishore Sen is the whole-time director and senior executive vice-president at Larsen and Toubro Limited (L&T). He is the chairman of several units of L&T related to power, steel, infrastructure, and aviation, and is also engaged with the company's foreign operations. A civil engineering graduate from IIT Kharagpur, he holds a postgraduate degree in business management from XLRI Jamshedpur. His previous experience includes working with Tata Steel as well as in Malaysia. He was the project director of Mumbai International Airport. He is also the chairman of the National Council on

Roads, Highways and Transportation, ASSOCHAM. His versatility, demonstrated by his experience of having worked across domains such as design and engineering, business development, tendering, and construction, is one of his core strengths.

Harry Dhaul

Shri Harry Dhaul is the director general of the Independent Power Producers Association of India (IPPAI). As the guiding spirit behind the organisation, he has made IPPAI's annual retreat extremely popular among regulators, producers, and others connected with the power sector. The retreat serves as an occasion for free and frank exchange of ideas, and some of the contributors for this book have been regular attendees. IPPAI is the oldest non-profit organisation in the energy sector that works in the policy and regulatory space, focussing on issues such as the energy–water nexus, rural–urban shifts, energy security, the geopolitics of energy, regulated versus free-market debates, security concerns in smart grids, cybersecurity, content versus carriage debates, etc. His goal is to demystify the power sector and develop holistic solutions.